20 SUTTON PLACE, Eastern Boulevard,
Cor. East 59th St., New York, May 12, 1879.

To Correspondents, Contributors, and others interested in the Pilgrim Record Series:

DEAR FRIENDS: We are glad to announce our having put to press the FARWELL ANCESTRAL MEMORIAL, another volume of the Series for which collection of materials commenced soon after our marriage—this 12th May, 1879, being the FORTIETH ANNIVERSARY—a number answering to forty thousand dollars we have advanced in this research.

Of one other volume we have 450 pages already stereotyped, and of several others our records of items not subject to change are reduced to the same solid form, ready for their just position in the volumes to be severally published, as means therefor may be equitably advanced by living members. In general, each volume is independent of the twelve others, and may be so purchased and read.*

While grateful for continued life and health, we are reminded that one decade more, if vouchsafed, will complete a half century since the commencement of these labors; and, that to publish the remaining ten volumes of the Series in style corresponding with the past issue, personally preparing the indexes and charts, arranging and proof reading the pages, and adding to the branches of each of the ten volumes the items derived from a correspondence constantly *alive* to the changes by birth, marriage, and death in the respective families, it becomes very important, if the volumes are to be issued, that the necessary means should be assured by liberal subscription from those therein represented, and from those favorable thereto; thus obviating those diversions and distractions which, in us unaided, would result in the non-completion of the work.

We shall at all times be glad to have any of you examine at your own convenience our published books, or our manuscript pages, tables, diagrams, and charts completed, and those in preparation; and as some of the days of this FORTIETH ANNIVERSARY YEAR, we especially name any and all the hours of the second Tuesday of each month, 1879, day and evening.

Very respectfully yours,

DAVID-P⁷. HOLTON, M.D.

---

* It will be seen that seven letters are found in FARWELL—an eminent number in all historic times, in literature and science, religious and secular; and it becomes expedient that three hundred descendants of Henry¹ Farwell, during this fortieth anniversary of these genealogical researches, in their purchase of the "ANCESTRAL" at $3 per copy, should each add seven (7) dollars, making an even ten, a number which extensively harmonizes with the decimal system, which is rapidly extending in various departments of mensuration in all lands.

These three hundred persons thus advancing to Wm-D⁵. Farwell, 115 Worth Street, New York, as their trustee, a total of $3000, will thereby secure the complete volume of Henry¹ and his descendants. Let this be done at once, that the fields pleasant to view from our Pisgah may be promptly entered and possessed, not for ourselves only, but for posterity.

FARWELL ANCESTRAL MEMORIAL.

HENRY¹ FARWELL,

OF CONCORD AND CHELMSFORD, MASSACHUSETTS,

AND ALL HIS

DESCENDANTS TO THE FIFTH GENERATION:

TO WHICH ARE ADDED

THREE BRANCHES—THE FAMILIES OF

DANIEL,⁵ OF GROTON AND FITCHBURG, MASS.,
1740——1818;

BETHIAH,⁵ OF MANSFIELD, CONN., AND WESTMINSTER, VT.,
1747——1813;

ELIZABETH,⁵ OF NORTH CHARLESTOWN, N. H.,
1751——1840,

AND THEIR DESCENDANTS TO 1879.

BY

DAVID-PARSONS' HOLTON, M.D., A.M.,

LIFE MEMBER OF THE NEW ENGLAND HIST. GEN. SOCIETY AND OF THE NEW YORK GENEALOGICAL & BIOG. SOCIETY; AND SEC'RY OF THE PILGRIM RECORD SOCIETY,
AND OF THE AMERICAN PHILOLOGICAL SOCIETY,

AND HIS WIFE,

FRANCES-K.' (FORWARD) HOLTON,

RESIDENT MEMBER OF THE NEW YORK GENEALOGICAL AND BIOGRAPHICAL SOCIETY.

NEW YORK:
D-P.' HOLTON, M.D., PUBLISHER,
20 SUTTON PLACE, EASTERN BOULEVARD, COR. EAST 59TH ST.
1879.

Entered according to Act of Congress in the year 1879, by DAVID-PARSONS' HOLTON, M.D.,
in the office of the Librarian of Congress, at Washington, D C.

READ & MOYNAHAN, PRINTERS.

PRESS OF J. J. LITTLE & CO.,
COR. ASTOR AND LAFAYETTE PLACES.

PREFACE.

Individual isolation contravenes the will of heaven, as shown in every characteristic of man's physical, intellectual and moral nature. Equally so of families and nations. Progressive discoveries, in the laws of mind and matter, made since the parable of the "Good Samaritan" was spoken, and harmonizing therewith, tend to unify the human race, whether near or distant in space or time. More and more the individual parent is brought to realize himerself* as a responsible connecting link in the great family circle; and this growing conviction has, within the last half of a century, added great impulse to genealogical and biographical studies.

Hon. Daniel Webster said : "It is wise for us to recur to the history of our ancestors. Those who do not look upon themselves as a link connecting the past with the future, do not perform their duty to the world."

Hon. John Winslow in a recent address, speaking of the value of family histories as contributory sources to more general history, said :

"Family histories are of great importance as primary sources of local or town histories. It is the histories of the families that make that of the town; those of the towns make up the history of the State, and those of the States the nation. It has been said that the utility of the great libraries in Europe may be best understood if we consider their vast number of books, not as books to be read seriatim, but like words in a dictionary, to be consulted as occasion may require; and so it may be said of family and town histories. They are like words in a vast lexicon; like rivulets that swell the streams, the streams the river, and the river the mighty sea. It is clear that to attain accuracy and a good understanding, we must begin at the first round of the ladder, and so know more about—if not the "forests primeval"—at least the families primeval, so far as human records or traditions will permit. If we start right here, we have data from which may be made safe inferences and clear generalizations.

"Let not the objection be thought well taken, that inasmuch as we live in a young country, we can feel no special interest in genealogy. The fact is, that for all purposes of genealogical studies we live, in a proper sense, in as old a country as can be found. In a broad sense our life in this is but a continuance of race life in the older countries from which our ancestors came. If then we would well understand

---

* See foot note on p. 219.

the forces that make our institutions, we must look back to the times of our European ancestors of whatever nationality. In the study of influences that shape and give tone to human affairs, how narrow is the limit of a single generation. There can be no thorough study of history that does not comprise genealogical researches. The extent to which such researches are carried is largely a measure of refinement and real culture among the people."

The compilers of this Memorial Volume were in the early times of their investigations encouraged and aided by Governor Leonard-J. Farwell of Wisconsin; and the numerous descendants of Henry[1] Farwell, an early settler of Concord, Mass., have for many years been aware that their memorial volume has been in a state of great forwardness for the press, waiting their equitable co-operation; but now, through the recent liberal aid of John-V[6]. Farwell, Esq., of Chicago, Ill., it has been made possible to issue this portion of the collection, which will be of common interest to all the branches, containing records of their several Farwell ancestors of the first four generations in America, and generally those of the fifth, born prior to 1760. This little book brings the record down to include the birth of most of the descendants who participated in the struggle for the Independence of the United States—an ANCESTRAL BOOK OF AMERICAN FARWELLS. To these pages of *common interest* to all Farwells, have been added samples of branch development to the present date, 1879.

The members of the second generation in America are recorded on the 6th page; those of the third are found on the 7th and 12th pages; those of the fourth on 13th, 14th, 16th, 19th, 20th, 21st and 22d pages. Their descendants of a later generation are to be readily found by following successively their respective serial number references. Taking for example the serial number 341 on page 35, Daniel[4] followed by a reference number [511], and turning to that number in the serial order found on page 72 the reader will find the full development of this Daniel[5]; and on page 84, his nine (9) children, from serial number 512 to 520 inclusive, each of whom, except the 6th and 8th (Benjamin[6] and Anna[6]) who died young, are severally referred for their respective development.

Again, in the Index, page 190, is to be found Paul-Theodore[9] Cheritree, serial number 939, answering to page 146, a child of Almira[8] (Farwell) and Theodore-Frelinghuysen Cheritree ; grandchild of Lyman[7] Farwell, serial number 928, page 143. For his ancestral line see the reference number in brackets [583], page 92, under serial number 577, p. 91 ; where this Lyman[7] is seen to be the son of Daniel[6] and Dorcas (Wetherbee) Farwell.

In like manner Paul-Theodore's line is traced through Daniel[5] [511], p. 72; Daniel[4] [340], p. 35 ; Joseph[3] [45], p. 13 ; Joseph[2] [4], p. 6, to Henry[1] [1], p. 1, the emigrant ancestor.

PREFACE.

As with Paul-Theodore⁹, so may be done in tracing the genealogy of any of the descendants of Henry¹ recorded in this book.

On the 250th page is placed a Calendar which will serve posterity to A.D. 5,999. A hope was expressed in 1876 that Russia would compliment the United States by making the centennial of our Independence, the occasion of her adopting the New Style common to other Christian nations. Now, the hope is that she will adopt it on or before the bi-centennial 1976. †

Readers of these Memorials can now purchase, for fifty cents, this Calendar and its slide in working order, which, with due care, can be practically used by their posterity for several generations. [See *Winslow Memorial*, Vol. I, page 349.] .

English correspondents have kindly aided the compilers by giving trans-atlantic records of Farwell families. These have been arranged in Chart I, which was designed for this work; but as several points need further confirmation before our Henry's English line can be satisfactorily established, its publication is deferred to the completed volume.*

Inviting the reader carefully to regard the explanations referred to in the " Supplemental Index," page 240, it may not be amiss to suggest that the perfections of the book should be credited to the promptness, fullness, clearness and accuracy of the forces that make our institutions, we must look back to the times of our European ancestors of whatever nationality. In the study of influences that shape and give tone to human affairs, how narrow is the limit of a single generation. There can be no thorough study of history that does not comprise genealogical researches. The extent to which such researches are carried is largely a measure of refinement and real culture among the people."

The compilers of this Memorial Volume were in the early times of their investigations encouraged and aided by Governor Leonard-J. Farwell of Wisconsin; and the numerous descendants of Henry¹ Farwell, an early settler of Concord, Mass., have for many years been aware that their memorial volume has been in a state of great forwardness for the press, waiting their equitable co-operation; but now, through the recent liberal aid of John-V⁸. Farwell, Esq., of Chicago, Ill., it has been made possible to issue this portion of the collection, which will be of common interest to all the branches, containing records of their several Farwell ancestors of the first four generations in America, and generally those of the fifth, born prior to 1760. This little book brings the record down to include the birth of most of the descendants who participated in the struggle for the Independence of the United States—an ANCESTRAL BOOK OF AMERICAN FARWELLS. To these pages of *common interest* to all Farwells, have been added samples of branch development to the present date, 1879.

ERRATA.

On page 15, the arc above Joseph² should have been removed, leaving an open space from Mary² to Olive², as seen on pages 80, 81; and on pages 52, 53. A similar error is to be seen on page 185, where Joseph² is by the arc cut off from that free intercourse with his descendants which, on page 82, John² Holton is seen to have with his children of the third generation; see also the open space above Nathaniel⁵ Winslow in the miniature radial facing page 135.

The sixteen pages next following the 104th were found to contain so many typographical misputtings that, after the corrections were made, this portion was reprinted; but in the binding the imperfect sixteen were included instead of the *corrected* ones. Compare the concluding three words of the 113th and the first four lines of the 114th page with the corrections as here made:

Henry^A Bright, bap. 20 Dec. 1560, and wife Mary; Thomas^B, buried 1 Sept. 1587, and wife Margaret, of Bury St. Edmunds; Walter^C, buried 25th Jan. 1551, and wife Margaret, of Bury St. Edmunds; and John^D, of Parish of St. Mary's, Bury St. Edmunds, Co. Suffolk, England. Reign of Henry VII.

The mistake of the binder is less to be regretted as this correction brings the reader, at an early stage, to consider and apply the American system of designating transatlantic ancestors, as published in 1870. [See page 78, FARWELL ANCESTRAL MEMORIAL.]

William⁴ Farwell, serial number 423, p. 50, should there have had reference number 77, which is found on page 20.

Bethiah⁵ Farwell, p. 50, should have reference number 521, found on page 84.

PREFACE. vii

As with Paul-Theodore⁸, so may be done in tracing the genealogy of any of the descendants of Henry¹ recorded in this book.

On the 250th page is placed a Calendar which will serve posterity to A.D. 5,999. A hope was expressed in 1876 that Russia would compliment the United States by making the centennial of our Independence, the occasion of her adopting the New Style common to other Christian nations. Now, the hope is that she will adopt it on or before the bi-centennial 1976. †

Readers of these Memorials can now purchase, for fifty cents, this Calendar and its slide in working order, which, with due care, can be practically used by their posterity for several generations. [See *Winslow Memorial*, Vol. I, page 349.]

English correspondents have kindly aided the compilers by giving trans-atlantic records of Farwell families. These have been arranged in Chart I, which was designed for this work; but as several points need further confirmation before our Henry's English line can be satisfactorily established, its publication is deferred to the completed volume.*

Inviting the reader carefully to regard the explanations referred to in the "Supplemental Index," page 240, it may not be amiss to suggest that the perfections of the book should be credited to the promptness, fullness, clearness and accuracy of correspondents, and of the worthy town and county clerks of former years; while all the omissions, discrepancies and errors, as well as any apparent dilatoriness in its publication, should be set to the account of the compilers.

Readers discovering errors are respectfully invited to state the same by early correspondence that the completed volume may indeed be complete.

20 Sutton Place, Eastern Boulevard, cor. E. 59th St.,
NEW YORK, 18 June, 1879.

Since writing the above we conclude to print herewith a portion of the chart, page viii, hoping our English correspondents and others may continue their friendly aid in this research.

† THE CALENDAR.—On the 250th page are placed side by side, immovably, the two parts of the Calendars. The recipient of the book can, on card-board or other thick paper, make with the pen a SLIDE in *precise* imitation of that in the book, which can be used on page 250 as directed on page 251. Should any prefer to send the publisher fifty cents, he will send by mail a calend r with a *slide* in working order, thus furnishing an almanac for all the past years of the Christian era, as well as for the time to A.D. 5999.

ENGLISH FARWELL FAMILIES.

In the preface of the Farwell Ancestral Memorial allusion is made to the collection of records during our visitations in England, and through transatlantic correspondence. Thus far the results of our efforts have not been conclusive as to the English pedigree of our Henry[1] of Concord, Mass.

With a view to enlist co-operation and to facilitate supplemental research we here print a few of the detached notes taken from the Harleian Manuscripts, Burke's Landed Gentry, Playfair's British Antiquities, Pigot's Commercial Directory, and other books, and from our notes of travels and correspondence, whether looking Henry-ward or otherwise. We hope some of the standpoints here presented may be occupied by intelligent co laborers Should the result fail to establish our long sought pedigree of Henry[1], which we cannot believe, suggestive points may be planted which, we trust, more successful investigators in other branches will cultivate and develope, and which ere long will be extended in directions to show the yet undiscovered point joining our worthy immigrant to his true ancestral vine.

Rev. Thomas Gataker, rector of Rotherhithe, b. 4 Sept. 1574; m. as 3d wife, Dorothy, daughter of George Farwell, Esq., of Hill Bishop, in Somersetshire, and sister of Sir George and Sir John Farwell, by whom, who d. 1627, he had two daughters; Elizabeth, who m. Wm. Draper, Esq., and Esther.

Maria Farwell, dau. of George of Hill Bishop, Somersetshire, m. Andrew Walton, son of William and Thomazine, and in 1620, his children were Walter, his first-born, aged 14 ; Arthur, his second son, aged 9 ; William, 3d son; Sylvester, Philip, Maria and Susan.

Elizabeth Farwell. dau. of Richard of Somersetshire, m. as 1st wife. Humphrey Venner of Hundscott (son of William of Chittlehampton and Elizabeth, dau. of Humphrey Copleston of Instow) and had Ann and Elizabeth. [See Richard in Chart B.]

Miss Farwell of Holbrook House * near Wincanton, Devonshire. m. Robert Woodford, Canon of Wells and Rector of Yeovilton, who died at Wells, 1762, aged 87. He was son of Rev. Samuel Woodforde, D.D., F.R.S., Prebendary of Winchester and Rector of Hartly Mauduit and Sheldon, in Hampshire.

Arthur Farwell. m. Mary Monk, daughter of Rev. Nicholas, Bishop of Hereford, brother of George Monk, the celebrated General under Cromwell, who was created baronet 1670. The mother of Mary Monk was Susanna Rayne.

The family of Le Moyne or Monk was of great antiquity in the County of Devon, and in that shire they had, from a remote period, possessed the manor of Potheridge.

The Monks were lineally descended from Arthur Plantagenet, Viscount L'Isle, son of King Edward IV, thus :

CHART I. [A]

ARTHUR PLANTAGENET=Elizabeth, sister and co-heir of John Grey, and widow of Edward Dudley.

Thomas Monk of Potheridge=Frances, for her 2d husband.

Anthony Monk=Mary, dau of Richard Arscott, Esq. of Dunsland.

Sir Thomas Monk, Kt.,=Elizabeth, dau. of Sir George Smith, Kt.

Thomas. George, the celebrated General under Cromwell, who, for his exertions in restoring the monarchy, was created by King Charles II, 7 July, 1670, Baron Monk of Potheridge, Earl of Torrington, Duke of Albemarle. [See Chart B]

Rev. Nicholas,=Susanna, daughter of Thomas Rayne, Bishop of Hereford. Esq.

Curwen Rawlinson.=Elizabeth. Mary, m. Arthur Farwell.

* The residence of this lady at Holbrook House suggests the probability that she was a descendant of John of Holbroo.. [See Chart B.]

Extracts from the Correspondence of Col. C. T. J. Moore, Frampton Hall, Near Boston, England.

DR. HOLTON, DEAR SIR:

About the same time as I received your letter, I got one also from Mr. John V. Farwell, of Chicago, in reply to one from myself about the Farwell pedigree.

I shall be very glad to receive the MEMORIAL and particulars you kindly offer to send me, and shall gladly give you all the information in my power about the English ancestors of the Farwells.

I am not quite certain about having found the right HENRY[1] FARWELL; but I can discover only one Henry in the English branch, and as all trace of him is lost I have presumed that he went to America.

The family in England seems to have been scattered over the country, and can be traced from the earliest period; but Yorkshire appears the place where they chiefly settled, and in the reign of Edward I (circa 1280) Richard Farwell married the heiress of Elias de Rillestone and brought Rillestone and several other estates into the family. These continued in the male line until the reign of Henry VII (circa 1500), when they passed through an heiress to the family of Radcliff, although some portion remains to this day in a family who call themselves Farwell, and bear the same arms and claim direct descent from Richard Farwell. The name is and has been spelt Fauvell, Favell, Varwell, Farewell and Farwell.

About the same time as the large estates passed by marriage to the Radcliffes, Simon Farwell migrated from Yorkshire and settled in Somersetshire and built at Bishop Hill near Taunton, the Mansion House, on which were carved the Farwell arms, quartering de Rillestone and others; and, although it cannot now be discovered, a pedigree was in the possession of his great grandson, showing the descent and alliances of the family for many generations. [See Harleian Mss. for this pedigree.] This Simon married Julia, dau. of —— Clark:

CHART I [B]

Simon Farwell of Hyl-Bishop, E qr., d. 1545 = Julia Clark.

Simon of Hill Bishop, Esq , = Dorothy, d. and heiress of Sir James Dyer, Speaker of House of Commons and Judge. She died 1580.
died 1568.

Simon. | John of Holbrook, Esq; m. Ursula Philipps. He sold Bishop Hill to his bro. George. This branch extinct in the male line.* | George, b. 1533; d. 1609; of Hill Bishop. = Philippa, d. of John Parker, Esq. died 1620. | Richard.§ | Christopher, from whom a long line of Christophers & the Devonshire branch desc'd to this day. [See chart I c.] | 4 daughters.

Sir George, Kt., of Hill Bishop; died 1647. He had 20 children, of whom we give six. = Lady Mary, dau. of Sir Edward Seymour, Duke of Somerset; brought Plantagenet blood in the family and died 1660. | Elizabeth = Sir John = Jane. | —— = Arthur

John. Charles. James.

Thomas. John = Dorothy, dau. of Sir John Routh. | George = Ann, daughter of Richard Brown | Nathaniel. Edmund. James. +. +.

Henry.
[Col. Moore can trace nothing of this Henry and suggests that he may be the one who settled in America, whose first son was born about 1639. See Seize Quartiers Chart, page 134a FARWELL ANCESTRAL MEMORIAL.]

John.

—— = Arthur Farwell married Mary Monk, daughter of Nicholas, Bishop of Hereford, niece of George Monk, the celebrated General under Cromwell. | Philip.

*John Farwell married Ursula Phelps or Phelipps, daughter of Sir Thomas who d. 1565 and Agnes (Smith) who died 1564. Thomas, brother of Ursula, born 1500, built the present house at Montacute in Somersetshire, considered one of the finest specimens of the Tudor style of architecture. Wm. Phelps, Esq., born 14 October, 1823, in 1846 had his seat at Montacute House.

§ Among the early descendants of Samuel[1] Farwell in America the name Richard frequently occurs, and suggests this as their ancestral line, there being none of the name Richard among the early generations of our Henry[1]. [See page viii.]

CONTINUATION OF THE ENGLISH FARWELL FAMILIES.

DEVON OR TOTNESS BRANCH.

CHRISTOPHER FARWELL of Totness, Esq.═Mary, relict of Barber, 1605,

Christopher of Totness, Esq. b. 1609; d. 1672, M.P. for ═Jane ——, only known as "Madame Jane Dartmouth in the long Parliament. Farwell," died 1676,

| Christopher Esq. of Totness. Born 1644; died 1729. ═Mary Southcott, died 1701. | Elizabeth, married Richard Belfield, Esq. 1652. | Sarah, married William Searle, Esq 1683. |

Christopher, Esq.═Catharine, d. of Arthur Ayshford of Wonwell Court, Esq. by Margaret daughter of Servington Savery, Esq. | Mary, married Francis Drake, Esq. 1690.

| Christopher, M. D., born 1706; died unmarried. | Arthur, Esq., born 1705. ═Grace, d. of Nicholas Piers, Esq. of Plympton 1740. | Katherine, 1708. |

| Arthur, Esq., born 1746, died 1809. ═Jane, dau. & heiress of James Taylor, Esq., by Ann, dau. of Thos. Acland, Esq. brother of Sir Hugh Acland. | Christopher. | George, m. Eliz. — & had Chas-F., Capt R. N. | Cutharine. |

| Colonel Christopher, Esq., of Totness, born 1774; died 1837. ═Elizabeth, dau. of John Bent, Esq., of Ivybridge. | Rev. Arthur b. 1776; d. 1809. Arthur | George, b. 1783; d. 1859. ═Maria, d. of John Bent, Esq., of Ivybridge. | Jane, m. Richard Marshal M. D. |

| Frederick, mar. Louisa Whitbread, and had Frederick, George and Gerald. | Maria, unm. | Emily, unmarried. | Georgian, married Gordon Whitbread, Esq. |

| William, rector of St. Austens, Cornwall, born 1805; died 1876.* ═Mary, d. of Wade Browne, Esq. of Chapel Allerton, Yorkshire, | George, s.p. Arthur, s.p. Christ.James,s.p. John-Bent, s.p. | Frank. | Anna-Maria, m. H. R. Roe, Esq. | Ellen Belfield m. J-W-C. Whitbread.† |

| Christopher-Wade, Captain in Army, unmarried. | Robert, Major in Army, unm. James. | Rev. H-Farwell, rector | Arthur, Capt. R. N. | F-M-V., m. Col. C-T-J. Moore, of Frampton Hall, F.S.A. | Ada-M., m. Admiral Glasse. | Camilla, m. Rev. George Heath. |

† Capt. Jacob-William-Carey Whitbread, of Loudham Park, Co. Suffolk, m. 14 Nov. 1832, Ellen-Belfield Farwell, third d. of Col. Christopher of Totness, and had Gordon-Carey b. 1 Jan, 1834; Howard, born 25 November 1836; Benjamin-Evelyn, b. 13 May, 1840; Charles-Frederick, b. 19 Sept. 1841; Jacob-Albert-Robert, b. 22 Jan. 1843; Elizabeth-Maria and Irene-Ellen.

* Rev. William Farwell, Rector of St. Austens, Cornwall, married Mary, dau. of Wade Brown and Eliz. (Jones) of Leeds; Wade Brown, Merchant, Magistrate, Deputy Lieut. of Co. York, &c., b. 1780, at Chapel Allerton, County York; d. 1821, and was succeeded by his only son, Wade Brown, Esq., of Monkton Farleigh. The seat of the Manor House, Monkton Farleigh, Bradford, Wilts.

☞ For the completed FARWELL MEMORIAL we have charts of other ENGLISH FARWELL FAMILIES, to which we shall add records forwarded to us, especially if they tend to establish the lines of Henry[1] and Samuel[2] Farwell. Communications are solicited, which may be addressed to

DAVID-P. HOLTON, M.D.

18 June, 1879. 20 Sutton Place, Cor. East 59th Street, New York.

FARWELL MEMORIAL.

HENRY¹ FARWELL.

HENRY[1] FARWELL was one of the first settlers of CONCORD, MASS., which was incorporated 2 September, 1635. Shattuck, in his History of Concord, writes of him as "probably the common ancestor of the name in New England." [George Farwell of Boston, one of the adherents of Andros, who was imprisoned in 1689, probably left no posterity in America.]

History gives us little authentic information concerning the private and public life of this ancestor. More might have been disclosed, had not the church records of Concord prior to 1738, and most of the town records prior to 1696, been irrecoverably lost.

To get an idea of the probable character of the man, his purposes and position, and the hardships endured for the rights of conscience, let us recur to the history of the place and circumstances in which his lot was cast, and, as we find him associated with worthy, God-fearing men, endeavoring to establish for posterity a home and a government beyond the control of despotism in civil as well as religious affairs, let us draw our inferences as to his individual life, aspirations, and efforts.

At the commencement of the seventeenth century the Indians of New England were able to bring into the field more than 18,000 warriors, but about the year 1612 they were visited with a pestilential disease, whose horrible ravages reduced their number to about 1,800. Some of their villages were entirely depopulated. This great mortality was viewed by the first Pilgrims as the accomplishment of one of the purposes of Divine Providence, by making room for the settlement of civilized man, and by preparing a peaceful asylum for the persecuted Christians of the old world. In what light soever the event may be viewed, it, no doubt, greatly facilitated the settlements, and rendered them less hazardous.

The original Indian name of Concord for a long time before it was settled by our fathers, was Musketaquid, and had been one of the principal villages of the Massachusetts tribe. Nanepashemet was the great king or sachem of these Indians. His principal place of residence was in Medford, near Mystic Pond. "His house was built on a large scaffold six feet high, and on the top of a hill. Not far off he built a fort with palisadoes thirty or forty feet high, having but one entrance, over a bridge. This also served as the place of his burial, he having been killed about the year 1619, by the Tarrantines, a warlike tribe of Eastern Indians, at another fort which he had built about a mile off." He left a widow—Squaw Sachem, and five children. Squaw Sachem succeeded to all the power and influence of her husband, as the great queen of the tribe. Her power was so much dreaded, when she was first visited by the Plymouth people in 1621, that her enemies, the sachems of Boston and Neponset, desired protection against her, as one condition of submission to the English.

The situation of Concord, though then considered far in the interior and accessable only with great difficulty, held out strong inducements to form an English settlement, and early attracted the attention of the adventurous pilgrims.

Traditionary authority asserts that the settlement was first projected in England.

Nearly all the first settlers were immigrants directly from England; and a greater number of original inhabitants removed, during the first fifteen years after the settlement, to other towns in the colony, than permanently remained there. This sufficiently characterizes it as one of the "mother towns." It was the first town settled in New England above tide waters; and was in fact, as it was then represented to be, "away up in the woods," being bounded on all sides by Indian lands, and having the then remote towns of Cambridge and Watertown for its nearest neighbors.

The first settlement commenced in the Fall of 1635, fifteen years after the Pilgrims landed at Plymouth, and five after the settlement of Boston.

Many of the first settlers were men of acknowledged wealth, enterprise, talents, and education, in their native country. Several were of noble families, who, having been persecuted in their native country, and deprived of the liberty of worshipping God and enjoying His ordinances, agreeably to their views of scripture and duty, accounted no temporary suffering or sacrifices too great to be endured, in order to be restored to their natural rights, and to freedom from religious oppression. Though some were men of fortune and eminence, and from their infancy had been unaccustomed to hardship, they cheerfully gave up all their personal comforts, crossed the ocean, and planted themselves in this lonely wilderness to endure suffering, for which no pecuniary compensation would have been adequate. No purpose of worldly gain could have prompted so hazardous and expensive an enterprise.

It was emphatically a religious community seeking a quiet resting-place for their religious enjoyments and religious hopes. The remark, in reference to the whole colony, that "God sifted a whole nation that he might send choice grain over into this wilderness," might, with propriety, be applied to the resolute and pious fathers of this town. Though they came from various parts of England, they were united, and had high hopes of happiness and religious prosperity, and emphatically lived in CONCORD.

The following extract is from Johnson's "Wonder-working Providence":

After they have thus found out a place of aboad, they burrow themselves in the earth for their first shelter under some hill-side, casting the earth aloft upon timber, they make a smoaky fire against the earth at the highest side. And thus these poore servants of Christ provide shelter for themselves, their wives and little ones, keeping off the short showers from their lodgings, but the long raines penetrate through to their great disturbance in the night season. Yet in these poor wigwams they sing psalmes, pray and praise their God, till they can provide them houses, which ordinarily was not wont to be with many till the earth, by the Lord's blessing, brought forth bread to feed them.

From this general view of the place and condition of the early settlers we proceed to gather up the few items personal to Henry¹, the immigrant ancestor of most if not all the Farwells in America.

He was made freeman, according to Savage, 14 March, 1639—according to Shattuck's History of Concord, 1638. [Probably 1638-9.]* In 1644 we have evidence of his being a member of the Church in Concord by the following petition:

"To the Honoured Court. The Petition of the Church of Concord in behalfe of our brother, Mr. Ambrose Martin.

Your humble Petitioners do intreate, that whereas some years ago our said brother, Mr. Martin, was fined by the Court for some unadvised speeches uttered against the Church-covenant, for which he was fined £10, and had to the value of £20 by distress taken from him, of which £20 there is one-halfe remayning in the hands of the country to this day, which £10 he cannot be perswaded to accept of, unless he may have the whole restored to him (which we doe impute unto his infirmitye and weakness). We now, considering the great decay of his estate, and the necessityes (if not extremityes) which the familye is come unto, we entreat that this honored Court would please to pittye his necessitous condition, and remit unto him the whole fine which was layd upon him, without which he cannot be perswaded to receive that which is due to him. Wherein if this honored Court shall please to grant this our petition, we shall be bound to prayse God for your tender compassion toward this our poor brother.

Peter Bulkeley,	Luke Potter,
John Jones,	Joseph Wheeler,
Richard Griffin,	Thomas Foxe,
Simon Willard,	William Busse,
Robert Merriam,	Henry Farwell,
Thomas Wheeler,	James Hosmer,
George Wheeler,	John Graves.
Robert Fletcher,	

*About the years 1718 and 1719 the *double dating* for the months of January, February and March was very much neglected, and during the twelve or fifteen years, commencing with 1741, it was omitted almost entirely. There is consequently an ambiguity of one year in most dates from January 1 to March 25, during those periods. But various circumstances indicate that the old form of date was intended, and, in the opinion of the copyist, it would be more safe to adopt this conclusion, and in a large majority of cases, would be certainly correct. [*Copied from the Concord (Mass.) Town Record Book.*]

"The 5th of the 4th month, 1644. The case appears to the magestreates to be now past help through his own obstinacye; but for the overplus upon sale of the distress he or his wife may have it when they will call for it.

Jo. ENDECOTT, Gov."

The following action of the town indicates the location of his homestead in Concord:

On the 8th of March, 1654, nine men were appointed to consider in what way the second division of lands in Concord should be made. After "much weariness about these things" it was decided to make the division into three parts or quarters. * * * "The limits of ech quarter as foloweth: The north quarter by their familyes are from the north part of the training place to the great river and all on to the north sid thereof.—The east quarter by there familyes, are from Henry Farweles all eastward with Thomas Brooke, Ensign Wheeler, Robert Meriam, Georg Meriam, John Adames, Richard Rice.—The south quarter by there familyes are all on the south and southwest side of the mill brooke except those before acsprest, with Luke Potter Georg Heaward, Mihel Wood, and Thomas Dane"

Regulations were established in each quarter, similar to those in wards of a city. Each chose its own officers, kept its own records, made its taxes, etc.

On the 29 Jan., 1663, at a town meeting, it was agreed that a new book should be procured.—"what is in the old booke that is useful shall be transcribed into the new* with all lands which men do hold"—; "that every man that hath not his proportion of lands laid out too him, that is due to him shall gitt it laid out by an artis" before 1665;—and that each one should give to the town clerk a description of their lands, approved at a meeting of the inhabitants of the quarter in which he lives, and certified by the quarter clerk.

From these records Lemuel Shattuck, Esq., author of the "History of Concord" (from which work we have largely copied as above) compiled a table, giving the greater part, though not all of the names of proprietors of the town at that time. In this table we see that *John* Farwell of the *East Quarter* had 18 lots containing 280 acres, but as the name of Henry does not appear it seems probable that he had removed to Chelmsford, leaving his son John in possession of his lands in Concord. J. B. Hill, who has given much attention to the genealogies of some of the Concord families, says that Henry[1] removed to Chelmsford at the incorporation of that town in 1654. The date of his marriage and maiden surname of his wife, Olive, we have not been able to ascertain. They both died in Chelmsford, he, the 1 Aug., 1670, and she, 1 March, 1691-2.

We here give a copy of his Will, dated 12 July, 1670, made three weeks before his death:

In the name of God, amen. I, Henry Farwell of Chelmsford, in the County of Middlesex, Taylor, being of perfect and sound memory, I praise my God, I make this my last will and testament in manner and form as followeth, First, I will and

---

*Doubtless many items which *then* seemed to the transcribers not "useful," would at this date be exceedingly so as relating to personal history, and highly prized by posterity.

earnestly desire, that all my debts be paid and satisfied, as shall appear legally or reasonably to be due, upon or by bond, bill or book, or otherwise however out of my estates with what convenient speed, the same can be raised, paid and satisfied.

SECONDLY. It is my will and I do give and bequeath unto Olive Farwell, my beloved wife, my housing with the upland about it, which I have now in possession, with convenient medow to keep 4 cows, during the time of her natural life.

THIRDLY. I give and bequeath unto Olive my wife all my movables to be at her dispose.

FOURTHLY. I bequeath unto Olive my now wife 3 cows and my mare for her own proper use.

FIFTHLY. I bequeath unto Olive my wife, all my service for her own proper use.

Thirdly. I give and bequeath unto my sonne John Farwell all my accommodation at Concord which he hath in present possession, to him and to his heirs forever of his own body lawfully begotten, always provided, and my will is, that my sonne John Farwell, shall pay forty shillings a year unto Olive Farwell my now wife, during the term of her natural life.

Secondly. I bequeath unto my sonne John Farwell one year old heifer and my coult.

Fourthly. I bequeath unto my son Joseph Farwell, all the land he hath in present possession wt 20 acres of upland lying at little tadmuck, 6 acres of upland lying in the new field.

Fifthly. My will is that Joseph Farwell my sonne shall have the remainder of my accommodations in Chelmsford, after my wife's deceese, only two small parcels of meadow, namely one acre lying in the river meadow, joining to the meadow of William Fletcher, I give and bequeath to Mary Bates my dauter, and one acre and a half of meadow lying at little tadmuck, joining to the meadow of James Heldreth, to Olive Spaulding my daughter, my will is in case Joseph my son dies before Olive his mother, then the lands at his mothers decease, I give to the heirs of Joseph my sonne. I give and bequeathe unto Joseph my son the remainder of my wearing apparell. My will is that Joseph my son, shall pay ten shillings a year to Olive his mother during the term of her natural life. Further, my will is that Joseph my son shall pay thirty pounds to his three sisters, namely ten pounds within half a year after my decease, namely three pounds six shillings and eight pence to Elizabeth Wilber, three pounds six shillings and eight pence to Mary Bates, and three pounds six shillings and eight pence to Olive Spaulding my daughter; my will is that my son Joseph shall pay six pounds and a mark to Elizabeth Wilber within a year after the decease of my wife, and six pounds and a mark to Mary Bates within two years after my wifes decease, aand six pounds and a mark to Olive Spaulding within three years after my wifes decease. I give and bequeath to Olive my wife a third part of the fruits of my orchard, during the time of her natural life, and a third part of the fruits to Joseph my sonne, and a third part of the fruit to Mary Bates and Olive Spaulding my daughters for five years, to be equally divided; and when the five years are expired my will is that that part shall return to Joseph Farwell my sonne.

Sixthly. My will is that Olive Farwell my now beloved wife and Joseph my sonne to [be] my sole executors, to this my last will and testament, and my will is that the remainder of my stock, I leave with my executors to the payment of my debts, and the payment of the first part of the legacies and all these legacies my will is should be paid, at the now dwelling house of my son Joseph in price current or corne or cattle. Lastly my will is that Hannah Farwell my daughter my son Joseph's wife, shall have the third part of the land after her husband's decease. This I do declare to be my last will and testament, revocking and disclaiming all other whatever by these presents, in testimony whereof I the said Henary Farwell have hereunto set my hand and seale ye 12th day of July in the year of Our Lord according to the computation of New England one thousand six hundred and seventy.

HENRY FARWELL.

JOHN FISKE, Jr.

INVENTORY OF HIS ESTATE.

	£.	s.	d.
Movable goods	209	11	00
House lot	38	00	00
Meadow	43	00	00
Four acres arable	08	00	00
In Wilderness land	48	00	00
	343	11	00

The children of Henry[1] and Olive Farwell were probably all born in Concord:

2. 1. JOHN[2], [7] b. abt. 1639; m. Sarah Wheeler; m. 2d, Sarah Fisk.
3. 2. MARY[2], [9] b. 26 Dec. 1640; m. John Bates.
4. 3. JOSEPH[2], [15] b. 20 Feb. 1642; d. 31 Dec. 1722; m. Hannah Learned.
5. 4. OLIVE[2], [25] b. ——; m. Benjamin Spaulding.
6. 5. ELIZABETH, m. —— Wilbur. [*See Will of her father.*]

Shattuck referring to Henry[1], says—"His sons Joseph, John and *James* lived in this town (Concord) where the name has been preserved; the latter married Sarah Wheeler 1658"; but J-B. Hill, Esq., of Mason, N. H., who has given the subject much study, says: "Shattuck must have been wrong and wrote James instead of John. There is no evidence as to any son James, and he is not mentioned in the Will." Again this gentleman writes—a son James "never was born." Three queries meet us in discussing this point. Was there a son James? If there was such a son, did he die before his father? Or did John[2] and James[2] marry the same Sarah Wheeler? These queries may eventually be answered, but we are unable to do so at present. Shattuck says—James married Sarah Wheeler, 1658; Savage says—John married Sarah Wheeler 1658. They cannot both be right, as the year is identical; and as John is a "fact," all through the search, and James is nowhere to be found, the fair presumption is, that no son James existed save in the imagination of Shattuck. [*There were two Sarah Wheelers born in Concord about the same date, and if there was a James, he might also have married a Sarah Wheeler.*] Savage, in his list of children, says, "Henry, perhaps." Fox, in his Hist. of Dunstable, gives, "Henry, from

Chelmsford ; a son of Henry Farwell of Concord." If there was a Henry among the children of Henry¹, he must have died before his father, as no child of that name is mentioned in the Will ; but Henry of Dunstable lived till 1738. Savage probably followed Fox, though doubtfully or with less assurance. It is singular that Fox should have entirely ignored Joseph², s. of Henry¹, and father of Henry³ of Dunstable, when said Joseph² was the last twenty-two years of his life an inhabitant of Dunstable and filled important town offices nearly, if not every year, from 1701 to 1717, and in his will appointed his son Henry one of the executors [15]. His gravestone also is still standing in the old Dunstable cemetery bearing this inscription : "Ensign Joseph Farwell died Dec. 31, 1722, in the 82d year of his age."

We find no mention of any Henry², son of Henry¹, except by Savage and Fox, as above, and believe the number of children as given by us is correct.

7. JOHN², [2] (*Henry*¹,) b. 1639 ; m. acc. to Concord Records, 4 Nov. 1658, Sarah Wheeler, who d. 23 May, 1662. The precise date of her birth, and the names of her parents are not known. The records of Concord give a Sarah to both George and Timothy Wheeler, of whom one was born 30 March, 1640, and the other 22 June, of the same year. He m. 2d, Sarah Fiske. He testified in Court, acc. to Middlesex Court files, 6m. 29d, 1669, and was then thirty years of age. In 1666 he was taxed in Concord for 18 lots, 280 acres. Probably this was the portion his father received in the division of lands in Concord, lying in the east quarter of the town and on which the son seems to have resided, or to have held it in possession in 1670, the date of his father's will, who bequeathed to him, " All my accommodations at Concord which he hath in present possession." He was coroner in the case of drowning of John Howard, Sen., 1m. 30d. 1671. Was made freeman 11 Oct. 1682. Chelmsford records mention a grant of 12 1-2 acres of land to John Farwell in 1682 [J.-B. H.] We have no record of his death. According to the *New England Historical and Genealogical Register* he owned land in Concord in 1696.

Res. *Concord, Mass.*

Child by first wife :

8. 1. SARAH³, [31] b. 2 May, 1662 ; m. Concord, Mass., 5 March, 1681, *Concord Rec.*, John **Jones.**

9. MARY², [3] (*Henry*¹,) b. 26 Dec. 1640 ; married, according to Chelmsford records, 22 Dec. 1665, John **BATES.** Her father bequeathed to her "one acre of land lying in the river meadow joining to the meadow of William Fletcher " ; also to her and her two sisters, thirty pounds. The "legacies to be paid at the residence of my son Joseph in Chelmsford, at price current or corn or cattle."

Their children were :

10. 1. MARY³, b. 8 May, 1667.
11. 2. JOHN³, b. 22 Dec. 1668.
12. 3. ELIZABETH³, b. 22 Dec. 1671.
13. 4. LYDIA³, b. 25 Feb. 1673.
14. 5. REBECCA³, d. 16 July, 1682.

15. Ensign JOSEPH², [4] (*Henry*¹,) b. 20 Feb. 1642, Concord, Mass.; d. 31 Dec. 1722, Dunstable. His gravestone in the old Dunstable burying-ground bears this inscription : "Ensign Joseph Farwell died Dec. 31, 1722, in the 82d year of his age." The *New England Historical and Genealogical Register* gives a Joseph Farwell, s. of Henry, b. in Concord, 26 Dec. 1640. We know not how to reconcile this date with the inscription above. The date is precisely that of his sister Mary's birth. We can see but two possible solutions of the difficulty, one, an inaccurate statement in the inscription, and the other, the possibility that the Joseph b. 26 Dec. 1640, was twin of Mary and died in infancy ; and the next child born, our Ensign Joseph, was named after the deceased brother. According to Mr. J-B. Hill[*], he accompanied his parents on their removal from Concord to Chelmsford about 1654 at the incorporation of that town. He inherited by will of his father "The land that he hath in present possession wt 20 acres of upland lying at little tadmuck, 6 acres of upland lying in the new field," and "The remainder of my accommodations at Chelmsford after my wife's decease" only two small parcels of meadow, namely, one acre lying in the river meadow joining to the meadow of Wm. Fletcher, "I give and bequeath to Mary Bates my dauter and one acre and half of meadow lying at little tadmuck joining to the meadow of James Hildrike, to Olife Spaulding my daughter. (*See Will of Henry*¹ *Farwell.*)

He seems to have remained with his mother in Chelmsford till her death in 1691, when according to that will he would come into full possession of his father's bequest. We have no positive information concerning his disposal of the Chelmsford estate ; he does not mention it in his will, but it will be observed that he states before signing that instrument : "it is to be understood that all my other children, both sons and daughters, have received their full portions of me already." Possibly his son Joseph whose first two children were born, or recorded, in Chelmsford, may have received his portion in Chelmsford property, as might also his two daughters, Elizabeth and Sarah who married gentlemen of C. However that may be, about 1699 he removed from Chelmsford and became an inhabitant of Dunstable, where he was a large land holder and prominent in town affairs. He was selectman 1701, '2, '5, '7, '10; was Surveyor of Highways 1706, and served on important committees during the years 1712, '14, '15, '17.

The place of Mr. Farwell's adoption does not appear to us now, as one, at that time, very desirable. It was a frontier town and so exposed to the incursions of the Indians that few or no improvements could be made ; and during the twenty years previous the population had even diminished, so that in 1701 there were but twenty-five families—five less than in 1680. Perhaps our worthy ancestor foresaw for his posterity in the peaceful future the valuable lands they would enjoy, and braved the difficulties and dangers of the times for their eventual advancement and prosperity.

The sad condition of the settlers of Dunstable in 1701 will be seen by the following petition to the General Court presented by Mr. Farwell and his associate select-

---

[*] We are greatly indebted to Mr. J-B. Hill, a venerable lawyer of Mason, N.H., and a Farwell descendant [379°] who, by very thorough search among the records, and the gravestones of cemeteries of Concord, Chelmsford, Dunstable and the several towns once included in the limits of Old Dunstable, has been able to correct long existing errors in the histories of Concord and Dunstable concerning the early Farwells, and to aid essentially in determining several lines of ancestry.

men of the town, and shows the situation at this period, as well as the custom of the times.

"To his Majesty's most Honorable Council and Representatives in the Great and General Court now assembled in Boston by adjournment.

"The Petition of the selectmen of Dunstable in behalf of the inhabitants there settled, Humbly Sheweth :—that whereas the wise God, (who settleth the bounds of all our Habitations,) hath disposed ours, but an handful of people, not exceeding the number of twenty-five families, in an outside plantation of this wilderness, which was much depopulated in the late war, and two-third parts of them, though living upon husbandry, yet being but new beginners, and their crops of grain much failing of wonted increase, are in such low circumstances as to be necessitated to buy their bread corn out of town for the support of their own families, whence it comes to pass that they are capable of doing very little or nothing towards the maintenance of a minister here settled : and our non-resident Proprietors being far dispersed asunder, some in England, and some in several remote places of this country, and making no improvement of their interest here, most of them for divers years past have afforded nothing of assistance to us in so pious a work ; there having also in some years past been some considerable allowances for our help herein out of the Public Treasury, (for which we return our thankful acknowledgements,) the continuance whereof was never more needful than at this time:

"These things being duly considered we think it needful hereby to apply ourselves to your Honors. Humbly to request the grant of such an annual Pension out of the Country Treasury, for the support of the ministry in this place, as to yourselves may seem most needful, until our better circumstances may render the same needless.

"Moreover having been lately informed, by a Representative from a neighboring town, that Dunstable's proportion in the Country rate newly emitted was £6, coming from the multiplication of 20s. six times, but finding by the printed paper lately come to us that we, *the smallest town in the Province*, are assessed £9, being £3 beyond Stow which we deem in respect of the number of inhabitants may exceed us at least one-third part : We humbly hereupon desire that the original assessment may be revised, and if there be any mistake found in the proportion assigned to us, (as we judge there may be,) that it may be rectified ; and we shall remain your honors' Humble Servants,

ever to pray for you.

JOSEPH FARWELL,
ROBERT PARRIS,
WILLIAM TYNG."

The petition was answered and £12 were allowed from the treasury in September of the same year.

In November, 1711, the inhabitants still lived principally in Garrison-houses, where soldiers under the pay of the Colony were stationed constantly for their defence. From a return of the number, location and situation of these garrisons made to the General Court at that time, it appears that there were seven, containing 13 families and eighty-six persons, in Dunstable, one of which was Mr. Henry Farwell's garrison-house, containing 3 families, 8 male inhabitants, 2 soldiers, making a total of 28 persons. It is presumed that at the advanced age of Ensign Joseph Farwell at this date he would be one of the three males occupying the garrison-house of his son, "Mr. Henry Farwell," above mentioned. According to the His. of Dunstable, these garrisons to which the inhabitants fled in time of danger and where they usually spent the nights, "were environed by a strong wall of stone or of hewn timber built up to the eaves of the houses, through which was a gate fastened by bars and bolts of iron. They were lined either with brick or plank. Some of them had port-holes for the discharge of musketry. They were generally built of logs, and had the upper story projecting three or four feet beyond the lower story walls, for the purpose of greater security."

The town records of Dunstable give the following, copied by Mr. Fox in his history of that town :

"Sept. 26th, 1717, voted that the Rev. Jona. Parepoint (Pierpoint of Reading, Mass., grad. Harv. Col., 1714) should have a call in order for settlement. Also, voted that the minister should have £.80 a year salary, and one hundred pounds for his settlement. Voted that Maj. Eleazer Tyng and Ensign Farwell should acquaint Rev. Mr. Pairpont with what is voted at this meeting."

Mr. Farwell, with Thomas Colburn, bought the Waldo Farm, extending from the Tyng farm, near Tyngsboro' meeting house, up the river, to the farm lately owned by Deacon Jonathan Howard, nearly two miles ; and back from the river one mile or more, which was one of the most valuable intervals on the Merrimac River. On this farm he and his son Henry[2] lived ; and portions of it have been owned and occupied by some of his descendants to the present time.

His will is as follows :

In the name of the Lord God, Amen. I, Joseph Farwell Sen[r] of the Town of Dunstable in the County of Middlesex in the Province of Massachusetts Bay in New England, Yeoman, being of sound and perfect memory praise be given to God for the same Yet knowing the uncertainty of this life on earth and being desirous to settle things in order doe make and ordain this to be my last Will and Testament, thereby revoking all former Wills by me made and signed to be null & of none effect. In primis.—My soul I give unto the hands of Almighty God that gave it in sure and certain hope of eternal life through our alone Lord and Saviour Jesus Christ, and my body to the earth from whence it came to be decently interred at the discretion of my executors hereafter named and after my funeral expenses and debts satisfied and paid, what worldly goods it hath pleased God to endow me withall I do give & bequeath in manner as followeth.

Item—I do give unto my beloved wife Hannah Farwell all my movable goods both within the house and abroad of all sorts whatsoever to be at her disposal forever except one paire of Andirons

Item—I do give and bequeath to my son Oliver Farwell and to his heirs, executors, administrators forever the one-half of my housings and lands which I have

---

This house was the mansion of Ensign Joseph[2] used as a garrison on account of its commanding position.

now in my possession when he shall attain the age of twenty-one years—Also I do give to him one paire of Andirons ; also I do give and bequeath to him my son Oliver Farwell and to his heirs the other part of all my housings and land which I have in possession after my decease and after the decease of my wife Hannah Farwell if in the meane time of our lives he doth take the whole care of us both and to provide all things comfortable and necessary for us both in sickness and in health and to bestow upon us or either of us a decent burial : Hereby authorizing and fully empowering my beloved wife Hannah Farwell and my son Henry Farwell to be whole and sole executors jointly and severally of this my last Will and Testament.

In witness whereof I have hereunto subscribed, as witness my hand and seal the thirteenth day of November Anno Domini, one thousand seven hundred & eleven, and in the tenth year of her Majesties Reign &c.

Signed, sealed and published to be the last Will and Testament of Joseph Farwell in presence of us.
    AMES CHEEVER
    SAML MOODY
    JOHN MERIAM, Jr.

Before, signing and sealing it is to be understood that all my other children both sons and daughters have received their full portions of me already.

    JOSEPH FARWELL.

The above Will was proved Jan. 16, 1722.

He married 25 Dec. 1666, Chelmsford, Mass., Hannah[2] Learned, b. 24 Aug. 1649, Woburn, Mass., [*Woburn records*] d. of Isaac and Mary (Stearns) of Woburn, afterwards of Chelmsford [*Bond Gen. p.* 133]. She is mentioned in the distribution of her father's estate as "daughter of Isaac Learned and wife of Joseph Farwell."

[Isaac[2] Learned, father of Hannah (Learned) Farwell, was born in England, s. of William[1] who, with his wife joined the church in Charlestown, Dec. 1632, being the first admitted after its separation from the Boston church. Savage thinks he may have come to America two years before. Said William[1] was made freeman 14 May, 1634 ; was selectman 1636 ; removed to Woburn 1641, and was the first selectman of that town. He d. 1646.

Isaac[2], the only son of William[1] was born in England ; was made freeman 1647 ; removed to Chelmsford, probably between 1650 and 1653, as his three children, Mary, b. 7 Aug. 1647, Hannah, b. 24 Aug. 1649, and William, b. 1 Oct. 1650, are recorded in Woburn ; and his daughter Sarah, b. 1653, and other children, Isaac and Benoni, were recorded in Chelmsford. He was a selectman in C. ; d. there 1657. He m. 9 July, 1646, Mary Stearns, eldest child of Isaac and Mary of Watertown, Mass., 1630. She was baptized 6 Jan. 1627, at Neyland, Co. Suffolk, which was the seat of the family in England. She m. 2d, 9 June, 1662, John Burge of Chelmsford, and d. next year.

Savage says Isaac Stearns came, probably, with Sir Richard Saltonstall in the fleet of Winthrop, having been "not a distant neighbor of the Gov. in their native land." He was admitted freeman, 18 May, 1631. He d. 19 June, 1671. His will, made four days before his death, provides for the children of his daughter Mary (Stearns) Learned deceased, besides special remembrance of Isaac and Mary Learned. His widow d. 2 Apr. 1677.] Res. Concord, Chelmsford and *Dunstable, Mass.*

The children of Joseph² and Hannah (Learned), born in Chelmsford, were as follows:

16. 1. HANNAH³, [36] b. 20 Jan. 1667-8 ; m. Samuel **Woods**, Jr. ; m. 2d, Capt. Peter Joslin.
17. 2. JOSEPH³, [45] b. 24 July, 1670 ; d. 21 Aug. 1740 ; m. Hannah Colburn.
18. 3. ELIZABETH³, [56] b. 9 June, 1672 ; m. 31 Jan. 1693-4, John² **Richardson.**
19. 4. HENRY³, [64] b. 18 Dec. 1674 ; d. 1738; m. 23 Jan. 1695-6, Susanna Richardson of Chelmsford, Mass.
20. 5. ISAAC³, [73] d. 28 June, 1753 ; m. Elizabeth Hyde.
21. 6. SARAH³, b. 2 Sept. 1683 ; m., *Chelmsford rec.*, 5 Sep. 1707, Jonathan **Howard** of Chelmsford, Mass.
22. 7. JOHN³, b. 15 June, 1686.
23. 8. WILLIAM³, [79] b. 21 Jan. 1688; married Elizabeth ———.
24. 9. OLIVER³, [86] b. 25 Nov. 1692; d. 5 Sep. 1724; m. Mary Cummings.

25. OLIVE², [5] (*Henry¹*) m. acc. to Chelmsford rec., 30 Oct. 1668, Benjamin **SPAULDING**, b. 7 Apr. 1643, Braintree, Mass., s. of Edward and his second wife Rachel of Chelmsford, Mass.

By reference to her father's will it will be seen that he bequeathed her from his Chelmsford estate "one acre and half of meadow lying at little tadmuck joining to the meadow of James Hildrike," and a legacy "to be paid in corn or cattle" at the residence of son Joseph in Chelmsford [1].

Mr. Spaulding is not mentioned in his father's will, probably because he had given him his portion which he had invested in lands in Plainfield, Windham County, Conn., to which place he removed after 1670. He purchased a large tract of land in the northerly part of Canterbury, a town adjoining Plainfield on the north west in the same county, now called Brooklyn. His family homestead was transmitted to his son Edward, and in process of time to Edward's son Ebenezer. Mr. Spaulding died before 1708.

[See "Spaulding Memorial, a Genealogical History of Edward Spaulding of Massachusetts Bay, and his descendants, by Samuel J. Spaulding, Newburyport, Mass., Boston. Alfred Mudge & Son, Printers, No. 34 School St., 1872."]

Res. Chelmsford, Mass., and *Plainfield, Ct.*

The children of Benjamin Spaulding and Olive² (Farwell) were:

26. 1. SARAH³, b. 4 Jan. 1669; m. John **Miriam.**
27. 2. EDWARD³, [91] b. 18 June, 1672; d. 29 Nov. 1740; m. Mary Adams.
28. 3. BENJAMIN³, [102] b. 6 July, 1685.
29.   ELIZABETH³, m. Ephraim **Wheeler.**
30.   MARY³, m. Isaac **Morgan.**

31. SARAH⁴, [8] (*John², Henry¹*,) b. 2 May, 1662; m. Concord, Mass., 5 Mar. 1681, *Concord Rec.*, John² JONES, b. 6 July, 1656, s. of John¹ and Dorcas of Cambridge and Concord. He d. 1726. In 1699-1700 he was one of the board of selectmen, also in 1702-4 and 6. Sept. 1700, John Jones is credited "expense of his house by ye selectmen when met to make ye county rate for entertainment 2s. 11d." He appears to have borne the title of Ensign in 1707-8; was then paid by the town for "going to visit a sick woman, Hannah Ganders in Billerica." 24 March, 1711-12, Ensign Jones was appointed one of a committee of four to "manage ye affaire in order to ordination of Mr. Whiting." Res. *Concord, Mass.*

Children :

32. 1. SARAH⁴, [105] b. 4 June, 1686; m. 1705, Lieutenant Daniel Hoar.
33. 2. JOHN⁴, [110] b. 6 Jan. 1690; d. 12 Mar. 1762; m. Anna Brooks.
34. 3. TIMOTHY⁴, b. 6 Apr. 1694; killed by a log falling on him, 10 March, 1697-8.
35. 4. BARTHOLOMEW⁴, [116] b. 15 Feb. 1697-8; d. 16 Sep. 1738; m. July, 1723, Ruth Stow.

36. HANNAH³, [16] (*Joseph², Henry¹*,) b. 20 Jan. 1667-8, Chelmsford, Mass.; m. according to Chelmsford records, 30 Dec. 1685, Samuel WOODS, Jr., of Groton, Mass. Inventory of estate taken 1 Apr. 1712. She m. 2d after 1709 Capt. Peter JOSLIN, b. 22 Feb. 1666, Lancaster, Mass., s. of Nathaniel² and Sarah (King) and gr. s. of Thomas¹ of Hingham, who came from London 1635 in the *Increase*, bringing with him wife Rebecca, son Nathaniel² aged 8 years, and other children, and after some years settled in Lancaster. His son Nathaniel² of Hingham, removed, 1654, to Lancaster ; m. Sarah, d. of Thomas King of Marlboro, and had large family. On the 18 July, 1692, while Peter³ Joslin was at work in the field, a party of Indians attacked his house, murdered his wife and four children and took his wife's sister, Elizabeth How, captive. He m. 2d, Hannah³ (Farwell) [Woods] as above, and outlived a fourth wife. He d. acc. to Savage, 8 Apr. 1759. Res. *Groton, Mass.*
[See Radial Chart, page 15.]

Children of Samuel and Hannah³ (Farwell) Woods recorded in Groton, except Samuel :

37. 1. SAMUEL⁴, [124] d. 10 Apr. 1778; m. Groton, Mass., 29 Nov. 1720, Patience Bigelow, who died 23 Jan. 1771.
38. 2. SUSANNA⁴.
39. 3. RACHEL⁴.
40. 4. ALICE⁴, b. 26 Dec. 1700, Groton, Mass.
41. 5. ABIGAIL⁴, b. 12 Sept. 1703, G.
42. 6. ESTHER⁴, b. 13 Nov. 1705, G.
-43. 7. JOSEPH⁴, b. 21 June, 1707, G.
44. 8. MARTHA⁴, b. 15 Apr. 1709, G.

45. JOSEPH³, [17] (*Joseph², Henry¹*,) b. 24 July, 1670, *Middlesex rec.*; d. 21 Aug. 1740, aged 70, Groton, Mass.; m. 23 Jan. 1695-6, Hannah Colburn, prob. dau. of Edward of Chelmsford. The Chelmsford records give the following: "Joseph Farwell and Hannah Colburn of Chelmsford entered into covenant of marriage January 23d, 1695-6, before Mr. Thomas Clark."

This form of marriage record is unusual, but probably was that adopted by Rev. Thomas Clark the minister of Chelmsford.

According to Savage an Edward Colburn came in the *Defence* 1635, age 17; was living in 1692.

Fox, in his History of Dunstable, gives "Thomas Colburn probably from Chelmsford and a son of Edward of Chelmsford." It will be observed that a Thomas Colburn shared with Joseph² Farwell in the purchase of the "Waldo Farm" in Dunstable. These several statements and the business and family relations of the Farwells and Colburns suggest that both Thomas and Hannah might be children of Edward of Chelmsford. We have no means at present of proving the correctness of this impression, but hope some reader may be able to throw more light on the subject.

Mr. Farwell removed to Groton, Mass., and became the founder of one of the Groton Farwell families. The precise date of removal we have not been able to ascertain; but, from the fact that his first two children were the only ones recorded in Chelmsford, and that the third was recorded in Groton in 1701, it seems probable that it may have been a little previous to that date. [See Radial Chart, page 15.]

Res. Chelmsford and *Groton, Mass.*

Children, all recorded in Groton, except the first two, were:

46. 1. JOSEPH⁴, [138] b. 5 Aug. 1696; m. Mary Gilson.
47. 2. THOMAS⁴, b. 11 Oct. 1698, at Chelmsford; m. Groton, Mass., 24 Dec. 1723, Elizabeth Pierce, b. 24 July, 1698, Groton, d. of Ephraim and Mary (Whitney) of Groton, Mass. They had son Thomas, b. 26 July, 1725, G., and d. 8 Sept. 1725.
48. 3. HANNAH⁴, [147] b. 6 May, 1701; m. Eleazer Gilson; m. 2d, Ephraim Sawtell.
49. 4. ELIZABETH⁴, [220] b. 31 Dec. 1703 or 4; m. John Stone, Jr.
50. 5. EDWARD⁴, [265] b. 12 July, 1706; m. Anna ——.
51. 6. MARY⁴, [271] b. 5 Feb. 1709; m. Dea. James Stone.
52. 7. JOHN⁴, [Appendix*] b. 23 June, 1711; m. Sarah Sawtell.
53. 8. SAMUEL⁴, [329] b. 14 Jan. 1714; m. Elizabeth Moors.
54. 9. DANIEL⁴, [340] b. 20 May, 1717; m. Mary ——.
55. 10. SARAH⁴, b. 26 Feb. 1721; d. 4 July, 1721, Groton, Mass.

56. ELIZABETH³, [18] (*Joseph²*, *Henry¹*,) b. 9 June, 1672; d. 9 May, 1722; m. 31 Jan. 1693-4, John³ **RICHARDSON**, b. 14 Feb. 1669, s. and fifth child of Josiah² and Remembrance Underwood of Chelmsford, Mass., and grandson of Ezekiel and Susanna of Charlestown and Woburn. He d. 13 Sept. 1746. He was brother of Susannah³ Richardson who m. Henry³ Farwell [64]. [See Radial Chart.]

---
*We have numerous records of *some* John Farwell and know not how to distribute them among the several of the name born about the same date, and we solicit information that, before our Appendix to the several branches of the Farwell family is reached by the printer, all may be marshalled in order. * * * *It is pleasant to watch the dissipation of darkness at the approach of the morning dawn.*

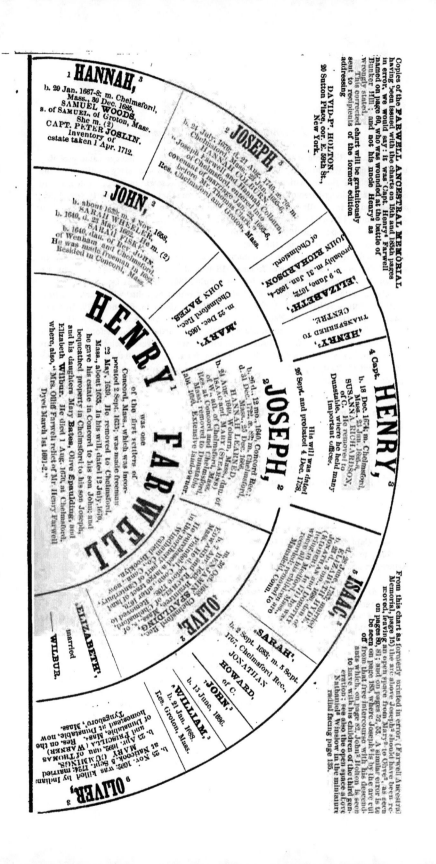

Descendants of Joseph¹ Farwell.

[Ezekiel¹ Richardson was born in England; according to Savage came probably in the fleet of Winthrop 1630, with wife Susanna. He was early admitted to the first church in Boston which was gathered in Charlestown in 1630. He, his wife Susanna, and thirty-three others, were dismissed from that church 11 or 14 Oct. 1632, and embodied into a distinct church, now the First Church in Charlestown. They were dismissed from the Charlestown church, together with his two brothers, Thomas and Samuel, supposed to be younger, June 1642, to help form the church at Woburn. The three brothers lived on the same street, long known as Richardsons row, and among their descendants have been many valuable members of the church and citizens of the town. Ezekiel¹ was freeman 18 May, 1631; was appointed constable by the court 1633, and representative by the people 1635. He d. 21 Oct. 1647.

Capt. Josiah² Richardson, s. of Ezekiel¹ and father of John³ who married Elizabeth³ Farwell, was baptized at Charlestown, 7 Nov. 1635; m. 6 June, 1659, Remembrance Underwood, b. 25 Feb. 1640, d. of William and widow Mary (Deane) [Pellet] Underwood of Concord, Mass., 1638, afterwards of Chelmsford, to which town he removed 1654. Capt. Josiah² was town clerk four years; selectman, fourteen years; representative in 1689-90. The Indians, for the good will they bore him, gave him a tract of land, a portion of which has always been owned and is now in possession of, and occupied by, his descendants]. [*Savage, J-B. Hill and His. of Woburn.*]

Res. *Chelmsford, Mass.*

The children of John and Elizabeth (Farwell) Richardson, according to J-B. Hill, were seven:

57. JOHN, who married Esther ——.
58. HENRY, who married Priscilla Spaulding.
59. SARAH, m. John **Colburn** of Dracut.
60. SUSANNA, m. Henry **Spaulding.**
61.
62.
63.

64. Capt. HENRY³, [19] (*Joseph²*, *Henry¹*,) b. 18 Dec. 1674, Chelmsford, Mass.; d. 1738; m. 23 Jan. 1695-6, Susanna Richardson of Chelmsford, d. of Josiah and Remembrance (Underwood) and sister of John Richardson [56]. *J-B. H.* "Henry Farwell and Susanna Richardson entered into covenant of marriage Jan. 23, 1695-6, before Mr. Thomas Clark." [*Chelmsford rec.*]

He removed with his father from Chelmsford to Old Dunstable about 1699, where his name appears on record as one of the first settlers. He lived on the "Butterfield farm," a part of the "Waldo farm" mentioned under serial number 15, in that part of the town afterwards set off as Tyngsboro. His homestead was not far from that occupied by his father. He seems to have held a prominent position in town affairs; was a selectman of the town most if not all of the years from 1706 to 1730; was surveyor of highways 1702; constable in 1723; moderator of town and proprietors meetings sixteen times between 1719 and 1730, and was appointed twenty-eight times on important committees in the business affairs of the town. Of some of these are the following taken from the History of Dunstable:

"January 16th, 1717, voted that Henry Farwell and Serg't. Cummings are to endever to get a minister as soon as they can, and to see after Mr. Weld's place (the old parsonage) to by it if it be to be had."

In 1724 the town was again called upon to assist in keeping "the great bridge in Billerica in good repare," and chose Henry Farwell "to jine with the committy appinted" for that purpose. 1729 they united with Dracut, Chelmsford, and Billerica in further repairs, and 1731 expended £.3 10s. for the same purpose. This bridge was over the Concord river on the main road to Boston and of great importance.

"In consideration of the universal scarcity of money, the General Assembly of Massachusetts issued bills of credit in 1721 to the amount of £50,000, to be distributed among the several towns in proportion to the public taxes. They answered the purpose of money for the time. —Nov. 7, 1721, Lt. Henry Farwell and Joseph Blanchard were appointed trustees to receive and loan out "the share" of this town, in such sums that "no man shall have more than five pounds, and no man less than three pounds," and shall pay *five per cent.* interest for the use of the same to the Town."

As illustrating in some measure the social position of some of the early families of Dunstable we quote from Fox' History of Dunstable the following:

"But even among our grave and simple forefathers luxury and ambition crept in. March 2, 1720, it was 'voted that Lt. Henry Farwell and Joseph Blanchard should hav the libety to erect for themselves two Pewes on there own charge at the west end of the Meeting House.' The example was contagious, so dangerous is a precedent. If Lt. Farwell and Capt. Blanchard could afford 'Pewes' why might not others ? May 18, 1720, it was 'voted that there be four pewes erected in our Meeting House; one on the back side of the lowermost seats, and one seat to be taken up; Sargt. Colburn, one pew; Sargt. Perham, one pew; Nathaniel Cummings, one pew; Oliver Farwell, one pew.'"

It will be noticed that these several parties were of names allied with the Farwell family. Mr. Farwell bore the title of Lieutenant and Captain and also of Deacon of the church. His will dated 26 Sept. 1738, showing that he was possessed of quite a fortune for that period, considering the high value of money at that date, is as follows :

In the name of God Amen ! The twenty-sixth day of Sept Anno Domini 1738, I, Henry Farwell of Dunstable in County of Middlesex in the Province of Massachusetts Bay in New England, Gentleman, being sick and weak, but of perfect Mind & Memory thanks to God therefor, calling to mind the mortality of my body and knowing that it is appointed for men once to Dye, do make and ordain this my last Will and Testament, and first, I recommend my soul to God who gave it and my body to the dust to be decently buried by my executors hereafter named—And as for the things of this world wherewith God hath blessed me withall—I give and bequeath in manner & form as followeth. And first I give and bequeath unto my beloved wife Susannah the improvement of all my movable Estate and personal Estate, as goods, chattels, etc., and also the improvement of all my homestead, house & buildings during the time she remains my widow, and if she shall marry again then to have no more of my estate than what the law allows her in case of intestate Estates.

Item—I give and bequeath to my Grand Daughter, Hannah Farwell, the daughter of my son Josiah Farwell, deceased, the sum of *three hundred* pounds of good bills of credit, of the aforesaid Province, after the rate of twenty-six shillings per ounce in silver, to be paid by my executors hereafter named to her at her marriage. If she is married before she is twenty years old or otherwise at the time she comes to be twenty-one years old, which I intend as the full of her portion of all my estate. Then I give and bequeath to my three Grand Children, the son & daughters of my son Jonathan Farwell, deceased—viz to Jonathan, Susannah & Rachel Farwell the sum of one (£100) hundred pounds in Bills of Credit of the aforesaid Province, after the rate of Twenty six shillings per ounce in silver, to be paid by my said executors at the time of their marriage, or at the age of twenty-one years, Each, their equal proportion of the said hundred pounds.

Item, I give and bequeath unto my daughter Susanna Brown, the wife of Benjamin Brown of Reading, the sum of Eighty pounds in good bills of credit after the rate of twenty six shillings per ounce, in silver to be paid by my executors hereafter mentioned within one year after my decease—she having already had one hundred and twenty pounds of my estate.

Item—I give and bequeathe unto my daughter Sarah Parker, the wife of Henry Parker of Dunstable, the sum of one hundred & five pounds in good bills of credit after the rate of twenty six shillings per ounce in silver, I having already given her ninety five pounds, to be paid by my executors hereafter named, within one year after my decease.

Item, I have already given to my daughter Elizabeth Bancroft the wife of Timothy Bancroft the sum of two hundred pounds to make her equal with the rest of my daughters in portion.

Item, I have already given unto my daughter Hannah Cummings, wife of Jeremael Cummings the sum of two hundred pounds which is equal to what I have given to the rest of my daughters.

Item,. I give and bequeath unto my two sons, Henry Farwell & Isaac Farwell, and to their heirs and assigns forever to be equally divided between them all my homestead house and buildings, after my wifes decease, making the said Henry Farwell & Isaac Farwell, my sole Executors of this my last will & testament, giving and granting unto my said executors full power and authority to grant, bargain and sell so much of my outlands as will pay out all the aforesaid legacies—Satisfying and confirming this to be my last Will & Testament.

In witness whereof I have hereunto set my hand and seal, the day and year above mentioned.

HENRY FARWELL

This Will was presented for probate Dec. 4th, 1738.

Col. Bancroft, gr. s. of Capt. Henry and his wife Susanna, states that his grandmother Susanna was so much affected by the sad death of her two sons and other troubles that she became insane, and (probably after the death of her husband) went to live with her daughter, Mrs. Cummings, in Hollis, N. H., where she died and was buried, though Mr. J.-B. Hill is unable to find any monument in the graveyard of Hollis erected to her memory. Nearly all of the early Farwells of Dunstable are buried in the Old Dunstable graveyard now included in the town of Nashua.

[See Radial Chart, page 15.]

Children born in Dunstable, except the first two:

65. 1. HENRY[4], [349] b. 14 Oct. 1696, Chelmsford, Mass.; m. Esther Blanchard.
66. 2. JOSIAH[4], [353] b. 27 Aug. 1698, Chelmsford; d. 8 May, 1725; m. Hannah Lovewell.
67. 3. JONATHAN[4], [355] b. 24 July, 1700; m. Susanna Blanchard.
68. 4. SUSANNAH[4], b. 19 Feb. 1703; m. Dea. Benjamin Brown, of Reading, Mass.
69. 5. ISAAC[4], [359] b. 4 Dec. 1704; m. Sarah ——.
70. 6. SARAH[4], b. 4 Dec. 1706; m. Henry Parker, of Dunstable, Mass. They removed from Dunstable to Wilton, N. H. [J.-B. Hill].
71. 7. ELIZABETH[4], [366] b. 1715; d. 23 Sept. 1754; m. Timothy Bancroft.
72. 8. HANNAH[4], [385] b. 4 Apr. 1719; m. Jeremael Cummings; m. 2d, Dea. Stephen Jewett.

73. ISAAC[3], [20] (Joseph[2], Henry[1],) born in Chelmsford, Mass.; d. 28 June, 1753, probably at Mansfield, Conn. He married Elizabeth Hyde, b. 23d. 3m. 1680, d. of Jonathan Jr. and Dorothy (Kidder) of Cambridge village, now Newton, Mass., and granddaughter of Jonathan, Sen., b. 1626, and Mary (French) of Cambridge village.

[Jonathan Hyde, Sen., was of Cambridge village 1647. In 1661 he and his wife Mary French, (daughter of William of Billerica and his wife Elizabeth) were admitted to the church in Cambridge; was freeman 1663. He bought a large tract of land, some of which was very near the centre of Newton. His dwelling house stood about seventy rods north of the centre Meeting House. He bought and sold much land, and in some of his deeds was styled "*Sergeant.*" A few years before his decease he settled his own estate by making deeds of gift of his real estate to eleven of his children; the first was dated 1698, and the last 1710, conveying in all about four hundred acres with several dwelling houses thereon; his other twelve probably had died before him. In his deed to his son Samuel, he put a condition that he was not to "sell it to a stranger, except through want or necessity, but to one of said Jonathan Sen.'s heirs, by the name of Hyde."

His first wife Mary French d. at the birth of her son Joseph (12th or 14th child) 27 May, 1672, aged 39. In 1673—2d. 11mo., he made with John Rediat and son, of Marlboro, a marriage covenant, stipulating that Jonathan Hyde should marry Mary, dau. of said John Rediat, and, that in case he should die before her, she should have his house, barn and one hundred acres of land. In case she had no children by him then the one hundred acres should pass to the children of his first wife. She d. 5 Sept. 1708; and he d. 5 Oct. 1711, age 85.

The father of Mary (French) Hyde came with Harlakenden in the *Defence*, 1635; settled in Cambridge where the births of several of his children are recorded. He was freeman 1636. About 1653 he became one of the first settlers of Billerica, and was the first representative of that town; was Lieutenant and Captain; was engaged in the cause of Indian instruction.

His daughter Mary was recorded in the London Custom House before embarkation as two and half years of age.

Dorothy Kidder, b. 1651, at Cambridge, was d. of James of Cambridge, 1649, who was b. at East Grinstead, Co. Sussex, Eng., about 1626, and son of James and wife Ann, d. of Elder Francis Moore of C., freeman 1639, and his wife Catharine.

Mr. Farwell settled in Medford, Mass., where the births of his children are recorded. March 6, 1710, he was chosen one of the "viewers" of fences; was taxed in Medford for poll, real estate and personal estate, Sept. 20, 1711. At what date he removed to Mansfield, Conn., we are not advised, neither do we know the date of his wife's death.

Children, all recorded in Medford, were:

74. 1. ELIZABETH[4], b. 15 June, 1707.
75. 2. MARY[4], [408] b. 19 Nov. 1709; m. Edmund Hovey.
76. 3. JOHN[4], [417] b. 23 June, 1711; d. Oct. 1756; m. Dorothy Baldwin.
77. 4. WILLIAM[4], [423] b. 28 Dec. 1712; d. 11 Dec. 1801, Charlestown, N. H.; m. 7 Nov. 1744, Bethiah Eldridge.
78. 5. DOROTHY[4], b. 23 Apr. 1715.

79. WILLIAM[3], [23] (*Joseph*[2], *Henry*[1],) b. 21 Jan. 1688, Chelmsford, Mass.; d. probably 14 Feb. 1754; m. acc. to His. of Groton, Elizabeth ———; acc. to Joseph-Rust Farwell and Elijah Scott he married Esther Patterson.

Res. *Groton, Mass.*

Children recorded in Groton, were:

80. 1. ELIZABETH[4], b. 2 Nov. 1713; m. perhaps [*Groton rec.*] 12 Jan. 1730–1, in Watertown, Mass., Jonathan Gates of Stow.
81. 2. WILLIAM[4], Jr., [437] b. 1 Feb. 1715; m. probably Sarah Parker.
82. 3. JOHN[4], [Appendix] b. 16 Oct. 1717; d. 17 Dec. 1814, Harvard, Mass., æ 97; m. 13 July, 1742, Sarah Sawtell, acc. to Wyman and O-P. Farwell.
83. 4. OLIVER[4], [446] b. 13 Jan. 1722; m. Groton, Mass., Rejoice Preston.
84. 5. HENRY[4], [457] b. 21 July, 1724; m. Lydia Tarbell; m. 2d, Sarah Taylor.
85. 6. JOSIAH[4], *acc. to Elijah Scott.*

86. OLIVER[3], [24] (*Joseph*[2], *Henry*[1],) b. 25 Nov. 1692, Chelmsford, Mass.; m. Mary Cummings, b. 25 Apr. 1692, d. of Thomas and Priscilla Warner of Dunstable, Mass. [See Radial Chart, page 15.]

On the 5th Sept. 1724, Lieut. French with ten men under his command, started for the rescue of two of their friends and townsmen, Thomas Blanchard and Nathan Cross, who had been carried off by the Indians the evening previous. Oliver Farwell was one of this company. On arriving at the place where the two men had been laboring, they found evidence that the men had been carried off alive, and concluding the captors and their prisoners could not be far distant, decided on instant pursuit. They therefore bent their way up the Merrimac, till they reached what is now Thorntons Ferry. There they were waylaid, fired upon by the Indians, and all killed except Josiah Farwell [66], nephew of Oliver, who was vigorously chased by them for some time without either gaining much advantage, till he darted into a thicket, where they lost sight of him, and fearing he might have reloaded, abandoned the pursuit. Thus he alone escaped—to fall by the hand of the same savage enemy the next year. Fox says in Hist. of Dunstable, the captors were a company of French Mohawks, about seventy in number. A company immediately mustered and proceeded to the place to secure the bodies of their friends and townsmen. Eight were found, placed in coffins and buried in one capacious grave in the ancient Cemetery of Old Dunstable, now in the south part of the City of Nashua. Of the slain was Oliver³ Farwell, and on a small stone about two feet high [*J. B. Hill*] is the following inscription: OLIVER FARWELL WHO DIED SEPT. 5, 1724, IN THE 33D YEAR OF HIS AGE.

By reference to the will of his father Joseph² [15] it will be seen that Oliver was chosen to take care of him and his wife during their natural lives; and if "he doth take the whole care of us both and to provide all things comfortable and necessary for us both in sickness and in health, and to bestow upon us, or either of us a decent burial," he was to receive all his "housings and lands which I have in possession." The father died nearly two years before the untimely death of his son Oliver. Whether the mother was living to mourn the loss of him on whom she had leaned for support and solace in the decline of life, we are not informed.

Mary Cummings, wife of Oliver Farwell, b. 25 Apr. 1692, was daughter of Thomas and Priscilla (Warner) Cummings of Dunstable, and granddaughter of John, Sen., and Sarah (Howlet) Cummings of Rowley, Mass. John, Sen. was freeman 1673, rem. to Dunstable 1684; 1685, was one of the founders of the Dunstable Church; selectman and town clerk. The parents of Sarah Howlet were Thomas and Alice (French) Howlet of Boston. Said Thomas Howlet is said by Savage to have come in the fleet with Winthrop 1630. He went with John Winthrop, son of Gov. W., early in 1633 to plant Ipswich was freeman 3 Mar. 1634, and Rep. 1635.

Children born in Dunstable:

87. 1. MARY⁴, b. 8 May, 1716.
88. 2. OLIVER⁴, [465] b. 19 Nov. 1717; d. 12 Feb. 1808; m. Abigail Hubbard.
89. 3. BENJAMIN⁴, b. 14 May, 1720; d. 20 Mar. 1772, aged 52; acc. to grave-stone, 56. A Benjamin died 20 Mar. 1772, and J-B. Hill finds no other Benjamin of this generation or date, and it is probable the mistake was made in the cutting of the inscription. His name is mentioned in the list of town officers of Dunstable, and Tyngsboro, Mass. 1747-9.
90. 4. SARAH⁴, b. 8 May 1724.

91. EDWARD³, [27] (*Olive²* (*Farwell*) Spaulding, *Henry¹*,) b. 18 June 1672; d. 29 Nov. 1740, aged 67. *Canterbury, Conn. records say* 1739; m. Mary Adams who d.

20 Sept. 1754, aged 78. He was the third settler of Brooklyn Conn. He bought lands north of Canterbury bounds at the foot of Tadwick Hill, in 1707. Was one of the first committee of the religious society organized in 1731.

Children, all of whom were born in Canterbury, except Benjamin, who was born in Chelmsford, Mass.:

92. 1. BENJAMIN⁴, [473] b. 20 July, 1696; m. Abigail Wright, m. 2d, Deborah Wheeler.
93. 2. ELIZABETH⁴, b. 15 Aug. 1698; m. William Darbe.
94. 3. EPHRAIM⁴, [484] b. 3 April 1700; m. Abigail Bullard.
95. 4. JONATHAN⁴, b. 15 April, 1704; m. Eunice Woodward, d. of David of Plainfield, Conn. They had one child Edith, b. 24 Oct. 1726.

Res. Plainfield, Conn.

96. 5. EZEKIEL⁴, [495] b. 8 Sept. 1706; m. 24 Nov. 1837, Martha Kimball.
97. 6. RUTH⁴, b. 27 Sept. 1710; m. John Bacon.
98. 7. ABIGAIL⁴, b. 10 March, 1713; m. Benaijah Douglas.
99. 8. EBENEZER⁴, [500] b. 24 June, 1717; m. Mary Fasset.
100. 9. THOMAS⁴, b. 7 Aug. 1719; m. 1 Nov. 1742, Abigail Brown.
101. 10. JOHN⁴, b. 1 Dec. 1721.

102. BENJAMIN³, [28] (*Olive²* (*Farwell*) Spaulding, *Henry¹*,) b. 6 July, 1685.

Children:

103. 1. OLIVE⁴, b. 17 July, 1709.
104. 2. SARAH⁴, b. 8 Oct. 1711; m. 30 March, 1730, Samuel Coitt.

105. SARAH⁴, [32] (*Sarah³* (*Farwell*) Jones, *John²*, *Henry¹*,) b. 4 June, 1686, at Concord, Mass.; m. 1705, Lieut. Daniel HOAR, b. about 1680, Concord, son of Daniel and Mary (Stratton,) of Concord. He d. 8 Feb. 1773, aged 93. [For his line of ancestry and connections see chart V].

"March 3, 1709—10. The select men order the town treasurer to pay Daniel Hoar Jr., a small bill of 6s:

"Whereas the select men of the town gave old Cooksey an ordre to take up a shirt cloth (viz.) two yards and an half of coutton and lining of Daniel Hoar Jr., comming to 6 s. sometime lately, the select men doe now order ye town treasurer to pay him the said sum out of the town treasury: That is to say to said Daniel Hoar Jr."

24 Feb. 1712—13. "To Daniel Hoar, Jr., for what he did for old Cooksay in sickness and health £1,7s,6d."

3 March, 1728—9. Daniel Hoar, Jr. was chosen one of the surveyors of highways and bridges. Was tithing man 3 March, 1729—30.

John Hoar, grandfather of Lieut. Daniel, Jr., was born in England; settled in Scituate, Mass., where he bore arms in 1643; practiced there as a lawyer till his removal to Concord in 1660. "He was distinguished for bold, independent mind and action." "By the bold and successful exertions of Mr. John Hoar of Concord, in connection with Tom Doublet, and Peter Conaway, Christian Indians of Concord,"

CHART V.—DANIEL[4] HOAR.

Patronymic Ancestral Line of Lieut. DANIEL[4] HOAR, with some of his Descendants.

JOANNA ——. She died at Braintree. Mass., probably at the residence of her daughter Joanna, who married the second Col. Edmond Quincy of B. = ——[1] HOAR, according to tradition a wealthy banker from London, who died soon after his arrival in Boston.
Mrs. Joanna Hoar, probably his wife, died in Braintree, Mass., 21 Dec. 1661.

24 June, 1648.
Joanna[2], d. 1680. = The second Colonel Edmund **Quincy**, of Braintree, Mass., born Eng. ab. 1628. He married 2d, and had 11, Edmund, born 1681, 12, Mary, m. Rev. Da'el Baker.

1, Mary[3], b. 1650, m. Ephraim **Savage**, ch. 4.
2, Daniel[3], b. 1651.
3, John[3], born 1652; died young.
5, Judith[3], b. 1655; m. Rev. John **Rayner**, Jr. of Dover.
6, Elizabeth[3], born 1656; m. 1689, Rev. Daniel **Gookin**, of Shirborne.
7, Edmund[3], born 1657; died young.
8, Ruth[3], b. 1658; m. 1686, John **Hunt**, of Weymouth.
9, Annie[3], born ——; died 1696.
10. Experience[3], married William **Savil**.
4, Joanne[3], b. 1654; d. 18 May, 1695. = David **Hobart**, b, Aug. 1651, s. of Rv. Peter of Hingham. He m. 2d, 4 Dec. 1695, Sarah Joyce and had 6 children.

1. Judith[4], born 1681.
2, Peter[4], born 1684; died in three days.
3, Jael[4], born 1688.
4. Deborah[4], born 1690.
5, Rebecca[4], born 1693.

Margery[2], b. England; d. 10 Mar. 1687. = Rev. Henry **Flint**, of Braintree, b. England, came 1635, d. 1688.
10 ch.

Hezekiah of Scituate, acc. to Deane.

Alice ——, died 5 June, 1697. = John[2], b. Eng.; was of Scituate 1643–55. [*Hist. of Concord.*] He rm. to Concord about 1660; died 2 April, 1704.
+ 8 ch.

Daniel[2] of Boston; rt. to Eng 1653, & d. in London.

Bridget Lisle, dau. of John, one of Cromwell's commissioners of the Great Seal. She d. 25 May, 1723. = Leonard[2], b. in Eng.; grad. Harvard College, 1650, and in 1672, M.D.; was Prs. of H. C. 1672 to 1675. He d. 28 Nov. 1675.

23 Dec. 1675.
Elizabeth (2d wife), died 22 Sept. 1687. See Prescott Memorial, p. 46. = Captain Jonathan **Prescott**, born 1643; d. 5 Dec. 1721.

19 July 1677.
Mary Stratton, daughter of Samuel and Mary. = Daniel[3] of Concord, b. 1650; m. 2d. 16 Oct. 1717, Mary Lee.

Mary[3], m. 1668, Bej. **Graves**. s. of John of Concord.

Bridget[3], born in Cambridge, 13 Mar., 1673; married Rev. Thomas **Cotton**, a minister, of London, and liberal benefactor of Harvard Coll.
For her relationship with Lord John Russell, Duke of Bedford, and Sir Henry Houghton see Sav., p. 432.

John[4], b. 24 Oct. 1678.
Mary[4], b. 14 Mar. 1689.

Leonard[4].
Jonathan[4].
Joseph[4].
Benjamin[4].

1705.
Sarah Jones, b. 4 June, 1686, daugh. of John and Sarah[3] (Farwell) of Concord, Mass. = Lt. Daniel[4], b. ab. 1680; died 8 Feb. 1773. æ. 93. [See [105] p. 22. *

Samuel[4], b. 6 Apr. 1691.
Isaac[4], b. 18 May, 1695.
David[4], b. 14 Nov. 1698.
Elizabeth[4], b. 22 Fb. 1701.

Daniel[5], entered Harvard College, 1730, but did not graduate. [107]

Timothy[5], [serial number 109, p. 24.]

Elizabeth Cooledge of Watertown, Mass. = John[5], was in the battle of Concord, Mass. 1775. See ser. number 106, p. 23.

Jonathan[5], b. ab. 1720; gr. H.C. 1740 d. 1771, æ 52 [108]

Several daughters.

—— = Hon. Samuel[6], of Lincoln, Mass., born about 1744; died in 1832 in his 89th year; was representative, senator, and justice of the peace; was one of a committee to take a plan of the town of Lincoln for the Gen Court, chosen 21 Aug. 1794. He was a Lieutenant at Ticonderoga, 1776, and was at the surrender of Gen. Burgoyne.

Leonard[6] of Lincoln, Mass.

Hon. Samuel[7], b. 18 May, 1778; grad. 1802; Was admitted to the bar 1805, and settled in Concord. He was a member of the committee for revising the Constitution of the State, 1821, and of the Senate, 1825 and 1832.

Nathaniel-Pierce[7], born 2 Sept. 1784; gr. 1810; read law with his bro. in Concord. Com. practice at Portsmouth 1813; d. in C. 24 May, 1820.

* This Chart is designed to represent briefly the ancestry and some of the connections of Lieut. DANIEL[4] HOAR, whose descendants, by his marriage with Sarah Jones, daughter of SARAH[3] (FARWELL) JONES, are allied with the descendants of Henry[1] Farwell, of Concord and Chelmsford, Mass.

DAVID-P[7]. HOLTON, M.D., 18 June, 1879.

Mrs. Rowlandson, the wife of the minister of Lancaster, Mass., and her children, who, were captured by the Indians, 10 July, 1676, at the burning of that place, were redeemed after a captivity of three months.

Mr. John Hoar was deeply interested in the welfare of the Indians, and was charged by order of the council "with the government and tuition" of the Praying Indians of Nashoba, who sojourned in Concord. They lived "soberly, quietly and industriously, and could not be charged with any unfaithfulness to the English interest."

At the opening of King Philip's war, some of the inhabitants, and especially the soldiers, became prejudiced against them, and to the great grief of Mr. Hoar, and much personal loss and brave resistance, the Indians were forced away by the soldiers and carried to Deer Island to share in the sufferings of many others of their red brethren.

Mr. Hoar had begun to build for them a large structure as a workhouse and place of defence, "but he lost his building and other cost which he had provided" for their entertainment and employment. [*Gookin.*]

Res. *Concord, Mass.*

Children :

106. JOHN⁴, m. Elizabeth Coolidge of Watertown, Mass. He was in the battle of Concord, 19 Apr. 1776. His deposition was taken the 23d of the same month, before the committee chosen by the Provincial Congress to take depositions, of those who witnessed or participated in the battle, relating to the conduct of the British on the 19th inst. The evidence was transmitted to the Continental Congress and to England. The whole was published by order of the Provincial Congress, in a pamphlet of 22 pages, entitled "A Narrative of the Incursions and Ravages of the King's Troops under command of Gen. Gage, on the nineteenth of April, 1775, together with the Depositions taken by order of Congress to support the truth of it." The original depositions, about one hundred in number, with the signatures of the deponents, were, a few years since, in the Library of Harvard College.

A John Hoar was captured in an engagement at Fort Dummer, 14 July, 1748, and remained with the Indians three months. We suppose this captive to be our John⁴ Hoar, instead of his uncle of the same name, who was b. 1678, and would be far advanced in years at this time. We know of no other John Hoar of Concord at the above date.

107. DANIEL⁴, entered Harvard College 1730, but did not graduate.
108. JONATHAN⁴, b. about 1820; grad. Harvard College 1740. He was in the provincial service during the whole French and Indian war. In 1755 went as Major to Fort Edward; was Lieut. Col. in the expedition to Crown Point 1756, and aid to Major Gen. Winslow; 1760 he was Lieut. Col. in the expedition to Nova Scotia. He sailed for that place from Boston, May 10, 1762, as Colonel, with 500 men, 16 of whom were from Concord. After the peace of 1763 he went to England, and was appointed Governor

of Newfoundland and the neighboring provinces, but died on his passage thither in 1771, aged 52.

109.   TIMOTHY⁴, 20 Apr. 1778, he was one of nine men required by the General Court from Concord to serve as guard at North River for eight months; his bounty was £100.   Res. *Concord, Mass.*
[There were also several daughters of whom we have no records.]

110.   Ensign JOHN⁴, [33] (*Sarah³* (*Farwell*) Jones, *John²*, *Henry¹*,) born. 6 Jan. 1690, Concord, Mass.; d. 12 March, 1762, aged 72, "The husband of Anna." He married Anna Brooks, who d. 9 June, 1753. She was probably daughter of Daniel and Ann (Merriam), gr. dau. of Joshua and Hannah (Mason, d. of Capt. Hugh of Watertown,) and gr. gr. dau. of Capt. Thomas and Grace (———) of Concord.

[Capt. Thomas, said to have come from London, *Shattuck's History of Concord*; was freeman 7 Dec. 1636, when, acc. to Savage, he "was an inhabitant of Watertown and owned estates there, and in Medford, perhaps as early as 1634; was representative 1642 and six years more." He removed to Concord, where he d. 21 May, 1667. His wife Grace d. 12 May, 1664.]

Ensign John Jones is mentioned in the records of Concord, in relation to the division of lands, 10 Feb. 1732-3.

Res. *Concord, Mass.*

Children:

111.   JOHN⁵, b. 23 June, 1718; m. 1742, Abigail Wesson, who d. 19 Dec. 1805.
112.   OLIVE⁵, b. 10 Sept. 1724; m. Joseph Stow, perhaps s. of Nathaniel and Ruth (Merriam) of Concord, who were married 1690.
113.   EBENEZER⁵, b. 8 Dec. 1726; m. Mary.
114.   DANIEL⁵, b. 28 Dec. 1728; m. Rebecca Cary.
115.   FARWELL⁵, b. 18 Aug. 1734; d. 20 Dec. 1802, aged 69; m. Concord, Mass. 1 Jan. 1777, Hannah Hosmer, who d. 11 Dec. 1801, aged 62.

Res. *Concord Mass.*

116.   BARTHOLOMEW⁴, (*Sarah³* (*Farwell*) Jones, *John²*, *Henry¹*,) b. 15 Feb. 1697-8; d. 16 Sept. 1738, aged 42; m. July, 1723, Ruth Stow.

Children:

117.   TIMOTHY⁵, b. 17 April, 1725; d. 11 Sept. 1745.
118.   RUTH⁵, b. 2 May, 1727.
119.   SARAH⁵, b. 28 Jan. 1729—30.
120.   MARY⁵, b. 12 May, 1732.
121.   LYDIA⁵, b. 7 Aug. 1734.
122.   REBECCA⁵, b. 24 July, 1736.
123.   SILENCE⁵, b. 14 Sept. 1738.

124. SAMUEL⁴, [37] (*Hannah³* (*Farwell*) [WOODS] Joslin, *Joseph²*, *Henry¹*,) married at Groton, Mass. 29 Nov. 1720, Patience Bigelow, probably daughter of James and Elizabeth (Child,) of Watertown, [first wife was Patience Brown.] She was born 30 Sept. 1695; died 23 Jan. 1771. He d. 10 Apr. 1773. [*Groton records.*] Although the name and birth of Samuel⁴, are not recorded among the children of Samuel, Jr., and Hannah Farwell in Groton, we infer from a deed to "Samuel, 1st. son of Samuel and Hannah," recorded vol. 17, p. 295, that he may have been born before their residence in Groton. Samuel Woods' name frequently occurs in the History of Groton, but not as *Senior* till 1692, and as Samuel, who married Hannah Farwell 1685 in Chelmsford, is called Junior, and no *births* of their children are recorded in Groton till 1700, it may be possible that they did not take up their abode in Groton for several years after marriage.

We hope to obtain information concerning this matter before the issue of a second edition. Res. *Groton, Mass.*

Children born in Groton:

125. 1. ELIZABETH⁵, b. 29 Aug. 1721; m. Groton, 4 Feb. 1741-2, Ephraim **Divol**, of Lancaster,
126. 2. SAMUEL⁵, b. 2 Dec. 1722.
127. 3. HANNAH⁵, b. 1 Dec. 1724.
128. 4. ABIGAIL⁵, b. 11 December, 1726; m. Groton, 25 Nov. 1747, Oliver **Wheeler** of Acton, Mass.
129. 5. EUNICE⁵. b. 24 Feb. 1729.
130. 6. JAMES⁵, b. 22 Oct. 1731; m. Groton, 6 Feb. 1760, Abigail Howard.

*Children, all recorded in Groton, were:

131.   1. James⁶, b. 19 April, 1761.
132.   2. Nahum⁶, b. 14 Nov. 1763.
133.   3. Jotham⁶, b. 3 Mar. 1766.
134.   4. Abigail⁶, b. 20 Jan. 1769.
135.   5. Rachel⁶, b. 9 Apr. 1771; m. Bill-Wright Stevens.
136. 7. WILLIAM⁵, b. 17 Oct. 1735.
137. 8. MARY⁵, b. 16 Mach, 1738.

138. JOSEPH⁴, [46] (*Joseph³*, *Joseph²*, *Henry¹*,) b. 5 Aug. 1696, Chelmsford, Mass.; married, Groton, Mass. 4 December, 1719, Mary Gilson, b. 8 February, 1703,

---

*The question may arise in the minds of our readers as to the reason of our giving so few of the descendants of the fifth generation in some lines, while in other branches the descendants are so fully given to the present date. In reply we must say that the scope of this work does not embrace any beyond the fifth generation outside of the branch at whose expense the edition is published. When, however, only a few of the sixth and subsequent generations are found in our collections of records, we have chosen to add them; while more fully developed branches could not be inserted without carrying us into greater expense than the funds of the party appropriated to the publication of their own branch would warrant us. We sincerely regret our financial inability to do more, but are prepared to print any or all of the branches whenever sufficient sums are advanced for the purpose.

G., d. of Joseph and Elizabeth of Groton.

In the diary of Joseph⁴ Farwell is found this entry:

"Groton June ye 29, 1750 I was chosen into ye office of a Deacon in the first church in Groton, and on the first sabbath in July waited on that duty."

"May 6, 1754. Voted, that the meeting house committee provide one hogshead of rum, one loaf of white sugar, one quarter of a hundred of brown sugar. Also voted, that Deacon Stone, [271] Deacon Farwell, Lieut. Isaac Woods, Benjamin Stone, Lieut. John Woods, Capt. Samuel Tarbell, Amos Lawrence, Ensign Obadiah Parker and Capt. Bancroft, be a committee to provide victuals and drink for a hundred men." "Then voted that the selectmen provide some convenient place to meet in upon the sabbath until further orders."

These preparations were made for the raising of the fourth meeting house in Groton.

At a church meeting July 5, 1782, the four deacons Farwell, Stone, [271] Farnsworth and Bancroft, with Israel Robert, Esq., were chosen trustees of the twenty pounds given by Jonathan Lawrence for the benefit of the ordained minister or ministers of Groton, with power to take or receive the same of Samuel Dana the late pastor if need be, to sue him upon his bond given therefor. Also to offer the same to Rev. Daniel Chaplin, if he will receive it, otherwise put it out upon interest, and pay over to said Chaplin the interest thereon.

A Joseph Farwell of Groton deeded land in Lancaster to Samuel Willard of L., 24 March, 1729, [*Worcester records*]. We are unable to say whether this land was deeded by Joseph⁴, or by his father, Joseph³, who was living at the above date.

Res. *Groton, Mass.*

Children all recorded in Groton:

139. 1. ANNA⁵, b. 20 Feb. 1721; m. 11 Nov. 1741, Josiah Brown of Littleton.
140. 2. ISAAC⁵, b. 16 Mar. 1722; d. 10 May, 1740.
141. 3. JOSEPH⁵, b. 20 Sept. 1725; d. 27 Aug. 1758.
142. 4. JONATHAN⁵, b. 15 May, 1730; d. 29 Nov. 1761, at Charlestown, N.H.
143. 5. DEA. THOMAS⁵, b. 30 July, 1733, *Groton rec.;* d. 20 Feb. 1825, Washington, N.H.; m. Sarah Davis, b. 22 March, 1742, Harvard, Mass., who died 28 Feb. 1813, in Washington, N.H.
144. 6. OLIVER⁵, b. 24 June, 1735.
145. 7. MARY⁵, b. 4 Sept. 1738.
146. 8. SUSANNA⁵, b. 8 Aug. [*Groton rec.*] 1742; m. Groton, 6 Apr. 1763. John Cheney of Groton.

147. HANNAH⁴, [48] (*Joseph³, Joseph², Henry¹,*) b. 6 May, 1701, Groton, Mass.; d. 11 May, 1762; married, *Groton rec.*, 6 May, 1719, Eleazer GILSON. She married 2d, as second wife, 26 March, 1755, *Groton rec.*, Capt. Ephraim SAWTELL. His will was made in 1767. At a legal meeting of "Groton West Parish" 17 Jan. 1742, Eleazer Gilson was chosen parish clerk. This precinct or parish set off from Groton

Children of Eleazer and Hannah (Farwell) Gilson:

148. 1. ELEAZER³, b. 19 Feb. 1720; m. Groton West Parish, 21 July, 1748, Mary Hall; m. 2d, 30 Oct. 1758, Sybil Lakin. From the church records made by the Rev. Joseph Emerson, first pastor of the first church in Pepperell, under the title of "Remarkable Providences," we quote the following: "January, 1767. In the night the house of Eleazer Gilson was entirely consumed by fire. They could save but very little of their household stuff." In the list of contributions made by the church in Groton, recorded in one of the church books, is found this entry: "1767, For Eleazer Gilson of Pepperell about £5." Res. *Pepperell, Mass.*

Children all born in Pepperell:

149.   1. Mary⁴, b. Oct. 1749.
150.   2. Catharine⁴, b. Nov. 1751.
151.   3. Lydia⁴, b. Dec. 1753.
152.   4. Eleazer⁴, b. March, 1756.
153.   5. Nathaniel⁴, b. 17 Sept. 1759, of "Sybil."
154.   6. Elizabeth⁴, b. 9 Feb. 1762.
155.   7. Peter⁴, b. 28 Feb. 1764.
156.   8. James⁴, b. 4 April, 1766.
157.   9. Sybil⁴, b. 31 Aug. 1768.
158. 10. Hannah⁴, b. 8 Jan. 1770.
159. 11. Susanna⁴, b. 8 Aug. 1772.
160. 12. Anna⁴, b. 19 Jan. 1776.
161. 2. HANNAH³, b. 7 March, 1722; m. Simon Page. Res. Groton and *Shirley*.

Children:

162.   1. Simon⁴, Jr., b. 6 June, 1742, Groton, Mass.; m. *Groton rec.*, 15 Jan. 1767, Elizabeth Moors, b. 6 July, 1745, *Groton rec.*, d. of Timothy and Lydia (Nutting) of Groton. Res. Groton and *Shirley, Mass.*

Children, all born in Shirley, were:

163.   1. *Eunice*⁷, b. 17 Aug. 1767.
164.   2. *Sybil*⁷, b. 5 Sept. 1769; d. 18 Jan. 1784.
165.   3. *Elizabeth*⁷, b. 12 Oct. 1771.
166.   4. *Susey*⁷, b. 8 Jan. 1774.
167.   5. *Lyda*⁷, b. 27 Dec. 1776.
168.   6. *Hannah*⁷, b. 28 Feb. 1778.
169.   7. *Simon*⁷, b. 30 Oct. 1779.

170.   8. Joel⁷, b. 22 July, 1785.
171.   2. James⁵, b. 22 Apr. 1744; d. 23 Sept. 1775, *Groton rec.*
171ᵃ.   3. Hannah⁶, b. 31 May, 1746, Groton, Mass.
172.   4. Lydia⁶, b. 10 Dec. 1748,   "
173.   5. Jonas⁶, b. 2 Sept. 1750,   "
174.   6. Betty⁶, b. 22 May, 1752,   "
175.   7. Abel⁶, b. 15 Aug. 1759, Shirley, Mass.
176.   8. Peter⁶, b. 29 Sept. 1761, S.; drowned 8 July, 1773.
177.   9. Eunice⁶, b. 24 July, 1763, S.; d. 30 Apr. 1767.
178.   10. Betsey⁶, b. 27 Apr. 1765, S.; d. 10 June, 1776.
179.   11. Oliver⁶, b. 17 Apr. 1767.
180. 3. ESTHER⁵, b. 30 July, 1724; m. ——.

   Child:

181.   1. Sybil⁶.

182. 4. EUNICE⁵, b. 8 Nov. 1726, *Groton rec.*; m. Benjamin **Blood**, b. 22 Aug. 1719, *Groton rec.*, son of Nathaniel and Hannah (Shattuck) of Groton.

   Children born in Groton:

183.   1. Eunice⁶, b. 9 July, 1747.
184.   2. Benjamin⁶, b. 1 July, 1749.
185.   3. Edmund⁶, b. 16 June, 1751; m. *Groton rec.*, 24 Nov. 1772, Catherine Blood, b. 27 Oct. 1753, *Groton rec.*, d. of Simon and Anna (Shattuck).
186.   4. Deborah⁶, b. 1 Oct. 1753.
187.   5. Joshua⁶, b. 26 Jan. 1756.
188.   6. Rachel⁶, b. 13 Apr. 1758.
189.   7. Ann⁶, b. 20 Nov. 1760.

190. 5. SAMUEL⁵, b. 7 Jan. 1728, *Groton rec.*; m. Pepperell, Mass. 20 Feb. 1752, Elizabeth Shed, b. 9 May, 1724, *Groton rec.*, dau. of Daniel and Abigail (——)

   Children recorded in Pepperell:

191.   1. Samuel⁶, b. 23 Dec. 1752; was of Chelmsford in 1810.
192.   2. Elizabeth⁶, b. 19 Dec. 1754; m. acc. to Mr. Wyman, ——**Crosby**.
193.   3. Sarah⁶, b. 18 Jan. 1757; m. acc. to Wyman, ——**Brown**.
194.   4. Rachel⁶, b. 13 Dec. 1759.
195.   5. John⁶, b. 7 Mar. 1762.
196.   6. Hannah⁶, b. 26 May, 1764.
197.   7. Joel⁶, b. 26 Mar. 1767.
198.   8. Alice⁶, b. 12 Apr. 1769.
199.   9. Mary⁶, b. 7 May, 1771.
200.   10. Rebecca⁶, b. 20 June, 1773.
201.   11. Joseph⁶, b. 30 July, 1775.

202. 6. SIMON⁴, b. 22 Dec. 1730; m., *Pepperell rec.*, 14 Apr. 1756, Sarah Fisk, b. 7 Oct. 1736, *Pepperell rec.*, d. of Josiah and Sarah (Lawrence) of P.
Res. *Pepperell.*

Children all born in Pepperell:

203. 1. Jonas⁵, b. 19 Dec. 1756; d. 1 Oct. 1757, Pepperell.
204. 2. Sarah⁵, b. 24 Aug. 1758.
205. 3. Peter⁵, b. 21 Jan. 1761; d. 15 Nov. 1763, Pepperell.
206. 4. Hannah⁵, b. 1 May, 1763.
207. 5. Simon⁵, b. 9 Aug. 1765; d. 10 Mar. 1770, P.
208. 6. Eunice⁵, b. 1 Aug. 1767.
209. 7. David⁵, b. 21 Sept. 1769.
210. 8. Submit⁵, b. 11 Aug. 1771.
211. 9. Josiah⁵, b. 27 Oct. 1773; d. 14 March, 1776, P.
212. 10. Simon⁵, b. 24 Apr. 1777.

213. 7. PETER⁴, b. 3 Feb. 1732, *Groton rec.*, married, *Groton rec.*, 27 May, 1756, Sybil Whitney, b. 31 March, 1731, *Groton rec.*, d. of Timothy and Submit (——) of Groton. She married 2d, *Groton rec.*, 3 May, 1764, Oliver Lakin, b. 24 Feb. 1733-4, s. of William and Miriam, *Groton rec.*

Children recorded in Groton:

214. 1. Sybil⁵, b. 18 Jan. 1757; m. Levi **Woods** of Pepperell, prob. s. of Jonathan and Mary and b. 10 May, 1753, *Groton rec.*
215. 2. Lydia⁵, b. 28 Aug. 1759; d. 29 Nov. 1847, Waltham, Mass.; married, Groton, Mass., Zaccheus **Farwell**, b. 27 June, 1753, Groton, s. of Daniel and Mary. He d. 28 June, 1811, Fitchburg, Mass. [347].

216. 8. LYDIA⁴, b. 17 Sept. 1735, *Groton rec.;* married, Groton, 27 Sept. 1759, Peter **Stevens**.
Res. *Groton.*

Children recorded in Groton:

217. 1. John⁵, b. 12 May, 1760.
218. 2. Peter⁵, b. 23 March, 1762
219. 3. Simon⁵, b. 2 Apr. 1764.

220. ELIZABETH⁴, [49] (*Joseph³, Joseph², Henry¹,*) b. 31 Dec. 1703, Groton, Mass., d. 11 May, 1762; married, *Groton rec.*, 22 or 26 Dec. 1722, John **STONE**, Jr., b. 23 Sept. 1699, s. of John and Sarah (Nutting) of Groton. His will was probated 29 Dec. 1784. He married 2d, 28 April, 1763, Rachel Pierce.
Res. *Groton, Mass.*

Children, born in Groton, were:

221. 1. JOHN⁵, b. 5 Nov. 1723; married, *Groton rec.*, 7 July, 1747, Anna Pratt, who d. 10 Nov. 1756, Groton. He married 2d, 11 Jan. 1759, widow Jerusha Woods.
Res. *Groton, Mass.*

Children born in Groton:

222.   1. Abraham⁶, b. 8 May, 1748.
223.   2. John⁶, b. 17 June, 1750.
224.   3. Israel⁶, b. 17 Feb. 1752.
225.   4. Nathaniel⁶, b. 11 Dec. 1754; d. 14 Nov. 1756.
226.   5. Anna⁶, b. 4 June, 1755; d. 29 Oct. 1756.
227.   6. Anna⁶, b. 6 July, 1760.
228.   2. ELIZABETH⁵, b. 26 Sept. 1725; married, *Groton rec.*, 27 June, 1745, Moses **Blood**, b. 25 Nov. 1724, s. of John and Joanna (Nutting).
                Res. Groton and *Pepperell, Mass.*

Children, all recorded in Pepperell, were

228ª.   1. Elizabeth⁶, b. 6 July, 1746.
228ᵇ.   2. Sarah⁶, b. 16 Mar. 1748.
228ᶜ.   3. Moses⁶, b. 29 Apr. 1750.
228ᵈ.   4. Abel⁶, b. 17 Sept. 1752.
228ᵉ.   5. Anna⁶, b. 7 Apr. 1755.
228ᶠ.   6. Rachel⁶, b. 11 Nov. 1757.
228g.   7. Anna⁶, b. 15 Sept. 1760.
228h.   8. Nathaniel⁶, b. 21 Aug. 1762.
228i.   9. Sewall⁶, b. 24 May, 1765.
228j.   10. Mary⁶, b. 4 Apr. 1770.
229.   3. DAVID⁵, b. 7 Aug. 1728; d. 10 Oct. 1758, Groton, Mass.; married 1 April, 1752, Lydia Pratt.

Children born acc. to Groton records, in Groton:

230.   1. Lydia⁶, b. 12 March, 1753.
231.   2. Anna⁶, b. 16 Aug. 1755; died 7 May, 1756, Groton.
232.   3. David⁶, b. 19 Feb. 1756; died 6 Nov. 1756,   "
233.   4. MINDWELL⁵, b. 10 Apr. 1731; married, according to Groton records, 8 Feb. 1747-8, Moses **Wentworth**.   Res. *Groton, Mass.*

Children recorded in Groton:

234.   1. Elizabeth⁶, b. 11 Jan. 1748-9.
235.   2. Eunice⁶, b. 18 Dec. 1750.
236.   3. Phœbe⁶, b. 26 Feb. 1753.
237.   4. Oliver⁶, b. 8 Feb. 1762.
238.   5. NATHANIEL⁵, b. 27 Sept. 1733; d. Sept. 1811; married, *Groton rec.*, Sybil **Stone**, b. 16 Oct. 1733, d. of Joseph and Mary (Prescott) of Groton.
                    Res. *Groton, Mass.*

Children:

239. 1. Nathaniel⁶, b. 1 Sept. 1759.
240. 2. Sybil⁶, b. 24 Nov. 1761.
241. 3. Hannah⁶, b. 10 Oct. 1763.
242. 4. Olive⁶, b. 15 Jan. 1766.
243. 5. Rhoda⁶, b. 22 Oct. 1767.
244. 6. Joseph⁶, b. 19 Dec. 1769; d. 10 Nov. 1772.
245. 7. Molly⁶, b. 29 Dec. 1771.
246. 8. Isaac⁶, b. 6 Jan. 1774.
247. 9. Joseph⁶, b. 7 Feb. 1776.

248. 6. SARAH⁵, b. 20 October, 1735; married, according to Mr. Wyman, William Jones.
249. 7. THOMAS⁵, b. 18 May, 1739.
250. 8. ABEL⁵, b. 9 April, 1742; married 11 Aug. 1763, Lydia Whittaker, *Groton rec.* Res. *Groton, Mass.*

Children born in Groton:

251. 1. Betty⁶, b. 25 Dec. 1763.
252. 2. Abel⁶, b. 8 March, 1765.
253. 3. Lucy⁶, b. 12 August, 1766.

254. 9. ESTHER⁵, b. 18 June, 1744; married, *Groton rec.*, 11 March, 1766, Ephraim Pierce.
255. 10. ASA⁵, b. 13 July, 1748; married Patty (——). Res. *Groton, Mass,*

Children recorded in Groton:

256. 1. Asa⁶, b. 21 January, 1777.
257. 2. Patty⁶, b. 15 March, 1779; d. 15 August, 1782.
258. 3. Emma⁶, b. 10 June, 1781.
259. 4. William⁶, b. 3 June, 1783; died 11 February, 1784,
260. 5. William⁶, b. 26 February, 1785.
261. 6. Patty⁶, b. 5 Sept. 1787.
262. 7. Sukey⁶, b. 21 Nov. 1789.
263. 8. John⁶, d. 28 Sept. 1784.
264. 9. Rachel⁶, d. 7 Nov. 1784.

265. EDWARD⁴, [50] (*Joseph³, Joseph², Henry¹,*) b. 12 July, 1706, Groton, Mass.; married Anna (——).

Children born in Groton:

266. 1. EDWARD⁵, b. 21 November, 1731, Groton; died, 25 Aug. 1819, aged 88, at Mason, N.H.; married, 9 March, 1768, (bans published 23 Dec. 1767, at Lincoln, Mass.) Rachel Allen, b. 25 June, 1747 (*Bond Gen.*) daughter of Benjamin and Eunice (Gale) of Lincoln, Mass. It is supposed he removed from Groton to Townsend, Mass, and thence to Mason, 1790, where he and his wife died.

Res. Groton and Townsend, Mass., and *Mason, N.H.*

267. 2. SUBMIT³, b. 19 December, 1733, Groton; married, Groton, 30 Apr. 1752, Jonathan Adams, of Concord.

Children:

268. 1. Submit⁶, b. 8 June, 1753.
269. 2. Alice⁶, b. 19 Jan. 1756.
270. 3. Jonathan⁶, b. 5 Mar. 1759.

271. MARY⁴, [51] (*Joseph³, Joseph², Henry¹,*) b. 5 Feb. 1709, Groton, Mass.; married, Groton, 28 Dec. 1726, Deacon James **STONE**, b. 23 Jan. 1701, Groton, son of John and Sarah (Nutting) of Groton. He died 27 Feb., *Groton rec.*, Dec., by other authorities, 1783.

He was chosen deacon at a church meeting in Groton, held 23 Sept., 1742 [see 138]. Until 1761, no articles of faith or church covenant appear on the Groton records, but soon after the election of the Rev. Samuel Dana as pastor, one was presented, and accepted by Mr. Dana as "pastor elect," and James Stone, moderator, on behalf of the church, June 1st of the same year. In 1782 he was chosen one of the trustees of a fund given by Jonathan Lawrence for the benefit of the ministry of Groton. [see 138.] Res. *Groton, Mass.*

Children born in Groton:

272. 1. JAMES⁵, b. 11 Aug. 1727; married, 13 Feb. 1748, Deborah Nutting, b. 30 Sept. 1728, Groton, d. of Jonathan and Mary (Green) of Groton.
Res. *Groton, Mass.*

Children:

273. 1. James⁶, b. 31 May, 1749.
274. 2. Jonathan⁶, b. 24 Oct. 1750.
275. 3. Lemuel⁶, b. 23 Aug. 1753.
276. 4. Eunice⁶, b. 10 Jan. 1760.
277. 2. MARY⁵, b. 23 Feb. 1728-9; married, 5 March, 1752, Elnathan **Sawtell**, b. 21 Oct. 1728, Groton s. of Hezekiah and Joanna (Wilson) of Shirley.
Res. *Shirley, Mass.*

Children recorded in Shirley:

278. 1. Elnathan⁶, b. 14 Sept. 1753.
279. 2. Joseph⁶, b. 25 Nov. 1755.
280. 3. Molly⁶, b. 13 Sept. 1757.
281. 3. JONATHAN⁵, b. 12 Dec. 1731; m., 9 July, 1755, Susan or Susanna Moors, *Groton rec.*, b. 4 Aug. 1735, Groton, d. of Abraham and Elizabeth (Gilson) of Groton. Res. *Groton, Mass.*

Children, all recorded in Groton, were:

282. 1. Susanna⁶, b. 3 Dec. 1756.
283. 2. Jonathan⁶, b. 10 Apr. 1758.
284. 3. Eunice⁶, b. 10 Feb. 1760.

285.   4. Molly⁶, b. 26 Dec. 1761; d. 17 Jan. 1762.
286.   5. Solomon⁶, b. 7 Feb. 1763.
287.   6. Moses⁶, b. 4 Nov. 1764.
288.   7. Molly⁶, b. 6 Feb. 1767.
289.   8. Sally⁶, b. 9 May, 1769.
290.   9. Oliver⁶, b. 27 Nov. 1770; died 10 Aug. 1775.
291.   10. Abraham⁶, b. 6 Dec. 1772; died 4 Aug. 1775.
292.   11. Oliver⁶, b. 16 Nov. 1778.
293.   4. WILLIAM⁵, b. 27 Feb. 1733-4, Groton; died young.
294.   5. ABIGAIL⁵, b. 2 Dec. 1736, Groton; married, 22 Dec. 1757, *Groton rec.*, Ephraim Sawtell, b. 18 Jan. 1734, Groton, s. of Hezekiah and Joanna (Wilson) of G.   Res. *Groton, Mass.*

Children born in Groton:

295.   1. Abigail⁶, b. 3 Nov. 1758.
296.   2. Lucy⁶, b. 20 Jan. 1760.
297.   3. Josiah⁶, b. 3 Jan. 1762.
298.   4. Molly⁶, b. 3 Dec. 1763.
299.   5. Eli⁶, b. 26 Nov. 1765.
300.   6. Josiah⁶, b. 24 Jan. 1768.
301   7. Ephraim⁶, b. 23 June, 1770.
302.   8. Sarah⁶, b. 20 Nov. 1772.
303.   6. SARAH⁵, b. 12 June, 1739, Groton, Mass.; married, *Groton rec.*, 15 February, 1763, William Jones, of Lunenburg, Mass.
304.   7. JOEL⁵, b. 1 May, 1742, Groton; married, *Groton rec.*, 31 Jan. 1765, Eunice Holden.

Child recorded in Groton

305.   Joel⁶, b. 30 Oct. 1765.
306.   8. SALMON⁵, b. 17 April, 1744, Groton, Mass.; married, *Groton rec.*, 11 Nov. 1767, Susanna Page, b. 29 June, 1747, Groton, d. of Joseph and Abigail (Shed) of G.

Child:

307.   Ede⁶, b. 24 June, 1768, *Groton rec.*; died 29 Oct. 1768.
308.   9. HANNAH⁵, b. 29 Oct. 1747, Groton; married, Groton, 2 Feb. 1769, Phineas Page, of Shirley, b. 24 May, 1745, Groton, s. of John and Mary (Parker) of G.   Res. *Shirley Mass.*

Children recorded in Shirley :

309.   1. Theophilus⁶, b. 12 Dec. 1769.
310.   2. Phineas⁶, b. 5 Nov. 1771; died 22 May, 1772.
311.   3. Phineas⁶, b. 16 March, 1773.
312.   4. Levi⁶, b. 18 Aug. 1775.
313.   5. Edmund⁶, b. 3 Mar. 1778.

314. 6. Ede⁶, b. 19 July, 1780.
315. 7. Eli⁶, b. 19 Sept. 1783.
316. 8. Walter⁶, b. 15 Nov. 1785.
317. 9. Augustus-Dole⁶, b. 12 Mar. 1799.
318. 10. LEVI⁵, b. 16 May, 1750, Groton, Mass.; died 4 Feb. 1830, aged 79, *Groton rec.*; married Lydia (——), who died 13 Feb. 1830, *Groton rec.*
                    Res. *Groton, Mass.*

  Children recorded in Groton:

319. 1. Sally⁶, b. 24 Dec. 1776.
320. 2. Lydia⁶, b. 22 Jan. 1778.
321. 3. Lucy⁶, b. 8 Nov. 1779; died 24 Aug. 1781.
322. 4. Lucy⁶, b. 1 Jan. 1782.
323. 5. Levi⁶, b. 17 March, 1784.
324. 6. Betsey⁶, b. 28 March, 1786.
325. 7. James⁶, b. 28 April, 1788.
326. 8. Hannah⁶, b. 9 Dec. 1789; died 27 Sept. 1792.
327. 9. John⁶, b. 11 Jan. 1792; died May, 1812.
328. 10. Samuel⁶, b. 1 Dec. 1798.

329. GEN. SAMUEL⁴, [53] (*Joseph³, Joseph², Henry¹,*) b. 11 or 14 Jan. 1714, in Groton, Mass.; m., acc. to Groton records, 23 June, 173–, according to George H. Jefts, 1735, Elizabeth Moors, b. 5 Feb. 1719, Groton, d. of Abraham and Elizabeth (Gilson) of Groton. We have not the date of his death, but are informed by Mrs. Ramsey, dau. of his youngest son Isaac-Moors, who was born 1757, that it occurred a few months previous to the birth of Isaac-Moors. His widow married —— Russell, and died when said Isaac-Moors was three years old. Her father Abraham Moors in his will, lodged in 1780, mentions his grandchildren, Isaac-Moors and Joseph Farwell and Lydia Ireland.   Res. *Groton, Mass.*

  Children recorded in Groton :

330. 1. SAMUEL⁵, b. 10 April, 1736; probably married at Concord, Mass., 9 Dec. 1765, Mary Parker, of Concord. [Concord Records.]
331. 2. ELIZABETH⁵, b. 10 Jan. 1739.
332. 3. EUNICE⁵, b. 12 Oct. 1741.
333. 4. ABRAHAM⁵, b. 18 Aug. 1743, Groton, Mass.; died 29 Aug. 1829; married, July, 1770, Priscilla Thurston of Fitchburg, Mass., who died 30 Dec. 1837. She was daughter of John and Lydia (——) of Fitchburg, Mass.
334. 5. DEA. JOHN⁵, b. 27 January, 1745; died 28 April, 1806, Fitchburg, Mass.; married, Lunenburg, Mass., 16 March, 1769, Sarah Hovey, born 30 Nov. 1746, Boxford, Mass. who died 23 April, 1829, Chelmsford, Mass.
  His will signed 24 April, 1806, gives to wife Sarah, whom he makes his executrix, all his furniture and use of all his estate real and personal, so long as she remains his widow, with leave to sell if necessary to her support: mentions sons John, Joseph, Abraham, Moses, and James, and

grandson Abel Cowden, son of his daughter Sarah deceased, the estate to be equally divided between them.

335. 6. SARAH⁴, b. 26 Dec. 1747. A Sarah Farwell of Groton was married by Joshua Wheeler, 22 Feb. 1763 to Silas Rand of Harvard, Mass.

336. 7. LYDIA⁴, b. 4 Aug. 1749; probably married —— Ireland.

337. 8. SUSANNA⁴, b. 20 July, 1751.

338. 9. JOSEPH⁴, b. 27 March, 1754, Groton; removed to Fitzwilliam, N.H., and afterward to Bridgewater, N.Y., where he died March, 1818. He married 27 Aug. 1777, Eunice Goodridge of Fitchburg, Mass., who died in Manlius, N.Y., March, 1811. He served during the whole Revolutionary war, a portion of the time in the body-guard of General George Washington.

339. 10. DR. ISAAC-MOORS⁴, b. 12 Apr. 1757, Townsend, Mass.; died 11 Aug. 1840, Paris, Oneida Co., N.Y.; married at Fitzwilliam, N.H., 6 Dec. 1785, Thankful Brigham, b. 13 June, 1760, Fitzwilliam, d. of Major Asa and Mary (Newton) of Shrewsbury, Mass., afterwards of Fitzwilliam, N.H. She died 28 July, 1849, aged 89 years and forty-five days.

Dr. Farwell was educated at Dartmouth College; studied medicine with Dr. Preston of New Ipswich, N.H.; removed to what is now the City of Utica, when it contained but three log houses; thence removed to Paris, where he practiced his profession till near the time of his death.

340. DANIEL⁴, [54] (*Joseph³, Joseph², Henry¹*,) b. 20 May, 1717, Groton, Mass.; married Mary ——. The surname of his wife and the date of his own death and also that of his wife Mary we have been unable to ascertain. A descendant thinks he died about 1805 or '6. Another descendant, Mr. Peter⁷ Farwell, thinks he lived to be 96 years of age, which would bring the date about 1813. [See Radial Chart IV. page 86].

Res. *Groton, Mass.*

Children all recorded in Groton:

341. 1. DANIEL⁵, [511] b. 22 April, 1740; died 17 May, 1815; married Sybil Page.
342. 2. ANNA⁵, [Com. Vol.*] b. 4 May, 1742; married 22 Oct. 1754, Silas Snow.
343. 3. ISAAC⁵, [Com. Vol.] b. 28 March, 1744; d. 31 Dec. 1791; m. Lucy Page.
344. 4. TIMOTHY⁵, [Com. Vol.] b. 21 Feb. 1745; m. 3 Oct. 1771, Sarah Page.
345. 5. MARY⁵, b. 6 Feb. 1747.
346. 6. EDMUND⁵, [Com. Vol.] b. 3 or 13 (old or new style) July, 1750; married Mary Russell.
347. 7. ZACCHEUS⁵, [Com. Vol.] b. 27 June, 1753; married Lydia Gilson.
348. 8. BENJAMIN⁵, [Com. Vol.] b. 2 July, 1756; married Lucy Collier.

---

*It is some years since we collected records for a complete "Memorial Volume of the Farwells of America." We continue to add thereto later records as obtained, and shall be ready to print a book of over 500 pages embracing records of the latest twigs of the vine, when a sufficient number of subscriptions are received to secure the publication.

Any branch will be printed to order at a charge proportionate to that of the complete volume. The bracketed [Com. Vol.] refers to the complete volume.

EXPLANATION OF THE RADIAL CHART III, HENRY[1], JOSEPH[2], JOSEPH[3] FARWELL, TO BE SEEN ON PAGE 15.

A. The initial ancestor,[1] occupying the first zone of this chart is Henry[1] Farwell.

B. Of his five children, Joseph[2], being the representative link in the descending genealogical chain with which Vol. I of the FARWELL MEMORIAL is chiefly occupied, is placed in the centre of the zone containing the second generation. His brother John[2] and his sister Mary[2] are on the left; his two sisters Olive[2] and Elizabeth[2] are upon the right.

C. The six sons Joseph[3], Henry[3], Isaac[3], John[3], William[3] and Oliver[3], also the three sisters, Hannah[3], Elizabeth[3], and Sarah[3], (the nine children of Joseph[2]) occupy the third zone, of whom the second in the order of birth is first placed *second* in the series, in small letters, and is transferred to the *centre*, as JOSEPH[3] in large letters. This central transfer shows that the chart continued will contain only his descendants.

EXPLANATION OF CHART IV, TO BE SEEN ON PAGE NEXT FOLLOWING SERIAL NO. 511, DANIEL[4] AND SYBIL (Page) FARWEI

The description above given of the chart on page 15 applies to the three initial zones of chart IV.

D. The fourth belt of the latter chart, contains the ten children of Joseph[3], of whom the ninth child, Daniel[4], is placed *without transfer* or *repetition* directly in the centre, intimating that any additions to *this* chart will contain *only* his descendants.

Our full sized Charts have a radius of twelve inches, with from nine to twelve zones, or even more if needed, instead of four, as above; and give, as far as practicable, the dates of births, marriages, and deaths, and the places of residence.

* RADIAL CHARTS,—as proposed by David-Parsons[7] Holton, M.D.—Of ancestors and descendants under consideration, the successive generations from the initial point in view are arranged in semi-circular belts of progressively increasing radii ; constituting what, for convenience of description, reference, and correspondence, are named " Genetic Zones."

1. The initial ancestor shown occupies the first zone resting on the *central portion* of the base line which sustains the genetic semi-zones.

2. The entire second generation, sons and daughters, recorded in the order of birth, from left to right, are represented in the second semi-zone.

The particular member who is the representative of the line (whose descendants in subsequent zones are to be represented; is recorded in small letters, signifying that the name is transferred in large letters to the centre of said zone, where are given fuller details. In some cases the lineal representative is placed directly (*i.e.*, without *transfer or repetition*) in the centre section of the zone.

3. The third zone contains the record of the sons and daughters of said lineal representative in the previous generation, arranged on the system above named, having an analogous transfer of the lineal representative or representatives for whose descendants the chart is specially formed.

4. In like manner the successive genetic zones are constructed, till we come down to an ancestor three or four generations preceding the ultimate twigs of the branches proposed to be represented. From *this* point *all* the descendants in male and female lines, as far as known, are fully represented by constituting each descendant a representative centre, from which are developed sections of subsequent and outer zones; and thus onward to the outermost genetic zone. The genetic belts instead of being semi-zones may conveniently be extended to form a larger part of a circle, thus giving more space for the development of the later generations, without producing the visual distraction created by following zones of the full sphere.

5. That which is peculiar to the invention of the subscriber, is the transferrence of the lineal representative to the central section, or other appropriate section, of successive genetic zones ;— thus showing in the clearest possible way the line of ancestors, with the brothers and sisters of each representative link in the ancestral chain.

6. The form and arrangement of this radial chart, originally designed for genealogies, are equally adapted to the illustration or presentation of any department of science. The division of any subject of study or instruction into classes, genera, species, varieties, and other subdivisions, may be advantageously shown by single charts or series of charts, constructed on the plan here above specified, having *successive transfers* to show the derivative line in the scientific series analogous to the ancestoral and descendental lines of the above-described genealogical series. Radial charts varied in structure according to the above rules, become useful instruments to facilitate the study and presentation of the facts of science. They are permanent apparatus adapted to varying circumstances of theory and facts, confirming that this invention as a valuable aid in many departments of education.

GRAND FOLIO. It is our desire to complete a large folio of 1000 pages, 20x30 inches, each right hand page containing a grand radial chart, faced by biographical sketches on the preceding left-hand page. Such a book would be for posterity *a bequest currently, prospectively and increasingly beneficial.* It can be completed only by co-operation.

349. HENRY⁴, [65] (*Henry³ Joseph², Henry¹,*) b. 14 Oct. 1696, Chelmsford, Mass.; married Esther Blanchard, b. 24 July, 1699, *Dunstable rec.*, daughter of Capt. Joseph and Abiah (Hassell) of Dunstable, Mass. He was one of a number of men who, 20 Feb. 1725, under command of Capt. John Lovewell, surprised and killed a party of ten Indians, at what has since been called "Lovewell's Pond," which is at the head of a branch of Salmon Falls river in the township of Wakefield. The Indians were from Canada, and within two days march of the frontier; were well armed, and had good supply of blankets, moccassins and snow-shoes for the accommodation of the prisoners they expected to take. Considering the extreme difficulty of finding and attacking the Indians in the woods, and the judicious manner in which they were so completely surprised, it was considered a most remarkable exploit. [*Hist. of Dunstable*].

In the fall of 1727, his wife's father, Capt. Joseph Blanchard, who had been the inn-keeper of the town for many years, died; and as the County-court, which granted license to inn-keepers, was not in session, Mr. Farwell petitioned the General Assembly for that position, which was granted.

His name is on the tax list of Dunstable in 1743. We infer from the His. of Dunstable that he was one of the famous "ROGERS RANGERS," a company which belonged to Col. Joseph Blanchard's regiment, which was raised for an expedition against the French at Crown Point in 1755. Their captain was Robert Rogers, and John Stark (afterwards General) was their Lieutenant. "There is scarcely in the annals of America a company of troops more famous than 'Rogers Rangers.' Their life was one scene of constant exposure, and their story reminds one of the days of romance. The forest was their home, and they excelled even the Indian in cunning and hardihood. Everywhere they wandered in search of adventures, fearless and cautious, until their very name became a terror to the enemy. Even in the post of danger, when the army was advancing, they scouted the woods to detect the hidden ambush, and when retreating, they skirmished in the rear to keep the foe at bay. If any act of desperate daring was to be done, the *Rangers* were 'the forlorn hope.' At midnight they traversed the camp of the enemy, or carried off a sentinel from his post as if in mockery. Their blow fell like lightning, and before the echo had died away or the alarm subsided, another blow was struck at some far distant point. They seemed to be omnipresent, and the enemy deemed that they were in league with evil spirits. The plain unvarnished tale of their daily hardships and perilous wanderings, their strange adventures and 'hair breadth 'scapes' would be as wild and thrilling as a German legend.

Of this company, and of others similar in character, a large number belonged to Dunstable," among whom were Jonathan Farwell, Eleazer Farwell, Bunker Farwell, and Henry Farwell.—*Hist. of Dunstable.*

Col. Blanchard was brother of Esther, wife of Mr. Farwell.

Res. *Dunstable, Mass.*

Children:

350. 1. ELEAZER⁵, b. 7 Oct. 1726, *Dunstable rec.*, married Mary Cummings. He was a soldier in the French war, and one of "Rogers Rangers" in 1756. [see 349, 363, 358.] His house in Dunstable, now Tyngsboro, was still

standing since the memory of G-H. Shed, husband of his granddaughter, b. 1809. Res. *Tyngsboro, Mass.*

351. 2. ESTHER², b. 16 May, 1730.
352. 3. OLIVE², b. 19 July, 1732.

353. LIEUT. JOSIAH⁴, [66] (*Henry³, Joseph², Henry¹,*) b. 27 Aug. 1698, Chelmsford, Mass.; died 8 May, 1725 in the Indian fight at Piqwacket. He married Hannah Lovewell. Her date of birth is unknown to us, and very conflicting statements are made by different authors in regard to her parentage. Allen's Biographical Dictionary states that she was the daughter of Capt. John, the hero of Piqwacket, and that she married Capt. Joseph Baker, of Pembroke; but Capt. Lovewell's only daughter Hannah was not born till 1721. Capt. Lovewell had a sister Hannah, b. between 1691 and 1701, but Fox, in his Genealogies of the settlers of Dunstable, makes her the wife of Capt. Joseph Baker of Roxbury. We are inclined to favor a transfer of Capt. Baker from the sister of Capt. L. to his daughter; and as the age of the sister is consistent for her to be the wife of Lieut. Josiah Farwell, conclude to call her the daughter of John¹ Lovewell, who is said to have been an Ensign in the army of Cromwell and to have left England on account of the Restoration of Charles II in 1660. Fox says he settled in Dunstable some years before 1690. His wife's name was Hannah.

Lieut. Josiah Farwell was one of the "party of ten of the principal inhabitants" of Dunstable (the only surviving one) who started Sept. 5, 1724, in pursuit of the Indians who had captured two of their neighbors the previous evening. Had his advice to their leader been heeded the calamitous result might have been avoided. [86.]

"Lieut. Josiah Farwell was in the company of Capt. Lovewell in the battle with the Indians at Piqwacket in May, 1725. In this battle he was shot through the body. His men endeavored to get him home, and on their way coming to a meadow in which they found some cranberries, they gave him some to eat. Finding that they came out at the open wound, he was satisfied that it was mortal, and insisted that they should leave him and make the best of their way home. They built a camp for him, and placed in it what they could provide for his comfort, and so this brave man was left to die alone in the wilderness. Fox states that he held out till the 11th day, during which time he had nothing to eat but water and a few roots which he chewed. His camp was readily found the next season by friends looking for the remains of the killed, by his handkerchief which he had tied to the top of a sapling bent down for that purpose. They took up his body and buried it in the forest." [Narrative of Col. Bancroft copied by J-B. Hill]. For further details of these thrilling scenes than our space will admit, see histories of Dunstable and Groton, New Hampshire His. Coll., Farmer's N.H. Gazateer. Res. *Dunstable, Mass.*

Child:

354. 1. HANNAH⁵, b. 27 Jan. 1722–3, Dunstable, Mass.; married, according to Col. Ebenezer Bancroft [378], John **Chamberlain**, who lived at the "Mills at

the mouth of the Souhegan river in Merrimac." Her grandfather, Henry¹, bequeathed to her £300, in good bills of credit of the Province of Massachusetts Bay, at the rate of 26 shillings silver per ounce [64].

355. JONATHAN⁴, [67] (*Henry³, Joseph², Henry¹*.) b. 24 July, 1700, Dunstable, Mass.; married, Charlestown, Mass., 27 May, 1723, Susanna Blanchard, born 29 March, 1707, d. of Capt. Joseph and Abiah (Hassell) of Dunstable, and sister of Esther, wife of Henry⁴ Farwell [349]. He was surveyor of highways, 1724; fence-viewer, 1725; constable, 1726; and treasurer, 1727; he owned a part of the farm in Tyngsboro on which he lived, and on which Colonel Bancroft lived in 1825. He was drowned probably 1780, Amoskeag Falls. His children were remembered in the will of his father, Henry³ of Dunstable [64]. Res. *Tyngsboro, Mass.*

The children of Jonathan⁴ and Susanna were:

356. 1. SUSANNA⁵, b. 17 Jan. 1723-4, Dunstable, Mass.
357. 2. RACHEL⁵, b. 19 Feb., 1727-8; married, 24 Nov. 1748, Col. Nehemiah Lovewell, b. 9 Jan. 1726, s. of Capt. John the hero of Piqwacket, [353] and Hannah (——). They removed to Corinth, Vt., where he died 23 March, 1801, and was there buried. She was buried in Newbury. He was Lieut. in 1756, in Col. Blanchard's regiment, Capt. in 1758 and '60, and one of the famous "Rangers" [349]. Res. Dunstable, and *Corinth, Vt.*
358. 3. JONATHAN⁵ b. 28 Aug. 1729, Dunstable, Mass.; married, probably, 19 Feb. 1761, Mercy Johnson. Little is positively known of this Jonathan⁵, but as the name is very seldom found on the records, and only two are known to us in this fifth generation, or whose ages would warrant the application of certain items in our collections, we have, after such investigation as our sources of information furnish, decided to give our impressions in this as in some other cases, that they may awaken inquiry and secure correction if we are in error. The other Jonathan⁵ will be found at serial number 142; and in his case some of his descendants have assisted us towards our conclusions. Of Jonathan⁵, b. 28 Aug. 1729, we have failed to find such aid; but Mr. J-B. Cheeney, a Farwell descendant in another line, finds on the Dunstable records the marriage of "Jonathan Farwell to Mercy Johnson, 19 Feb. 1761," and that a Jonathan Farwell was a prominent man in town, doing official business 1788-9; but finds no record of children.

Fox, in History of Dunstable, says: "It was about this time, (1747) probably, that Jonathan Farwell and Taylor were taken captive by the Indians while hunting in the south part of this town. They were carried to Canada and sold to the French, where they remained in captivity three years; but finally succeeded in obtaining their release and returned to their friends. A daughter of Farwell, Mrs. Rachel Harris, a granddaughter also of Noah Johnson, one of Lovewell's men, is still (1840) living in this town."

The Historical and Genealogical Register gives a Jonathan Farwell taken captive at New Gloucester, 1755. Susanna applied for his redemption.

As Jonathan⁵ of Dunstable, b. 28 Aug. 1729, had mother and sister of that name it seems probable this Jonathan⁵ was the captive spoken of and the same as mentioned by His. of Dunstable. It will be observed that his father Jonathan⁴ died about 1730, certainly before his father's death in 1738, as he is spoken of in his will, dated 1738, as deceased, and could not therefore have been the captive in either case [64]. He had, too, a sister Rachel, but she could not have been the grand-daughter of Noah Johnson, if her mother was Susanna Blanchard, and her grandmother Farwell was Susanna Richardson. We therefore conclude that these several statements are applicable to this Jonathan⁵, and that he may have had daughter Rachel, though no record of her birth has been found. Res. *Dunstable, Mass.*

359. ISAAC⁴, [69] (*Henry³, Joseph², Henry¹*,) b. 4 Dec. 1704, Dunstable, Mass.; married Sarah (———). In 1723 he was one of the six Dunstable men "in the company of Lieut. Jabez Fairbanks of Groton, which was scouting up and down the Nashua." Dunstable was then a frontier town and much exposed to the enemy. Upon a petition from the selectmen of the town that they should be allowed to stay at home to guard it, they were all discharged on condition that they should perform duty at Dunstable. The following in relation to Isaac⁴ of Dunstable is communicated by J-B. Hill, Esq. "In a memorandum now before me taken from the lips of Col. Bancroft in 1825, of Isaac⁴ he says, 'He settled on the Eppes farm, (one near Col. B's) and which his father Henry³ owned, then removed to the farm where Capt. Isaac Parker lived in Hollis, N.H., thence removed to Amherst, and from that place went to Penobscot,' a term which Col. B. often applied to the whole State of Maine. In another place Col. B. says 'he went to Vassalboro,' (Vassalboro and Winslow are adjoining towns, and no doubt V., at the time referred to by Col. B. included Winslow) Me. This statement shows that Isaac⁴ was a moving planet and would very likely after trying a single winter in Maine return to New Hampshire."

Children born in Dunstable:

360. 1. Elizabeth⁵, b. 12 March, 1726, Dunstable, Mass.
361. 2. Josiah⁵, b. 17 Aug. 1728, Dunstable, Mass.; d. at Charlestown, N. H. He married Lydia Farnsworth, probably of Groton. Two Lydias of this name were born in Groton, one to Ebenezer Farnsworth and Elizabeth (Whitney), 20 Dec. 1729, and one to Isaac Farnsworth and Sarah (Page), 5 July, 1730. He probably removed to Chester, Vt., soon after the birth of his daughter Mary, who was b. 8 Nov. 1756. Her birth is recorded in Groton, as were the births of his three elder children. His removal to Charlestown, N.H., was on the 22 September, 1766. We hope the incertitude connected with the history of Josiah⁴, as here stated, may elicit more accurate information before his branch of the family shall be published.

362. 3. RELIEF⁵, b. 4 Oct. 1730, Dunstable, Mass.
363. 4. BUNKER⁵, b. 28 Jan. 1732, Dunstable. He was in the military service, during the French war, and one of the famous "Rangers" [*His. of Dunstable*]
364. 5. ABIGAIL⁵, b. 11 March, 1734, D.
365. 6. ISAAC⁵, b. 18 Feb. 1736, D.; married, probably, 24 Apr. 1769, Mary Horn, [*Dover, N. H., rec.*]

366. ELIZABETH⁴ [71] (*Henry³, Joseph², Henry¹,*) b. 1715, Old Dunstable, now Tyngsboro; died 23 Sept. 1754, Tyngsboro, aged 39; married Lieut. Timothy⁵ BANCROFT, b. 14 Dec. 1710, son of Capt. Ebenezer² and Abigail (Eaton, probably dau. of John and Elizabeth, of Reading, now Wakefield, Mass.) and grandson of Thomas¹, b. in Eng. 1622, and 2d wife Elizabeth (Metcalf,) b. St. Benedicts Co., Norfolk, Eng., dau. of Miguel and Sarah. The first wife of Thomas¹ was Alice Bacon, dau. of Miguel of Ireland. Acc. to J-B. Hill, John of Lynn was bro. not father of Thomas¹.
Lieut. Bancroft married 2d. Mary (Newhall) and had Rachel and Timothy, as found on p. 42. He died at Tyngsboro, 21 Nov. 1772. His farm was the first after crossing the Massachusetts line on the old post road from Nashua to Boston.
Res. Dunstable, now *Tyngsboro, Mass.*

Children:

367. 1. TIMOTHY⁵, b. 23 Nov. 1733, Dunstable; d. unmarried, 12 Aug. 1754, D.
368. 2. ELIZABETH⁵, b. 16 Dec. 1735, D.; m. Ezra **Thompson.** She died soon after the birth of twin daughters, one of whom died unmarried, and the other married Dea. William Blodgett of Tyngsboro and removed West.
369. 3. Col. EBENEZER⁵ [378], b. 1 Apr. 1738; m. Susanna Fletcher.
370. 4. ABIGAIL⁵, b. 9 May, 1740, Dunstable; died 28 March, 1818; married Silas **Thompson,** who died 25 April, 1806. Res. *Chesterfield, N.H.*
371. 5. SARAH⁵, b. 6 Sept. 1743, Dunstable; died 28 June, 1798; married, (published) 8 Feb. 1766, James **Robertson,** b. 8 March, 1741, Waltham, Mass. He settled in Chesterfield, N. H., had large family, and died 19 March, 1830. Farmer. Res. *Chesterfield, N.H.*
372. 6. JAMES⁵, b. 26 Oct. 1745, Dunstable, Mass.; died 2 Mar. 1832; married Lucy Whitney, b. 1754, daughter of James and Lucy (——). She died at Montpelier, Vt., 22 May, 1840, aged 85 years, 5 months. He is said to have been on secret service in the Revolutionary war. Farmer.
Res. Nelson, N. H., and *Rockingham, Vt.*
373. 7. LOIS⁵, b. 10 May, 1748, Dunstable; m. Dunstable, Mass. 6 Oct. 1767, Samuel **Pearsons** of Reading, now Wakefield, Mass. Res. *Wakefield, Mass.*
374. 8. Dea. JONATHAN⁵, b. 11 Aug. 1750, Dunstable; died 15 July, 1815; m. 6 Apr. 1773, Martha Green of Groton, b. 30 April, 1749, Groton, d. of Isaac and Martha; she died 10 March, 1843. He lived on a part of his father's farm in Dunstable, now Tyngsboro, adjoining that of his brother, Col. Ebenezer⁵, now occupied by his grandson Jonathan⁷, although his buildings were on the Massachusetts side of the line between Massachusetts and New Hampshire. He was in the Revolutionary army, *His. of Dunstable.*
Res. *Tyngsboro, Mass.*

375. 9. HEPSIBAH³, b. 5 June, 1753, Dunstable; died, Reading, Mass.; married Samuel **Cook** and resided in Windsor; m. 2d John **Pratt**, and removed to Reading, Mass.
376. 10. RACHEL⁵, b. 18 Apr. 1758; m. 9 Jan. 1777, John **Hawkes**.

Res. *Lynnfield, Mass.*

377. 11. TIMOTHY, b. 15 July, 1759; d. 1848; married Abigail Taylor.

Res. *Nelson, N.H.*

378. Col. EBENEZER⁵, [369] (*Elizabeth⁴* (Farwell) **Bancroft,** *Henry³, Joseph², Henry¹*,) b. 1 April, 1738, Old Dunstable, now Tyngsboro, Mass.; died, 22 Sept. 1827, Tyngsboro; married, Dunstable, 5 May, 1763, Susannah Fletcher, b. 27 Oct. 1743, D., dau. of Dea. Joseph and Elizabeth (Underwood) of Dunstable. She died 4 Oct. 1823, Tyngsboro, Mass.

Col. Ebenezer⁵ was an ensign in the French and Indian war in 1758; was Captain in Col. Bridges' regiment in the battle of Bunker Hill; was Major in the regiment of Col. (afterwards Gov. of Mass.) Brooks in which he served at White Plains; and Lieut. Col. in command of troops from Middlesex Co., stationed at Rhode Island, 1781. One of his commissions, dated 19 May, 1775, was signed by Joseph Warren and another, dated 1 July, 1775, from Gen. Washington, by order of, Congress, signed by John Hancock, Pres., and Charles Thompson, Secretary. He received wounds in the battle of Bunker Hill, for which he was an invalid pensioner of Massachusetts, and afterwards of the United States. His personal narrative of the battle of Bunker Hill, in which he won a high reputation for bravery and skill and prepared the way for subsequent promotion, is exceedingly interesting, and we deeply regret that the scope of the present work will debar us the privilege of inserting it, but hope to do so in our complete Memorial of the Farwell family, perhaps in the Appendix to this volume. The present brief sketch, with the record of a limited number of his descendants, is given in grateful appreciation of the interest manifested and information given by his grandson, our much esteemed friend and helper, John-Boynton⁷ Hill, Esq., of Mason, N.H. [378°]

Res. on a portion of his father's farm in *Tyngsboro, Mass.*

Children of Col. Bancroft:

378ᵃ. 1. ELIZABETH⁶, b. 2 Mar. 1764, Tyngsboro, Mass.; died 14 July, 1859; married (published) in Dunstable, 23 Oct. 1784, and certified 24 Jan. 1785, Joseph **Butterfield**, Esq., b. 18 Aug. 1754, Dunstable, now Tyngsboro, son of Joseph and Elizabeth of Dunstable. They removed to Milford, Me. He was a farmer. They had no children. In his will he bequeathed his property to his adopted son John Butterfield, who resided, 1872, in Milford, Me., and had a large family.

378ᵇ. 2. SUSANNAH⁶, b. 26 May, 1766, Tyngsboro; d. 8 Jan. 1838, Tunbridge, Vt.; m. probably, T., Rev David-Howe⁵ **Williston**, b. 8 Jan. 1768, West Haven, Ct., son of Rev Noah⁴ and Hannah (Payson) of West Haven. He gr. Y. College, 1787; received honorary degree of A.M. from D. C. 1793; ordained, Tunbridge, Vt., 26 June, 1793, and died there 29 Oct. 1845.

[*See Memorial Volume of Cornet Joseph¹ Parsons*] Mr. Williston was brother of Rev. Payson Williston, of Easthampton, Mass.; of Hannah, who married Rev. Ebenezer Kingsbury; and of Sarah who married Rev. Richard Salter Storrs, of Longmeadow, Mass. The Hon. Samuel Williston of Easthampton, Mass., founder of the Williston Seminary and a liberal donor of Amherst College, was his nephew, as is also Prof. Whitney of Yale College, and others eminent for learning and piety.

378°. 3. CHLOE⁶, b. 8 Nov. 1768, Tyngsboro; died 17 Jan. 1807; married Oliver Richardson.   Res. *Chelmsford, Mass.*

378ᵈ. 4. REBECCA⁶, [378¹] b. March, 1771, Tyngsboro; d. 12 July, 1797, Mason, N. H.; m. T., 6 Jan. 1790, Samuel Howard, of Chelmsford, Mass. She m. 2d, Rev. Ebenezer Hill of Mason, N.H.

378°. 5. LUCY⁶, b. 7 June, 1773, Tyngsboro; d. 14 Apr. 1849, Stoddard, N.H.; m. 27 Jan. 1795, Gardner Towne, b. 1 May, 1765, s. of Israel and Lucy (Hopkins) of Milford, N.H. He was a merchant, inn-holder, justice of the peace, and active and enterprising in business. He died 16 Dec. 1815, Stoddard, N. H. She married 2d, Capt. Levi Warren of Alstead, N. H., who died at Stoddard.   Res. *Stoddard, N.H.*

378ᶠ. 6. MARY-DANDRIDGE⁶, b. 14 Nov. 1775, Tyngsboro; d. 21 Nov. 1859, Alstead, N.H.; m. Jonathan Barron of Chelmsford, Mass., b. 1769, C., son of Oliver. He died Aug. 1821. She m. 2d Benjamin Brooks of Dalton, N.H.

"The origin and choice of the name DANDRIDGE appears in the following extract from the Essex Gazette of 18 Jan. 1776. 'Jan. 7. This morning the sixth daughter of Capt. Bancroft of Dunstable was baptized by the name of Martha Dandridge, the maiden name of his excellency, General Washington's lady. The child was dressed in buff and blue with a sprig of evergreen on its head, emblematic of His Excellency's glory and provincial affection.' The name recorded in the family Bible is Mary Dandridge, not Martha as stated in the paper." [*J-B. Hill.*]

378ᵍ. 7. EBENEZER⁶, b. 19 Oct. 1778, Tyngsboro; d. 5 May, 1858, T.; m. Hannah Towne sister of Gardner [378°]; b. 28 Aug. 1776, Milford, N.H., d. of Israel and Lucy Hopkins, of Milford; she d. 13 Oct. 1870, T.   Res. on the homestead of his father in *Tyngsboro, Mass.*

378ʰ. 8. JOSEHH-FARWELL⁶, d. 8 July, 1850, Tyngsboro, and was buried in Tyng's burying ground ; m. Sarah-Tyng Farwell, born 9 March, 1789, T. d. of John and Elizabeth-Hunt (Smith) of Tyngsboro [472]. She died 14 Jan. 1861, T., and was buried in Tyngs' burying ground.

378ⁱ 9. REBECCA⁶, [378ᵈ] (*Ebenezer⁵, Elizabeth⁴* (Farwell) Bancroft, (*Henry³, Joseph², Henry¹*) b. 5 March, 1771, Tyngsboro; d. 12 July, 1797, Mason, N.H.; m. Tyngsboro, 6 Jan. 1790, Samuel Howard of Chelmsford, Mass., who died May, 1790, Tyngsboro. Farmer in Tyngsboro. She married 2d, 18 November, 1795, Dunstable, now Nashua, N. H., as 2d wife, Rev. Ebenezer⁵ Hill, b. 31 January, 1766, Cambridge, Mass., s. of Samuel and Sarah (Cutler) of Cambridge. He graduated, H. C. 1786; was ordained at M., 3 Nov. 1790, and settled there as pastor of the Congregational church, where he died 20 May, 1854, in the 64th year of his ministry.

[John-B"⁶ Hill, Esq., as a descendant from Henry¹ Farwell is of the *seventh* generation; but through his grandmother Sarah⁴ (Cutler) Hill, is of the *sixth*: James¹ Cutler, b. 1606, Eng.; John², b. 19 March, 1663; Ebenezer³, b. 24 July, 1700; Sarah⁴, b. 15 Sept. 1735, m. Samuel Hill; Ebenezer⁵, b. 31 Jan. 1766, m. Rebecca (Bancroft) [878d]; John-Boynton Hill⁶⁷, Esq., b. 25 Nov. 1796. Res. Mason, N.H.]

Rev. Ebenezer Hill m. as first wife Mary Boynton, dau. of Nathaniel and Rebecca (Barrett) who died 2 March, 1794, leaving three children. He m. 2d, Rebecca⁵ Bancroft, gr. d. of Elizabeth⁴ Farwell, as before said. He m. 3d, 22 Sept. 1799, Abigail (Jones) Stearns, widow of Edward who was husband of her deceased sister Polly⁷ (Jones).* They were daughters

---

* We have very extended records of the FARWELL-JONES families, embracing by intermarriage, many families of distinction: Whittemore, Meriam, Ames, Shattuck. Spaulding, Wood, Messenger, Davis, Cutler, Fletcher, Barrett, Love, Wilson, Wheeler, Harwood, Fry, Mellish, Brush, Sahler, Hodgman, Pratt, Kimball. Cragin, Hall—records too numerous for insertion in this volume.

As the family of the REV. EBENEZER HILL, by reason of his marriage with his second and third wives, each a descendant in different lines of Henry¹ Farwell, of Concord, appears in our book, we have thought it not improper to add, in a note, this brief sketch of his life, ancestry and of his family by his first wife. He was born in Cambridge in January, 1766, the second son of Samuel and Sarah (Cutler) Hill. Of the parents, age, and ancestry of his father nothing is with certainty known. He was undoubtedly a descendant of Abraham Hill of Malden, the common ancestor of the numerous families in Malden, West Cambridge, and that vicinity. On his mothers side he was of Puritan descent, traced as follows: JAMES¹ CUTLER born in England in 1606, settled in Watertown in 1634. About 1651 he removed to his farm in what was then called "Cambridge farms," afterwards Lexington, now Lincoln, where he died May 17, 1694. John² Cutler his ninth child and the first of his third wife Phebe Page, born March 19, 1663. His mother was the daughter of JOHN and PHEBE PAGE, who came from Dedham, England, 1630. He married, January 1, 1694, Mary Stearns, b. Oct. 8, 1663, d. Feb. 24, 1733. She was the daughter of Isaac and Sarah² (Beers) Stoarns. Isaac² Stearns was born in Watertown January 6, 1632-3. His father ISAAC¹ STEARNS born in England, came to America in 1630, in the same ship with Winthrop and Saltonstall. He was the common ancestor of the very numerous families of the name in New England. Her father Captain RICHARD¹ BEERS came from England, settled in Watertown, admitted freeman 1636-7, was selectman and representative of Watertown from 1544 to 1675. He was slain in battle with the Indians September 4, 1675, at Northfield. Their third child Captain Ebenezer³ Cutler was born July 24, 1700. He married March 3, 1723-4, Ann Whitney of Concord, born May 22, 1702. He died at Lincoln, January 17, 1777. She died August 24, 1798. She was the daughter of Jonathan² Whitney. His father Jonathan² Whitney born in England in 1634, came with his father John¹ Whitney, who sailed from London in the *Elizabeth* and *Ann* in April, 1635. Sarah⁴ Cutler their fifth child, born Sept. 15, 1735; m. Samuel Hill. They resided in Cambridge. He died at Mason June 21, 1798, aged 66 years. She d. at Mason, Dec. 30, 1808. Their only children were born in Cambridge; Samuel⁵ in 1764 and Ebenezer⁵, 31 Jan. 1766. Samuel⁵ was a carpenter; d. at Mason, May 23, 1813. Ebenezer⁵, b. 31 Jan. 1766; grad. H.C. 1786; after graduation taught the town schools in Westford two years; licensed to preach Oct. 23, 1788; ordained at Mason Nov. 3, 1790; died May 20, 1854, in the 64th year of his ministry. His published funeral sermons and discourses are in number thirteen. He married first, Feb. 2, 1791, Molly (Mary) Boynton, daughter of Nathaniel and Rebecca (Barrett) Boynton, born in Westford, March 20, 1765. She died March 2, 1794. Their children were: 1. Ebenezer⁶, b. Oct. 14, 1791. 2. Polly⁶ and Sally⁶, twins, b. Jan. 13, 1793, Ebenezer [see 878a], printer and publisher, settled at Fayetteville, Tenn. where he died in 1875; m. Feb. 12, 1834, Mary T. Bryans. She died April 19, 1871, aged 72 years. Their children were three sons and three daughters, all of whom excepting one are now living. 2. Polly, m. Jan. 17, 1813, Timothy Wheeler, b. 16 Jan. 1783; d. Jan. 21, 1854. Farmer. Resided in Mason. Their children eleven, eight sons and three daughters, of whom four died in infancy and two of full age unmarried. 3. Sally, m. Oct. 10, 1813, Josiah Merriam, born in Mason, April 20, 1790. Blacksmith and farmer. Res. at Mason, afterwards at Exeter and Garland, Maine, where he d. 17 Aug. 1874. Their children, five sons and one daughter. Two of the sons died in infancy.

of Col. Timothy⁵ and Rebecca (Bateman) **Jones,** son of John⁴ and Abigail (Wesson) [111], John⁴ and Anna (Brooks) [110], John³ and Sarah² (Farwell) **Jones** [31], John² FARWELL, Henry¹ of Concord, Mass. John² Jones was son of John¹ and Dorcas of Cambridge and Concord.

Children:

378ʲ.   1. Rebecca⁷, b. 25 Oct. 1790, Tyngsboro, Mass.; died 25 Aug. 1793, T.
378ᵏ.   2. Rev. Joseph-Bancroft, b. 25 Nov. 1796, Mason, N.H.; graduated at Harvard College, 1821; was admitted to the Bar in Lincoln county, Tenn, in 1830; resided at Fayetteville, with his eldest half-brother Ebenezer Hill, a printer and publisher [See note 378ᵈ.]; engaged in preaching in Tennessee and neighboring States, also in printing newspapers, books, almanacs, etc. till 1840, when he returned to New England and was colleague pastor with his father, of the Congregational church at Mason, from 20 Oct. 1841 to 23 Apr. 1847.

He became pastor of the Congregational church at Colebrook, N.H. in Oct. 1847, where he remained ten years; and afterwards at West Stewartstown, N.H. till 1862, when he removed to Temple, N. H., where he purchased a small farm which was his residence till death.

In March, 1864, he joined the Army of the Cumberland in the service of the Christian commission, to which cause he devoted himself with great zeal and fidelity, till he met his death by a railroad accident at Chattanooga, Tenn. 16 June, 1864. He married, Antrim, N.H., 26 Aug. 1845, Harriet Brown, b. 20 June, 1819, at Antrim, d. of —— and Sarah (Flagg) of Antrim, afterwards of Temple, N.H.

Res. *Temple, N.H.*

Children:

378ˡ.   *Charles-Ebenezer⁸*, b. 7 Feb. 1848, Colebrook, N.H. He left Dartmouth college 1871 before completing his senior year on receiving the appointment of Assistant Professor at the U.S. Naval Academy, Anapolis, Md.
378ᵐ.   *William-Bancroft⁸*, b. 17 Feb. 1857, Colebrook, N.H. Attended Appleton's Academy, New Ipswich, N.H. In 1878, a Sophomore in Cambridge University. 1878. Res. *Temple, N.H.*
378ⁿ.   *Joseph-Adna⁸*, b. 5 May, 1859, West Stewartstown, N.H. In 1878, is a student in the Exeter Academy, N.H.

Three children died in infancy.

278ᵒ.   3. John-Boynton⁷, twin of Joseph-Bancroft⁷, b. 25 Nov. 1796, Mason, N. H.; married, Hollis, N.H., 10 August, 1829, Acsah Parker, born 24 June, 1799, Hollis, daughter of Capt. Isaac and Olive (Abbot) of H. She died 6 May, 1831, Exeter, Me.

Mr. Hill graduated Harvard college 1821, and for two years was Principal of Garrison Forest Academy, near Baltimore, Md.; studied law and was admitted to practice, Hillsborough county, N.H., 7 Oct. 1826. Followed his profession at Nashua, N.H., Townsend, Mass., and from 1835 to 1862 at Exeter and Bangor, Me. He removed to Bangor 1835, which town he represented in the Maine legislature, 1853-4-5. He retired from practice 1862 and returned to the old homestead in Mason 1865, where he has since resided. Mr. Hill has published "Memoirs of his father Rev. Ebenezer Hill, p.p. 113," "Proceedings of the Centennial celebration of Mason, N.H., pp. 115," and "History of Mason, N.H. 8vo., pp.324," *History of Old Dunstable N.H. and Mass.* 1878. An edition of only 100 copies, rapidly disposed of.

Child :

878,   1. *Isaac-Parker*, born and died March, 1881.

The children by the 3d marriage, were :

379.   1. EDWARD-STEARNS⁸, born 19 July, 1800 ; died 24 March, 1874 ; married 28 June, 1827, Catharine Houghton of Milton, Mass., b. 4 Oct. 1806. Children, four sons and three daughters—eighteen grandchildren. Of the sons, Ebenezer-Bancroft⁹ served in the war of the Rebellion two years and eight months as engineer of the gunboats Lafayette and Benton, and was at the taking of Vicksburg. He subsequently married and was engineer of the St. Louis Water Works. His brother Charles-Walter-Houghton⁹ also served in the war, in Co. A, 115th Reg't Ill. Volunteers, 1874, Mrs. Hill resided with her daughter Mrs. Cragin N.Y. City.

379ᵃ. 2. REBECCA-HOWARD⁸, born 13 March, 1802. In 1878 was residing on the homestead at   *Mason, N.H.*

380.   3. ABIGAIL-JONES⁸, born 7 February, 1804, Mason ; died 9 September, 1829, Fitzwilliam, N.H. ; married, Mason, 2 June, 1825, John **Kimball** of F., b. 17 December, 1798, Temple, N.H., son of Isaac and Sally (Cutter). He married 2d, Fitzwilliam, 24 Jan. 1831, Jane-Sophronia Richardson, b. 21 November, 1802, Royalston, Mass., by whom he had: 1, John-Richardson, b. 24 Nov. 1831 ; 2, Charles-Edward, b. 26 April, 1834 ; 3, Abigail-Hill, b. 10 Jan. 1838, and 4, Eliza-Jane, b. 11 Nov. 1839. He d. 7 May, 1866, at Fitzwilliam.

Children of John and Abigal-Jones (Hill) Kimball :

1. Maria-Frances⁹, born 29 August, 1826, Fitzwilliam ; married there, 16 Oct. 1850, Charles Whittemore of F., born 15 February, 1828, F., son of Dexter and Betsey (Wright) of Fitzwilliam, grandson of John and gr. grandson of Josiah Whittemore.

Merchant, firm of Whittemore Bros., manufacturers of looking-glasses 579 Broadway N.Y.

Children :

1. *Charles-Erving*¹⁰, born 18 August, 1856, Fitzwilliam.
2. *William-John*¹⁰, born 26 March, 1860, New York City.
3. *Frances-Maria*¹⁰, born 11 Nov. 1862,   "

2. John-Edward⁹, b. 9 Jan. 1829, F.; died 25 Sept. 1829, F.
881.   4. MARIA⁸, born 14 December, 1806 F.; died 10 September, 1835; married, 4 June, 1829, Oliver-Hosmer Pratt of Mason. Their only child Ebenezer-Hill died 11 March, 1833, aged 2 years 3 months.

1878, res. *Townsend, Mass.*

381ᵃ.   5. TIMOTHY-JONES⁸, born 15 March, 1808; died 8 July, 1810.
381ᵇ.   6. LUCY-SYLVANIA⁸, b. 14 June, 1810 ; died 13 Aug. 1827.
382.   7. ADELIZA⁸, born 9 July, 1812 ; married, New York City, 4 April, 1833, Benjamin-Wheeler Merriam, born 8 May, 1803, Mason, son of Samuel and Lucy (Wheeler) of M. Merchant, manufacturer of Mirrors, 577 Broadway, New York.   Res. 312 Fifth Ave., *New York.*

[Adams-Brooks Merriam, brother of Benjamin-Wheeler, m. Hannah Matilda Wentworth, gr. gr. dau. of Susanna⁵ (Winslow) and Edward Wentworth [See 4228 Winslow Memorial] and the niece of Mrs. H. M. Merriam, Miss Maud Wentworth, is writing a sketch of Thomas-Handford Wentworth, Earl of Strafford and Lord Lieutenant of Ireland.]

Children :

1. Adeliza-Frances⁹, born 3 March, 1835 ; married, Orange, N.J. 22 June, 1865, Rev. Daniel-Dubois Sahler. Pastor of Presbyterian Church, Carmel, N.Y.

   Children :
   1. *Henry-Hasbrouk*¹⁰, born 14 March, 1867 ; died 26 July, 1868.
   2. *Emma-Frances*¹⁰, born 5 May, 1869.
   3. *Florence-Louise*¹⁰, born 15 September, 1871.

2. Maria-Hill⁹, born 9 August, 1837 ; married 2 December, 1862, Walter-Franklin Brush; who died 5 June, 1865. Commission Merchant.

Res. *New York City.*

   Children :
   1. *Addie-Frances*¹⁰, born 15 December, 1863.
   2. *Walter-Franklin*¹⁰, born 27 September, 1865.

3. Harriet-Wheeler⁹, born 3 September, 1839 ; died 10 Feb. 1845.
4. Abbie-Caroline⁹, born 8 November, 1841 ; married 3 November, 1870, William-Nevins Crane. Book publisher and stationer N.Y. City.
5. Henry-Everett⁹, born 30 March, 1844. Merchant, in partnership with his father.
6. Emma-Rebecca⁹, born 10 April, 1850 ; died 9 October, 1873.
7. Annie-Louise⁹, born 24 November, 1852.
8. Sarah-Wheeler⁹, born 1 September 1854.

383.   8. MARTHA⁸, born 31 October, 1816; died 2 May, 1854; married 17 September, 1846, Rev. Edwin-Ruthven Hodgman, born 21 October, 1819, Camden, Me.

He graduated Dartmouth coll. 1843 ; at Andover Theol. Sem. 1846; was ordained at Orford, N.H., 17 May, 1849. She had four children, one of whom died in infancy. The son Edwin-Rutherford-Hill⁶, gr. D.C. 1869. The two daus. are Harriet-Mehetabel, born 8 December, 1851 and Martha. 1878. Res. *Westford, Mass.*

384. 9. Rev. TIMOTHY⁵, born 30 June, 1819; married, St. Louis, 2 November, 1854, Frances-Augusta Hall, born 26 August, 1821, Minnisink, Orange co. N.J.

He gr. D.C. 1842, and Union Theological Sem. N.Y.; was ordained Pres. minister St. Louis, Mo. Was settled at Shelbyville and Rasomond, Ill. and Kansas city, Mo. District Secretary of Home Missions. They have had five children, two of whom died infants, Frances-Lewis⁶, b. 17 Sept. 1858, died 12 May, 1866, John-Boynton⁶, born 3 Nov. 1860, and Henry-Edward⁶, born 9 Feb. 1863. Res. 1878, *Kansas City, Mo.*

385. HANNAH⁴, [72] (*Henry³, Joseph², Henry¹,*) born 4 April, 1719, Dunstable, Mass.; m. Jerahmael CUMMINGS, b. 10 October, 1711, Groton, Mass., s. of Samuel and Elizabeth of G. He d. in Hollis, N.H. She married 2d, Dea. Stephen JEWETT of Hollis, who died 23 May, 1803, aged 76. [*Hollis Records.*] Res. *Hollis, N.H.*

Children :

386. 1. HANNAH⁵, b. 2 July, 1737; married James **Hobart** of Hollis, and removed to Plymouth, N.H. about 1764.

387. 2. Rev. HENRY⁵, D.D., H.C., b. 16 Sept. 1739, Hollis; died 5 Sept. 1823, aged 84. He graduated H.C. 1760, was ordained minister of Billerica, Mass., 26 Jan. 1763. After toiling 51 years he received Nathaniel Whitman as his colleague, 26 Jan. 1814. He died Sept. 5, 1823, aged nearly 84. He was frequently called to preach on public occasions. Among his occasional discourses published are the following : "At the election 1783," "Dudleian lecture 1791," "At a Thanksgiving 1798," "Before a charitable society 1802," "Half-century discourse 1813." [*Allen's Biog. Dict.*] Res. *Billerica, Mass.*

388. 3. JOTHAM⁵, b. 29 Dec. 1741, Hollis; married 27 Apr. 1763, Anna Brown, and is supposed to have removed and settled at Plymouth, N.H. 1764.

389. 4. CATY⁵, (Catharine) b. 28 Feb. 1744, H.; married 27 Sept. 1764, Thomas **Pratt** of Hollis. Res. *Hollis, N.H.*

Children recorded in Hollis:

390. 1. David⁶, b. 2 June, 1765.
391. 2. Caty⁶, b. 9 May, 1767.
392. 3. Hannah⁶, b. 29 July, 1769.
393. 4. Jerahmael⁶, b. 12 Apr. 1772.
394. 5. Betty⁶, b. 13 Jan. 1774.
395. 6. Molly⁶, b. 17 June, 1776.
396. 5. BETTY⁵, (Elizabeth) b. 17 July, 1746.
397. 6. Dea. STEPHEN⁵, b. 14 Oct. 1753, H.; married, 10 Nov. 1778, Elizabeth **Pool** of Hollis. Res. *Hollis, N.H.*

Children recorded in Hollis:

398. 1. Elizabeth⁶, b. 18 June, 1779.
399. 2. Stephen⁶, b. 11 July, 1781.
400. 3. Nancy⁶, b. 16 May, 1783.
401. 4. Hannah⁶, b. 7 Feb. 1785.
402. 5. William-P⁶., b. 26 Feb. 1787; died 11 July, 1788.
403. 6. William-P⁶., b. 11 Feb. 1789.
404. 7. Sarah⁶, b. 24 Feb. 1790.
405. 8. Polly⁶, b. 8 July, 1792.
406. 9. Noah⁶, b. 13 Dec. 1794.
407. 10. Samuel-Gibson⁶, b. 29 Oct. 1798.

407ª. 7. REBECCA⁵, b. 14 Jan. 1756.
407ᵇ. 8. NOAH⁵, b. 11 Feb. 1758.
407ᶜ. 9. JONATHAN⁵, b. 25 July, 1760.
407ᵈ. 10. LOIS⁵, b. 21 May, 1763.

408. MARY⁴, [75] (*Isaac³, Joseph², Henry¹*,) born 19 November, 1709, Medford, Mass.; died 27 January, 1746-7; married, 8 Feb. 1727-8, Edmund HOVEY, born 10 July, 1699, *Malden, Mass. rec.*, son of James and Deborah of Mansfield, Conn. He married 2d, 16 April, 1747, Ann Huntington, born 15 November, 1714, daughter of Thomas.

Mr. Hovey removed late in life from Mansfield, Conn. to Norwich, Vt. where he died 21 January, 1788. His wife Ann died 16 April, 1797, Thelford, Vt. His children by his second marriage were: 1, ANN, born 20 January, 1747-8, died March, 1825. 2, WILLIAM, born 6 July, 1749, died 1836. 3, PRISCILLA, born 17 April, 1751, died 1 May, 1847, married —— Whittaker, married 2d, John Slafter the husband of her deceased half-sister Elizabeth [416]. 4, AMOS, born 9 April, 1753, died 11 July, 1840. 5, MARY, born 24 September, 1755, died 14 March, 1846. [*See Slafter Memorial.*] Res. Mansfield, Conn. and *Norwich, Vt.*

Children of Edmund and Mary⁴ (Farwell) Hovey recorded in Mansfield, were:

409. 1. EDMUND⁵, b. 19 Nov. 1728; d. 14 February, 1767, Manchester, Mass, ; m. 15 Dec. 1749, Mary Gilbert, d. of Noah. She d. 3 Nov. 1754, Mansfield, Ct. He m. 2d, Margaret Knowlton, who d. 1789, Norwich, Vt., aged 59. His will is recorded in Essex county.
410. 2. ISAAC⁵, b. 7 Aug. 1730; died Aug. 1761.
411. 3. MARY⁵, b. 8 Nov. 1732; died 6 Nov. 1749.
412. 4. AARON⁵, b. 22 Apr. 1735; died 10 March, 1812, North Mansfield, Ct.; married 15 Jan. 1761, Olive⁵ Farwell, [418] b. 24 July, 1740, daughter of John and Dorothy (Baldwin). She died 29 July, 1764, and Mr. Hovey married 2d, 18 Feb. 1768, Abigail Freeman, b. 20 May, 1743, daughter of Edmund and Martha (Otis). Mrs. Abigail Hovey died 12 Feb. 1831, North Mansfield, Conn. Res. *North Mansfield, Ct.*
413. 5. JAMES⁵, b. 14 Aug. 1737; died unmarried, 8 Jan. 1766.

414. 6. WILLIAM⁵, b. 29 May, 1740; died 28 Apr. 1748.
415. 7. ELIJAH⁵, b. 30 Sept. 1741; died, 22 March, 1748.
416. 8. ELIZABETH⁵, b. 22 June, 1744, Mansfield; died 1 Jan. 1811 ; married, 26 March. 1767, John Slafter, b. 26 May, 1739, Mansfield, Ct., son of Samuel and Dorothy (Fenton) of M. Mr. Slafter m. 2d, Priscilla (Hovey) Whittaker, b. 17 April, 1751, daughter of Edmund and Ann Huntington of M. [408] Mrs. Slafter died 1 May, 1847 in her 97th year. Mr. Slafter died 8 Oct. 1819, Norwich, Vt. [See Slafter Memorial.]
Res. *Norwich, Vt.*

417. JOHN⁴, [76] (*Isaac³, Joseph², Henry¹.*) b. 23 June, 1711, at Medford, Mass.; died Oct. 1756 ; married, 7 June, 1739, Dorothy Baldwin. Res. *Mansfield, Ct.*

Children of John and Dorothy (Baldwin) Farwell were :

418. 1. OLIVE⁵, born 24 July, 1740; died 21 July, 1764; married 15 January, 1761, Aaron² Hovey, born 22 April, 1735. [412.]
419. 2. JOHN⁵, born 5 September, 1741, Mansfield, Conn.; died in Dorset, Vt., 24 Aug. 1823, to which place he had removed in August, 1772. He married in Mansfield, Conn. 25 August, 1763, Esther Dimmick, born in M. 1742, daughter of Shubael and Esther [——], of Mansfield. She died in Dorset, 11 Aug. 1831. Res. Mansfield, Ct. and *Dorset, Vt.*
420. 3. ISAAC⁵, born 7 February, 1744–5 ; died April, 1833, Dorset, Vt.; married Mary daughter of Skiff Freeman. s.p. Res. *Dorset, Vt.*
421. 4. THOMAS⁵, born 17 June, 1751 ; died Mansfield, Ct., 1 May, 1831; married 26 April, 1780, Hannah Topliff, born Mansfield, 5 February, 1763, dau. of Calvin of M. She died 1 April, 1822 at Mansfield. Farmer and shoemaker. Res. North Parish in *Mansfield, Ct.*
422. 5. ASA⁵, born 4 January, 1755 or 7; died 16 June, 1815; married 1780, Keziah daughter of Skiff Freeman, born 25 April, 1761 ; died 2 Dec. 1843.

423. WILLIAM⁴, b. 28 Dec. 1712, Medford, Mass, admitted freeman 25 April, 1738; died 11 December, 1801, Charlestown N.H.; married Mansfield, Conn. 7 Nov. 1744, Bethiah Eldridge, b. 1726, dau. of Elisha, Eldredge of Cape Cod, Mass. She died 5 Jan. 1812, at Charlestown, N.H. Mr. Farwell removed from Mansfield, Conn. to Westminster, Windham co. Vt., and thence, but at what date is uncertain, to Charlestown N.H. Res. Mansfield Ct. Westminster Vt. and *Charlestown, N.H.*

Children of William⁴ and Bethiah (Eldridge) Farwell were :

424. 1. WILLIAM⁵, born Mansfield, Conn , 4 April, 1746 ; died 9 April, 1749, [*Mansfield rec.*]
225. 2. BETHIAH⁵, [ ] b. 18 September, 1747, Mansfield, Ct.; died 3 February, 1813, Westminster, Vt.; married Joel² Holton, born 10 July, 1738, Northfield, Mass. son of John¹ and Mehetable (Alexander) of Northfield. Mr. Holton died at Westminste, Vt. 12 August 1821 [See Winslow Memorial Vol I page 322 serial number 3814]

F   *Descendants of William⁴ Farwell.*   51

426. 3. Rev. WILLIAM⁵, b. 16 Jan. 1748-9, Mansfield; died 11 Dec. 1823, Barre, Vt. married Phebe Crosby of Charlestown, N.H., where he resided till late in life, when he removed to Barre, Vt. We have records of his numerous descendants residing in Barre, Montpelier and Barton, Vt.; Compton, Stanstead, Ascott, Sherbrook, and Bury, in Dominion of Canada; Chicago, McComb, and Quincy, Ill.; Wisconsin, California, and other parts of the Union; for which we refer to the completed volume of the FARWELL MEMORIAL*. An extended and very interesting biography of Rev. William⁵ Farwell is to be found in the History of Charlestown, N.H.

427. 4. ELIZABETH⁵, [534] b. 1 Aug. 1751, Mansfield, Ct.; died 9 Sept. 1840, North Charlestown, N.H.; married, Walpole, N.H., Elijah **Parker**.
[See the Farwell-Parker Radial Chart, pages 52, 53.]

428. 5. JEMIMA⁵, b. 5 Apr. 1753, Mansfield, Ct.; died young.

429. 6. ELISHA⁵, born 1 July, 1754, Mansfield; married according to History of Charlestown, N.H., Sarah Farnsworth. Their first four children born after 1775, are recorded in Charlestown. He probably removed from C. to Springfield, Vt., where two children are recorded in 1785 and 1787, and thence to Georgia, Vt., where his son Francis-C. was b. in 1791. He afterwards emigrated to Genesee County, N.Y., and died about 1826-8. Some of his descendants are living in Ohio, Michigan, and in Oakland, California.

430. 7. JOSEPH⁵, b. 29 March, 1756, Mansfield, Ct.; married Polly Carpenter of Westminster, Vt., born 1783; died 30 July, 1813. They removed from Charlestown to Dalton, N.H.—date to us unknown. The History of Charlestown gives records of birth of only the first three children from which might be inferred that their removal occurred previous to the birth of the fourth child born in 1799. The family suppose the children were all born in Charlestown. Mr. Farwell died in Dalton, 15 Nov. 1833, aged 77. Farmer. *Res. Dalton, N.H.*

431. 8. JOHN⁵, b. 30 June, 1758, Mansfield, Conn.; married Phebe Spafford. He removed to Genesee Co. N.Y.; had no children.

432. 9. DOROTHY⁵, b. 29 June, 1760, Mansfield; died in Westminster, Vt.

433. 10. ISAAC⁵, b. 29 Oct. 1763, in Walpole, N.H.; married 6 Nov. 1785, Prudence Allen, b. 14 May, 1768 (1769, *His. of Charlestown*) daughter of Benjamin and Peggy (Spafford) of Charlestown. They removed from C. to Rochester, N.Y., and in 1826 to Pecatonica, Ill., where he died 18 Feb. 1846. She died 17 Nov. 1848. *Pecatonica, Ill.*

---

* After many years of research for the pedigree and biographical records of the Farwells of America and those of their descendants of other names; and after great expenditure of finance therefor, we find our collection ample for a volume of over six hundred large octavo pages; and for a folio of grand Radial Charts, bound atlas-form, the octavo volume bearing to the folio relations analogous to those which a descriptive geography bears to an atlas or collection of bound maps.

Of course separate branches of the Farwell family will be printed, only in the order in which persons whose records are embraced, shall advance the funds requisite therefor. If by single or united subscription a sum should be raised sufficient to secure at once the entire volume, it would be to the authors a very agreeable result.

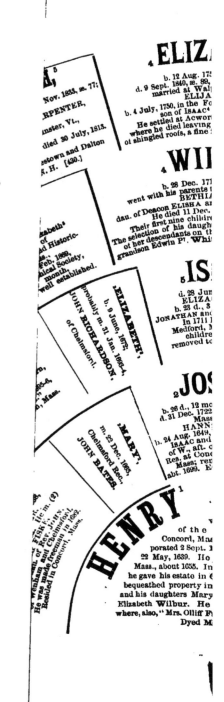

ABETH,[5]

, Mansfield, Conn.;
North Charlestown, N. H.;
ole, N. H., 3 Nov. 1769;
[3] PARKER,
t at No. 4, now Charlestown,
nd MARY PARKER.
h; thence removed to No. 4,
one of the best farms, an acre
amily, and a good name. [427.]

8 JOH
b. 30 June,
married
PHEBE
SPAFFORD.
s. p. [431.]

LLIAM,[4]

t, at Medford, Mass.;
e Mansfield, Ct.; m. 7 Nov. 1744,
H ELDRIDGE,
il ——— (MULFORD) of Cape Cod.
1801, and she 5 Jan. 1812.
n were recorded in Mansfield.
er Elizabeth[5] for full development
..s chart, is in compliment to her
more, a liberal contributor. [423]

m
childr
wide
and his brothe
the records o

AAC,[3]

e, 1753; married
BETH HYDE,
mo., 1680, dau. of
: DOROTHY (RIDDER).
e was living in
ass., where all his
n are recorded;
Mansfield, Conn.

4 Capt. HEN
b. 18 Dec. 16; m. 2
Mass., 25 Jan. 1
SUSANNA RICHA
of C. He removed
Dunstable, where he he
important offices.
26 Sept. and probated 4 Dec. 1
He was o

SEPH,[2]

, 1640, Concord Rec.;
æ. 82; m. Chelmsford,
, 25 Dec. 1666,
H LEARNED,
Woburn, Mass., dau. of
MARY (STEARNS)
f Chelmsford, Mass.
ord and Chelmsford,
oved to Dunstable
xtensive land-owner.

m. 30 Oct. 1688,
BENJAMIN SP
b. 7 Apr. 162 Brainte
EDWARD and BEATRI
Mass. He d.
Plainfield, Conn. after
He purchased a large tract of l
in the northerly part of Canterbury,
Windham Co., Conn., now
called Brooklyn.

FARWELL

was one
f first settlers of
s., which was incor-
835; was made freeman
removed to Chelmsford,
his will, dated 12 July, 1670,
Concord to his son John; and
Chelmsford to his son Joseph,
Bates, Olive Spaulding, and
died 1 Aug. 1670, at Chelmsford,
arwell relict of Mr. Henry Farwell
March 1st 1691-2."

434. 11. DAVID⁵, b. 6 March, 1766, Westminster, Vt.; removed from Charlestown to Canada, probably Stanstead, where he lived for many years, according to the recollections of his niece, Mrs. Bethiah (Holton) White [529], now in her 97th year. She remembers his visit to Westminster in 1806 when she was eighteen years of age, and was impressed by his pleasing manners and appearance. He emigrated to the "Genesee Country," N.Y. and settled in Rochester or Wheatland, in which latter place he is supposed to have married. Late in life (1838 acc. to a descendant of his brother Elisha [429]) he removed with two sons and a daughter from N.Y. State to Hillsdale county, Michigan. By other authorities he removed from Rochester, N.Y. to Jonesville, Mich. where he died about 1855—if so at the advanced age of 99 years.*

435. 12. JESSE⁵, born 12 July, 1768, Charlestown, N.H.; died there 21 Oct. 1844; married, 13 March, 1792, Abigail Allen, b. 8 Feb. 1764, C. d. of Benjamin and Peggy (Spafford) of Charlestown. She died 14 Oct. 1849, at C.

"Mr. Farwell's whole life was spent in North Charlestown, where he established a character and exercised an influence that rendered him a highly esteemed and valuable member of the community. As a man he has been described as conscientious, upright and honorable in all his dealings, and as having, to the close of life, sustained, in every respect, an unblemished reputation. In religious belief he was a Universalist of the Murray school, in which faith he lived and died. He made many friends, and his memory, by the aged in that section of the town where he dwelt, is still warmly cherished."—*History of Charlestown, N.H. by Rev. Henry-H. Saunderson.*

436. 13. JUDGE ELDRIDGE⁵, born 6 March, 1770, Charlestown, N.H.; married, 25 Sept. 1799, Fairfield, Franklin Co., Vermont, Polly Richardson, born in 1782, who died Oct. 1821, at Clarenden, Genesee county, N.Y. He m. 2d, 23 March, 1823, in Barre, Vt., Submit Lee, widow of —— Andrews, b. 17 May, 1791, Wardsborough, Windham county, Vt., daughter of Judge John and Sarah (Wheat) of Barre.

Mr. Farwell emigrated to the "Genesee country" in 1808 and settled in Clarkson, Monroe county; thence removed in 1811, to Clarendon, Orleans county, N.Y., a place earlier called Farwell's Mills, he being one of the first settlers of the county. Postmaster many years and owner of a flouring mill and saw mill. He died 15 Oct. 1843, Somerset, Niagara county, N.Y., while on a visit to his son Elisha; was buried in Clarenden. His widow resided 1870, at Stafford, Genesee county, N.Y.

For the records of the descendants of William⁴ Farwell [423], we are largely indebted to his granddaughter Bethiah⁶ (Holton) White; and in deference to this venerable lady whose intelligence and sound judgment still honor humanity, we here reproduce a letter addressed to her some three years ago:

---
* We shall be happy to receive additional information concerning the four brothers Elisha⁵, John⁵, Isaac⁵, and David⁵ who went West, and of their descendants, to the latest twigs in both male and female lines.

436ª. One hundred years after Henry¹ Farwell assisted in the settlement of Concord, the General Court of Massachusetts, 1735, appointed a committee to procure a survey of the lands between the Merrimac and the Connecticut rivers, from the northwest corner of Rumford on the former, to the Great Falls [Bellows' Falls] on the latter ; and on both sides of the Connecticut from the northern limit of the "equivalent lands."

One year later, petitioners, mostly residing in Taunton, having obtained of the General Court a grant to township "NUMBER ONE," on the west side of the river, south of the great falls, about twenty miles north of Fort Dummer, assembled 14 Jan. 1736, in the school house at Taunton, as "proprietors" and appointed a committee to proceed to their newly acquired township and lay out sixty-three "house lots" and sixty-three "interval lots," a "mill lot," a "burying place," and a "meeting house lot."

COUNTER CLAIMS TO THE TERRITORY.

December 2, 1740, the proprietors of " No. One" assembled in the school-house at Taunton, Mass ; [Their township west of the Connecticut and south of the great falls began to be called "NEW TAUNTON"] and appointed Lieut. Morgan Cobb, Jas Williams, Lieut. John Harvey, Dea. Samuel Sumner, Lieut. Eliphalet Leonard, a committee " to ascertain the circumstances of said township, as to the settlement of the Hampshire line, and what is the opinion of the General Court in the premises."

1742, April 5th, the proprietors at Taunton appoint Joseph Eddy to consult a committee from the General Court upon the difficulties arising from the transfer of New Taunton (No. One) to the Government of New Hampshire.

1753, Oct. 29, The Proprietors at Westminster, (a name substituted for that of "New Taunton") met at Fort Dummer, and, agreeably to a settlement between the Governments of Massachusetts and New Hampshire, voted that those having purchased rights under the Massachusetts grant, and holding the same, should have their lots and first division meadows, where they had them before the government transfer.

1760, Dec. 3d, A Proprietors' meeting was called at the house of John Averill, (where was born the first white child in the settlement) to see whether the Proprietors will give encouragement to any person or persons to build a mill or mills in said town ; and to see what the Proprietors will do toward agreeing with Josiah Willard about the old mill lot—the mill lot to which the Proprietors voted 8 July, 1740, to build a road. On this lot Mr. Barney *commenced* to build a mill, but being interrupted by Indian difficulties, he hid his mill irons and fled.

It does not appear on the records that any mill was built previous to 1760. Soon after which Joel⁵ Holton [¹2], who subsequently married Bethiah⁴ Farwell, the eldest daughter of William⁴ Farwell [423] erected on Holton's Brook a saw mill some two

---

* The letter of Mrs. White, granddaughter of William⁴ Farwell named as of this page. is to be found on page 57.

(Isaac³, Joseph², Henry¹)

miles west of the settlement, and it is probable Mr. Willard built one south of the "plain" about the same time. [See Vol. I of the Winslow Memorial, page 323.]

The establishment of the northern boundary of Massachusetts so far south as to leave "Number One" out of that State discouraged new settlers from coming. The grants made or confirmed by New Hampshire were from the Governor, as agent of the King of England and, strange as it may appear, the Governor of New York, acting under the same English government—claimed the right to require of the grantees a *second* purchase—a condition equivalent to a proprietor having two agents, each demanding and receiving full payment for the land.

Notwithstanding these clouds new settlers came, among whom was William⁴ Farwell, from Mansfield, Conn., whose ninth child, Dorothy⁵, died at Westminster, and whose eleventh child, David⁵ Farwell, was nere born ; and whose second child the eldest daughter, Bethiah⁵ [521] married Joel⁵ Holton. [For a detailed showing of the trials of the Pioneers of the Green Mountain State under the triple allegiance demanded of them, see Hall's and other histories, a resumé of which is prepared for the forthcoming Memorial Volume of Dea. William¹ Holton of Hartford and Northampton.]

We clip from a Vermont paper, the Windham county *Reformer*, of 23 August, 1878, under Local Items, the following:

WESTMINISTER, VERMONT.

At a social gathering at S. S. Stoddard's, Wednesday, there were present representatives of four generations of the descendants of the first Holton family that settled in this town, the oldest person being Mrs. Bethiah (Holton) White, aged 97 (a granddaughter of William⁴ Farwell) [423], and the youngest, seven years. The dinner was enlivened by songs and by anecdotes of old times related by Mrs. White, whose voice retains much of its youthful vigor. She is the mother of the late Rev. Pliny-Holton⁷ White [1230], and great-aunt of Dr. H-D⁸. Holton of Brattleboro.[1188]

MR. EDITOR : There are few villages in the Connecticut valley better adapted for the summer visitor than this quiet village of Westminster. The village, like many others of New England, is made up of comparatively few buildings. The more compact portion lies about a mile south of the depot, and all along the main road are neat looking houses with their beautiful door yards and gardens ; and scattered here and there on the back roads and hills are the substantial farm houses, surrounded by fields and meadows well filled with cattle, grain, and fruit, all showing evidence of that thrift and application which are proverbial with the New England farmer. The straight, broad road presents to the eye a very attractive and pleasing drive, as well as an enjoyable stroll. In the cemetery stands the monument erected to French, the first man to fall in the Revolution. The old town records are in a good state of preservation. [Under the careful supervision of S-S. Stoddard, Esq.]

Mrs. Bethiah[6] (Holton) White,
Westminster, Vermont.

Dear Aunt,

In the Providence of God, there has been vouchsafed to you an extension of the time usually alloted to humanity in the flesh.

Born the 7th of March 1782, and now in your 94th year, you, without doubt, gratefully recall the varied blessings you have enjoyed for so long a period—a period, which, since the landing of our Pilgrim Fathers, (since the birth of Peregrine White,) has been repeated only one and two-thirds times. Twice and two-thirds your present age measures a period equal to that extending from the first permanent settlement in New England to the present time [accurately stated, to 1868].

Fruitful as were the earlier years of New England's experience, it has been your privilege to behold astonishing progress in the discovery of laws in the realms of mind and physics; to behold new applications of law in the various spheres of human acts and relations.

When your ancestor, Deacon William[1] Holton united his fortunes with the first settlers of Hartford Conn., and nineteen years subsequent thereto became one of the small party that first established a settlement at Northampton Mass., how impossible would it have been for him to have anticipated the present condition of progress, northward, southward, eastward and westward.

Three of his grandsons were active in the settlement of Northfield, Mass.—one of them was William[3], who married Abigail Edwards, the grandparents of your father Joel[5] Holton, born 10 July, 1738.

When your father came from Northfield, Mass., by an Indian trail, or paddled his canoe up the Connecticut river, then bordered by a dense wilderness, could he have credited a prophesy even remotely approximating to what his daughter now sees in this progressive valley?

What wonders hath God wrought within the period of your happy life!

You, Dear Aunt, the last remaining of the twelve (12) children of your father, are permitted to count great, great grandchildren of your parents, Joel[5] and Bethiah[5] (Farwell) Holton. That is, your father Joel[5] was the fifth generation of the line of Holtons in America; and his descendants have already reached to an equal number of generations subsequent thereto, even to the tenth (10th) American generation.

One of the members of this tenth generation, residing in Illinois, is named Centurius-Holton, born 26 July, 1871, precisely one hundred years from the birth of his great, great grandfather, William[5] Holton, your brother, born 26 July, 1771, one of the twelve (12) children of his father—he, himself, also, having twelve (12) children, of whom one, likewise, had twelve children—three representative families of three successive generations, each family including twelve children.

[Joel[5] Holton, born 10 July, 1738, had 12 children; his son William,[6] born 26 July, 1771, had 12 children; his son William,[7] born 31 Oct., 1801, had 12 children.] Here presents the thought of the possibilities of the labors of the genealogist who may undertake, some fifty years hence, to search out and arrange the family records of your ancestor, Deacon William[1] Holton and his numerous progeny, down, to include the tenth generation.

While some families of his descendants count more than twelve children, the average number should be accepted as not exceeding half a dozen.

Without recurrence to actual statistics, let us for a few moments assume the progressive average to be *five*; and on this basis run the calculation to estimate the number of descendants of the said Deacon William[1] Holton of Hartford and Northampton. On this basis we should find the number of descendants:

In the second generation... 5
 "   " third   "   25
 "   " fourth   "   125
 "   " fifth   "   725
 "   " sixth   "   3,625
 "   " seventh   "   18,125
 "   " eighth   "   90,625
 "   " ninth   "   453,125
 "   " tenth   "   2,265,625

Total number of nine generations................................ 2,832,005

On the supposition above offered, the genealogist who may hereafter undertake to complete the family records of the first nine generations of the descendants of this Deacon William[1] Holton will have for his study the records of two million, eight hundred and thirty-two thousand, and five persons. [2,832,005.] The ratio *five* is evidently too large to represent the probable rate of increase, in fact. Well, to prove our liberality, let us count, as true, one hundredth part of the above result, and even then, such a genealogist would have to include the records of twenty-eight thousand, three hundred and twenty persons as descendants of the good Deacon. This last [28,320] is not above that which the facts will justify.

Assuming it to be the duty of parents, to give, as far as possible, the knowledge of the ancestral line of their progeny, it is apparent that quite a duty devolves upon us of the *present*, to do what we can to preserve from oblivion, the records of the *past*, and to put them in form most available for the service of *posterity*.

It is of record that your ancestor, William[1] Holton, the first elected Deacon of the first church in Northampton, made the first motion in Town Meeting to prohibit the sale of intoxicating drinks ; and that he was the first Commissioner to the General Court at Boston in this Temperance effort.

Counting that moral forces increase in revolving years for good or evil of the numerical increase of persons, it is not strange, Dear Aunt, that three years ago you were found an active participant at Westminster, Vermont, 18th June, 1872, in the Jubilee celebration of the fiftieth anniversary of the formation of a Temperance Society, commenced on "Apple Oven Ledge," 18th of June, 1822.

Your father and your elder brothers, in their labors in their saw-mill, the first one erected in Westminster, occasionally invited the youth of the village to a pic-nic of fruits baked in an oven excavated in a ledge near the mill.

Subsequently some youth, 18th June, 1822, met upon this "Apple Oven Ledge," and to each other made a Temperance Pledge, the first known Society in America, pledged to total abstinence from intoxicating drinks. It is proposed there to celebrate the fifty-fourth anniversary of this Pledge, 18th June, 1876.

Under the imperfections and losses of public and family records, and the dispersion of branches in the remote parts of our expanding Republic, we shall probably never gather details for a complete enumeration of your said ancestors' descendants ; and, more surely, will remain unknown to mortals on earth, the sum total of moral influences flowing onward from the earnest efforts of Deacon Holton in founding the early institutions of the Connecticut Valley.

Hoping, Dear Aunt, to meet you in Philadelphia at the Centennial of the Great Republic—also, on "Apple Oven Ledge," at the fifty-fourth (54th) anniversary of the Pledge there made ; or, if earlier called hence, may we meet in joy, where vision present and retrospective will not be "through a glass darkly."

Your affectionate Nephew,

19 Great Jones St.,
New York, 18 June, 1875.

DAVID-PARSONS[7] HOLTON.

DEA. WILLIAM[1] HOLTON,
OF
HARTFORD AND NORTHAMPTON,
DIED 12 AUG., 1691.

JOHN,[2]
OF
NORTHAMPTON,
DIED 14 APR., 1712.

WILLIAM,[3]
OF
NORTHFIELD,
DIED 1755.

JOHN,[4]
OF
NORTHFIELD
BORN 24 AUGUST, 1707; DIED 25 OCTOBER, 1798.

JOEL,[5]
OF
WESTMINSTER, VT.,
BORN 10 JULY, 1738; DIED 12 AUGUST, 1821;
MARRIED BETHIAH[5] FARWELL,
BORN 18 SEPTEMBER, 1747; DIED 3 FEBRUARY, 1818.

JOEL,[6]
OF
WESTMINSTER, VT.,
BORN 5 OCTOBER, 1769; DIED 10 DECEMBER, 1846;
MARRIED PHEBE[6] PARSONS,
BORN 27 FEB., 1780; DIED 25 JAN., 1838;
DAUGHTER OF BENJAMIN[5] PARSONS AND MIRIAM[4] WINSLOW.

PHEBE-HELEN,[7]
BORN 27 DECEMBER, 1816; DIED 5 SEPTEMBER, 1817.

MIRIAM[7] HOLTON,
BORN 31 OCT., 1807;
DAUGHTER OF JOEL[6] AND PHEBE[6] (PARSONS) HOLTON;
For many years a Teacher in New England; and subsequently Proprietor and Principal
of a Boarding and Day School for Young Ladies in New York City.
She was married at Sumpterville, S. C., 10 March, 1855, to

HENRY-SMITH BROWN, M.D.,
BORN 26 DECEMBER, 1807; SHE DIED AT LE CLAIR, SCOTT CO., IOWA, 8 OCTOBER, 1865.

UNDER PROVISIONS OF HER LAST WILL AND TESTAMENT,
THIS MONUMENT IS

𝕰𝖗𝖊𝖈𝖙𝖊𝖉.

437. WILLIAM⁴, [81] (*William³, Joseph², Henry¹*,) b. 1 Feb. 1715, Groton, Mass.; married probably Sarah Parker, acc. to *Groton rec.* and *Mr. Wyman*, born 27 Nov. 1719, Groton, daughter of Phineas and Abigail, of Groton. Removed probably to Shirley after 1751, as the birth of their sixth child was there recorded in 1757. We have no record of his death, but his will made in 1775 was "lodged" 28 Feb. 1776. In it are mentioned sons William, Henry, and Phineas, also " Father Parker deceased."

His name or that of his father William³, appears March 1, 1747, as one of the 33 petitioners of Groton for the separation of the south-west part of the town as a distinct precinct or district. This petition commenced the separation of Shirley from Groton. The following is the petition and the names of the petitioners as given in Hist. of Groton.

"To the inhabitants of the town of Groton, assembled in town meeting on the first day of March, 1747.

The petition of us, the subscribers, being all inhabitants of the town of Groton aforesaid, humbly showeth, that your petitioners all live in the extreme parts of the town, and by that means are incapacitated to attend the public worship constantly, either ourselves or families ; and being sensible that our being set off in order for a precinct will be of great service to us, we desire that we may be set off by the bounds following, viz. : beginning at the mouth of the Squawnacook river, and so run up said river till it comes to Townsend line, and thence by Townsend and Lunenburg lines till it cometh to Groton south-west corner, and so by the south line of said town until it cometh to Lancaster river, and then down said river till it cometh to Harvard corner, and then about a mile on Harvard north line, then turn north and run to the waste brook in Coicois (Cauicus or Nonacius) farm, where people generally pass over, and from thence to the mouth of Squawnacook river, where we first began ; and your petitioners as bound in duty shall ever pray, &c.

John Whitney	Jacob Williams	Henry Farwell
John Williams	William Farwell	Josiah Farwell
David Gould	Jonas Longley	John Russell
John Kelsey	Oliver Farwell	James Park
Phineas Burt	Isaac Holden	Daniel Page
Joseph Wilson	Jerahmael Powers	Joseph Dodge
Thomas Laughton	Philemon Holden	Moses Bennet, Jr.
James Patterson	Stephen Holden, Jr.	Caleb Bartlett
Jonathan Gould	William Simonds	Francis Harris
Robert Henry	William Preston	Caleb Holden
John Williams, Jr.	William Williams	Hezekiah Sawtell, Jr.

"The above petition was read at the anniversary meeting in Groton, March 1, 1747, and the prayer thereof granted, except the land on the easterly side Lancaster river, and recorded.

THOMAS TARBELL, Town Clark."

Res. Groton and *Shirley, Mass.*

Children of William⁴ and Sarah (Parker) Farwell were :

438. 1. EUNICE⁵, b. 20 Apr. 1742, Groton, Mass.; married —— **Conant.**
439. 2. ELIZABETH⁵, b. 13 Apr. 1744, Groton; married —— **Gould.**
440. 3. HENRY⁵. b. 15 May, 1746, Groton ; married ——.
441. 4. SARAH⁵, b. 28 Nov. 1748, Groton ; married —— **Todd.**
442. 5. SUSANNA⁵, b. 28 Jan. 1751, Groton; married —— **Solendine.**
443. 6. SYBIL⁵, b. 1 Jan. 1757, Shirley, Mass.
444. 7. WILLIAM⁵, b. 23 Sept. 1761, Shirley, Mass.
445. 8. PHINEAS⁵.

446. OLIVER⁴, [83] (*William³, Joseph², Henry¹,*) b. 13 Jan. 1722, Groton, Mass.; married 22 July, 1742, Groton, Mass., Rejoice Preston. He was one of the 33 petitioners for the organization of the southwest part of Groton into a separate precinct in 1747. See [437].

Children :

447. 1. WILLIAM⁵, b. 12 Dec. 1744.
448. 2. ISAAC⁵, b. 8 Dec. 1746.
449. 3. JONATHAN⁵, b. 25 Sept. 1748; died 18 Jan. 1819; married, 26 Aug. 1771, *Groton rec.*, Priscilla Smith, born 10 July, 1751, daughter of Nathan and Rebecca (Bixby). Res. *Chesterfield, N.H.*
450. 4. ABIGAIL⁵.
451. 5. OLIVE⁵.
452. 6. BENJAMIN⁵.
453. 7. LEVI⁵.
454. 8. NANCY⁵.
455. 9. ELIZABETH⁵.
456. 10. CALVIN⁵.

457. CAPT. HENRY⁴, [84] (*William³, Joseph², Henry¹,*) born 21 July, 1724, Groton, Mass.; died 1803; married, Groton, 6 Dec. 1749, Lydia Tarbell, b. 9 Oct. 1727, daughter of Samuel and Lydia (Farnsworth) of Groton. She died ; he married 2d, 3 June, 1761, Sarah Taylor, of Westford, Mass. He was a soldier in the French war, said by some of his descendants to have been in the company of the famous "Rogers Rangers" [349] ; "was captain of one of the companies of minute men in Groton at the commencement of the revolutionary war. He marched with his company, on the 19th of April, 1775, to Cambridge ; was in the battle of Bunker Hill, in Col. Prescott's regiment, and was severely wounded. A musket-ball passed through his body, lodging near the spine, whence it was extracted in the evening after the battle. He engraved upon the ball the figures 1775, and kept it as a precious relic. He was a man of small stature, but very strong and athletic, and of undaunted courage." [*Hist. of Groton.*]

The ball with which he was wounded is in the possession of his grandson, James-Brazier Farwell. He has also a powder-horn curiously engraved, and the

the strap as worn on the battle field. [A Capt. Henry Farwell of Groton, married 12 Oct. 1800, Hannah Worcester of Groton. We shall be pleased to receive further information of this Capt. Henry.] Res. *Groton, Mass.*

Children, recorded in Groton, were :

458. 1. ANNA⁵, b. 17 Oct. 1750; died 20 February, 1754, Groton, Mass.
459. 2. SAMUEL⁵, b. 21 May, 1752 ; probably died in infancy.
460. 3. WILLIAM⁵, b. 16 Feb. 1754, *Groton rec.*
461. 4. LYDIA⁵, b. 25 Oct. 1762 ; d. 16 Dec. 1763, *Groton rec.*
462. 5. SARAH⁵, b. 4 Dec. 1763; d. 1810 ; m. James Brazer of Charlestown, Mass. who died 1818, in Groton. He was Lieutenant and Captain, receiving his commission from John Hancock. Merchant, justice of the peace and of the Quorum, and representative of Groton, to General court 1810.
463. 6. LYDIA⁵, b. 14 Oct. 1765. Res. *Groton, Mass.*
[A Lydia Farwell married 25 Dec. 1788, John White of Pepperell, b. Pepperell, 21 Aug. 1763, son of John and Sybil (Shattuck) of Pepperell.]
464. 7. JONATHAN⁵. b. 6 Dec. 1767 ; died 1 Apr. 1845, and was buried in Milford, N.H.; married 25 Jan. 1801, *Groton rec.*, Sybil Sawtell of Shirley, Mass., born there perhaps 6 Dec. 1763, daughter of Richard and Elizabeth (Bennett) of Shirley [see Shirley rec.] She died 26 March, 1839, Milford, N.H., and was there interred. Res. Groton, Mass. and *Milford, N.H.*

465. OLIVER⁴, [88] (*Oliver³, Joseph², Henry¹,*) born 19 Nov. 1717, Dunstable, Mass.; died 12 Feb. 1808, Dunstable "in the 91st year of his age," acc. to gravestone ; married Lunenburg, 25 Dec. 1738, Abigail Hubbard, b. 25 June, 1721, Groton, Mass., dau. of Jonathan, called " of Groton," and Rebecca (Brown, called "of Townsend"). Mrs. Abigail Farwell d. 18 Aug. 1789, and was buried in Dunstable.

He resided on a farm about one mile north of the meeting-house in Tyngsboro, on the homestead of his grandfather Joseph², which his father Oliver³, [86] inherited by will of his father Joseph² [15], [J-B. Hill]. In "Giles Memorial," Oliver Farwell is called in 1763, Yeoman of Merrimac, N.H.; but as a portion of Merrimac was originally included in the old town of Dunstable, which at first contained more than two hundred square miles, and as he died and was buried in Dunstable, it is not probable that he changed his residence, but continued to occupy the homestead till his death.

We insert the following transfer of property in which Mrs. Farwell had an interest, as not only personal to her but as corroberative of the place of her mother's home, and showing the connections and social relations of her family.

1763, Sept. 12. Josiah Willard, of Winchester, N.H., Esquire, and Hannah his wife ; Benjamin Bellows of Walpole, N.H., Esquire, and Mary his wife ; Oliver Farwell of Merrimac, N.H., yeoman, and Abigail his wife ; Rebecca Blanchard of Dunstable, widow; and Ruth Stearns of Lunenburg, widow, for £30 lawful money sell to James Giles of said Lunenburg, yeoman, the second division lot in Townsend, No. 82, containing fifty acres, being in that part of Townsend called Bayberry Hill.

These five ladies were all sisters and daughters of Major Jonathan Hubbard of Groton, afterwards of Townsend, where he died April 7, 1761.

Josiah Willard was Col Willard formerly of Lunenburg. His son Josiah m. Mary Jennison. Benjamin Bellows was Col. Bellows of Walpole, N.H. Rebecca Blanchard was widow of Col. Joseph Blanchard [466] of Dunstable. Ruth Stearns was widow of Rev. David Stearns of Lunenburg. Res. *Tyngsboro, Mass.*

Children born in Dunstable :

466. 1. REBECCA[4], b. 9 Oct. 1739; died 20 Aug. 1811, aged 72 ; m. Hon. and Gen. Jonathan[5] **Blanchard**, b. 18 Sept. 1738, Dunstable, son of Col. Joseph[4] and Rebecca (Hubbard) of D. [349].

"July 16, 1788, died Hon. Jonathan Blanchard, aged 50 years. He was the son of Col. Joseph Blanchard, and was born September 18, 1738. He had not the advantage of a collegiate education, but was early initiated by his father, into the active business of life. After the death of his father which occurred in his 20th year, he was called upon to fill his place as proprietors' clerk and surveyor, and was soon deeply engaged in the management of town affairs and other public business." He was buried in the old south burying-ground at D. [*Hist. of Dunstable.*]

Mr. Blanchard was one of the delegates to a convention at Exeter, that adopted a constitution for N.H., bearing date 5 Jan. 1776, which was considered a virtual declaration of independence. Was representative, or a member of the council of twelve (which with the House of Delegates, constituted the executive government of the State of New Hampshire) in 1776, 7, 8, 9, and perhaps other years, as the names of representatives are not preserved from 1782 to 1798.

In 1777, he was appointed Attorney General in conjunction with Col. Nathaniel Peabody ; Jan 6, 1778, was appointed a member of the "Committee of safety"; 1784, was appointed *Judge of Probate* for Hillsboro co. N.H. ; 1786, March 6, appointed one of the committee to give instructions to representatives; and in 1787 he was a delegate to the Continental Congress. "In October, 1776, Gen. Blanchard was sent by the Legislature to recruit our regiments, which had been wasted by sickness, suffering and defeat at Ticonderoga."

He was agent of the Masonian proprietors to manage and dispose of all unsettled lands in New Hampshire; and conveyed most of the lands within the State. *Res. Dunstable, Mass.*

467, 2. OLIVER[4], b. 28 June, 1741, Dunstable, Mass.; died 1822 in Merrimac, N. H.; married Albigail Danforth who died at New-Boston, N. H., 1 May, 1840. Inn keeper, *Res. Merrimac, N.H.*

23 Dec. 1771, Oliver Farwell of Dunstable deeded lands in Hubbardtown, formerly called Rutland to Andrew Beard [Worcester, Reg'r of Deeds]. We are not able to say whether this relates to Oliver[5] or his father, Oliver[4] who was living at that date.

468, 3. MARY[5], b. 10 Jan. 1745. D.; died 24 Nov. 1835, "aged 93,"? Married,

17 Dec. 1767 Gen. Noah **Lovewell**, b. 1741, D., son of Zaccheus and Esther. (——), grandson of John' and nephew of John² the hero of Piqwacket.

He took an active part in the war of the Revolution, and in the civil affairs of the State and country. Nov. 26. 1776, Capt. Noah Lovewell was a delegate to a convention held at Dracut to petition Congress and the State Legislature, "that the resolves of the Continental Congress of 1775, respecting prices &c., be enforced more strictly." In Dec. 1776, he was Quartermaster in Col. Gilman's Regiment and ordered to N.Y.

Aug. 1778. Colonel L. went from Dunstable with fourteen volunteers to R.I. In Dec. same year, was chosen Representative; being the first sent from the town under the new constitution. Feb. 1776, at the annual meeting warned in the name of the people of New Hampshire, (not in his Majsesty's name), he was chosen one of the delegates to a County Congress and one of the "Committee of Safety." Dec. 1782, was one of a Committee to state the reasons for rejecting the Bill of Rights and Plan of government of the State. He served as Representative 1779, 80, 94, 96, and 1802.

Gen. Lovewell's residence seems to have been in that part of Dunstable which is now Nashua, N.H., at "The Harbor," and after his death, which occurred on 29th May, 1820, was occupied by his son-in-law Hon. Jesse Bowers. He was the first Post-Master of Nashua, ap. in 1803.

469. 4. ABIGAIL⁵, b. 13 Apr. 1747, D.; died, 4 Feb. 1786, m. 28 Feb. 1769, Dea. Samuel **Wilkins**, son of Rev. Daniel and Sarah (——) of Amherst, N. H. He was chosen Deacon of the Cong. ch. 5 Jan. 1774, and resigned 1816, He married 2d, Dorcas Towne, 25 Nov. 1788. He d. in Dec. 1832, aged 90. [Rev. Daniel was the first settled minister of Amherst.]
470. 5. JOSEPH⁵, b. 22 June, 1750, *Duns. rec.;* d. 1 Nov. 1750.
471. 6. SARAH⁵, b. 3 Apr. 1753.
471ᵃ. 7. JOSEPH⁵, b. 3. Apr. 1753; died 13 Apr. 1754, (*J. B. Hill*).
472. 8. Dea. JOHN⁵, b. 8 Dec. 1755; d. 12 Feb. 1838, "aged 84;" married, Gorham, Me., 24 Dec. 1784, Elizabeth-Hunt Smith, b. 7 Aug. 1766, dau. of Rev. Peter Thatcher and Elizabeth (Wendall) of Windham, Me. She died, 27 Nov. 1807. He married 2d, 12 Sept. 1820, Dorothy Porter, b. 5 Jan. 1756, whose parents were of Topsfield, Me.

Res. Tyngsboro, Mass.

473. BENJAMIN⁴, [92] (*Edward³, Olive² (Farwell)* **Spaulding**, *Henry¹*,) b. 29 July, 1696, Chelmsford, Mass.; married 7 March, 1719–20, Abigail Wright, dau. of Ebenezer of Chelmsford. She died 6 Jan. 1727. He married 2d, 30 Oct. 1727, Deborah Wheeler. *Res. Plainfield, Conn.*

Children born in Plainfield were:
474. 1. BENJAMIN⁵, b. 22 Feb. 1721; d. 19 Mar. 1807, Moretown, Vermont; m 29

Jan. 1756 Rachel Crary or McCrary, b. 20 Jan. 1729, Plainfield, Ct. d. of John and Prudence. She died 14 July, 1824 Saranac, N. Y.

Mr. Spaulding was a Quaker, and his wife a congregationalist. They removed from Conn., to Sharon, Vt., and thence to Moretown, Vt. They had ten children, three of whom died young; seven married and had large families. Rev. Horace[7] Spaulding, son of Wright[6], of Jacksonville, Ill., was a grandson of Benjamin[5], as also were the brothers Rev. Nathan-Benton[7] and Rev. Newell-Stevens[7], sons of Royal[6] Spaulding; Rev. Justus[7], once a Missionary of the M. E. church to Rio Janeiro, son of Levi[6], and his brother, Rev. Enos-Wilder[7] Spaulding who was much interested in collecting material for a Spaulding Genealogy to be published in the form of a Magazine; which collections were purchased, after his death in 1868, by the compiler of the Spaulding Memorial.

475. 2. ABIGAIL[4], b. 20 Feb. 1723.
476. 3. OLIVE[4], b. 25 Jan. 1725.
477. 4. EBENEZER[4], b. 8 Dec. 1726 ; d. 26 March, 1727.
478. 5. ASA[4], b. 26 March, 1729 ; d. about 1776 ; m. 4 Sept. 1755, Grace Rowland, dau. of Samuel of Fairfield, Conn.; grad. Y.C. 1752. He settled in Fairfield, where he was an inn-keeper. His buildings were all consumed when Gov. Tryon's soldiers burned the town. His children were five sons and four daughters; his son David[5], the only son who left descendants, was grandfather of Dr. David-C[7], a graduate of the University of Michigan, who was assistant surgeon of the 6th Mich. Vol. cavalry, and afterward surgeon of the 10th Mich. cav. till the close of the war.
479. 6. OLIVER[4], b. 25 Jan. 1731 ; d. 24 Feb. 1731.
480. 7. MARY[4], b. 17 Jan. 1732 ; m. 20 Feb. 1754, Rev. David-Sherman Rowland, and had two children; Wm-Frederick[5], a graduate of D.C. 1784, and Henry-Augustus[5], who grad. D.C. 1785.
481. 8. SARAH[4], b. 6 Dec. 1733.
482. 9. DAVID[4], b. 27 March, 1736.
483. 10. ALICE[4], died 6 Jan. 1808; married 26 March, 1759, Isaac Morgan. He was commissary in the Rev. war. A part of General Lafayette's men were quartered on his farm a few days, and the bedroom in which the illustrious General slept is still distinguished as the Lafayette room.

Res. *Plainfield, Conn.*

484. EPHRAIM[4], [94] (*Edward[3], Olive[2] (Farwell)* Spaulding, *Henry[1]*,) b. 3 Apr. 1700, Canterbury, Conn.; m. Abigail Bullard of Plainfield, Ct. which place became his residence, and place of birth of all his children.

Children :

485. 1. JOHN[5], b. 8 Aug. 1724 ; died 29 May, 1768 ; m. 22 Jan. 1744, Elizabeth Sanger, who died 14 April, 1808, at Plainfield, N.H. Some of his family settled in Plainfield, N.H. and some in Morristown, Vt.

His son Amasa⁶ had twelve children who all lived till the youngest was 55 years of age. Of these,

Josiah⁷, the fifth child, b. 3 Dec. 1791, in Plainfield, N.H., was justice of the peace, twice representative to General Court and held various town offices. In the war of 1812 he enlisted Sept. 1814, and served in several grades till his discharge 1819. His sons John⁸ and Herbert-Eustis⁸ were volunteers in the late war of the rebellion.

Jason⁷, another son, b. 1795, had seven children, among whom was Rev. Nathaniel-Goodell⁸, graduate of Union College, 1852; ordained as pastor in M. E. church in West Troy, N. Y.; afterwards preached in several places, and was subsequently elected principal of Amenia Seminary and latter a President of Fort Plains Female College, which position he resigned 1866 on account of impaired health, purchased "Fountain Dell" at Schodac Landing and accepted an agency in the Home Life Insurance Co., Albany, N. Y.

486. 2. PHINEAS⁵, b. 25 Mar. 1726; died 18 Aug. 1751. His widow married a Mr. Stow of Granville, Mass.

487. 3. REUBEN⁵, b. 26 Feb. 1728; (or 24 Feb. 1727, died Jan. 1755, Tyringham, Mass., [acc. to tradition], m. 1 Oct., 1747, Mary Pierce, b. 15 Nov. 1728, d. of Timothy and Mary. She died 1826. They had five children, two of whom d. in childhood. Of those remaining the daughter Mary m. Ebenezer Parkhurst, one of the sons Azel⁶ removed to Canada, and the other Dea. Reuben⁶ to Sharon, Vt. 1769, and resided on the same farm till his death in 1849.

He was a member of the Congregational church of Sharon sixty-one years, and sustained the office of Deacon forty-two years. His devotion to the cause of Christ was sincere and earnest, and the church of which he was an honored member is a witness to his faithfulness. He died in 1849 aged 91 years.

Dea. Spaulding had twelve children, nine sons and three daughters, and all married and had families. Of his sons :

Hon. John⁷ was President of the Bank of Montpelier, also President of the Vermont Mutual Insurance Company; served seven years as State Treasurer, and was for several years assistant Judge of Washington Co. Court. He died at Montpelier in 1870, aged 80 years, 8 months and 10 days. Charles-Carrol⁸, s. of Hon. John, grad. Univ. of Vt. 1847, and was connected with the Boston *Post.*

Dr. James⁷ Spaulding, another son of Dea. Reuben⁶, an "Eminent physician and surgeon" at Alstead and Claremont N.H. and Montpelier, Vt., graduated at Dart. Med. Inst., 1812; was a member of Vermont State Medical Society more than forty years, and Secretary over twenty years; was elected its President 1846, 7, 8—Cor. Sec. 1850; Librarian 1854. He was also, a member of the Board of Fellows of the Vermont Academy of Medicine, besides holding many offices in the Sate connected with science, literature, temperance, etc.

His life was that of the good Samaritan, a life of toil, prayer, and sympathy for others; and it is hoped his mantle will fall on many who will as faithfully devote their lives to the best interests of their fellow-beings, and as highly honor their adopted professions.

He had nine children, six daughters and three sons :

James-Reed[8], who grad. Univ. of Vermont, 1840, and has been connected with the New York *Courier and Inquirer*, N.Y. *World*, and the N.Y. *Times*.

Dr. Wm-Cooper[8], who grad. N.Y. University 1847 ; surgeon in 29th Reg't Wis. Vol. Inf., and since, in practice at Watertown, Wis. ; and

Rev. George-Burley[8], who grad. Univ. of Vermont 1856, studied law in Florida, grad. And. Theol. Sem. 1861, Ord. Vergennes, Vt., 5 Oct. 1861.

Dr. Phineas[7] was born 1799; grad. M.D. at Dartmouth college, 1823; a lecturer on surgery in Vermont Medical college. He had three daughters and one son. One of his daughters m. James-H. Fowler of N.Y. city, another Henry-D. Jones of N.Y.

Dr. Reuben[7], b. 1807; grad D.C. 1832, Middlebury college, 1835, and Harv. Univ. Med. school, 1836 ; in 1872, was in practice at Worcester, Mass. He had three children, all sons, viz. : Rev. Henry-George[8], grad. Harv. Univ. 1860 ; Divinity school Har. Univ. 1866 ; ordained pastor o of first Parish Church Framingham, Mass. 1868.

Frederick[8] was Lieutenant in 2d U.S. Sharpshooters, in McDowell's corps 1861-2, afterward served in the war department till 1874, when he was appointed assistant paymaster in the Navy ; and

Edward-Reynolds[8], grad. Har. Univ. 1844, studied medicine Harvard medical school, Med. Assistant in the Insane Asylums of Hartford, Conn. and Northampton, Mass.

Dr. Jason-Carpenter[7], grad. as M.D. at Dart. college 1828, practised in Dixfield, Me. and Spencer, Mass, till 1836, when he returned to the homestead in Sharon, Vt. to take charge of his aged parents, where he remained till his death 1847, aged 46. At his funeral in the mansion, where the 12 children had their birth, were present the surviving eleven, who, with their aged father, were all gathered for the first and last time around the paternal table.

Azel[7], b. 1803, gr. A.M. Middlebury college, 1835, practised law in Montpelier, Vt.; had 2 daughters who died young, and son Azel-Wainwright of Atchinson, Kan.

The other three sons of Dea. Reuben are :

Pierce[7] of Warren, Vt., b. 1786 ; d. 1852.

Charles[7] of Montpelier, b. 1812; d. 1857; and

Levi[7] a merchant of Derby Line, Vt., b. 1805, whose son Stephen-Foster[8] grad. Univ. of Vt. 1860, studied law first at Derby, then in N.Y., where he was a student when the war commenced. He enlisted

Apr. 1861, in 7th N.Y. Battery. Was Lieut. of Co. B, 8th Vt. Reg. and acted as Captain under Gen. Banks and Gen. Butler at New Orleans; promoted Adjutant 1863, and fell in the second assault on Port Hudson, 14 June, 1863.

488, 4. JOSIAH[5], b. 7 Dec. 1729, Plainfield, Conn.; d. 18 Dec. 1809, Ashford, Conn. aged 80; m. 24 Dec. 1755, Priscilla Paine, b. 31 Aug. 1735, who died, 19 Oct. 1817.

They had six sons and four daughters, all of whom married. Of his sons:

Solomon[6], b. 1761, Ashford, Conn.; d. 1816 at Pittsburg or Amity, Pa. He m. 1795, Matilda Sabin, but had no children. He was a soldier in the Revolutionary Army; read law with Judge Zephaniah Swift of Windham, Conn.

After a change in his religious views he sought the ministry, and entered the Sophomore class of Dartmouth college at the age of twenty-one; graduating there in 1785, he studied divinity and became a licentiate of the Windham Conn. Cong. Association, 9 Oct. 1787; preached eight or ten years, and ordained an evangelist, received several calls, but on account of failing health declined a pastorate.

Soon after 1795 he engaged with his brother Josiah[6] in mercantile pursuits at Cherry Valley, but removed to Richfield, N.Y. in 1799, when they purchased large tracts of land in Penn. and O., and Solomon removed to Salem O. to superintend that interest. The war of 1812 deranged their plans and caused great losses.

His brother Josiah[6] visited him in Salem and found him in poor health and low spirits; and for diversion, writing a novel suggested by the opening of a mound, in which were found human bones and some relics indicative of a former civilized race.

According to Josiah's statement in 1855, then 90 years of age, his work was entitled "Historical Novel" or "Manuscript Found," and in it he imagined the fortunes of the extinct people.

He soon after removed to Pittsburg, probably in 1814, where he was followed by Sidney Rigdon, a printer and afterwards a noted morman, who, with his employer, borrowed the manuscript and desired to print it; but Spaulding refused to allow its publication. From subsequent circumstances it is believed Rigdon copied it and surreptitiously obtained the original to avoid future exposure, as having used it for the basis of the forthcoming

MORMON BIBLE.

Thus unwittingly and innocently an evangelical clergyman became the medium of one of the most monstrous and fatal delusions of the age. For further details and the entire statement of his brother Josiah, see "Spaulding Memorial."

Josiah⁶, brother of Rev. Solomon above, was b. 1765, Ashford, Ct.; m. 1806, Jemima Bosworth, who d. Eastford, 1837. They removed from Eastford to Richfield, N.Y. about 1818, where their only child Josiah⁷ was born who d. unmarried. He returned to Ashford where he died, 1859, aged 94 years, 8 m. 4 days.

A grandson of Josiah⁵, Rev. Erastus⁷ Spaulding, son of Reuben⁶, graduated at Brown Univ. in 1821; m. 1831, Laura-Maria Wooster, who died in 1853; studied law, was admitted to the bar, and commenced practice in Rochester. N.Y. He soon changed his purpose in life, and in 1831, commenced studying for the ministry in the Prot. Epis. Church, under the Rev. H-B. Whitehouse, D.D.; was ordained Deacon by Bishop Onderdonk, 1833, and priest by the same, 1835. Three of his four sons, Henry-Whitehouse⁸, Erastus-Wooster⁸, and Charles-Nelson⁸ graduated Hobart College, Geneva, New York; the first two were ordained Deacons and Priests in the Epis. Church; Prof. Charles-Nelson was ordained Dea. in the Epis. ch. and appointed ass't minister of St. Paul's church, Evansville, Ind.; took charge of Discipline and the Dep't. of Math. Burlington, N.J.; and, 1872, was Prof. of Math. Racine Coll. The fourth son Edward-Bigelow⁸ was ordained Dea. in Epis. church in 1870, and has been Headmaster of Racine College, Wis.

A Brother of Rev. Erastus⁷, Josiah⁷, graduated Yale Coll. 1813, and became an eminent lawyer of St. Louis.

Another of the grandsons of Josiah⁵, Rev. Josiah⁷, son of Elisha⁶, was a minister in the Christian connection and preached in Royalton and Pembroke, N.Y. and in 1837 settled in what is now Summit, Mich.

Of the great grandsons of Josiah⁵ quite a number served in the late war and still bear the scars of wounds received; among whom are Josiah-Sawyer⁸, son of Rev. Josiah⁷, and Joseph-Rodney Little, a son-in-law of the same, both of Newton, Jasper, Co. Iowa; and of those who sealed their love of country by the sacrifice of their lives on the altar of freedom are Capt. William-Lawton⁸ Spaulding son of Reuben⁷, grandson of Reuben⁶ and the brothers Elisha-Abbott and Asa Blodgett, sons of Solomon⁷, and grandsons of Elisha⁶ Spaulding.

489. 5. EZEKIEL⁵, b. 30 Sept. 1731, Plainfield, Conn.; m. 26 March, 1754, Sarah-Morgan. They had seven children.

Dr. Luther-Spaulding⁷ who practiced twenty years in Erie co. N.Y., and Dr. Parley-Joslyn⁷ of Adrian, Mich. were gr. sons through his son Parley⁶. The latter commenced the study of medicine with his brother, Dr. Luther⁷, took his degree of M.D. at Fairfield Med. college, N.Y. in 1838-9, practised two years with Dr. Luther' near Buffalo, and, in 1832, removed to Adrian, where he has since resided.

490. 6. PELATIAH⁵, b. 19 March, 1734; died 3 Oct. 1750.
491. 7. ABIGAIL⁵, b. 16 March, 1736; married 19 May, 1756, Capt. Samuel Hall.
492. 8. OLIVER⁵, b. 30 Sept. 1739, Plainfield, Conn.; d. May, 1795 or '96, Scipio,

N.Y.. m. 17 June, 1762, Mary Witter of Preston, Conn., b. 12 May, 1740; killed by her brother in a fit of insanity, 24 Apr. 1781.

He married 2d, 9 May, 1784, Rebecca Bolton, who died in 1816, at Scipio. He removed from Connecticut to Cayuga Lake, N.Y. about 1788.

He was a soldier in the "old French war" and made the campaign of 1759 with the Conn. troops. in N.Y.. His order book passed into the hands of his son Frederick⁶, and is now held by his grandson Frederick-Austin⁷. of Ann-Arbor, Mich.

He had twelve children, five sons and seven daughters. Lyman-Austin⁷ Postmaster at Lockport and his brother Erastus-Holmes who built the first flouring mill in the village of Dowagiac, Mich. are grandsons through his son Erastus⁶ Spaulding.

Dr. Volney⁷, s. of Frederick⁶ who m. Pamelia Grant cousin of President Grant is also his grandson. James Franklin⁸, son of Ephrain-Hall⁷, grandson of Ephrain⁶, founder of Spaulding's Commercial college is a gr. grandson. Delos⁸ Spaulding another gr. grandson through Alexander-Hamilton⁷ and William-Witter⁸ is a noted musician and composer, known as "Frank Howard;" and still another great grandson through Robert⁷ and William Witter⁸ viz: Israel-Putnam⁸ was mortally wounded in the battle of Gettysburg.

493. 9. Mary⁵. b. 16 May, 1744, Plainfield; married, 16 May, 1762, John **Larrabee**.

494. 10. Ephraim⁵, b. 24 May, 1747, Plainfield; d. 1811; m. 20 May, 1773, Esther Snow, d. 17 July, 1806 in the 61st year of her age. He m. 2d, 1 Sept. 1808, Hannah Stowell. She died 9 March, 1823 in her 65th year. They had five children; two of his gr. grandsons in the line of his son Edmund⁶, and grandson Alva⁷, viz: William-Wallace⁸ and his brother Alexander⁸, resided with their families in New York City.

Res. *Ashford, Conn.*

495. EZEKIEL⁴, [96] (*Edward³, Olive² (Farwell)* Spaulding *Henry¹*) born 8 Sept. 1706, Canterbury, Conn.; m. 24 Nov. 1737, Martha Kimball.

They resided in *Canterbury, Conn.*

Children all born in Canterbury were:

496. 1. Mehetabel, b. 26 Aug. 1738.
497. 2. Elizabeth⁵, b. 24 July, 1749.
498. 3. Ezekiel⁵, b. 8 Sept. 1756; died 29 Jan. 1758.
    4. Twin daughter, b. and died 8 Sept. 1756.
499. 5. Lydia⁵, b. 8 Jan. 1759; died 31 July, 1759.

500. EBENEZER⁴, [99] (*Edward³, Olive² (Farwell)* **Spaulding**, *Henry¹*) born 24 June, 1717, Canterbury, Conn.; d. 18 June, 1794; m. 24 Feb. 1748, Mary Fasset, b. 17 Sept. 1723, dau. of Josiah Fasset. She died 22 May, 1790.

They lived upon the farm inherited from his father Edward⁸, consisting of two hundred and fifty fertile acres in Canterbury, now in the limits of Brooklyn, the shire town of Windham co., Conn.

Children :

501. 1. MARY⁴, born 6 Dec. 1743: d. 10 Feb. 1820; married, 6 Oct. 1762, Daniel Cady of Brooklyn, Conn.
502. 2. EBENEZER⁴, b. 15 Nov. 1745; d. 13 July, 1746.
503. 3. SAMUEL⁴, b. 22 June, 1747; d. 19 Sept. 1754.
504. 4. PRISCILLA⁴, b. 8 June, 1749: d. 8 Dec. 1850.
505. 5. EBENEZER⁴, b. 13 July, 1751, O.S. in Canterbury, Conn., now Brooklyn, Windham co. Conn.; was drowned 2 Jan. 1788; m. 29 May, 1783, Molly Payne, dau. of Solomon and Polly (Bacon) of C. She d. 23 Oct. 1821, Resided on the homestead of his father and grandfather, Brooklyn, Ct. He had three children: a daughter Polly who married William Putnam, grandson of Major General Israel Putnam; and two sons, Bela-Payne and Dr. Luther.

Bela-Payne⁶ was father of Dr. Benjamin-Bacon⁷ Spaulding who received the degree of M.D. in Y.C. 1835; and of Ebenezer⁷, a graduate of Y.C. 1838; of Cambridge Law School 1839; settled in St. Louis, Mo., where he died of cholera 17 Aug. 1866.

Dr. Luther⁶ graduated at Y.C. 1810; as A.M. 1822, attended lectures at the University of Pennsylvania in 1813, served for a time in the war of 1812, and was in the hospital at New London, Conn., he practiced at New Braintree, Mass, Brooklyn, and Windsor, Conn., and from 1822 or 3, at Stow Corners, O. where he died.

506. 6. LYDIA⁴, b. 30 Apr. 1753; died 17 Sept 1754.
507. 7. SARAH⁴, b. 15 Mar 1755; died 11 Dec. 1775.
508. 8. ASA⁴, b. 20 May, 1757, Brooklyn, Ct.; d. 13 Aug. 1811, Norwich, Ct.; m. by Rev. Joseph Strong, 21 Nov. 1787, Lydia Shipman of Norwich.

He grad. at Yale Coll. 1778, received the degree of A.M. from Harv. univ. 1791, and studied law with Judge Adams of Litchfield, Ct.

He settled at Norwich, Ct. in the practice of law, and by force of native ability, sound judgment and integrity, acquired a very extensive patronage.

At the date of his settlement there he was extremely poor, living in a small house, under a system of riged economy, and although the price for managing cases at law was only from six to fifty-four shillings, by his dilligence and prudence, he accumulated one of the largest estates in the eastern part of Conn. In his later years he owned and occupied the spacious mansion with majestic portico and massive pillars erected by Gov. Samuel Huntington.

He filled various offices of trust and honor, was a sound lawyer, unremitting in his attention to business, tenacious of the rights of his clients, and just in all his dealings. His only child Maria-Elizabeth, the idol of his affections, died two years before him, aged 12 years. His estate of $150,000 was divided equally between his sister Mary Cady and his brothers Ebenezer, Rufus and Luther, who survived him.

509. 9. Dr. RUFUS⁶, b. 8 Jan. 1760, Brooklyn, Ct.; died, 22 Aug. 1830. Norwich, Ct., m. 10 Jan. 1782, Lydia, dau. of David Paine Esq. of Canterbury. She d. 10 Dec. 1834.

Dr. Spaulding practised his profession at Mansfield, Ct.; and from 1787 to 1812 at Martha's Vineyard, and subsequently at Norwich, Ct. where he died.

In addition to an extensive practice at Martha's Vineyard, he kept a house of public entertainment, was Postmaster, Justice of the Peace, School-director and Librarian.

He was of genial temperament, had an inexhaustable fund of anecdote and was quick at repartee.

He had ten children, two sons and eight daughters who were well trained and faithfully educated. Nine of them publicly professed the Christian religion.

His son Hon. Rufus⁷, b. 3 May, 1798 grad. Y. Coll. 1817; studied law with Hon. Zephaniah Swift, Chief-Justice of Conn., whose daughter, Lucinda-A. he married in 1822. After her death he married in 1859, Nancy-Sargeant, eldest dau. of Dr. William-S. Pierson of Windsor, Ct.

He migrated to Ohio where he became eminent as a lawyer and statesman. In 1841, he was chosen speaker of the house of representatives, and in 1848 was elected Judge of the Supreme Court of Ohio for the term of seven years.

Hon. William Lawrence, M.C. and reporter of the decisions of the Supreme court while Mr. Spaulding was on the bench, wrote of him: "It is at least no disparagement to others to say that Judge Spaulding never had a superior on the bench of the State."

On retiring from the bench he resumed the practise of law in Cleveland, O., and as an advocate and counsellor maintained the highest rank in the State.

In politics, he was an active and devoted member of the Democratic party from the days of Andrew Jackson until the passage of the Fugitive slave bill in 1850, when he threw all his energy and influence into the ranks of the free soil or Anti-Slavery party.

In 1862, Judge Spaulding was chosen a Representative to the 38th Congress of the United States, and continued there six years, having been twice re-elected: so that he participated in the important legislation of the last two years of the war of the Rebellion, and in the exciting work of reconstruction that followed, until 4th March, 1869, when he retired of his own choice, from the public service very much to the regret of his constituents.

Judge Spaulding has for many years been a communicant in the Episcopal church, and one of the Vestry of Trinity church of Cleveland.

Hon. Thaddeus Stevens once remarked to Hon. Benjamin Wade, "Spaulding is the right bower of intellectual liberty."

Of his seven children, three were sons; one died young; his son Zephaniah-Swift[7], late a Lieut. Col. in the 27th Ohio Infantry, was subsequently U.S. Consul at Honolulu, Hawaiian Islands.

His son Geo-Swift[7] entered the U.S. Service at the age of sixteen; was commissioned 2nd Lieut. in the 27th Ohio Volunteer Infantry, to date from the battle of Corinth, Oct. 4, 1862; entered the regular army, 28 July, 1866, and was subsequently Brevet Captain and 1st Lieut. of what was once the 33rd Reg't, afterwards the 8th U.S. Infantry.

Rufus-Claghorn[7] Spaulding, paymaster in the U.S. Navy, is son of Luther-Paine[6], brother of Hon. Rufus-Paine[6] Spaulding.

510. 10. LUTHER[5], b. 22 March, 1762, Brooklyn, Ct.; died, 3 Feb. 1838, at Norwich Town, Conn.; married, 24 March, 1796, Lydia Chaffee of Canterbury who d. 1 June, 1847.

Mr. Spaulding was an attorney at law, and Judge of New-London Co. Court. At the death of his brother Asa[5] he assumed the management of his estate as Executor and principal trustee. In 1812, he purchased from the heirs of his brother Asa[5] the "Huntington House" in which he lived till his death.

His eldest son, George, grad. Y.C. in 1818.

His second son, Charles, preferred the career of a tradesman and manufacturer; of the firm of Barnes and Spaulding, proprietors of the cork-cutting machine. He had two daughters, one of whom died in infancy and the other unmarried.   [*Spaulding Memorial*].

511. DANIEL[5], [341] (*Daniel*[4], *Joseph*[3], *Joseph*[2], *Henry*[1],) born 22 April, 1740, Groton, Mass.; married, Groton, 8 December, 1763, Sybil[5] Page, born 28 Aug. 1740, acc. to Groton rec., daughter of John[4] and Mary[4] (Parker) of G. She died 26 Sept. 1804. He died 17 May, 1815, Fitchburg, probably intestate. [See Seize-Quartiers Chart No. viii and the Radial Chart at the end of this serial number.]

The deaths of Daniel[4], his son Daniel[5], and Daniel[6], son of Daniel[5], occurring at dates so near each other, have rendered it difficult to locate or appropriate certain items gathered from Worcester co. probate records, as delay in settlement of one estate, and promptness in that of another might bring dates of accounts rendered by administrators into the same period of time. [See Radial chart X,

"Joseph Downe, Jr., administrator on the estate of Daniel Farwell, late of Fitchburg, deceased," rendered first account 6 Jan'y, 1818. We conclude this refers to Daniel[5]. See serial No. 577.

[Thus far we have sought to give the descendants of Henry Farwell of Concord, Mass., through the second, third, and fourth generations, in male and female lines, equal attention to the several branches.
At this point, page 72, serial No. 511, we (for the present) leave all the members of the FARWELL FAMILY in the fifth, sixth, seventh, eighth, ninth and tenth generations, except Daniel[5] [511], Bethiah[5] [521], and Elizabeth[5] [534], and their descendants; to which three several divisions we are called by special payments from one or more members thereof; and we hope members of other divisions will soon order their respective branches that the "completed volume" may ere long appear. . .
See foot notes on pages 25, 35, 36, and 51.]

F   *Brief Pedigree of Sybil Page, wife of Daniel^5 Farwell.*   73

John^1 Page of Watertown, Mass. acc. to Savage, came in the fleet with Winthrop in 1630, bringing with him son John and another child. He was from Dedham, Co. Essex, England. He was made constable 19 Oct. 1630; admitted freeman 18 May, 1631. His wife was Phebe Payne, sister of William of Ipswich, who came in the Increase from London, 1635, aged 37, with wife Ann, 40, and several children. He removed to Boston, had large estate, and "used it in a public spirit"; died 10 Oct. 1660. His will made 9 Oct. 1670, makes very liberal bequests to his wife, children, grandchildren and to his sister Phebe, "to my sister Page £3 per annum, to her five children, John, Samuel, Elizabeth, Mary and Phebe, £5 each."

John^2 of Watertown, born in Eng.; m. 12 May, 1664, Faith Dunster, who, acc. to prob. rec. was cousin of Henry Dunster, first president of Harvard College; removed to Groton where he was town clerk 1661 (or perhaps his father); was the first represen'ative from G. at the first session held in Boston in 1692.

"Groton, April 12, 1693. Know all people by these presents that John Page, Senior, doth fully and clearly acquit the town, selectmen and constables for serving the town as a representative at the first [Session] held in Boston in 1692 as witness my hand. [f*]

JOHN PAGE, Senior."

"Paid to John Page, Sen. two pounds sixteen shillings and nine pence in money,"

He had a son John of Groton, 1711, and therefore might be called John "Senior,"

His son Jonathan had among other children a son John, born 30 Jan. 1712; m. 12 Sept. 1733, Mary^4 Parker, of Groton, and had eight children of whom Sybil, the third child, b. 28 Aug. 1740; m. as above, Daniel^5 Farwell. . . . See Sieze-quartiers chart, page 75.]

The mother of Sybil, Mary^4 Parker of Groton, born 12 Oct. 1716, was dau. of Joseph^3 and Abigail Sawtelle, m. 24 Jan. 1715-16; gr. dau. of Joseph^2 according to Shattuck, p. 376, and his second wife Hannah Blood [g*] and gr. gr. dau. of Joseph^1, brother of Capt. James Parker of Groton, and wife Margaret. Savage does not know whose son was Joseph^2 who m. Elizabeth —— and Hannah Blood, but says "probably son of James." Capt. James^1 did not in his will mention son Joseph or any of his descendants. [See under serial number 534.]

The Joseph Parker born 1689, who m. Abigail Sawtelle, according to Shattuck was son of Joseph^2 and Hannah Blood, and grandson of Joseph^1 and Margaret. But to reconcile Savage and Shattuck, may it not be that Margaret was the first wife and had Joseph, b. 1653, and Ann, born 2 Feb. 1655; and by marriage of Rebecca Reed, 24 June, 1655, had Ann, b. 2 Feb. 1656, Mary, 28 Oct. 1657, the precise date of the Mary, dau. of Jos.^{1}, as by Shattuck. Savage is confused but Shattuck gives the line which we believe correct; Margaret being the mother of Joseph, born 1653, whatever other wives there may have been.—[534] [g*].

Abigail^4 Sawtelle was daughter of Obadiah^3 [h*] and Hannah^2 Lawrence, b. 24 Mar. 1662, d. of George of Watertown, Mass. [i*] and Elizabeth Crispe who was b. 8 Jan. 1637, m. 29 Sept. 1657 and was dau. of Benjamin Crispe of Watertown, and wife Bridget.

---

* Letters with asterisks in brackets refer to the same on a seize quartiers chart.

In Bond's Genealogies it is stated that Crispe was a servant of Major Gibbons, and perhaps came as early as 1629. He removed rather late in life to Groton, but before 1682 had returned to Watertown having married 2d wife Joanna, widow of Wm. Longley. The father of Obadiah² Sawtelle was probably Obadiah² who married Hannah, and was son of Richard of Watertown, 1636, and wife Elizabeth. Richard was one of the early proprietors of Groton, was town clerk the first three years in which records were made. Many of his descendants have sustained offices of trust in the town, church and militia. He returned to Watertown, perhaps driven back by Indians and died there 21 Aug. 1694. In his will he names wife Elizabeth, son Obadiah and other children.

Explanation of Charts VIII and IX.—Pedigree of Henry⁷ and Nancy⁷ (Jackson) Farwell.

By chart viii it is seen that Henry⁷ was grandson of Daniel⁵ and Sybil⁵ (Page) Farwell, also of Abraham⁵ and Priscilla⁵ (Thurston) Farwell; that Joseph³ was grandfather [ayle]* of both Daniel⁵ and Abraham⁵, and grandson [oye] of Henry¹ of Concord, Mass.

It is seen that Priscilla⁵ was great-great granddaughter [tresoye] of Daniel¹ Thurston ; that her American ancestors named in the first or left-hand column were THURSTON, PELL, SPOFFORD and BIXBY; that Sybil⁵ was tresoye of John¹ Page, and that her American ancestors named in the said column were PAGE, PAYNE, DUNSTER, PARKER, BLOOD, SAWTELL, LAWRENCE and CRISPE.

The great grand parents of Priscilla [her besayles] were Daniel² and Mary Thurston, Samuel² and Sarah (Bixby) Spofford ; Sybil⁵ had as her besayles John² and Faith² (Dunster) Page⁴, Joseph² and Hannah (Blood) Parker ; Obadiah² and Hannah (Lawrence) Sawtell.

It is to be seen that Simeon⁶ Farwell married his second cousin Hepzibah⁶ Farwell, as they severally had a common great grandfather [besayle] Joseph³ Farwell. [See FARWELL MEMORIAL page 13, serial number 45, also radial chart iii on page 15] This Joseph³ was an oye of Henry¹ and Olive Farwell, also of Isaac² and Mary² (Stearns) Learned.

The children of Simeon⁶ and Hepzibah⁶ (Farwell) Farwell were:

1. Hepzibah⁷, b. 28 Feb. 1794 ; m. George Turner, m. 2d, David Allen.
2. Henry⁷, b. 3 Dec. 1795; d. 4 Jan. 1878; m. 5 Oct. 1819, Nancy⁷ Jackson. [See chart ix.]
3. Benjamin⁷, b. 25 May, 1798 ; m. 6 July, 1826, Hannah-Mary Knox.
4. Peter⁷, b. 24 June, 1800 ; m. Catherine Boutelle, 2d, Maria Patch, 3d, Elizabeth-Smith Burridge.
5. Mary⁷, b. 15 Oct. 1802 ; m. 30 Sept. 1835, Elias-Coolidge Lane.
6. Miriam-Thurston⁷, b. 14 July, 1806 ;·m. 30 Apr. 1827, Stephen Bemis.
7. Simeon⁷, b. 28 Feb. 1809 ; m. 10 June, 1831, Mary-Ann Downe.

By this chart it appears that Henry¹ Farwell was grandfather (or *ayle*) of Joseph³ who married Hannah Colburn ; was besayle of Gen'l Samuel⁴ who married Elizabeth⁵ *

---
* For explanation of the use of the raised index letters see American system of Nomenclature, page 78

SEIZE QUARTIERS CHART, representing the American Ancestry of **HENRY FARWELL**, born 3 December 1795, Fitchburg, Mass.; d. 4 Jan. 1873, at Chicago, Ill. By DAVID P. HOLTON, M.D., 20 Eastern Boulevard, New York City.

THURSTON, Daniel[1]; { Daniel[2], b. 18 Jan. 1661; m. Mary. } { Jonathan[3], b. 16 Mar. 1701. } { John[4], m. Lydia. } { Priscilla[5], d. 80 Dec. 1837. [a*] }

PEEL, ... Ann[2].

SPOFFORD, John[1]; Samuel[2]. ...... Lydia[3], b. July, 1700.

BIXBY, ... Sarah.

MOORE or MOORES .... Abraham[3]. His will lodged 1780. [b*] } { Elizabeth[4], b. 5 Feb. 1719. } { Abraham[5], b. 18 Aug. 1743; d. 29 Aug. 1829. Had nine children. } { Hepzibah[6], b.15 Oct. 1771; d.15 Oct. 1811 }

GILSON, ... Joseph[1] { Joseph[2], b. 8 Mar. 1667; m. Olive; } { Joseph[3], b. 1642. [15] }

CAPER or CAPEN, Mary } { Hepzibah; m. 2d, Elizabeth[c*] acc. to E. Hubbard }

FARWELL, Henry[1], of Concord, Mass. 1635; m. Olive; d. 1 Aug. 1670. } { Joseph[2], b. 24 Jul.1670 } { Gen. Sam'l[4], b.1714 He had 10 ch. [329] Res. Groton, Mass. } { Daniel[5], b. 20 May, 1717; m. Mary. Had 8 ch. [340] } { Daniel[6], b. 22 Apr. 1740; d. 17 May, 1815, Fitchburg, Mass. [511] } { Simeon[6], b. 28 Oct. 1766; d. 31 Aug. 1808, Fitchburg, Mass. [557] }

LEARNED, William[1]; Goodith. } { Isaac[2]. } { [d*] Hannah[3], b. Aug. 1649. }

STEARNS, Isaac[1]; .... Mary[2].

COLBURN, Edward (?) [e*] .... Hannah.

PAGE John[1].................. { John[2]. [f*] }

PAINE; Phebe, sister of Wm. } { Jonathan[3], m. Mary. } { John[4], b. 30 Jan. 1712; m. 12 Sept. 1738. }

DUNSTER, ... Faith.

PARKER, Joseph[1], m. Margaret. } { Joseph[2], b. 30 Mar. 1658. } { Joseph[3], b. 1 Mar. 1689; m. 24 Jan. 1715-16 } { Mary[4], b. 13 Oct. 1716. } { Sybil[5], b. 28 Aug. 1740; d. 26 Sept. 1804. }

BLOOD, [g*] .... Hannah.

SAWTELL, Richard[1]; ...... Obadiah[2]; ...... [h*] Obadiah[3]. } { Abigail[4], b. 13 Mar. 1697. }

LAWRENCE .... [i*]..........George[2]; Hannah[3]

CRIPE, Benjamin[1]; Elizabeth, b. 1637. } { b. 1662. }

Simeon[6] and Hepzibah[6] had seven children:
1. Hepzibah[7] [Turner] Allen.
2. Henry[7], m. Nancy Jackson.
3. Benj[7]. m. Hannah M. Knox.
4. Dea. Peter[7], m. three times.
5. Mary[7] Lane.
6. Miriam-Thurston[7] Bemis.
7. Simeon[7], m. Mary-A. Downe

Henry[7], b. 3 Dec. 1795; m. 6 Oct. 1819, Nancy[7] Jackson. They had six children: Henry-Jackson[8], Charles-Benjamin[8], John-Villars[8], Simeon[8], Simeon[8], Maria-Louisa[8]. J-V[8], their 3d son, has 5 children; the 4th, Arthur-Lincoln[9], b. 17 Jan. 1867.

For explanation see pages 74 and 75.

CHART VIII
OF THE
FARWELL MEMORIAL.

IX. SEIZE QUARTIERS CHART, showing the ancestry of NANCY^7 JACKSON, b. 11 Jan. 1798, at Westminster, Mass., daughter of John^6 and Susannah (Sawyer). She married 5 Oct. 1819, HENRY^7 FARWELL. Res. 1879, Sterling, Whiteside Co., Ills.

By DAVID-P^7. HOLTON, M.D., A.M.; 20 Sutton Place, Eastern Boulevard, Cor. East 59th Street, N.Y.

Christopher^A JACKSON was a merchant in London, England, during the latter part of the reign of Queen Elizabeth, where were found on the White-chapel and Stepney Register, in 1851, by H. G. Somerby, Esq., the following entries:

"John, son of Christopher Jackson bapt. June 6, 1602.

"Edward, son of Christopher Jackson, bap. February 3, 1604."

We know nothing of his other children, if any he had.

Sawyer...Jonathan^a }
FLINT...Susanna^a } Susanna^b. j*

BAKER, John^1, 1634 of Ipswich; — Thomas^2, of Roxbury; — Sarah^3, b. 24 Apr. 1650. }
JACKSON, Edward^1, b. 3 Feb. 1604, m. Frances. } Sebas^2, m. Ap. 1671. k* Hannah^2, b. 1631 London, Eng. }
WARD, William^1, of Sudbury. Came in 1639. — John^2, b. abt. 1626; d. 2 July, 1708. }
} OVE Edward^3, b. 12 Sep. 1672; m. Mary; res. Newton.
} Hannah^3 m. 8 June 1670. l*
GREENWOOD.........................Thomas^1; d. 1 Sept. 1693.
} John^2; d. 29 Aug. 1737.
} BISOVE Isaac^4, b. Feb. 1701; d. 1769; k* m. July, 1729,
} Ruth^4, b. 12 Oct. 1701.

TROWBRIDGE, Thomas^1, of New Haven, Conn. — James^2, of Dorches'r, b. ab. 1636; m. 1659.
ATHERTON, Gen. Humphrey^1, of Dorchester; — Margaret^2, d. 17 June, 1672.
} Hannah^3, b. 15 June, 1672.
m*
John^3, b. 22 May. 1664; d. 1737; m. 27 Feb. 1708, as 2d wife,

WILSON, Nathaniel^1.............. n*
CRAFT, Griffin^1........ m. Alice............ } Margaret
} Joseph^2; b. 31 Jan 1655; m. Deliverance.
Sarah^3.
} Jonathan^4, b. 23 July, 1711; d. 1753.

TRESOVE Edward^5, b. 3 Sept. 1739; was among the first settlers of Westminst'r, Mass. Built the first house there.

t*

QUATROVE John^6, b. 19 July, 1767.

u*

QUINTOVE Nancy^7, b. 11 Jan. 1798; m. at Westminster, Mass., 5 Oct. 1819 Henry^7 Farwell, b. 3 Dec. 1795, at Fitchburg. [700].

JACKSON, Dea. John^1, bapt. 6 June, 1602. Had 5 sons & 10 d's. m. Marg'ret } Abraham^2, b. 14 Aug. 1655; m. 20 Nov. 1679. o*
Briscoe, Nathaniel^1; m. Elizabeth. } John^2, b. 1622;
Brittlestone, Thomas^1, of Cambr.; m. Elizabeth. } Elizab'h^2 d. 1685.
} Elizabeth^2, b. 1653.
} Margaret^3, b. 1685. Her sister Mary m. Daniel Cook. Her sister Elizabeth m. Col. Ephraim Williams, and was mother of Col. Ephraim, founder of Williams College. r*

Bright, Henry, b. 1602, Eng.; m. 1634. p*
Goldstone, H'y^1; m. Ann } Anna^2.
} Nathaniel^2. His sister Beriah m. Isaac Fowle and became gr. gr. grand mother of Pres. J-Q. Adams
Coolidge, Jno^1; m. Mary } Simon^2, m. 1657.
Barron, Ellis^1; Hannah^2.
} Mary^2, b. 11 Dec. 1660. q*
} OVE Henry^3, b. 16 Aug. 1684; d. Oct. 1756.

} BISOVE Jemima^4, b. 19 July, 1712. Had 5 ch. †

s*

TRESOVE Jemima^5, b. 21 Jan. 1745.

*Letters with an asterisk refer to the same in the explanation of this Chart, on p. 73 and elsewhere See pp. 74 and 77, FARWELL MEMORIAL.

Children of Henry^7 and Nancy^7 (Jackson) Farwell.

1. Henry-Jackson^8, m. Mahala-J. Baker.
2. Charles-Benjamin^8, m. Mary-E. Smith.
3. John-Villars^8, m. Abigail-Gates Taylor; m. 2d. Emerette Cooley.
4. Simeon^8, b. 28 Feb. 1828; d. 22 Sept. 1829.
5. Simeon^8, m. Ebenette-C.-M. Smith.
6. Maria Louise^8, m. 5 Mar. 1863, Epaphras-Wadsworth Edson.

† Jemima^4, dau. of Henry^3 and Margaret^3 (Jackson) Bright, b. 19 July, 1712, was great grand daughter of Dea. John^1 Jackson, and great grandmother of Nancy^7 (Jackson) Farwell, being 110 years junior of the former, and 86 years senior of the latter; and, as seen in the chart, united the Bright family with those of the two brothers John^1 and Edward^1 Jackson.

Moores, and of Daniel⁴ the father of Daniel⁵ who married Sybil⁵ Page ; also that he was great-great-great grandfather [quatrayle] * of Simeon⁶, b. 23 Oct. 1766, who married Hepzibah⁶ the quatroye of Henry¹ through her ayle, Gen. Sam'l⁴ the besoye of Henry¹.

In farther explanation of the chart we observe that Henry⁷ was one of seven children of Simeon⁶ and Hepzibah⁶ Farwell. These seven (four sons and three daughters) were quintoyes of Henry¹. In their paternal branch they were quintoyes through their besayle Daniel⁴ ; while in their maternal branch they were quintoyes of Henry¹, through their besayle Genl. Samuel⁴ Farwell.

Gen. Samuel⁴, besoye* of Henry¹ Farwell, married Elizabeth*ᵇ, dau. of Abraham*ᵃ Moores.

Daniel⁴, besoye of Henry¹ had eight children of whom Daniel⁵ (tresoye of Henry¹ married Sybil⁵ Page, tresoye of John¹ Page.

Sybil⁵ Page, b. 28 Aug. 1740, was daughter of John⁴ who married Mary⁴, besoye of Joseph¹ Parker, whose oye, Joseph³ married Abigail⁴ Sawtelle, besoye of Richard¹ Sawtelle.

---

*Ayle, In law, a grandfather. Besayle, a great grandfather. Tresayle, a great-great grandfather Quatrayle, etc. see *Webster's Dictionary*.

See recommendation of Wm-H. Whitmore in the Historical and Genealogical Register, read the 4th Feb. 1874; a system denoting relationship, a *word* system equivalent to the *numerical* symbols as filial measures proposed and published by David-P'. Holton, M.D. in 1870 *

To Mr. Whitmore the public are indebted for producing in tabular form the terms found in Blackstone, the English-French method of denoting relationship:

1. A.
2. Father.
3. Grandfather, ... Ayle.
4. Great grandfather, ... Besayle.
5. Great-great grandfather, ... Tresayle.
6. Great-great-great grandfather, ... Quatrayle.
7. Great-great-great-great grandfather, . . . Quintayle.
8. Great-great-great-great-great grandfather, . . Sesayle.
9. Great-great-great-great-great-great grandfather, . Septayle.
10. Great-great-great-great-great-great-great grandfather, Octayle.

He adds: In the same manner we can easily arrange a system for the descending series, the gr. children, gr. grandchildren, etc.

In Scotch-English we find the word "oye," meaning a grandchild; and this fortunate selection gives us a word corresponding to "ayle," and like it capable of joining well with prefixes; and he suggests therefore as parallel words :

        1   2   3   4   5   6   7
Father, Ayle—besayle—tresayle—quatrayle—quintayle—sesayle—septayle.
Son,   Oye—besoye—tresoye—quatroye—quintoye—sesoye—septoye.

Mr. Whitmore adds that, strictly speaking, it will be best to consider these terms as applicable to either sex, as equivalent respectively to "parent" and "child," and let the sex be determined by the accompanying names.

* For the system of numerical symbols, as FILIAL MEASURES or visible expose of degrees of consanguinity see page 79.

We here reproduce the AMERICAN SYSTEM of GENEALOGICAL NOTATION, by David-Parsons' Holton, M.D.

In Vol. I, p. 29 of the New York Genealogical and Biographical record, may be seen a system of notation of pedigrees adapted to American Genealogies, as proposed by Dr. Holton.

In the first section of this system of notation, *small capitals*, A,B,C,D,E,F, etc. are placed above and at the right of the name, as indices in trans-oceanic generations, commencing with the father^A of the first immigrants of the American family.

In the second section, the members of the American series are indicated by *numeral* indices, commencing with the immigrant children^1 of the father^A; thence by Arabic figures, progressively increasing, to show the successive generations down to the present.

In cases where as yet the line is *not* traceable back to the first immigrant, we use *small letters* of the alphabet, indexing the earliest known ancestor* as a; and the successive generations by the letters, b,c,d,e,f, etc. to the youngest born.

In case we subsequently extend our genealogical discoveries, each generation ascending is marked by affixing to the a regularly increasing *numerals*; a, a^1, a^2, a^3, a^4, etc., upward toward the ascertained immigrant^1.

For illustration, let us take Philip^a Parsons, who was in Enfield, Conn. in 1697; whose ancestry we are yet (1870) unable to discover; while we have on our *Memorial* Records thousands of his descendants. Hence, for the present, we adopt the following mode of notation for said Philip Parsons and his descendants:

Philip^a Parsons, of Enfield, Conn., was there in	1697
Nathaniel^b Parsons, born in Enfield, Conn.	1709–10
Shubael^c Parsons, died in Enfield, Conn.	1819
Eben^d Parsons, died in Enfield, Conn.	1844
Dr. Edward-Field^e Parsons, resides in Enfield, Conn.	1870
His son, Edward-Field^f Parsons, resides at Enfield, Conn.	1870

Search is still continued for the ancestral line of this Philip^a.

Should we discover his father a^1, we shall designate him as a^1; should we later find his gr. father, a^2, as of America, he will be a^2; unless this last be the immigrant^1, when he will receive the unit index; and his descendants will then be re-indexed with *numerals*, as in second section.

The first section in this system of pedigradation includes any father, having left the Eastern continent and having died upon the voyage, his children reaching America. He would, therefore, be pedigraded A, as of the first section; while his children, if any settled in America, would be pedigraded (1), as of the second section.

The illustration of the system may be more fully understood by the following: Edward-Field^f, Dr. Edward-Field^e, Eben^d, Shubael^c, Nathaniel^b, Philip^a. It is traditionally believed that this Philip^a was a grandson of Deacon Benjamin^1 Parsons, of Springfield, Mass, the immigrant ancestor.

Should this tradition *be proved* to be true then the pedigradation will run thus:

Edward-Field^8 Parsons, residing at Enfield, Conn.	1870
Dr. Edward-Field^7 Parsons, residing at Enfield, Conn.	1870
Eben^6 Parsons, died in Enfield, Conn.	1844
Shubael^5 Parsons, died in Enfield, Conn.	1819
Nathaniel^4 Parsons, born in Enfield, Conn.	1709–10
PHILIP^3 Parsons, was living in Enfield, Conn.	1697
——^{2},	
Deacon Benjamin^1 Parsons married at Windsor, Conn. Nov. 6, 1653; res at Springfield, Mass. and d. Aug 24,	1689

FILIAL MEASURES, IN FULL SERIES OR IN SECTIONS.
Symbols of degree of consanguinity in direct and allied lines.

Without special reference to the genetic index American or trans-oceanic, we frequently desire to state the relation of a person to a given ancestor; as son or daughter, grandson or granddaughter, great grandson or great granddaughter. . . . etc.

For this purpose, place after the said descendant and before the said ancestor *small* Roman numerals, symbolizing the relation of the said parties.

1. Let one i symbolize one generation of descent; and let each additional unit Roman numeral represent one additional descending generation.

[*In this system the small i, v, and x have the force of capitals used conformably to the style of Roman notation.*]

2. The numerals may be succeeded by *s.* for son or *d.* for daughter, when the writer thinks this will add to the perspicuity of the notation.

3. The symbols may be read by saying *son* or *daughter of* . . . . when one i is used; *grandson* or *granddaughter of* . . . . when *two* are used; and for any indicated number more than two, by speaking the word *great* as many times *save two* as the small Roman numerals signify.

The following examples may serve to illustrate the preceding rules:

Examples of the use of the Symbols in Filial Measures.

John-Villars^2 Farwell is a son of Henry^7 and great-great-great-great-great grandson of Henry^1; and also of Christopher Jackson.

His mother Nancy^7 (Jackson) Farwell was great-great-great-great granddaughter of Henry^1 Bright, who married Anna^2 Goldstone. [41 words].

The above may be symbolized thus:

John-Villars^2 Farwell i Henry^7 and vii Henry^1; and, also, of Christopher^1 Jackson. His mother Nancy^7 (Jackson) Farwell is vi Henry^1 Bright who married Anna^2 Goldstone. [26 words].

41—26—15, a saving of 15 words, and the economical form is, to the initiated, more readily comprehended than is the long one. Through vision, these roman numerical symbols convey definite ideas more quickly than do the literal words.

By the chart viii, on page 75, we see that Simeon^6 Farwell was a great grandson of Joseph^3 [Simeon^6 iii Joseph^3]; also, that Hepzibah^6 the wife of Simeon^6, was a gr. granddaughter of the same [Hepzibah^6 iii Joseph^3.]

Supposing that we desire to speak of Henry^7 Farwell, a quintoye of Henry^1, as connected with any intermediate member of the direct line; for example with Joseph^2 who m. Hannah^2 Learned, d*, we write it *Henry^7 Farwell* v *Joseph^2*, and not by the tedious process of words Henry^7 Farwell, great-great-great grandson of Joseph^2.

Again let it be required to express the degree of relationship between the said Henry^7 Farwell and Faith^a Dunster f* we should write it thus: Henry^{7}Farwell v Faith^a§ (Dunster) Page. In reading this last agreeably to the rule, from v before Faith^a we subtract two, leaving iii (3) the number of repetitions of the word *great* in the reading great-great-great grandson. [see rule 3 above.] Mary^4 g*, a besoye of Joseph^1 and Margaret Parker, as a descendant of Sawtelle h* may be seen to be great granddaughter of Obadiah^2, and this relationship is readily symbolized thus: Mary^4 Parker iii Obadiah^2 Sawtelle. The illustration of the rules might be extended, but enough has been said for those who wish for progress in nomenclature—for the other class farther explanation might be distasteful.

§ See American system of notation, p. 78.

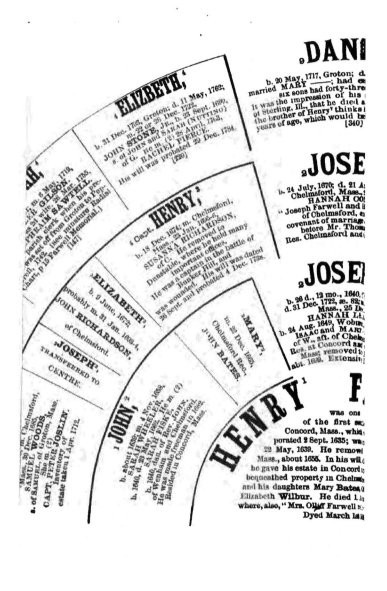

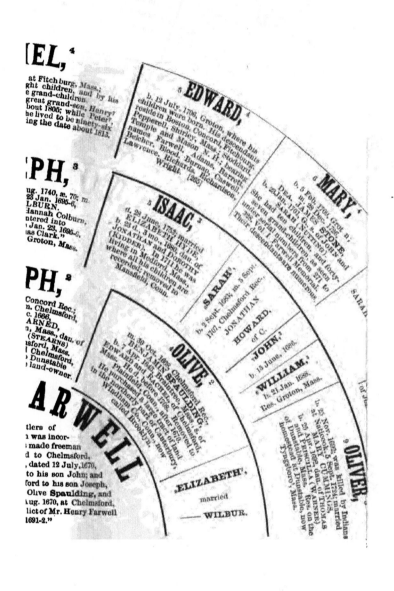

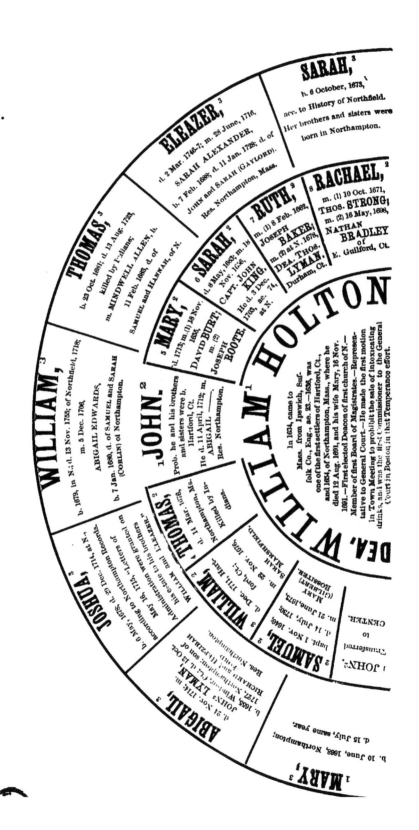

Col. Joseph Parker and Descendants

The emigrant ancestor of Elijah[5] Parker in America was Col. Joseph[1] who with Col. James[1] probably his brother, first settled in Woburn; and they were among the original grantees of Billerica, Chelmsford, Dunstable and Groton. "He was considered an inhabitant of Dunstable, probably in that part which was originally Chelmsford and subsequently included within the bounds of Pepperell. He owned a large estate in Groton and was the ancestor of most of the Groton families of the name. He was constable seven years, was a selectman and a member of the committee for managing town affairs." [*Shattuck's Memorial.*] He died in 1690, leaving large estate ; 700 acres of his land lay in Chelmsford and Groton. His wife's name was Margaret. [see seize-quartiers chart.]

Of his children Joseph[2], probably his only surviving son, b. 30 March, 1653; m. 1, Elizabeth ——; m. 2d, Hannah Blood; was first of Dunstable where he succeeded his father as constable in 1683. He was afterward an inhabitant of Groton where he died 19 Nov. 1725, leaving large estate. Of his seven children Lieut. Isaac[3] m. Ruth —— and lived in Groton till his removal to No. 4 N.H. in 1653. Nine children are recorded in G. His second son William was grandfather of Amos Abbott, and Samuel Lawrence. Three of his sons acc. to Hist. of Charlestown, Isaac, Jr., Nathaniel, and David settled in No. 4. Isaac, Jr[4]. married Mary who had 10 children and died 8 March, 1730. He died 1 Apr. 1760, in No. 4. Elijah, his ninth child, was born as above in Fort No. 4, 14 July, 1750, N.S.

"Lieut. Parker was among the most prominent men in the township. On the Proprietors' Records his name is found in connection with the most important business transactions—On the Town Records it is found six times as moderator, and eight times as one of the selectmen ; and when it is considered that he died April 1, 1762, only nine years after the organization of the town, it shows that he must have possessed the confidence of his fellow-townsmen to an unusual degree. He had been moderator, and had also been elected first selectman the March previous to his decease. Mrs. Parker died March 25th, 1759.

Lieut. Parker, Capt. John Spofford, and Stephen Farnsworth, were the first captives taken by the Indians from No. 4. They were taken on the 19th of April, 1746, and carried to Canada where they were retained through the following winter when they were returned to Boston under a flag of truce. [See Hist. of Charlestown, N.H.

Lieut. Parker was a member of Capt. Hobbs company in 1748, in which he held the position of First Lieut. and did his duty most bravely and manfully in the almost unexampled fight which they had with Sackett, on the 26th of June, 1748. He was also Lieutenant in Captain Phineas Stephens' company, which was stationed at No. 4, in 1750-51. He was also a Lieutenant in Colonel Meserve's regiment in 1756. After Capt. Stephens left for the war in Nova Scotia, Lieut. Parker was put in his place as commander of the post of Charlestown. The following is an extract of a letter from him while acting in this capacity, dated Charlestown, Oct. 3d, 1756. It was directed to Gov. Wentworth.

"This day arrived here one Enoch Byshop, an English captive, from Canada, who was taken from Contoocook, about two years since. He left Canada twenty-six days ago in company with two other English captives, viz.: William Hair late of Brookfield, entered into Shirley's regiment and taken at Oswego; the other name unknown taken from Penusylvania. They came away from Canada without gun, hatchet, or fireworks, and with no more than three loaves of bread and four pounds of pork. As they suffered much for want of provisions, his companions were not able to travel any further than a little on this side Cowass (Coos) where he was obliged to leave them last Lord's day, without any sustenance but a few berries. Six men were sent out this evening to look for them, but it is to be feared they perished in the wilderness."

The letter of Lieut. Parker also contained important information given by Byshop of the movements of the enemy confirming intelligence which had been previously received. The inhabitants of No. 4 having failed to gain the needed force for their protection from New Hampshire had, at the instance of Gov. Shirley, forwarded a petition to the king. Before an answer had been received the settlement still being in great danger, Lieut. Parker, Sept. 1st, 1757, had addressed a letter to Lord Loudoun informing him of the circumstances of its situation. To this he received the following answer :

New York, Sept. 12, 1757.

Sr. I am commanded by His Excellency the Earl of Loudon to acquaint you that he has Received your letter of the first instant and to assure you that he will give proper orders for the protection of the Inhabitants in your part of the country. I am likewise to acquaint you that His Lordship has Received the Petition of the Inhabitants back from England with Directions thereupon.

I am Sr. Your Most Humble Serv't,
JO. FORBES, Adjutant General.

To Mr. Isaac Parker, at
No. 4 on Connecticut River.

Children of Daniel³ and Sybil³ (Page) Farwell born in Fitchburg, were:

512. 1. SYBIL⁴, [549] b. 29 Apr. 1765; d. 11 May, 1845; married Jacob **Osborne**.
513. 2. SIMEON⁴, [557] b. 15 Aug. 1766; died 31 Aug. 1803; married Hepzibah Farwell.
514. 3. ASA⁴, [565] b. 15 July, 1768; died 10 Aug. 1843; married Vashti Carter.
515. 4. POLLY⁴, [572] b. 24 July, 1770; married John **Hartwell**.
516. 5. DANIEL⁴, [577] born 14 May, 1772; died 15 Sept. 1816; married Dorcas Wetherbee.
517. 6. BENJAMIN⁴, b. 15 April, 1774; died 1776.
518. 7. LEVI⁴, [585] born 23 March, 1776; died 18 July, 1840; married Betsey Carter, m. 2d, Beatrix Carter.
519. 8. ANNA⁴, b. 23 July, 1778; died aged 7 days.
520. 9. ANNA⁴, [596] b. 9 Apr. 1780; m. Thomas Carter, m. 2d, Nathaniel Carter.

521. BETHIAH⁴, [425] (*William⁴, Isaac³, Joseph², Henry¹,*) born 18 Sept. 1747, Mansfield, Ct. d. 8 Feb. 1813, Westminster, Vt.; married Joel⁵ **HOLTON**, (*John⁴, William³, John², William¹,*) b. Northfield, Mass. 10 July, 1738, son of John⁴ and Mehetable (Alexander) of Northfield.

Mr. Holton was in the military service in 1759. From March 31 to Dec. 25, served in Capt. John Burk's company, Col. Timothy Ruggles' regiment in the expedition to Ticonderoga and Crown Point.

From Greenfield, Franklin co., Mass. Rec. of Deeds we have the following: "1766, Joel Holton of Westminster, N.Y. to Jonathan Belding of Northfield, Hampshire co. a tract of land in Northfield."

Joel⁵ Holton was one of the twelve men who settled in Westminster, Vt. then the bone of contention between New York State and New Hampshire—each claiming it as belonging to its own territory. [See page 55 this book and 324 Winslow Memorial.] This, with other unsettled affairs, rendered the condition of the pioneers peculiarly unfortunate. They were subjected to great privations—their progress in providing conveniences and comforts was retarded [see serial number [436ª]. They were obliged for some time to take their grain to be ground at Northfield, and when Mr. Holton was so unfortunate as to break his leg he was carried there a distance of thirty miles for its treatment. The passage was comparatively easy being in a boat on the Connecticut river.

After a time the courage of the pioneers was rewarded, and by force of character and industry, they overcame the obstacles in their progress and made themselves possessors of some of the best farms in the fertile valley of the Connecticut. Mr Holton erected one of the first saw mills, if not the first, in the town, and devoted himself mostly to the making of lumber. He died 12 Aug. 1821, in his 84th year.

He settled his estate in his life time, and considering a collegiate education as valuable as a farm he allowed his sons to choose their several portions accordingly. Three of his sons, the three youngest, chose education, and John [632], Alexander [634], and Isaac [640] were graduates of colleges.

[The names of the one hundred first settlers of Hartford, Conn. are engraved on Forefathers' Monument in the cemetery of the Central Church of that city, in which list is found WILLIAM HOLTON. We have not been able to learn where he spent the time from his arrival till his settlement in Hartford, 1635, nor the surname of his wife. His children were undoubtedly all born there, and he resided there till 1654, when he removed to Northampton, Mass. and assisted in the settlement of that new town. He was much employed in the business of the town—was deacon of the first church, erected by contract the first house of worship, was one of the magistrates to try small cases, and introduced a motion in the General Court at Boston for the suppression of intemperance—the first known in American history. The marriage of one of his daughters is recorded in 1654, the first in Northampton; and a second daughter's marriage in the following year was the second recorded.

In Hotten's List of Emigrants to America from 1600 to 1700 he is given as WILLIAM HAULTON aged 23. The name is second on the list headed "IPSWICH. A Note of the names and ages of all the Passengers which tooke shipping In the *Francis*, of Ipswich, M' John Cutting, bound for new England the last of Aprill, 1634." The name is variously spelled on the records, sometimes *Holten*, and in one instance the name of one of his sons is spelled *Houghton*. In sundry English records we find *Holton* and *Houghton* interchangeably used in the same family.]

Children of Joel⁵ and Bethiah.⁵ (Farwell) Holton, were :

522. 1. JOEL⁶, [606] b. 5 Oct. 1769, Westminster, Vt.; died 10 Dec. 1846; married 2 Dec. 1802, Westminster, Phebe Parsons.
523. 2. WILLIAM⁶, [612] b. 26 July, 1771, W.; died 12 April, 1857, Bethel, Ill.; m. Olive Rockwood, m. 2d, Mrs. Keziah Shaw.
524. 3. ZOETH⁶, [625] born 21 Jan. 1773, W.; d. 25 June, 1859; married Amanda Loomis.
525. 4. JEMIMA⁶, b. 18 Jan. 1775, W.; died at Westminster, 18 Aug. 1778.
526. 5. JOHN⁶, [632] b. 11 Feb. 1777, W.; died Springfield, Vt., 28 Nov. 1815; m. Harriet Richards.
527. 6. ALEXANDER⁶, [634] b. 19 Jan. 1779, W.; died, Vevay, Ind. 4. Aug. 1823; married Harriet Warner.
528. 7. ERASTUS⁶, b. 6 Feb. 1781, W.; died there 12 Feb. 1781.
529. 8. BETHIAH⁶, [638] b. 7 Mar. 1782, W; m. 6 Sept. 1821, John **White**.
530. 9. ERASTUS⁶, b. 19 Feb. 1784, W.; d. there 3 May, 1800.
531. 10. JEMIMA⁶, born 28 May, 1786, W.; died in W. 7 July, 1865 ; was a teacher many years in Westminster, Vt. and subsequently principal of a young ladies Seminary at S. Berwick, Me.
532. 11. ELISHA⁶, b. 1 March, 1788, W.; died there 1 Feb. 1790.
533. 12. ISAAC⁶, [640] b. 13 March, 1790, W.; died at Hillsgrove, Ill. 26 June, 1850; married Phebe Arnold.

534. ELIZABETH⁵, [427] (*William⁴, Isaac³, Joseph², Henry¹,*) b. 12 Aug. 1751, Mansfield, Conn.; died 9 Sept. 1840, North Charlestown, N.H., aged 89 ; married 8 Nov. 1769, Walpole, N.H., Elijah⁵ **PARKER**, b. in the block house or fort of No. 4 Charlestown, N.H., 14 July, 1750, *His. of Charlestown*, son of Isaac⁴ and Mary (——) of Groton, Mass. and Charlestown, N.H. He died 17 (25th His. of C.) Dec. 1804, North Charlestown, N.H. [See radial chart, page 52.]

Mr. Parker removed with his young wife to Acworth, N.H. where his first two children were born. Here he was principally engaged in making shingles, which found ready sales in the river towns. He appears however to have returned before the birth of the third child to what is now North Charlestown, where he spent the remainder of his life.

By dilligence and enterprise he acquired a competency for the enjoyment of his old age ; his farm was one of the best on the Connecticut river, and his buildings of a fine order are said to have covered an acre of land—quite a contrast to his circumstances and the amount of his worldly goods, when, according to the tradition in the family, he started in life, removing his bride and their effects on a hand sled to Acworth.

He was one who volunteered to clear the land for the erection of Dartmouth College, at Hanover, N.H. In 1782 he was one of the committee chosen by the town to raise £50, and apportion it among the several school districts of the town.

Mr. Parker was a descendant in the fifth generation from Joseph[1], an original proprietor of Groton, Mass. and his wife Margaret ; of Joseph[2] and Elizabeth ; of Lieut. Isaac[3] and Ruth of Groton and, 1746, of No. 4, now Charlestown, N.H.; and of Isaac[4] Jr. and Mary, who removed after the birth of their seventh child recorded in Groton, to No. 4, in the last named year.

Joseph[1] according to Shattuck's Memorial, was brother of Captain James[1] of Groton, one of the most active and conspicuous of the early inhabitants of that town.

The descendants of the name have been very numerous in Groton and difficulties arise in distinguishing members of the same Christian name of different families; and different opinions have been entertained by Savage, Shattuck and others, but we believe after a careful investigation our line will be found to be correct.

Joseph[1] is called Captain by Shattuck who says he was the ancestor of the most numerous branches of the Parker families of Groton; that he had large estate, leaving at his death in 1690, in Chelmsford and Groton, about 700 acres of land ; that he served the town as selectman ; one of the "committee for managing town affairs," and was Constable of Dunstable from 1675 to 1682. He was considered an inhabitant of D. in the section originally Chelmsford and now Pepperell.

His son Joseph succeeded him as constable in 1683 but was subsequently considered as of Groton, where he died leaving large estate.

Lieut. Isaac[3] was among the most prominent men in the township of Charlestown, N.H. He was one of the first captives taken by the Indians from No. 4, 19 Apr. 1746, and was carried to Canada and retained nearly a year when he and his companions were returned to Boston under a flag of truce. On the Proprietors' records his name is found in connection with the most important business transactions. On the town records it is found six times as moderator, and eight times as selectman ; and when it is considered that he died April 1st, 1762, only nine years after the organization of the town it shows that he must have possessed the confidence of his fellow-townsmen to an unusual degree—He had been moderator, and had also been elected first selectman the March previous to his decease.

His son Isaac[4] Parker, Jr., was also a useful and respected citizen and would probably have stood before the public much more prominently had it not been for the overshadowing influence of his father which appears to have been second only to that of Capt. Phineas Stevens. He was still placed often on important committees, and entrusted with business of such consequence as would at least be adapted to show the confidence of the public, both in trustworthiness and ability. He died about two years before Lieutenant Parker, and in his death and that of his father subsequently, a loss was experienced which doubtless affected the little settlement greatly. For thereby was removed not only an exemplary member of the church which had been but a short time formed, but a citizen of much promise. [His. Charlest'n, N.H.]

Children of Elijah and Elizabeth (Farwell) Parker, were :

535. 1. ISAAC⁶, b. 9 April, 1770, Acworth, N.H.; d. 20 Sept. 1818, at Waterbury, Vt.; married, Claremont, N.H. in the fall of 1794, Catharine Green, of C. b. 26 Feb. 1769, Providence, R.I. from which place she removed with her parents at the age of 14, to Claremont. They removed to Waterbury, Mar. 1795, where there nine children were born. She died 13 Aug. 1824.
Res. *Waterbury, Vt.*

536. 2. DOLLY⁶, b. 15 May, 1772, Acworth, N.H.; m. 15 May, 1793, *Hist. of Charlestown*, Lemuel Cone, of Westminster, Vt., son of Samuel. He was a merchant in W.; removed West, and it is supposed was murdered by a legal opponent, though no direct proof of it could be elicited. According to the History of Charlestown, N.H. Mrs. Cone married 2d, Benjamin Bellows of C. She d. Mar. 1819, at Caledonia, N.Y.

537. 3. ELIZABETH⁶, b. 14 Apr. 1774, Charlestown ; died 17 Mar. 1789, of Measles, in C. [d. 20 Mar. 1791, acc. His. of Charlestown.]

538. 4. JACOB⁶, born 25 May, 1776, C.; died Sept. 1819, at Eight-Mile Creek near Lockport, N.Y.; m. Eliza Morse of Chester, N.H., who died about 1816, at Pembroke, N.H.

539. 5. ELIJAH⁶, b. 26 June, 1778, N. Charlestown, N.H.; died 7 Apr. 1859, Elyria, O.; m. Brandon, Vt. 4 Oct. 1806, Harriet Horton, b. 30 Apr. 1789, B., d. of Major Gideon and Thirza (Farrington). She d. 1 Jan. 1874, Elyria. Lawyer.

540. 6. ORRA-WEST⁶, [648] b. 30 Mar. 1780, N. Charlestown; died 14 June, 1828, No.Ch.; m. Giddings Whitmore.

541. 7. Col. DAVID⁶, b. 4 Apr. 1782, N.C.; died there 4 May, 1846 ; m. 1 May, 1810, Claremont, N.H., Fanny Jones, b. 3 April, 1792, Claremont, dau. of Maj. Ezra of Barre, Mass. and Esther (Rice) of Claremont, N.H. Col. of the 16th regiment of New Hampshire Militia, whence his title by which he was always called. Was a prosperous farmer on the homestead of his father. She res. 1878, with her dau. Fanny-Jones (Parker) Wilson, of Vergennes, Vt. [548]

542. 8. POLLY⁶, b. 19 June, 1784, [*Hist. of Ch.*] N. Charles'n; died 28 Aug. 1808, Brandon, Vt.

543. 9. ENOS⁶, born 1 May, 1786, N.Ch.; married, perhaps, Nelly Sperry, perhaps —— Barber.
Res. *Randolph, Vt.*

544. 10. MARTHA⁶, born 7 March, 1788, N.Ch.; m. Buffalo, N.Y. 12 Apr. 1820, John White who died 8 Oct. 1839, Waitsfield, Vt.

545. 11. PHINEAS⁶, b. 21 Apr. 1790, N.Ch.; married, but we have no further information of him. It is thought he resided in Rutherford co., Tenn. He was a taxpayer in Charlestown in 1812.

546. 12. SOPHIA⁶, b. 7 Feb. 1792, No.Ch.; d. 11 Feb. 1840, Unity, N.H.; married, at Claremont, N.H. 17 Nov. 1816, as 2d wife, Col. Nathan Huntoon of Unity, N.H. Was born 27 March, 1781, Unity, son of Patrick-Henry and Deliverance (Gaus) of U.

547. 13. JOHN⁶, b. 17 Feb. 1794, No.Ch.; died 23 June, 1856, Morristown, Vt.; m. Sept. 1814 [published acc. to Hist. of Charlestown, 8 Jan. 1815] Phila Farnsworth, b. 5 May, 1793, N. Charlestown, dau. of Ebenezer, of C.

She res. 1873, *Morristown, Vt.*

548. 14. SARAH⁶ or SALLY⁶, b. 9 Mar. 1797, N.H.; d. 2 Oct. 1842, Vergennes, Vt.; married, Charlestown, 10 Feb. 1717, Samuel Wilson, b. 30 Mar. 1791, C. son of Joseph of V. and Anne (Holden) of Charlestown, N.H. He m. 2d, 1 Jan. 1844, No. Ch., Fanny-Jones Parker, b. 3 Dec. 1812, No.Ch., dau. of Col. David and Fanny (Jones) of North Charlestown. [541]

They reside 1878, *Vergennes, Vt.*

549. SYBIL⁶, [512] (*Daniel⁵, Daniel⁴, Joseph³, Joseph², Henry¹,*) b. 29 Apr. 1765, at Fitchburg, Mass.; died 11 May, 1845, "aged 80 years and 12 days"; m. by Rev. John Payson, 10 May, 1786, acc. to family record of Mrs. Down, 2 Aug. *His. of Groton,* Jacob OSBORNE, b. Fitchburg, 18 Apr. 1766, and died 21 Apr. 1846.

Children :

550. 1. POLLY⁷, [656] b. 24 Apr. 1787; d. 20 Oct. 1821; married Benjamin Page.
551. 2. SUSAN⁷, [659] b. 24 Apr. 1787; m. 26 Apr. 1807, William Downe.
552. 3. SYBIL⁷, [675] b. 10 July, 1792; married 15 Sept. 1813, Asa-G. Porter.
553. 4. NANCY⁷, [698] b. 12 Nov. 1796, [*Mrs. Downe*]; 1798 [Farwell-O⁶. Cobb]; married Leonard Cobb.
554. 5. LOUISA⁷, [719] b. 22 June, 1801; married, 9 Mar. 1 24, by Rev. Seth Winslow [*Winslow Memorial.*] Jedediah Tuttle.
555. 6. DANIEL-FARWELL⁷, [725] b. 6 Aug. 1805; d. 1 Dec. 1851; married Sarah-Noyes Maynard.
556. 7. LEONARD⁷, [734] b. 6 July, 1809; married Eliza Holman; m. 2d, Sarah-Clapp Coby.

557. SIMEON⁶, [513] (*Daniel⁵, Daniel⁴, Joseph³, Joseph², Henry¹,*) b. 15 Aug. or 22 Oct. 1766, at Fitchburg, Mass.; died 31 Aug. 1808.; m. F. 28 May, 1793, Hepzibah Farwell, b 15 Oct. 1771, F., dau. of Abraham and Priscilla (Thurston) of F.

Mr. Farwell died intestate according to Worcester co. Probate Records : the "thirds" of the widow Hepzibah, appraised at $1050, were set off and a report thereof presented to N. Paine, Judge of Probate, 11 April, and accepted by him on the third Tuesday in May, 1809.

Joseph-Simonds was administrator on the estate, 1st Tuesday in June, 1810. Levi Farwell, guardian for the minors rendered his account as guardian of Mary Farwell, daughter of Simeon, 28 Oct. 1811.

Mrs. Hepzibah Farwell died 15 Oct. 1811. In her will dated 2 Sept. 1811, she bequeathed to her "five eldest children" the one-half of her estate, "and considering the probable expense of supporting my two youngest children, Miriam-Thurston, and Simeon till they are able to support themselves, I give and bequeath to the said Miriam and Simeon the other half of said remainder of my estate to be divided equally among them."—[See serial numbers 804 and 817.]

[The ancestral Farwell line of Mrs. Hepzibah Farwell traced back to its connection with that of her husband is Abraham^5 and Priscilla (Thurston), Gen. Samuel^4 and Elizabeth Moors, b. 5 February, 1719, dau. of Abraham and Elizabeth (Gilson); Joseph^3 Farwell and Hannah Colburn—the parents of both Gen. Sam'l^4 and Daniel^4.

The Gilson line descendant is Joseph^1 of Chelmsford, who m. 18 Nov. 1668, Mary Caper, and removed to Groton where their son Joseph^2 was b. 8 March, 1667, who m. 1st, Hepzibah and 2d, Elizabeth. Among the children of Joseph^2 and Elizabeth [c*] †, according to Edwin Hubbard of Chicago, was a daughter of Elizabeth who married Abraham Moors, [b*] and became mother of Elizabeth Moors, wife of Gen. Samuel^4 Farwell.

The pedigree of Priscilla^5 Thurston [a*]†, wife of Abraham^5 Farwell, is John^4 and Lydia, Jonathan^3 and Lydia Spofford, Daniel and Mary (perhaps Dresser, born 24 July, 1667, d. of John^1 of Rowley, 1643), Dan'l^2 and Ann Pell. [Ed Hubbard.]

Daniel^1 Thurston was of Newbury, Mass. According to Savage may have been the legatee of Daniel Thurston an early settler of Newbury who had grant of land Nov. 1748, and dying childless gave his estate to his "kinsman Daniel Thurston," before called junior.—He had a large family of whom Daniel^2 the third child, born 18 Jan. 1661, d. about 1737; when the lots in Buxton, Me. one of the townships granted to the soldiers of the Narragansett war were drawn by lot, recorded 17 Nov. 1735, Daniel Thurston, on the right of his father Daniel had lot No. 1, first division or "home lot" in "raing" D. by wife Mary. According to Savage and Coffin's Hist. of Newbury, he had seven children, the youngest being Jonathan^3, b. 16 Mar. 1701, who married according to E. Hubbard, Lydia Spofford, born 7 July, 1700, dau. of Samuel and Sarah (Birkbee or Bixbee).

[Daniel Thurston, Sen. witnessed a codicil to the will of Thomas^2 Hale of Newbury, 20 Feb. 1687-8.]

John^1 Spofford was of Rowley 1743. By wife Elizabeth had four sons and four daughters. His son Samuel^2, b. 31 Jan. 1753, m. Sarah Birkbee or Bixbee and had eleven children, one of whom Lydia^3, b. 7 July, 1700, is supposed to have married Jonathan^3 Thurston and became the mother of John^4 who was father of Priscilla^5 (Thurston) Farwell.]

In Gen. Reg. Vol. IX, p. 318, is related an anecdote of John^1 Spofford handed down by his son Samuel who lived to be ninety years of age, which we reproduce :

During a time of great scarcity of corn, probably from the great drought of 1662, John Spofford, then living with his family at Rowley, and being with his neighbors

† For starred letter references, see chart page 75.

much pinched by the famine, went all the way to Salem to buy corn.

A ship load of corn had lately arrived there, but the owner, foreseeing greater scarcity, and higher prices, refused to open his store and commence dealing it out. Spofford plead the necessity of himself and his neighbors, but his arguments were unheeded, and he had only the prospect of returning without being able to carry bread to his suffering family. After every plea was exhausted to no effect on the heartless merchant, he sternly *cursed him to his face!* The merchant, astonished to hear such language, had him arrested instantly, and arraigned before a magistrate, for profane cursing and swearing. The accused, nothing daunted, informed the magistrate that he had not cursed the merchant profanely, but religiously, and producing a Bible, he read, Proverbs, xi, 26.—"He that withholdeth corn, the people shall curse him, but blessing shall be upon the head of him that selleth it." The authority was deemed decisive, the accused was discharged, and, in accordance with the summary process of those days, the magistrate ordered that the merchant should open his store, and sell him as much corn as he desired at the current price.

Res. *Fitchburg, Mass.*

Children, born in Fitchburg, Mass.:

558. 1. HEPZIBAH[7], b. 28 Feb. 1794 ; died 2 June, 1859, Auburn, Me. s.p. ; m. 8 May, 1815, George Turner of Pembroke, Me. He died and she m. 2d, 6 Oct. 1824, David Allen, born 13 Aug. 1796, son of James and Hannah (——) of New Glouster, Me.
559. 2. HENRY[7], [747] born 3 Dec. 1795 ; died 4 Jan. 1873, Stirling, Ill. ; married Nancy Jackson.
560. 3. BENJAMIN[7], [778] b. 25 May, 1798 ; m. Hannah-Mary Knox.
561. 4. PETER[7], [789] born 24 June, 1800 ; m. Catharine Boutelle, 2d, Maria Patch, 3d, Elizabeth-Smith Burrage.
562. 5. MARY[7], [801] b. 28 Oct. 1802 ; married, 6 Sept. 1835, Elizabeth-Cooledge Lane.
563. 6. MIRIAM-THURSTON[7], [804] born 14 July, 1806 ; m. 30 April, 1827, Stephen Bemis.
564. 7. SIMEON[7], [817] b. 28 Feb. 1709 ; m. 10 June, 1831, Mary-Ann Downe.

565. ASA[6], [514] (*Daniel[5], Daniel[4], Joseph[3], Joseph[2], Henry[1]*,) born 16 July, 1768, Fitchburg, or as by his dau. Abigail, at Harvard, Mass. ; d. 10 Aug. 1843, F. ; m. at F. 28 May, 1796, Vashti Carter, b. 8 Mar. 1772, d. of Elijah and Jane (Goodrich) of Fitchburg. She died 9 Nov. 1853.

Mr. Farwell signed his will, 1 May, 1843, which was probated 18 Oct. 1843. In it he made bequests to his wife Vashti, to dau. Sophia Wheeler, wife of Micah-L., to dau. Jane wife of Benjamin Brown, to dau. Abigail, and son Charles, whom he names as his executor, appointed his son-in-law Benjamin Brown to hold the bequest of his daughter Sophia in trust for her use during her life, and after her decease, to render the same to her heirs. [Worcester co.prob records.]

CHART II. *Descendants of* SIMEON[1] *and* HEPZIBAH[1] FARWELL, *of Fitchburg, Mass.*

Hepzibah[1] Farwell, b. 15 Oct. 1771, Fitchburg, dau. of Abra.—Simeon[1] Farwell, b. 15 Aug. or 28 Oct. 1766, Fitchburg, ham[1] and Priscilla (Thurston). She d. 15 Oct. 1811. [333.] 28 May, 1793. Mass.; died 31 Aug. 1808. [657.]

1. Hepzibah[2], b. | 2. Henry[2], b. 8 | Hannah-Mary[2]—3. Benjamin[2], | 6 July, 1825. | 5. Mary[2], | 6 Sept. 1826. | 6. Miriam[2], | 30 Apr. 1827. | —Ste- | Eliza- | 3d, 26 Nov. 1829. | 1st, 21 Sept. 1823. | 10 Jan. 1831.
28 Feb. 1794; | Dec. 1795; d. 4 | Knox, b. 9 | b. 25 May, | Coo- | phen | beth- | Elizar—4. Dea.—Catha-Mary-—7. Sim-
m. 1st George | Jan. 1873, Ster- | Dec. 1806, | 1798. Res. | ledge b. 14 | Thurston[2]. | Smith | rine Ann | eon[2],
Turner; m. 2d | ling, Ill.; m. | Nancy[2] Jack- and Hannah | July, | Be- | b. 24 | Bou- | b. 28
David Allen. | Nancy[2] Jack- | son. [See p. 75] (Douglas.) | 1879, *Paint-* | Lane b. 1806; | mia, | June, | telle, | Feb.
s. p. [558.] | son. [See p. 75] | *ed Post, N. Y.* | [801.] | b. 24 Jan. 1840. | born | 1800. | b. 22 | 1809.
 | | [778.] | | | May, | He m. | Mar. | Res.
 | | | | | 1820, | Oct. | 1810. | *Detroit*
 | | | | | Apr. | 2d, | Res. | *Mich.*
 | | | | | 24, 20 | 1798, d. of | Polly | [817.]
 | | | | | d. of Joseph | Na- | (Hills) |
 | | | | | 1887, | and | than- | She
				Maria	iel	d. 17
				Patch	(Kil-	Sept.
				b. 5	bourn)	1835.
				June,	(Kil-	
				1804;	bourn)	
				d. 10		
				Feb.		
				1888.		
				s. p.		
				[789.]		

11 Apr. 1866 | 22 Jan. 1868 | 12 June, 1860 | 8 Oct. 1862 | 31 Jan. 1880 | 23 Dec. 1872
Hannah-Da-—1. Wil- | Harriet-Rose[3], —2. John[3], —2d, | 3. Mary- 4. Deida-—Wil- | 5. Ma- 1. Wallace-Far- | 8. Arthur- 9. Helen- —1. Henry-—2. Arte-
nelia[3] Ripley, | liam[3] | b. Feb. 1843. | Knox[3], | Char- Aurelia[3], | mia Knox[3], | liam ry-Au- | well[3], b. 8 Sept. | Burrage[3], Gertrude[3], Augusta Bouteller
b. 5 Jan. 1843 | Doug- | d. of Jas. and | b. 5 Jan. | lotte b. 28 Jan | Jas. relia[3], | Knox[3], relia[3], | 1863. [788.] | b. Oct. 1852 b. Dec. 1858 | Harris. b. 1835.
d. of Allen- | las[3], b. | Catharine | 1829, | Law- 1831; d. | b. 16 mon- | Solo- | | |
P. and Cor- | May, | (Castelline). | Big | ton. 15 Aug. | June, and Josiah | | | |
nelia Smith. | 1827. | She d. 1869. | Flats. | 1883. | 1835. Patch | | | |
 | | | | [784.] | | | | |

10 July, 1869 | 20 May, 1851 | 31 Aug. 1856 | 21 May, 1861
Hannah-Cor- | 1. Harriet[4], b. | 1. Douglas- 2. William- | 1. Sarah-—Silas-David | 2. George-Au- | Catharine—3. Alfred- 4. Elizabeth- 5. Annette—Joseph-Com-
nelia[4], b. 17 | 1869; d. 11 Aug. 1869 | Farwell[4], Benjamin[4], | Emory[4], b. Helen[4], b. | gustine[4], b. 3 | Isabel Allen[4], b. True[4], b. Dec. Elizabeth[4] stock Iones, Su-
Jan. 1867, at | [782.] | b. 26 May, 1861 b. 13 May, | Burrage[4], Edward[4], | June, 1835. | Morton. May, 1838 1848; d. 1644 b. Jul. 1846 perintendent
Buffalo, N. Y. | | [785.] 1864. [786.] | b. 1835. b. 1851. | | | | of Schools, East Saginaw, Mich.

4. Catha- | 5. Charles- 6. Emory- 7. George-
rine-Smith[4], | Emory[4], b. Edward[4],
William[4], | with STEEL 1845; d. '46 b. Feb. 1851
b. Mar. 1841 | b. Jun. 1843 |

3. Francis-—James-Nes-
William[4], | rine-Smith
b. Mar. 1841 | b. Jun. 1843

1. Isabella-—2. Ruth[5], b. 1. Edward-Horton[5],
Elizabeth[5], 6 Aug. 1872 b. 2 Feb. 1877. [827[5].]
b. May 1870 Downe[5]
 Jun. 1833
 [795.]

1. Frank-Farwell[5] 2. Edgar-David[5], 3. Charles-Sumner[5], 4. Alfred-Allen[5], 5. Ethel-S..., b.
b. 1853. [818.] b. 1855. [820.] b. 1857. [821.] b. 1859. [822.] 1863. [825.]

Asa Farwell was administrator on the estate of Zaccheus Farwell, and rendered his account 20 May, 1817, which was allowed, and he ordered to pay to the seven children who had attained their majority their portion of the estate. [Worcester co. probate rec.]

Res. *Fitchburg, Mass.*

Children all born in Fitchburg, were:

566. 1. SOPHIA⁷, [828] b. 11 Nov. 1797 married, Fitchburg, 28 Nov. 1824, Micah-Lawrence **Wheeler**, b. 4 July, 1794, son of Joseph and Elizabeth (Lawrence). He died 14 Apr. 1867.
567. 2. ASA⁷, b. 8 Apr. 1800; died 11 Nov. 1815, Fitchburg.
568. 3. JANE⁷, [839] b. 21 Jan. 1802; died 4 Mar. 1870, Boston, Mass.; m. Fitchburg, 25 Dec. 1828, Benjamin **Brown**.
569. 4. CHARLES⁷, [849] b. 21 Nov. 1803; d. 27 Apr. 1868; m. Ann-Elmira Sanderson; m. 2d, Hannah-Page Chaplain.
570. 5. ABIGAIL⁷, b. 23 Dec. 1807; unmarried; Res. Boston, d. 18 Mar. 1875.
571. 6. POLLY-OSBORNE⁷, b. 27 May, 1810; died 7 July, 1812, Fitchburg.

572. POLLY⁶, [515] *Daniel⁵, Daniel⁴, Joseph³, Joseph², Henry¹,*) born 24 July, 1770, Fitchburg, Mass.; married, 7 May, 1792, Fitchburg, John **HARTWELL**, of Lunenburg, [Worcester Co., records of returns from Fitchburg] b. 4 Sept. 1770, L. He died in 1817, L. She died, L., date unknown. Res. *Lunenburg, Mass.*

Children:

573. 1. MARY⁷, [855] b. 17 July, 1792, Lunenburg; d. 18 Sept. 1853, L.; married, Stephen **Gibson**.
574. 2. NANCY⁷, [889] b. about 1796, at Lunenburg; married, Samuel **Davis**, of Holden, Mass.
575. 3. JOSEPH⁷, [891] b. 19 Aug. 1798, Lunenburg; m. 1821, Clarissa Reed; m. 2d, Martha-Maria Bean.
576. 4. WILLIAM-BASCOMB⁷, b. Lunenburg, about 1810, acc. to his brother Joseph⁷, resides unmarried at Shirley, Mass.

577. DANIEL⁶, [516] (*Daniel⁵, Daniel⁴, Joseph³, Joseph², Henry¹,*) b. 14 May, 1772, Fitchburg, Mass.; d. 15 Sept. 1816, F.; m. F., 18 Dec. 1797, Dorcas Wetherbee, b. 27 Nov. 1775, F., dau. of Paul and Dorcas (Hovey) of Lunenburg, Mass. She died at the house of her daughter Mrs. Boutelle, [906] in Fitchburg, 17 Nov. 1855.

Mr. Farwell was a selectman in F. many years.

We have found no record of will, and conclude from the manner of settlement of his estate, he died intestate.

According to Worcester County probate records, an inventory of the estate of Daniel Farwell was ordered 19 Nov. 1816, returned 27th, and accepted 29th Nov. 1816.

The "thirds" of the widow Dorcas, were reported as appraised and set off 19 Dec. 1816.

Report of Elias Messenger, guardian of the heirs of "Daniel Farwell, late of Fitchburg, deceased," accepted by the judge, 1st Tuesday in Feb. 1817. He rendered his account of guardianship of Abel-W. Lyman, and George Farwell, and was ordered to pay to Micah Warren, guardian of Dorcas Farwell, $855.59, being one-fourth part of the balance of the estate.

The guardian of George, 6 July, 1830, was Francis Perkins,

Our collections from Worcester co. records do not give the name of the administrator, unless it may have been Joseph Downe, Jr. and no information from the family has enabled us to decide the question, see serial number 571. Farmer.

Res. *Fitchburg, Mass.*

Children of Daniel and Dorcas were :

- 578. 1. ASENATH⁷, b. 18 Sept. 1798, Fitchburg ; d. 16 Oct. 1816, F.
- 579. 2. JOSEPH⁷, b. 5 June, 1800, F.; d. there 2 Sept. 1803.
- 580. 3. MARIA⁷, b. 3 Mar. 1802, F.; d. there 12 Oct. 1816.
- 581. 4. DORCAS⁷, [906] born 13 Dec. 1804, F.; m. there 26 Jan'y, 1826, Nathaniel-Seaver **Boutelle**.
- 582. 5. ABEL-WETHERBEE⁷, b. 15 Nov. 1809, F.; d. 1 Aug. 1831. He once saved a boy from drowning at the imminent risk of his own life.

    He was called "of Pinckneyville, Mass., formerly of Fitchburg," on Worcester co. probate records, 27 Oct. 1831. Probably died there.
- 583. 6. LYMAN⁷, [928] b. 7 Sept. 1811, F.; m. 26 July, 1836, Eliza-Ann Adams.
- 584. 7. DANIEL-GEORGE⁷, [939] b. 10 July, 1815, F.; d. 19 Sept. 1850, St. Louis ; m. Charlotte Maynard.

585. LEVI⁶, [518] (*Daniel⁵, Daniel⁴, Joseph³, Joseph², Henry¹,*) b. 23 March, 1775, Fitchburg, Mass.; d. there 18 July, 1840; m. F. 27 May, 1801, Betsey Carter, b. 26 Aug. 1782, F., d. of Elijah and Jane (Goodrich) of F. Mrs. Betsey-C. Farwell died 14 Nov. 1808, and he married 2d, her sister Beatrix-Carter, b. 7 Sept. 1788, d. 29 Sept. 1839.

Mr Farwell held various town offices and was representative 1832-4.

The inventory of estate of Levi Farwell late of Fitchburg, deceased, returned by E. C. Farwell, administrator, 31 Oct. 1841. According to Worcester co. probate records, five of the older children had received advancements during the life time of the father, and the two younger had received none, being under age.

21 Oct. 1840, Nathaniel Wood of Fitchburg, guardian of Levi under 14, and same date Horace Newton, guardian of Henry-N. Farwell, sons of Levi, deceased.

Children all born in Fitchburg :

- 586. 1. ELIZA⁷, born 16 or 25 March, 1802; died 28 Aug. 1803.
- 587. 2. BETSEY⁷, [942] born 5 April, 1804; d. 28 Dec. 1870, Lynn, Mass.; married Abel **Baldwin**.
- 588. 3. ELIJAH-CARTER⁷, b. 25 March, 1806 ; married Putney, Vt. 30 Jan. 1833, Lydia Jones, born 20 February, 1809, Royalston, Mass. dau. of Amos and Lephe (Eastbrook) of Putney.

Mr. Farwell was administrator on the estate of his father, Levi⁴ Farwell—account rendered 20 Oct. 1841. "He has lived a quiet life and entered into no business for years." s.p.

589. 4. CAROLINE⁷, b. 28 Oct. 1808 ; d. 21 Aug. 1824, F.
590. 5. LEVI-LINCOLN⁷, b. 2 July, 1811 ; d. 9 Apr. 1825, F.
591. 6. ABEL-GOODRICH⁷, [955] b. 6 Feb. 1813 ; d. 26 Dec. 1863; married Susan-Walker Bartlett.
592. 7. DEXTER⁷, [958] born 27 Jan 1815; m. Olive Shaw.
593. 8. ASA⁷, [961] born 29 March, 1817; married Marcia Piper.
594. 9. HENRY-NEWTON⁷, [965] born 12 Jan. 1822 ; m. Clara Richardson,
595. 10. LEVI⁷, born 18 March, 1828 ; died 14 Oct. 1851, acc. to Boston rec, buried in Fitchburg, Mass. Was clerk in Boston, Mass.

596. ANNA⁶, [502] (*Daniel⁵*, *Daniel⁴*, *Joseph³*, *Joseph²*, *Henry¹*,) born 9 Apr. 1780 Fitchburg, Mass.; married 16 February, 1803, F., Thomas CARTER, born 15 Feb. 1774, F. son of John and Lydia (——). He died there 21 January, 1816. Farmer.
She married 2d, 9 April, 1822, Nathaniel CARTER, of Leominster, Mass., b. in L. 29 November, 1770, son of Nathaniel and grandson of Nathaniel, one of the first settlers of L. and Dorothy (Joslin) of L. He died 30 August, 1850, L. Farmer. She died 17 May, 1851, at Leominster, Mass.

Res. Fitchburg and *Leominster, Mass.*

Children:

597. 1. SAMUEL⁷, [970] born 1 November, 1804, F.; m. F. 18 May, 1828, Martha Litch ; married 2d, Elvira-A. Lancaster.
598. 2. SYBIL⁷, born 3 January, 1807, F. ; died 7 November, 1807.
599. 3. FARWELL-SIMEON⁷, born 25 August, 1808, F. ; died 2 Oct. 1810.
600. 4 SYBIL⁷, born 21 July, 1811, F. ; died 28 October, 1870 ; married 15 April, 1831, Leominster, Mass. Shepherd-Clark Wilder, of Leominster, s.p., born 12 July, 1806, son of Elisha and Polly (Parkhurst) of Hubbardstown, Mass. Farmer.
601. 5. ANNA-FARWELL⁷, [973] born 18 September, 1813, F. ; mar. 2 May, 1836, Leominster, Charles-Pinckney Dean.
602. 6. THOMAS⁷, [989] born 13 June, 1815, F. ; married 21 June, 1838, Mary Phelps.
603. 7. EUNICE-LINCOLN⁷, born 22 May, 1823, Leominster; died 8 Jan. 1857.
604. 8. ASA⁷, born 7 October, 1825 ; died 7 Oct. 1825.
605. 9. CHARLES-FARWELL⁷, [999] born 8 June, 1827 ; married 25 Apr. 1861, Leominster, Harriet May.

606. JOEL⁶, [522] (*Bethiah⁵* (*Farwell*) Holton, *William⁴*, *Isaac³*, *Joseph²*, *Henry¹*,) b. 5 Oct. 1769, Westminster, Vt., d. 10 December, 1846, W.; married 2 December, 1802, W, Phebe Parsons, born 27 February, 1780, Swanzey, N.H., daughter of Benjamin⁵ (*David⁴*, *Benjamin³*, *Ebenezer²*, *Benajmin¹* of Springfield, Mass.) and Miriam⁶ Winslow (*Thomas⁵*, *Thomas⁴*, *Kenelm³*, *Kenelm²*, *Kenelm¹* of Plymouth and Marshfield, Mass) [See

Winslow Memorial, pp. 319 and 332] Mrs. Holton d. 25 Jan. 1838, at Westminster.

Pedigree of Mr. Holton in his patronymic line :

William[1] Holton, of Hartford, Ct. and Northampton, Mass. and his wife Mary ; John[2] and Abigail ; William[3] and Abigail (Edwards) ; John[4] and Mehetabel (Alexander) ; Joel[5] and Bethiah[6] (Farwell) of Westminster, Vt.

[See *Winslow Memorial*, pages 27 and 329, where his death which occurred 10 Dec. 1846, is by mistake said to have occurred a year later, 1847.]

Mr. Holton died at Westminster, Vt. after an illness of only twenty-two hours. Shortly before the close of his sufferings, as he became conscious that death was fast removing him from all earthly scenes, taking the hand of a relative watching over him he said : "I am one of those who were present at the old people's party," referring to a party made for him on his 75th birthday anniversary, 5 Oct. 1844, and these were his last words.

The party was composed of persons over seventy years of age or having a partner over 70; and all of that class in Westport, Elizabethtown, Lewis, Willsboro, Essex, Moriah, and Crownpoint in Essex co., N.Y. were invited. The attendance was large, above sixty. Some were in their eighties, and some in their nineties, and one over a hundred years.

As the steamer from Whitehall the day previous (4th Oct.) approached the Westport wharf, the honored father and grandfather was received with songs of welcome by the pupils of the Seminary and the children of the two public schools of the village.

After having accompanied him to the house the youth were bountifully entertained with melons and fruits; and on the fifth, for half an hour previous to the anniversary dinner, formed in front of the house and sang pieces prepared for this patriarchal reunion, thereby furnishing great pleasure to the guests.

During the day and after a substantial dinner several of the guests recited early experiences in their newly forming villages, contrasted former and later customs, and offered sentiments appropriate to the present and future.

The venerable Dr. Livingston of Elizabethtown gave an address. A song composed for the occasion was sung in the tune of "Long Time Ago," and the guests bidding each other an affectionate *adieu* separated. It was an interesting and solemn scene . . . .

. . Twenty-two months passed, and as one after another had departed, it was natural that Mr. Holton should recall the event in the moments of his own departing.

Children all born in Westminster, Vt. were :

607. 1. ERASTUS-ALEXANDER[7], [1003] b. 9 Sept. 1803 ; d. 3 Aug. 1849 ; m. 2 Sept. 1834, Hannah-Brainerd May.
608. 2. MINERVA[7], [1013] born 18 October, 1805 ; died 30 June, 1875 ; m. Charles-Grandison **Gilchrist**.
609. 3. MIRIAM[7], [1043] b. 31 Oct., 1807 ; died 8 November, 1865, at LeClaire, Iowa ; m. Sumpterville, S.C., 10 March, 1855, Dr. Henry-Smith Brown.
610. 4. DAVID-PARSONS[7], [1044] born 18 June, 1812 ; m. 12 May, 1839, Frances-K. Forward.
611. 5. PHEBE-HELEN[7], born 27 December, 1816 ; died 5 Sept. 1817, Westminster.

CHART XVI.—THE PARSONS FAMILY.

Sarah (Heald) Leonard, wid. of John, of Spring- — DEA. BENJAMIN² PARSONS, bap. 17 Mar. — Sarah Vore, dau. of Richard, of Dorchester
field, 1689; she died 23 November, 1711.
21 Feb. 1675–7.
6 Nov. 1658.
1627–8, Sandford, Co. Oxford, Eng; d. 24 in 1688, and of Windsor before 1640. She d.
Aug. 1689, Springfield, Mass.
1 Jan. 1675–6, at Springfield.

---

1. Sarah³, b. 18 Aug. 1656; m. Spr., 1 Mar. 1676–7, James **Dorchester**, of Spr., prob. son of Anthony.

2. Benjamin³, b. 15 Sept. 1658; m. 29 Dec. 1680; m. 17 Jan. 1682, Sarah Keep, Springfield.

3. Mary³, b. 10 Dec. 1660; m. 27 Jan. 1682, John **Mynn**; m. 2d, 8 Oct. 1684, John Hitchcock, b. 30 Sept. 1666.

4. Abigail³, b. 17 Feb. 1662–3; m. 18 Mar. 1681, Hannah Hitchcock, b. 30 Sept. 1666.

5. Samuel³, b. 10 Oct. 1666; m. 18 Sept. 1702, dau. of Thomas and Hannah (Chapin) of Spr., b. 1666, s. of John. **Richards.**

6. Ebenezer³, 10 Apr. 1690.

7. Mary³, b. 17 Dec. 1670; d. 3 Dec. 1700; m. 1 Oct. 1691, Dea. Thomas **Richards**, of Spr., b. 1666, s. of John.

8. Hezekiah³, b. 24 Nov. 1672; d. 18 March, 1732; m. Sept. 1697, Abigail Phelps, of Northampton, b. Aug. 1673, d. 20 Feb. 1700–1; m. 2d, Hannah Cooley; m. 3d, Abigail of N.

9. Joseph³, b. 6 Dec. 1675; d. 21 Oct. 1733; m. 15 March, 1697.

---

1. Ebenezer⁴, b. 13 Jan. 1690–1; d. Aug. 1742; m. Nov. 1714, Martha Ely, b. 16 July, 1697.

2. Margaret⁴, b. 5 Sept. 1693; m. 31 Dec. 1713; drowned 1 July, 1706.

3. Jonathan⁴, b. 15 Sept. 1695; d. at Swanzey N.H., Rev. Daniel **Elmer**.

4. Benjamin⁴, 15 Aug. 1722.

5. Caleb⁴, b. 27 Dec. 1699; d. 28 Aug. 1786; m. 4 Oct. 1722, Miriam (Stebbins) Williston, wid. of Nathaniel (Cadwell). She died 24 July, 1766.

6. Sarah, b. 30 Jan. 1704, Peletiah **Hitchcock.**

7. Rev. Jonathan⁴, b. Nov. 1705; d. 1776; m. Dec. 1781, Phebe Griswold, b. 1716; d. 1723, Thomson, who d. 1772. He m. 2d, Oct. 1771, Lydia (Clarkson), who d. 1772.

8. Abigail⁴, b. 21 Oct. 1708; m. 19 Mar. 1723, Thomas **Day**.

---

1. Eleanor⁴, b. 29 Nov. 1726; m. May 1752; d. 31 (Bishop) 1755, in French war.

2. David⁴, b. 10 — Bathia bap. 10 Oct. 17; d. 2 May 1810; d. at Fort Edward, 8 Nov. 1755, in the French war.

3. Tabitha⁴, b. 4 Oct. 1729; d. 25 Nov. 1790; m. 17 Apr. 1766, Lt. Robert **McMaster**.

4. Benjamin⁴, bap. 10 Oct. 17; d. 2 May 1810; m. 1761, Mary Merrick, b. 17; bap. Oct. 1736; d. Mar. 1787; s. a. 8d, Joseph.

5. Jonathan⁴, b. 18 Dec. 1733; d. 2 May 1810; m. 1761, Mary Merrick, b. 17 Nov. 1782; m. 2d, at Havana, in m. Eleanor Allen.

6. Israel⁴, b. abt. 1740; d. 28 Oct. 1755 in Fr. war, Th. Damaris Whitcomb; m. 2d, 1787, Mary (Miles) Forbes, 2d cousin Ebenezer.

7. Aaron⁴, b. 21 July, 1745; d. 1814; m. 1771, ben. Daniel **Worthington**, bap. 19 Aug. 1783.

10. Joshua⁴, b. 15 Apr. 1749.

11. Abigail⁴, b. 21 July, 1745; d. 1814; m. 1771, ben. Daniel **Worthington**, bap. 19 Aug. 1783.

12. Margaret⁴, b. 1749; d. abt. 1832; m. 1773, Sarah (Higgins) of Harwich. She d. 8 Mar. 1830.

Phebe, died s.p.

Ebenezer⁵, b. Springfield, Mass.; m. (pub. 30 Aug. 1772,) Jane McMaster, b. abt. 1749; d. 10 Feb. 1827, Marcellus, N.Y. He served in the Revolutionary war.

Benjamin⁵, b. 5 Jan. 1753; d. 8 October, 1833. He served in the Revolutionary war. Res. Moriah, N.Y.

19 Apr. 1779, Miriam⁵ Winslow, [3808] b. 6 May, 1758, dau of Thomas & Sarah (Higgins) of Harwich. She d. 8 Mar. 1830.

---

1. Phebe⁵, [3814]—Joel **Holton.**
2. Benjamin⁵, d. 1796. [See Holton re- b. 30 Dec. 1785; gard.
3. Isaac **Stoddard.**
4. David⁵, d. inf. d. 10 July, 1856. 1776; d. 1848.
5. David⁵, d. s.a. bt. 3.
6. Philander; m. 1814, Sophia Lovell.
7. Philo⁵, [3808]— b. 1791; d. John.
Horace Lovell, of Carpenter.
8. Abigail⁵, [4005] m. 1835, Elijah
9. Polly⁵, [4010], 10. Elisha Winslow, b. 1800.

DESCENDANTS OF EDWARD[A] WINSLOW OF DROITWICH ENG.

1 — 4 Nov. 1594
Eleanor Pelham══Edward Winslow══Magdalene Ollyver.

Children of Edward Winslow:

Edward[1], b. 18 Oct. 1595, Droitwich, Eng.; d. 8 May, 1655; m. at Leyden, 16 May, 1618, Elizabeth Barker, who d. 24 Mar. 1621. He m. 2nd, 12 May, 1621, Susanna (Fuller) White, who died 1 Oct. 1680.

John[1], b. 16 Apr. 1597; d. 1674; m. 12 Oct. 1624, Mary Chilton, dau. of James. [See *Memorial of John[1] Winslow*.] Eleanor, b. 22 Apr. 1598; bap. 24 Apr. She remained in England.

Kenelm[1], b. 29 Ap. 1599; d. 13 Sep. 1672; m. June, 1634, Eleanor Adams, wid. of John. She d. 5 Dec. 1681. [See *Memorial of Kenelm[1] Winslow*.]

Gilbert[1], b. 27 Oct. 1600; came to New Eng. with his brother Edward in 1630. Returned to England. Elizabeth, b. 6 Mar. 1601-2; bap. 8 Mar.; buried 20 January, 1604-5.

Magdalen[1], b. 26 Dec. 1604; bap. 30 Dec. 1604. She remained in England. **Josiah[1]**, b. 11 Feb. 1605-6; d. 1 Dec. 1674; m. 1636, Margaret Bourne, who d. Oct. 1683. [See *Memorial of Josiah[1] Winslow*.]

Generation 2:

Damaris══**Kenelm[2]**, b. 1685, Marshfield; d. 11 Nov. 1715. — **23 Sept. 1667, Mercy Worden**, his cousin, b. 1641, dau. of Peter Worden, Jr.; d. 22 Sept. 1668.

Eleanor or Ellen[2], b. 1637, Marshfield; d. 1676; m. Samuel **Baker**.

Nathaniel[2], b. 1639; d. 1 Dec. 1719; m. 1664, Faith **Miller**.

Job[2], b. 1641; d. 1720; m. Ruth ——.

Generation 3:

Damaris[3], m. 1718, J. **Small** (or Smalley). Elis.[3], m. 1711, Andrew[3] **Clark**. Eleanor[3], m. 1719, Shubael **Hamblen**.

Kenelm[3], bapt. 9 Aug. 1668, Scituate; d. 20 Mar. 1728-9, in the 62d year of his age, as stated on his tombstone in the Winslow Yard. — **5 Jan. 1689-90, Bethia Hall**, dau. of Rev. Gershom[2] & Bethia (Bangs).

Josiah[3], b. 7 Nov. 1669, Marshfield. **Thomas[3]**, bapt. 3 Mar. 1672; d. 5 Apr. 1689.

Samuel[3], b. ab't 1674. **Mercy[3]**, b. ab't 1676; m. Melatiah **White**.

Nathaniel[3], b. ab't 1678. **Edward[3]**, b. 30 Jan. 1680-1; d. 25 June, 1760.

Generation 4:

Bethia[4], bap. 1691, H.; d. 1720; m. John **Wing**. Mercy[4], bapt. 1693, Harwich; m. Philip **Vincent**.

Rebecca[4], bapt. ab't 1695. H. **Kenelm[4]**, b. ab't 1700, H.

Thomas[4], b. ab't 1703; d. 1779. Thankful[4], bapt. ab't 1697; m. 1722, Theophilus **Crosby**. — **12 Feb. 1722-3, Mehetable Winslow**, b. 6 May, 1705, dau. of Edw.[2] & Sarah; d. 5 Mar. 1791.

Mary[4], bap. 1707, H.; m. Ebenezer **Clapp**. Hannah[4], b. 1713, H.; d. 1745.

Seth[4], b. 1715, Harwich; d. 12 Aug. 1754; m. 1st, 1735-6, Thankful **Sears**.

Generation 5:

Thomas[5], b. 29 Feb. 1723-4, Yarmouth. — **Sarah Higgins**, adopt. dau. of Mr. Sears.

Edward[5], b. 4 Mar. 1725-6, Yarmouth. Bethia[5], b. 19 Jan. 1729, Y.; d. 8 May, 1729-30.

Bethia[5], b. 11 Feb. 1730-1; d. 1731. Isaac[5], b. 22 Jan. 1732-3, Y.; d. 1733.

Sarah[5], b. 2 Feb. 1735-6; d. 1 Dec. 1736. Sarah[5], b. 24 Apr. 1737; d. 16 May, 1737.

Isaac[5], b. 7 Oct. 1738; d. 1738. Zenas[5], b. 1740; d. 1740. Zenas[5], b. 30 O. 1741; m. Abigail Clark.

Josiah[5], b. 26 Sep. 1744; d. 8 Oct. 1744. Joshua[5], b. 30 May, 1745; d. 11 Dec. 1748.

Generation 6:

Isaac[6], b. 1742; m. a lady of Bristol, Eng. Elisha[6], b. 1745; d. at Port Mahon, Minorca Island.

Mehetable[6], b. 13 July, 1747; m. Nathaniel **Clark**. Joshua[6], b. 1749; d. at sea, July, 1788; m. Rhoda Punney.

Sarah[6], b. 7 May, 1753; m. John **Hatch**. Priscilla[6], bapt. 24 Apr. 1757; m. 12 Dec. 1772, John **Webb**.

Miriam[6], b. 6 May, 1758; d. 8 Mar. 1835. — **19 Apr. 1799, Benjamin[5] Parsons**, b. 5 Jan. 1758; d. 8 Oct. 1812.

Hannah[6], b. 1761; d. 1832; m. Thomas **Ruggles**. Susanna[6], b. 1764; m. Phineas **Meigs**.

Generation 7:

Phebe[6], [3814], b. 27 Feb. 1780; d. 25 Jan. 1838, at Westminster, Vt. [See Holton Radial Chart.] [3814.] — **2 Dec. 1802, Joel[6] Holton**, b. 5 Oct. 1769, s. of Joel and Bethiah (Farwell). He d. 10 Dec. 1847 [See Holton Memorial.]

Benjamin[6], d. 14 June, 1789. Miriam[6], b. 30 Dec. 1785; d. 10 July, 1856; m. 23 Aug. 1810, Isaac **Stoddard**, b. 22 Oct. 1776; d. 1848. [3862.]

David[6], d. inf. David[6], d. ae. abt. 3 years. Philander[6], b. 15 June, 1789; d. 15 June, 1849; m. 14 Jan. 1814, Sophia Lowell, b. 21 Feb, 1791; d. 17 Nov. 1867. [3901.]

Phila[6], b. 13 Aug. 1791; d. June, 1862; m. 3 Aug. 1807, Horace **Lovell**. Abigail[6], b. 9 Mar. 1794; d. 16 Mar. 1871; m. 1, Jan. 1812, Elijah **Carpenter**, b. 8 Nov. 1787; d. 23 Sept 1851.

Polly[6], b. 11 Apr. 1797; m. 17 June, 1819, Augustus **Cook**, b. 12 Mar. 1792; d. 23 Aug. 1874. Elisha-Winslow[6], b. 11 Feb. 1800. He went to Canada [and is supposed to have been murdered there].

Generation 8:

Erastus-Alexander[7], b. 9 Sept. 1803; d. 30 Aug. 1849; m. 2 Sept. 1834, Hannah-Brainerd May, b. 4 Aug. 1807.

Minerva[7], b. 18 Oct. 1805; d. 30 June, 1875; m. 31 Dec. 1829, Charles-Grandison **Gilchrist**, b. 27 May, 1802.

Miriam[7], b. 31 Oct. 1807; d. 8 Nov. 1865; m. 10 Mar. 1855, Henry-Smith **Brown**, b. 26 Dec. 1809.

David-Parsons[7], b. 18 June, 1812; m. 19 May, 1839, Frances-Keturah Forward, b. 5 May, 1815.

Phoebe-Helen[7], b. 27 Dec. 1816; d. 5 Sept. 1817, [3819]. [3819]

612. **WILLIAM⁶**, [523] (*Bethiah⁵* (*Farwell*) Holton, *William⁴, Isaac³, Joseph², Henry¹*,) b. 26 July, 1771, Westminster, Vt.; d. 12 Apr. 1857, Bethel, McDonough Co., Ill.; married at Westminster, Vt., Olive Rockwood, b. 20 May, 1772, Winchester, N.H., dau. of William and Mary (Averill) Wilson, of Winchester. She died 14 Oct. 1836, Bethel, Ill. He married 2d, 27 May, 1837, at Macomb, McDonough Co., Ill., Mrs. Keziah Shaw. Farmer.

Res. Westminster, Vt., and *Bethel, Ill.*

Children all born in Westminster, Vt.:

613. 1. MARY⁷, b. 10 May, 1793; died unmarried, 1875. To her we are indebted for many of the records of her father's descendants.
614. 2. REUBEN-ROCKWOOD⁷, [1048] b. 16 June, 1795; married Rebecca-Baker Tower; m. 2d, Margaret-Albro (Whitehorne) Albee.
615. 3. ELIZABETH⁷, b. 14 Aug. 1797; died 3 Nov. 1825 at Westminster, Vt.
616. 4. BETHIAH⁷, b. 9 Aug. 1799; died 20 May, 1810 "
617. 5. WILLIAM⁷, [1065] b. 31 Oct. 1801; m. Betsey Mason; m. 2d, Sophia-Maria Waddell; m. 3d. Dorcas-Ford Hoyt.
618. 6. ELISHA⁷, b. 12 Sept. 1803; m. 5 Nov. 1827 at Saxton's River, Vt., Maria Granger, b. 1805, Westmoreland, N.H., dau. of Eldad and Susanna (Holmes) of W. He m. 2d, Rockingham, Vt., 17 June, 1840, Mary-Ann Wright, b. Nov. 1805, Westminster, Vt., dau. of Salmon and Ruth (Reed) of Westminster. She died 8 Oct. 1872. He has no children. Farmer.

1878, Res. *Troupsburg, Steuben Co., N.Y.*

619. 7. OLIVE⁷, [1112] b. 2 Apr. 1806; m. Joshua Ruggles.
620. 8. ISABEL⁷, [1166] b. 13 Aug. 1808; married John-Calvin Conant.
621. 9. ANSON⁷, b. 1 July, 1811; d. 12 July, 1811.
622. 10. REV. ISAAC-FARWELL⁷, [1170] b. 30 Aug. 1812; d. 25 Jan. 1874; m. Mary Susanne Warner.
623. 11. WEALTHY-ANN⁷, [1175] b. 24 Jan. 1815; m. Rev. Horace Worden.
624. 12. JOHN⁷, b. 6 July, 1817; m. Keosauqua, Iowa, 2 Apr. 1848, Harriet (Stannard) Chandler, b. 11 Oct. 1810, Newport, N.H., dau. of William and Hannah (Hagar) of Newport. s.p. Farmer.

Res. 1871, *Ashland Mills, Jackson Co., Oregon.*

625. **ZOHETH⁶**, [524] (*Bethiah⁵* (*Farwell*) Holton, *William⁴, Isaac³, Joseph², Henry¹*,) b. 21 Jan. 1773, Westminster, Vt.; d. at W., 25 June, 1859; m. 5 Feb. 1805, (pub. 3 Oct. 1804, *West Springfield, Mass., rec.*) Amanda Loomis, b. W. Springfield, 16 Aug. 1779, dau. of Noadiah and Thankful (Bagg) of Springfield, Mass. She died 5 Mar. 1859. Farmer. Res. on the homestead of his father Joel⁵,

Westminster, Vt.

[The line of ancestry of Mrs. Holton as by Loomis Genealogy is the following: Joseph¹ of Windsor, Conn.; John² of W.; Thomas³ of Hatfield, Mass.; John⁴ of Lebanon; Jonathan⁵ of Springfield, and Noadiah⁶ and Thankful (Bagg) of West Springfield, Mass.]

Children all born in Westminster, were:

626. 1. NOADIAH-LOOMIS⁷, [1179] b. 4 Dec. 1805; m. 16 Aug. 1847, Eliza Burroughs, of Alstead, N.H.
627. 2. ELIHU-DWIGHT⁷, [1183] b. 19 Feb. 1807; m. 21 Nov. 1831, Nancy Grout of Westminster, Vt.
628. 3. JULIA-ANN⁷, [1189] b. 3 Nov. 1809; married Hiram King; m. 2d, Darwin Wood.
629. 4. OLIVIA-ARNOLD⁷, b. 27 Dec. 1814; m. 5 Feb. 1839, by Rev. Sylvester Sage at Westminster, Vt., Mark-Richards Clapp, of Westminster. s.p. Farmer. Res. *Milford, Jefferson Co., Wis.*
630. 5. LAURA-WOLCOTT⁷, b. 10 Mar. 1818; died 8 Oct. 1854, Ashburnham, Mass.; married, Westminster, Vt., 8 Oct. 1848, Joseph-Parker Rice, b. Mar. 1819, s. of Joseph and Susan (Balcom) of Ashburnham. Mr. Rice enlisted in Co. H, 21st Regt., Mass. Vols., 21 Aug. 1861, was Captain till promoted Major, 28 Feb. 1862; was again promoted Lieut.-Colonel 16 May, and was killed at the battle of Chantilly, Va., 1 Sept. 1862. He married 2d, at Winchendon, Mass., 22 June, 1857, Emily-Maria Garnett, who was born in Lowell, Mass., 15 Dec. 1838. By this marriage he had two children, Frederick-William, b. 27 Sept. 1860, and Newbern, b. 15 Mar. 1862, the day of the battle of Newbern, in which his father, who named but never saw him, participated. These children we insert in compliment to the father's patriotism and the mother's kindness in furnishing the family record. Col. Rice was by occupation a chairmaker.
   Res. *Ashburnham, Mass.*
631. 6. ANN-JENNETTE⁷, b. 12 July, 1820; married, as 2d wife, at Milford, Wis., the residence of her sister, Mrs. Clapp, 8 Nov. 1860, Sylvester-Sage Stoddard, of Westminster, Vt., b. 24 Feb. 1804, Billymead, now Sutton, Vt., s. of Ezra⁷, b. in Westminster, and d. June, 1811, and Jerusha (Goodell), b. W. and d. 19 May, 1849, aged 72. Mr. Stoddard married 1st., at Westminster, 19 Mar. 1829, Mary Holton, b. 13 Sept. 1806, W., who died there 22 Feb. 1859, having previously buried all of her five children, of whom four died in early childhood or youth, and the eldest married Bradshaw-Horace Stone. She was dau. of Worthington⁵ Holton and Phebe (Phelps) Ranney of Westminster; granddaughter of Ebenezer⁵ of W. and Mary (Worthington of Springfield, Mass.); gr. granddaughter of Joshua⁴, killed by Indians 25 Apr. 1746, and Mary (Stebbins) of Northfield, Mass.; gr. gr. grand-daughter of Thomas³, killed by Indians 13 Aug. 1723, and Mindwell (Allen of Northampton) of Northfield; gr. gr. gr. grand-daughter of John² of Northampton, and later of Northfield, and Abigail; and gr. gr. gr. grand-dau. of Dea. William and Mary of Hartford, Conn., and Northampten, Mass. [521 p. 85.]

Mary⁷ Holton i Worthington⁶, ii Ebenezer⁵, iii Joshua⁴, iv Thomas³, v John², vi William¹ Holton of Hartford and Northampton. [See system of abbreviation by symbols of degree of lineal descent, page 79].

Mr. S. has been for many years a deacon of the Congregational Church at Westminster, has long been town clerk, and has held numerous positions of trust and honor to the entire satisfaction of his constituents. It was at his residence that the social gathering mentioned on page 56 was so heartily and profitably enjoyed, and by his co-operation in celebrating the Temperance Jubilee, page 57, he contributed essentially to the general enjoyment of the occasion.

632. JOHN⁶, [526] (*Bethiah⁵* (*Farwell*) Holton, *William⁴*, *Isaac³*, *Joseph²*, *Henry¹*,) b. 11 Feb. 1777, Westminster, Vt.; died, Springfield, Vt., 28 Nov. 1815; married, April, 1808, (pub. Apr. 3, 1808) Harriet Richards, b. 23 July, 1783, Westminster, dau. of Hon. Mark, Ex-Lieut.-Gov. and Anna (Ruggles) Dorr, dau of Joseph Ruggles and widow of Joseph Dorr. Mrs. Holton died 20 Aug. 1811.

Mr. Holton fitted for college at Chesterfield Academy, N.H., under Roswell S. Shurtliff, afterwards Prof. in Dartmouth College; graduated D. Coll. in 1805; read law with Hon. Stephen-Rowe Bradley of Westminster; settled in practice at Springfield, Vt., where he remained till his death.

[Among the classmates of Mr. Holton was Francis Brown, D.D., afterwards Pres. of Dart. College, Henry Colman, celebrated as a writer on agriculture, Rev. Dr. Samuel Osgood, long a pastor of Cong. Ch., Springfield, Mass., and Rev. Alpheus Harding, unitarian, of Salem, Mass.

Hon. Mark Richards was son of Abijah and Huldah (Hopkins) who was sister of Rev. Dr. Hopkins, the hero of Mrs. H. (Beecher) Stowe's "Minister's Wooing," and of another brother who was the author of a system of divinity, called after his name.]

Child:

633. 1. HARRIET-ANN⁷, [1199] b. 28 Nov. 1808, Springfield, Vt.; married Rev. John-Humphrey Noyes.

634. ALEXANDER⁶, [527] (*Bethiah⁵* (*Farwell*) Holton, *William⁴*, *Isaac³*, *Joseph²*, *Henry¹*,) b. 19 Jan. 1779, Westminster, Vt.; married at Hardwick, Mass. in 1805, Harriet Warner, b. 15 Jan. 1783, Hardwick, dau. of Gen. Jonathan and Hannah (Mandell) of Hardwich.

He fitted for college, as did his brother John, [632] at Chesterfield Academy under Roswell S. Shurtliff, and graduated at Dartmouth College in 1804; pursued the study of law under Hon. Stephen-R. Bradley of Westminster; practiced his profession in 1807 at Hardwick, afterwards in Hartland and Woodstock, Vt. In March, 1815, he removed to Vevay, Ind., whence, after, several years practice, he went to Vernon, Marion Co., Ind., where he died 4 Aug. 1823, aged 44.

Of his classmates we mention Job Lyman of Burlington, Vt., and Rev. George T. Chapman, D.D., of Newburyport, Mass.

Mrs. Holton has lived many years with her sons at Deep River, Lake Co., Ind. [For her pedigree see Appendix of WINSLOW MEMORIAL.] also p. 174 this book.

Children:

635. 1. JONATHAN-WARNER⁷, [1201] b. 30 July, 1807, Westminster, Vt.; married 7 Dec. 1829, Charlotte-Baily Perry.

636. 2. WILLIAM-AUGUSTUS-WARNER⁷, [1213] b. 15 May, 1809 : married Bernetta Vosburg.

637. 3. HARRIET⁷, [1222] b. Vevay, Ind., 1 Nov. 1818; married, 8 Jan. 1846, Asahel Albee.

638. BETHIAH⁶, [529] (*Bethiah⁵* (*Farwell*) Holton, *William⁴, Isaac³, Joseph², Henry¹,*) b. 7 March 1782, Westminster, Vt.; m. 6 Sept. 1821, Springfield, Vt., John WHITE, b. 19 June, 1760, in Douglass, Mass., son of Peter and Hepzibah, and grandson of David White. He died 4 May, 1826, Springfield, Vt. Lawyer and farmer. Mrs. White resides, 1878, with her niece, Mrs. S. S. Stoddard, Westminster, Vt. [See 631]

Child:

639. 1. PLINY-HOLTON⁷, [1230] b. 6 Oct. 1822, Springfield, Vt.; married Electa-Barber-Dickinson Gate:.

640. ISAAC⁶, [533] (*Bethiah⁵* (*Farwell*) Holton, *William⁴, Isaac³, Joseph², Henry¹,*) b. 13 Mar. 1790, Westminster, Vt.; died, 26 June, 1850, at Hillsgrove, McDonough Co., Ill.; married 5 Jan. 1827, Phebe Arnold, b. 29 Jan. 1798, Westminster, dau. of Seth and Esther (Ranney) of W.

Mr. Holton fitted for college at Deerfield Academy, Mass.; graduated at Vermont University, Burlington, Vt., in 1814, during the war. Constantine Gilman, Isaac Moore, Erastus Root, M.D.,* and Almon Warner were his classmates.

He read law with his brother John in Springfield, and subsequently with Hon. William C. Bradley of Westminster, Vt. After a brief law practice he resigned his profession for that of a teacher, in which calling he was eminently successful. He commenced teaching as Principal of Chester Academy, Vt., and successively filled the same position in the academies of South Berwick and Limerick, Me. and Bellows' Falls, Vt.; till about 1835 when he removed to Hillsgrove,§ Ill., where he spent the remainder of his life as teacher and farmer.

Children :

641. 1. SETH-ARNOLD⁷, [1236] b. Limerick, Me., 14 Nov. 1828 ; married Elizabeth Roe ; m. 2d, Margaret-Farley Shedd.
642. 2. REBECCA-RANNEY⁷, [1238] b. Limerick, 3 Sept. 1830 ; married Rev. Joseph Mason.

---

* Dr. Erastus Root, b. 9 Jan. 1789 at Guilford, Vt., having graduated at the Vermont University, subsequently received his medical diploma from the Medical Department of Dartmouth College, and practiced his profession at Betsburg, N.Y.
This is his pedigree : Dr. Erastus⁶ Root (Timothy⁵,† Samuel⁴, John³, Thomas², John¹ of Farmington, Conn.; John⁰ of Badby, Northamptonshire, England.
His father, Timothy⁵, was born in Fort Dummer, Brattleboro, Vt.; was one of the first settlers in Guilford and d. 12 Dec. 1843, aged 100 years. Of the sisters of Timothy⁵,
           Elizabeth⁶ married Judge Burt of Westminster, Vt.
           Sarah⁶   "   Elijah Bonny "   "
           Naomi⁶   "   Capt. Eaton   "   "

† See Genealogical Chart, page 347, VOL. I. WINSLOW MEMORIAL, where the line of Gideon³ of Southwick, Mass., cousin of Timothy⁵ Root, is given.

§ A place in McDonough Co., so named in compliment to Mrs. Hills of Westminster, Vt., a sister of Mrs. Holton.

643. 3. DR. JOHN-AMBROSE⁷, [1242] b. 12 Apr. 1832, Bellows' Falls, Vt.; marrie Adelaide Taylor.
644. 4. Rev. CHARLES-AUGUSTUS⁷, [1246] b. 8 Mar. 1834, Bellows' Falls; m. Mary ⌐linor Yeager ; m. 2d, Mary-Elizabeth Hopper.
645. 5. JULIA-ESTHER⁷, [1249] b. 28 Mar. 1836, Hillsgrove, Ill., married Hiram-Gano Ferris.
646. 6. ANNA-PHEBE⁷, b. 13 Dec. 1839, Hillsgrove, and d. there 30 Sept. 1849.
647. 7. JOEL-ALEXANDER⁷, b. 15 June, 1840, Hillsgrove; d. there 25 Apr. 1860.

648. ORRA-WEST⁶, [540] (*Elizabeth⁵ (Farwell)* Parker, *William⁴, Isaac³, Joseph², Henry¹,*) b No. Charlestown, N.H. 30 Mar. 1780, *Hist of Charlestown;* d. there 14 June, 1823; married, 24 August, 1806, *Hist. of C.*, Giddings Whitmore, of Newbury, Mass., b. 26 Jan. 1777, son of David and Lydia (Giddings) both of Newbury.

Mr. Whitmore served his time with his father, learning the trade of a ship carpenter, but left it after he attained his majority, for that of a house carpenter. He soon became a contractor, and thus earned and saved a competency.

First settling in Lebanon, N.H., and there remaining till after 1815, he removed to Charlestown and purchased a farm, on which he resided till he went to Springfield, Vt., and retired from active life, enjoying the fruit of his former industry.

He died 16 May, 1860, leaving, instead of a fortune for his sons, the example of a well-ordered life and an honorable memory.

[The Parker line of ancestry of Mrs. Whitmore is this : Capt. Joseph¹ and Margaret of Dunstable, Joseph² and Hannah (Blood) of Groton, Lieut. Isaac³ and Ruth of Groton and Charlestown, N.H., Isaac⁴ and Mary of Groton and Charlestown, Elijah⁵ and Elizabeth⁵ (Farwell) of Charlestown, who had fourteen children, of whom Orra-West⁶, the sixth child, married Giddings Whitmore.

The following is the ancestral line of Giddings Whitmore : Francis¹ and Margaret (Harty) of Cambridge, Mass., Joseph² and Mary (Kendall) of Woburn, Mass., Joseph³ and Elizabeth (Flagg) of Woburn, David⁴ and Lydia (Giddings) of Newburyport, Mass., who had twelve children, of whom Giddings⁵, the tenth child, married Orra-West⁶ Parker.]

Res. Newbury, Mass., Lebanon and Charlestown, N.H., and *Springfield, Vt.*

Children:

649. 1. EDWIN-PARKER⁷, [1258] b. 22 Jan. 1808, Lebanon, N.H.; married Mary-Elizabeth Chase.
650. 2. HAMLIN⁷, [1264] b. 5 Mar, 1809, Lebanon; married Seloma-Whiting Sawyer.
651. 3. ALBERT⁷, b. 3 May, 1810, Lebanon.

His education was principally obtained at the academy in South Berwick, Me., under the tuition of that eminent preceptor, Isaac⁶ Holton [640], an unusually large proportion of whose pupils have since occupied, or now hold, positions of honor and usefulness.

Mr. Whitmore chose the calling of a merchant, and was for some

XI.—WHITMORE PARALLEL CHART.

Isabel Parke, who died 31 March, 1665, daughter of Richard and Sarah (——) Francis¹ Whitmore of Cambridge, Mass., born 1625; ——Margaret Harty. She d. of Cambridge village (Newton). He may have been son of Henry of London. d. 12 Oct. 1685.* 1 March, 1698.

Elizabeth²—Daniel   Francis², b. 12 Oct. 1650; re- John², b.   Samuel², b. 1 May,   Abigail², born 3   ——Wilcox   Sarah², born 7 March, 1662; married
b. May 2, MARKHAM. moved to Middletown, Ct.   1 Oct.   1653; removed to   July, 1660.   William LOCKE, son of William
1649.   and left heirs.   1654.   Lexington.   13 Feb. 1698.   of Woburn.

Margaret³, born 9 September, 1668;   Frances³, born 3 March, 1671;   Thomas³, b. 1673; lived in Kil- Joseph³ of Wo-——Mary Kendall, dau. of Thomas She d. 19
married Thomas CARTER.   m. Jonathan THOMPSON.   lingly, Ct. and had ch.   burn, b. 1675.   Nov. 1760, aged 82.

                                Elizabeth Grover.——Joseph³ of Woburn, b. 17 Feb. 1699.——Elizabeth Flagg.
                                                          1   2

                                                5 Dec. 1726.
Joseph⁴, born 9 September, 1719.   David⁴, of Newbury, Mass.——Lydia Gid-   Jonathan⁴, b. 18 Oct. 1734.   Hannah⁴, born 28 May, 1743; m. ——
                                    b. 18 Oct. 1724; d. Lebanon, dings of   MORSE
Elizabeth⁴, b. 3 Mar. 1730; d. 1793. N. H. 19 Jan. 1828. He was   Newbury,   Nathan⁴, b. 16 Nov. 1736; d. 1756.
                                    a Ship-carpenter at N.; rm.   Mass. See   Dorothy⁴, b. 9 Feb. 1744; m. —— HUSK.
Mary⁴, b. 5 Sept. 1731;   to Lebanon, N. H.   Gr. Radial Ruth⁴, born 24 March, 1739;
m. —— RADCLIFF.   Chart, pp. m. —— FURLONG.   Thomas⁴, b. 1746; d. 1747.
                                                                 52, 53.
Phebe⁴, b. 6 Aug. 1733; m.—TITCOMB.   Ebenezer⁴, b. 14 Sept. 1740; d. 1760.   Abigail⁴, m. —— PROCTOR.

                                    David⁴, b. 17 Sept. 1763.   24 Aug. 1806.
Elias⁴, born 29 October, 1759; died 30 March, 1829.   Giddings⁴, b.—Orra-West Parker, born 30 March,
                                    Sarah⁴, b. 5 Dec. 1771; m. Edward KEYES.   26 January,   1780; died 14 June, 1828; dau. of
Ebenezer⁴, born 28 February, 1760.   1777; died   Elijah and Elizabeth (Farwell)
                                    Elizabeth⁴, b. 20 June, 1773; d. 1780.   16 May,   Parker. [648]
Jacob⁴, born 30 October, 1761; d. 6 Jan. 1811.   1860.
                                    Hannah⁴, born 11 May, 1779; married, John CARR
Lydia⁴, b. 10 Oct. 1763; m. Timothy GORDON.
                                    Joseph-F⁴., born 16 May, 1782; died 16 May, 1863.
Joshua-G⁴., b. 1765; d. 1765.

Mary⁴, b. 1766; d. 1895.

1. Edwin-Parker⁵, m.   2. Hamlin⁵, m. Seloma   3. Albert⁵,   4. Joseph-Flagg⁵, m.   5. Martha⁵ m. Henry-   6. Henry-Sylvester⁵, m.   7. Horace-Metcalf⁵,
   Elizabeth Chase.   -W. Sawyer. [1264]   1810-1847.   Maria Hayes. [1271]   H. SHERWIN. [655]   Mary-Ann Varney.   1821-1870. [655]

* See Will of Francis¹, page 95 Medford Genealogies, by Wm.-H. Whitmore of the Board of Directors N. E. Hist. Gen. Society, 18 Somerset St., Boston.
For more extended details see the "Whitmore Grand Radial," designed as a parlor ornament for the present and future generations, published by David
Parsons⁷ Holton, M. D., 20 Sutton Place, cor. East 59th St., N. Y. See serial number 1264, p. 153 FARWELL MEMORIAL.

years overseer of the sales department in one of the leading houses in New York City. He died of consumption at Springfield, Vt., 25 Oct. 1847.
652. 4. JOSEPH-FLAGG⁷, [1271] b. 22 Dec. 1811, Lebanon; married 15 Mar. 1837, Maria Hayes.
653. 5. MARTHA⁷, b. 3 Sept. 1815, Lebanon ; married, Springfield, Vt., 16 July, 1849, Henry-H. **Sherwin**, of Chester, Vt. She died 15 Oct. 1849, Chester.
654. 6. HENRY-SYLVESTER⁷, [1277] b. 28 Oct. 1818, Charlestown, N.H.; married 25 Oct. 1847, Mary-Ann Varney.
655. 7. HORACE-METCALF⁷, b. 25 Sept. 1821, North Charlestown, N.H.; d. 9 Mar. 1870, unmarried, at San Francisco, Cal.

He was one of the early adventurers in quest of wealth in the gold fields of California, where, after various vicissitudes of fortune, having realized his golden dreams, he was suddenly removed from the scenes of earth, leaving a large estate which is, 1878, under the management of his executor, Edwin-P⁷. Whitmore [1258].

656. POLLY⁷, [550] (*Sybil⁶* (Farwell) **Osborne**, *Daniel⁵*, *Daniel⁴*, *Joseph³*, *Joseph²*, *Henry¹*,) b. 24 Apr. 1787 ; died 20 Oct. 1821, Weathersfield, Vt.; married, as 2d wife, date not known, Benjamin **PAGE**, of Cavendish, Vt. She had one child which died aged nine months, and twins which died soon. Mr. Page married after her death, for third wife, a Widow Finney. His first wife was Sally Robinson by whom he had two children, which we give though outside of our regular system.

Res. *Cavendish, Vt.*

657. 1. SAMUEL-DANA, b. 7 May, 1805. Res. *Houston, Texas.*
658. 2. ROXALANA, b. 12 Aug. 1809.

659. SUSAN⁷, [551] twin of Polly⁷, (*Sybil⁶* (Farwell) **Osborne**, *Daniel⁵*, *Daniel⁴*, *Joseph³*, *Joseph²*, *Henry¹*,) b. 24 Apr. 1787; married 26 Apr. 1807, William **DOWNE**, of Fitchburg, Mass., who died 20 July, 1855. Mrs. Downe, by her grand-daughter, wrote in 1867 that "she had lived to see seven generations, and was the oldest of the Farwell race then living." She was residing, 1875, in *Fitchburg. Mass.*

Children:

660. 1. SUSAN⁸, b. 4 May, 1809; was married by John Albrough, 24 Oct., Abram Osborne, of Fitchburg, Mass., who died there 16 Mar. 1875.

Children:

661.   1. Hattie-Elizabeth⁹, b. 24 Aug. 1840, Fitchburg, Mass.
662.   2. Georgiana-Frances⁹, b. 21 July, 1844, F.; d. 11 May, 1845, F.
663.   3. Arvilla-Frances⁹, b. 25 Apr. 1848.
664. 2. WILLIAM-STILLMAN⁸, b. 13 Jan. 1812; died, Fitchburg, 6 Apr. 1859; m. 6 Nov. 1834, Betsey Eaton, of Fitchburg, who died 13 May, 1841, F. He married 2d, Lunenburg, 1 June, 1842, Louisa Henry of Lunenburg.

Children:

665.   1. Harriet-Augusta⁹, b. at Fitchburg, 23 July, 1838 ;. died 17 Dec. 1865 ; married by Rev. Alfred Emerson, 25 Feb. 1864, Julius **Whitney** of Ashby, Mass., son of Jonas-Prescott and Rebecca (Piper) of Fitchburg.
   He enlisted about the 1st July, 1861, and went into camp with Co. D, 21st Regt., Mass. Vols. as sergeant ; served as such till 1 Jan. 1863, at which time was promoted to orderly sergeant ; served till 18 June, 1864 ; was then promoted to 1st lieut. Re-enlisted 1 Jan. 1864, and went to Massachusetts on a furlough of thirty days. He participated in the following engagements :

Roanoke Island, N.C., 8 Feb. 1862.	Wilderness, Va., 6 May, 1864.
Newbern, " 14 Mar. "	Spottsylvania, Va., 10 May, 1864.
Camden, " 19 Apr. "	" " 12 May, "
2d Bull Run, Va., 30 Aug. "	" " 13 May, "
Chantilly, " 1 Sept. "	Shady Grove Road, Va., 31 May, 1864.
South Mountain, Md., 14 Sept. "	" " " " 1 June, "
Antietam, " 17 Sept. "	Cold Harbor, Va., 2 June,
Fredericksburg, Va., 13 Dec. "	Petersburg, " 16 June,
Blue Springs, Tenn., 10 Oct. 1863	" " 17 June,
Campbell's Station, Tenn., 16 Nov. 1863.	" " 23 June to 28 July, 1864
Siege of Knoxville, " 17 Nov. to 7 Dec. 1863.	" " 30 July, 1864.

He was discharged 30 Aug. 1864, when the regiment's term of service had expired. Res. *Brattleboro, Vt*

Child :

666.   1. *Herbert-Prescott*¹⁰, b. 10 Aug. 1865, Fitchburg.
667.   2. Herbert-Sumner⁹, b. 26 May, 1843, Fitchburg ; d. 5 May, 1845.
668.   3. Louisa-Frances⁹, b. 12 Apr. 1847, F. ; m. by Rev. Alfred Emerson, 12 June, 1867, Franklin-Miller **Whitney**, of Westminster, Mass., b. 23 Aug. 1843, s. of Joseph-M. and Dolly (Jackson). Res. *Fitchburg, Mass.*

Children :

669.   1. *Edith-Louisa*¹⁰, b. 7 Sept. 1869, F.
670.   2. *Ray-Elliot*¹⁰, b. 16 May, 1874, F. ; died F. 21 July, 1875.
671.   3. *Daisy-Christabel*¹⁰, b. 20 Sept. 1875, F.
672.   4. Mary-Emmeline⁹, b. 7 Jan. 1850, F.   Res. *Fitchburg, Mass.*
673.   3. SYBIL-ANN⁸, b. 10 June, 1816, F. ; died 3 Nov. 1816, F.
674.   4. SUMNER⁸, b. 1 Dec. 1817, F. ; m. Richmond, N.H., 1 Nov. 1845, Sarah-A. Narramore, and had

675.   1. William-Narramore⁹, b. 23 Sept. 1864 ; d. 15 Nov. 1864.

676. SYBIL⁷, [552] (*Sybil*⁶ (*Farwell*) Osborne, *Daniel*⁵, *Daniel*⁴, *Joseph*³, *Joseph*², *Henry*¹,) b. 10 July, 1792, Fitchburg, Mass. ; married 15 Sept. 1813, Asa-G. **PORTER**,

b. 5 July, 1788, Marlboro, N.H. He d. 1854, Madison, Wis.
She resided, 1875, *Winchendon, Mass.*

Children:

677. 1. JACOB-OSBORNE⁸, b. 30 Sept. 1814, Weathersfield, Vt.; d. 17 Sept. 1825.
678. 2. HENRY-ALBERT⁸, b. 12 Oct. 1817, Weathersfield; m. Troy, N.H., Apr. 1842, Czarina Forresttall, b. Troy, N.H., 1817, dau. of Joseph and Fanny (——) of Troy.

Children:

679. 1. Henrietta-Jane⁹, b. 2 Nov. 1849, Boston, Mass.
680. 2. Charles-Henry⁹, b. 1856, Troy, N.H.

681. 3. LEONARD-WARNER⁸, b. 14 Sept. 1820, Weathersfield, Vt.; married Jan. 1845, Waltham, Mass., Mary Hayward, b. Hopkinton, Mass., in 1827.

Children:

682. 1. Charles-Warren⁹, b. Dec. 1845, Waltham; died in Cambridgeport, Mass. in 1847.
683. 2. George-Henry⁹, b. Cambridgeport, 1847; died in Boston, 1850.
684. 3. Emma-Louisa⁹, b. Newton Corners, Mass., 1 Nov. 1849.
685. 4. George-Warren⁹, b. Boston, 1851; d. 1858, Troy, N.H.
686. 5. Frederic-Leonard⁹, b. 14 Sept. 1857, Boston.
687. 6. Nellie-Marie⁹, b. Nov. 1862, Boston.

688. 4. ALMIRA⁸, b. 1 Jan. 1825, Weathersfield, Vt.; married in New York City, June, 1847, Luke **Bemis** of Weston, Mass.

Child:

689. 1. George-Luke⁹, b. 29 May, 1850, Mason, N.H.

690. 5. LORINDA⁸, b. 25 Dec. 1829, Weathersfield, Vt.; married 16 Oct. 1845, Waltham, Mass., Amos-Warren **Buttrick**, b. Rindge, N.H., 5 Mar. 1821, son of Amos and Fanny (——) of Rindge.

Children:

691. 1. Warren-Elphonzo⁹, b. 28 May, 1847, Waltham, Mass.; died in Waltham 17 Feb. 1848.
692. 2. Helen-Viora⁹, b. 8 June, 1849, Newton Corners; married East Jaffrey, N.H., 4 June, 1867, Henry-Willard **Pierce**, b. 21 Mar. 1842, East Jaffrey, son of Samuel-Willard and Mary (——) Pierce of E.J.
693. 3. Frances-Lurenza⁹, b. 16 Sept. 1851, Winchendon, Mass.; d. in W. 8 May, 1854.

694. 6. LOUISA⁸, b. in Weathersfield, Vt.; married in Connecticut, Oliver-Henry **Smith**, b. Lexington, Mass., 1821, son of Josiah Smith of Lexington.

Children:

695. 1. Charles-Henry⁹, b. July, 1851, Lexington.
696. 2. Emma-Louisa⁹, b. in Waltham, and died in Westboro, Mass.

697.   3. Ella-Frances⁸, b. 1856 in Westboro.
698.   4. Albert⁸, b. in Natick, Mass., 1859.

699. NANCY⁷, [558] (*Sybil*⁶ (*Farwell*) **Osborne**, *Daniel*⁵, *Daniel*⁴, *Joseph*³, *Joseph*², *Henry*¹,) b. 12 Nov. 1796 or 1798 ; died 15 Mar. 1862, aged 64; married Leonard **COBB**, b. 21 July, 1800, Londonderry, Vt. He died 17 Apr. 1856, aged 56.

Children :

700.   1. Farwell-Osborne⁸, b. 10 Mar. 1824; married, 14 Mar. 1850, Louisa-Maria Woodward, b. Marlboro, N.H., 4 Feb. 1831, d. of Franklin and Louisa (Dyer) of Troy, N.H. Res. *Troy, N.H.*

Children :

701.   1. Henry-Albert⁹, b. 2 Jan. 1851.
702.   2. Charles-Frederic⁹, b. 9 Nov. 1852.
703.   3. George-Wallace⁹, b. 11 Nov. 1854.
704.   4. Frank-Eugene⁹, b. 11 Feb. 1860.
705.   5. Emma-Jane⁹, b. 22 Feb. 1862.
706.   6. Lizzie-Maria⁹, b. 16 Apr. 1865.
707.   7. Davis⁹, b. 11 May, 1867.

708.   2. Sybil⁸, b. 23 May, 1826 ; married, 1 Jan. 1849, Theodore-Jones **Dyer**, of Templeton, Mass., b. Athol, Mass., 3 July, 1825, s. of James and Mary (——) of Otter River, Mass. He served three years in the war for the Union, and d. 18 Sept. 1864. Res, *Templeton, Mass.*

Children :

709.   1. Walter-Alvin⁹, b. 2 Mar. 1851.
710.   2. Leonard-Farwell⁹, b. 17 Aug. 1859.

711.   3. Albert⁸, b. 11 Aug. 1829 ; married, 28 Nov. 1867, Myra Dyer, daughter of James and Almira of South Royalton, Mass. She was b. 10 Oct. 1845 at S. R. Mr. Cobb served one year, 1864, in the late war in the First New Hampshire Heavy Artillery. Res. *Keene, N.H.*
712.   4. Alvin⁸, twin of Albert, b. 11 Aug. 1829. Res. *Troy, N.H.*
713.   5. Leonard-Davis⁸, b. 14 May, 1832 ; m. 11 Oct. 1853, Mary-Ann Shae of Templeton, Mass., b. Ireland, 12 June, 1828, d. of Timothy and Elizabeth (Shae) of Ireland. Res. Gardner and, 1875, *Leominster, Mass.*

Children :

714.   1. Henry⁹, b. 3 Apr. 1855.
715.   2. Timothy⁹, b. 11 Aug. 1856.
716.   3. Mary-Ann⁹, b. 31 Aug. 1859 ; died 4 Jan. 1868.
717.   4. Hannah-Maria⁹, b. 17 June, 1862.
718.   5. Mary-Ann⁹, b. 31 July, 1865 ; died Aug. 1867.
719.   6. Lizzie-Jane⁹, b. 3 June, 1866.

720. LOUISA⁷, [554] *Sybil*⁶ (*Farwell*) **Osborne**, *Daniel*⁵, *Daniel*⁴, *Joseph*³, *Joseph*², *Henry*¹,) b. 22 May, 1801; married by Rev. Seth Winslow, Marlboro, N.H., 9 Mar.

1824, Jedediah **TUTTLE**, of Littleton, N.H., b. 24 Mar. 1792. He died 22 May, 1861, in Acton. Res. *Fitchburg, Mass.*

Children:

721. 1. Louisa-Osborne⁸, b. 22 Feb. 1828; married, 6 May, 1846, Thomas-Green-Fessenden **Jones**, b. 19 Jan. 1822, son of Silas and Lucinda (Wetherbee) of Acton, Mass. she d. 19 Oct. 1873; He d. 18 Nov. 1878.

Children:

722. 1. Orra-Louisa⁹, b. 16 Mar. 1848; married by Rev. Mr. Lumas of Littleton, Mass., 6 Sept. 1868, to Henry **Hanscomb** of Wilton, Me.
723. 2. Rozina-Tuttle⁹, b. 8 Oct. 1851; d. 21 Jan. 1867.
724. 3. Lizzie-Edna⁹, b. 21 Apr. 1856. m. Charles **Martin.**
725. 4. Carrie-Josephine⁹, b. 5 Apr. 1862.
726. 2. Albert-Austin⁸, b. 29 May, 1831; served in the war of the Rebellion five months. d. at Duluth, Minn. 29 Jan. 1871,

727. DANIEL-FARWELL⁷, [555] (*Sybil⁶*, (*Farwell*) **Osborne**, *Daniel⁵*, *Daniel⁴*, *Joseph³*, *Joseph²*, *Henry¹*,) b. 6 Aug. 1805; married, Sudbury, Mass., 1 May, 1828, Sarah-Noyes Maynard, b. S. 5 May, 1798, dau. of Samuel and Susa of North Sudbury, Mass. Mr. Osborne died at Marysville, Yuba Co., Cal., 1 Dec. 1851.

Marlboro, N.H.

Children:

728. 1. Daniel-Farwell⁸, b. 3 Sept. 1829, Marlboro, N.H.; m. 28 Dec. 1853, at West Newton, Mass., Elizabeth Finn, b. Boston, Mass., 8 Dec. 1835.

Children:

729. 1. George-Warren⁹, b. Waltham, Mass., 17 July, 1854.
730. 2. Frank-Maynard⁹, b. Waltham 6 Feb. 1856.
731. 2. George-Warren⁸, b. 4 Sept. 1831, Marlboro, N.H.; married in San Francisco, Cal., 5 May, 1859, Susan-Eveline Garfield, b. Waltham, Mass., 22 Dec. 1828, dau. of Alvis and Susan. Res. *San Francisco, Cal.*

Child:

732. 1. Charles-Pierson-Johnson⁹, b. 15 June, 1860.
733. 3. Sarah-Eveline⁸, b. Troy, N.H., 7 June, 1838; m. Waltham, 22 Dec. 1858, James-Lawrence **Butters**, b. Sangerville, Me., 6 Mar. 1836, son of James and Esther of Wilmington, Mass.

Children:

734. 1. Sarah-Ida⁹, b. 13 May, 1861, Waltham.
735. 2. Esther-Myra⁹, b. Waltham, 22 July, 1865; died W. 4 Oct. 1865.

736. LEONARD⁷, [556] (*Sybil⁶* (*Farwell*) **Osborne**, *Daniel⁵*, *Daniel⁴*, *Joseph³*, *Joseph²*, *Henry¹*,) b. 5 July, 1809; m. 1 Sept. 1829, Eliza Holman, b. 23 Oct. 1810,

dau. of Edward and Mehetable, of Fitzwilliam, N.H. She d. 1 Apr. 1850, and he married 2d, 20 May, 1851, Sarah-Clapp Coley, b. 9 July, 1820, dau. of Nathaniel and Lucinda-Clapp (Purrington) of Bath, Me. Res. Billerica and, 1878, *Leominster, Mass.*

Children :

737. 1. ELIZA-ANN[8], b. 10 June, 1831 ; died 10 July, 1840.
738. 2. LEONARD-WARREN[6], b. 14 May, 1833 ; married, Nov. 1852, Susan-Maria Foster, dau. of Francis and Susan (Packard) of Troy, N. H.

Res. *Troy, N.H.*

Child :

739. 1. Elizabeth-Maria[9], b. 1853.
740. 3. CYNTHIA-MELISSA[8], b. 13 Dec. 1834 ; died 25 Apr. 1841.
741. 4. CYNTHIA-ELIZA[8], b. 1 June, 1842 ; died 10 Apr. 1865 ; married, Feb. 1863, Sidney-Patterson Emery.

Child :

742. 1. Walter-Osborne[9], b. 31 Mar. 1865 ; died June, 1865.
743. 5. HELEN-GEORGIANA[8], b. 26 May, 1844 ; married, Nov. 1863, George-E. Litchfield of Leominster, Mass., son of Edward and Mary.

Child :

744. 1. Flora-Georgiana[9], b. 31 Oct. 1814.
745. 6. MARY-ELIZABETH[8], b. 3 Feb. 1847 ; died 16 Feb. 1867.
746. 7. SARAH-FRANCES[8], b. 11 Feb. 1850.

747. HENRY[7], [559] (*Simeon[6], Daniel[5], Daniel[4], Joseph[3], Joseph[2], Henry[1],*) b. 3 Dec. 1795, Fitchburg, Mass.; died 4 Jan. 1878 at Stirling, Whitesides Co., Ill.; married at Westminster, Mass., 6 Oct. 1819, Nancy[7] Jackson, b. 11 Jan. 1798, Westminster, daughter of John[6] and Susanna (Sawyer) of W.

Mr. Farwell moved from Massachusetts to Steuben Co., New York, about the year 1820, and engaged in the lumber business, which at that time was attended with great hardships. Lumber was then marketed by rafting down the Susquehannah River. He there continued in this business for twelve or thirteen years when he removed to Big Flats, Chemung Co., New York, and engaged in farming. In 1838, when the Western fever took so many of the pioneers of New York to the great North West, he was among the first to take part in opening this great agricultural bonanza to the world. In July, of that year he arrived with his family near Daysville in Ogle County, Illinois. As a sample of the hardships attending a pioneer's life, we give the following experience of Mr. Farwell's family. In less than two weeks all the family, except the mother and babe, were sick with fever-and-ague, together with the family of his sister, Mrs. Stephen Bemis [804] making in all fourteen persons in a log cabin, fourteen feet square. Less pluck would have given up the task of helping to open up a new country. A better log-house and better health came in due time, and, in a few years, a fine brick house was erected. The boys made the brick, cut the stones for the sills and caps and made a wagon to haul them by sawing large logs for wheels. The wagon was not ornamental in the least, but quite useful.

Mr. Farwell was several times elected as Co. Commissioner, and was among the early friends of Rock River Seminary where some of his children were educated. Was a member and an officer in the M. E. Church, and in all the relations of life had the respect of all who knew him. He often used to say, in connection with other peoples' troubles, that he was never sued but once, and that was as vestryman of an Episcopal church, which office he never knew that he held until thus called on to pay its debts.

Oct. 5, 1869, four years previous to Mr. Farwell's death, the celebration of their golden wedding took place, their home surroundings being in striking contrast with the picture above given of their early settlement in Illinois.

Among other grounds for congratulation and gratitude, and by no means the least, were the fruits of their careful, conscientious family training shown in the high moral character and useful positions of their offspring, verifying the promise of their covenant-keeping God—fruits in harmonious keeping with parental growth in Christian experience and the graces which adorn the evening of a well-ordered and useful life.

Mrs. Farwell still (1878) resides in Sterling, Ill. Her ancestry, as also that of her husband, may be seen in brief through the seize quartiers charts on the 75th and 76th pages. We cannot, however, refrain from inserting details of the several parties therein mentioned more fully than the size and character of the charts will permit, and shall give some extracts from *Jackson's Hist. of Newton* and other authorities which we believe will be interesting to the reader and useful to posterity.

It will be observed that Mrs. Farwell descends from the two sons of Christopher Jackson, Edward[1] and John[1], who were the immigrant ancestors of most of the name in this country, and the extracts given pertain to both lines of her ancestry.

Dea. John[1] Jackson,§ the elder of the two brothers, came in the *Defence* in 1635.

The following entry is given by Hotten in his "Lists of Emigrants," page 100: "July 6th, 1635, In the Defence, Thos. Bastocke Mr. Vrs., New England, John Jackson, 80 yrs, wholesale man in Burchenlane, per, cert from Sr. George Whitmore, and minister of ye parish."

He was the first settler of Cambridge Village, (now Newton) Mass., who remained and died there. He brought a good estate from England. His homestead which he bought of Miles Ives in 1639 was situate on the Roxbury road, very near the line which now divides Newton from Brighton. He took the freeman's oath in 1641; was one of the first deacons of the Church; gave the land on which the church was erected in 1660, which is the oldest part of the Centre Cemetery.

He had, in this country, by two wives, 5 sons and 10 daughters, and at the time of his death had about 50 grandchildren. He left an estate valued at £1,230, including 863 acres of land. The old mansion-house stood on the same spot, subsequently occupied by the dwelling of Edwin Smallwood, and was pulled down about 1800. The old pear-trees still standing were planted by his son, Abraham[2], the only son who left posterity.

§ See chart on page 76.

Dea. John[1] was ancestor of Col. Charles-G. Hammond of Chicago through his daughter, Hannah[2] Jackson, who married Elijah Henrick, Ann[3] Kendrick who married Isaac Hammond, and had Elijah[4], Col. Hammond's great-grandfather.

Abraham[2] Jackson, [o *] of Newton, had 8 sons and 7 daughters. One of these, Elizabeth, was the mother of Col. Ephraim Williams (her first born), the munificent founder of Williams' College.

Edward[1] Jackson, brother of Dea. John[1], was born in London, 1604, called "Naylor of Whitechapel;" came to Cambridge in 1648; caused an entry to be made on the County Records, of a certificate from the Treasurer, under an ordinance of the two houses of Parliament at Westminster, that he had brought in for them, light gold and money, to the amount of £95. He was freeman in 1645; in 1646 purchased the beautiful farm of 500 acres of Gov. Bradstreet for £140 which the latter had bought 8 years before of Thomas Mayhew for six cows.

He was Representative in the General Court for 16 years. At his death in 1681 he left 400 acres of land in Billerica to Harvard College. By his first wife, Frances, he had 5 sons and 8 daughters, the youngest son, Sebas, k* was b. on the passage to this country. In March, 1649, he married, for second wife, Elizabeth, wid. of Rev. John Oliver, and dau. of John Newgate, or Newdigate, a merchant from Southwark, near London Bridge, by whom he had four daughters and one son. Of these 13 children, five or six died young, but by the others he had some sixty grandchildren. His Inventory contained upwards of sixteen hundred acres of land, and amounted to £2477 19s. 6d. His daughter, Hannah[2], [k *] married John Ward, and was the gr. gr. gr. gr. grandmother [quintayle] of Nancy[7] (Jackson) Farwell. The generations from Hannah[2] (Jackson) Ward exceeded by one, as shown by the chart, those from her brother Sebas[2], who married Sarah Baker, and was quatrayle of the said Nancy.

Commodore Joshua[4] Loring of the British Navy, was a great-grandson of Edward[1] and second wife Elizabeth Oliver, through their son Dea. Edward[2], and grand-daughter Hannah[3], who married Joshua Loring. Hannah[4] Loring, daughter of the Commodore, married Joshua[5] Winslow, (*Joshua[4], Edward[3], Capt. Edward[2], John[1],*) [See John Winslow Memorial.]

Jonathan[3] Jackson son of Jonathan[2] and grandson of Edward[1] was a brazier, an importer of hardware, and the first manufacturer of nails in this country, as appears from his petition to the General Court in 1727. The House of Representatives passed a resolve, loaning said Jackson £10,000 for seven and a half years without interest, for his encouragement in the business, he giving security for the payment thereof, and obligating himself to make not less than forty tons in each and every year.

The council non-concurred, and Jackson went forward without aid from the General Court.

That he was successful appears from the inventory of his estate in 1736, which covers more than 20 pages on the records, and amounts to more than £30,000. His son Edward[4] married Dorothy Quincy, and had Jonathan[5] who was a member of the Provincial Congress early in the war; M.C., 1781, State Senator for the Co. of Essex, appointed by Washington first Marshal of Mass. Dist., Inspector of Excise, Supervisor, Treasurer of Mass., and Treasurer of Harvard College. He took an early

---

o* and k* etc. refer to parties found on the charts pp. 75 and 76.

and zealous part in the Revolution, was an ardent friend of liberty, and the owner of a slave. Seeing his inconsistency, he placed on record, in the Suffolk Probate office, the following document—A NOBLE TESTIMONY. "Know all men by these presents, that I, Jonathan Jackson of Newburyport, in the County of Essex, gentleman, in consideration of the impropriety I feel, and have long felt, in holding any person in constant bondage—more especially at a time when my country is so warmly contending for the liberty every man ought to enjoy—and having some time since promised my negro man Pomp, that I would give him his freedom—and in further consideration of five shillings paid me by said Pomp, I do hereby liberate, manumit, and set him free ; and I do hereby remise and release unto said Pomp, all demands of whatever nature I have against Pomp. In witness whereof, I have hereunto set my hand and seal this 19th of June, 1776.

"JONATHAN JACKSON. [Seal]

"*Witness*, Mary Coburn, Wm. Noyes."

This document is dated just two weeks before the glorious Declaration of Independence was issued, proclaiming all men to be born free. Pomp enlisted in the army as Pomp Jackson, served through the war of the Revolution, and received an honorable discharge.

The following is an extract from the will of Edward[1]:

"I do give and bequeath to my son Sebas, his heirs and assigns forever, that my house in which he at present dwelleth, with one hundred and fifty acres of land adjoining, as it is already bounded, also two gilded silver spoons." "That house was eighteen feet by twenty-two, with two stories, and stood on the same spot occupied by the mansion of William[7] Jackson, Esq., (*Wm*[6], *Timothy*[5], *Timothy*[4], *Joseph*[3], *Sebas*[2], *Edward*[1],) a cold water man, who continues to draw from the old well, a pure fountain, which has served seven generations, and is none the worse for wear. The old house was built about 1670, and enlarged before 1690, which increased its length to thirty-nine feet. It was demolished in 1809, having withstood the tempests of one hundred and forty years."

Sebas[2], [k*] son of Edward[1], died 6 Dec. 1690, leaving four sons and three daughters. Two of his sons had died young, and his son, Jonathan[3], went to sea and never returned. Through his sons Edward[3], Joseph[3] and John[3] he had numerous descendants. Joseph[3] was "famous for raising honey-bees and sweetened his minister and his neighbors with large donations of honey." Edward[3] had, besides others, Isaac[4], (gr. grandfather of Nancy (Jackson) Farwell) a carpenter, having served his time with Isaac Beach, who gave him four acres of land with house adjoing the burial place. He was Selectman five years, and d. Feb. 5, 1769, aged 68. He owned a large tract of land in Westminster, Mass., which, by his will, (1765) he gave to his sons Josiah, Edward, and Elisha, who settled upon it, being among the first settlers of Westminster.

Another son of Edward[3], and brother of Isaac[4] above, was Michael[4], the father of Col. Michael[5], who, at the breaking out of the Revolutionary war, was a private in a volunteer company of Minute Men in Newton. At the early dawn of the 19th of April, 1775, the signal was given that the British troops were on their march for Lexington. The company of Minute Men were early upon their parade ground, but none of the commissioned officers were present ; the orderly sergeant had formed the company, and a motion was made to choose a captain for the day, when Michael Jackson was nominated, and chosen by uplifted hands. He immediately stepped from the ranks to the head of the company, and without a word of thanks for the honor, or the slightest formality, he ordered the company to "shoulder arms" —"platoons to the right wheel"—"quick time"—forward march!" These words of command were uttered, and the company were on the march to join the regiment at Watertown Meeting-house. On their arrival there, the commissioned officers of the regiment were holding a council in the school-house, and he was invited to take part in their deliberations. He listened to their discussion, but soon got the floor, and made a *moving* speech. He told them that there was a time for all things, but that the time for talking had passed, and the time for fighting had come; not now the wag of the tongue but the pull of the trigger. This *pro tem.* captain accused the officers of wasting time, through fear of meeting the enemy. He told them "if they meant to oppose the march of the British troops, to leave the school-house forthwith, and take up their march for Lexington. He intended that his company should take the shortest route to get a shot at the British," and, suiting the action to the word, left the council, and took up his march. This blunt speech broke up the council, without any concert of action, and each company was left to act as they chose. Some followed Jackson, some lingered where they were, and some dispersed. Soon after, he received a major's commission in the Continental army. In an action with the British on Montressor's Island, in New York, he received a severe wound in the thigh by a musket ball, from which he never entirely recovered.

Sebas^2 Jackson left a will, giving all the estate to his wife for her maintenance and the well bringing up of his children, during her life, or so long as she continues to be his widow.

The estate remained in the hands of the widow seventeen years after his death, when it was divided and settled by agreement among his heirs.

Jonathan^4 Trowbridge [s *] gr. grandfather of Nancy' (Jackson) Farwell, [747] was of the fourth generation of the family in America.

His immigrant ancestor, Thomas^1, was of Dorchester, Mass., and engaged in the Barbadoes trade from 1637 to 1639. In 1640 he was of New Haven, Conn., but according to Savage "was prosecuting voyages to and from Barbadoes." He came probably from Taunton, Somersetshire, Eng., where his father founded a charity for poor widows, which is still administered for their benefit. [*Hist. of Newton.*]

Brought with him sons Thos. and Wm. and "perhaps" [*Sav.*] James, though the latter was baptized at Dorchester, 1638. In 1644 he returned to England, leaving his sons in charge of Sergt. Thomas Jeffries, and all his property in trust with his steward, Henry Gibbons, who kept the estates in his possession, till the matter was settled by law many years afterwards.

Thomas^1 never returned to this country and died at Taunton, Eng., 1672.

Dea. James^2, youngest son of Thomas^1, [m*] returned from New Haven to Dorchester, where he married 30 Dec. 1659, Margaret, dau. of Major-General Atherton.

After the birth of three of his children in D. he removed to Cambridge village, 1664. The Dorchester ch. records state that Margaret, wife of James Trowbridge, was "dismissed to the church gathered at Cambridge village, 11, 7, 1664." After the death of Dea. John¹ Jackson, father of his second wife Margaret Jackson, 1674-5 he was chosen deacon of the church. Dea. James was chosen one of the first Board of Selectmen at the organization of the town of Newton, 27 Aug. 1679, and continued in office nine years ; he was clerk of the writs, 1691, and 1693 ; was Commissioner, Lieutenant, and Representative to the General Court 1700, 1703. By his will, dated 1709, James Trowbridge, Sen., bequeaths what rights of lands he has in Dorchester, which came by his own father Thomas, to all his children equally, and all the rights to lands in D. which came by his father-in-law Atherton, to the children of his first wife equally. He had by wife Margaret Atherton among other children, a son ; John³ [m*] married Sarah Wilson and had Jonathan⁴, who married Jemima⁴ Bright, and they became the besaylest† of the above-named Nancy⁷ (Jackson) Farwell.

Henry¹ Bright came in the fleet with Winthrop, 1630, and settled in Charlestown, Mass., but soon removed to Watertown, where he m. 1634, Ann, dau. of Henry¹ Goldstone. He was freeman 6 May, 1635 ; deacon of the church ; was held in high esteem, and died 9 Oct. 1686, aged 84. He was probably from Ipswich, Suffolk Co., Eng. He had an elder brother, Thomas, of Ipswich, who mentions him in his will proved 1626. His sister Elizabeth (Bright) Dell bequeathed to him in 1657, £200, and to each of his seven children, £10.

His will, recorded in Suffolk Co., Mass., dated 25 Jan. 1680, and a codicil dated 25 Oct. 1685, were probated in Boston 13 Nov. 1686.

He had eight children, one of whom died young—his dau. Mary, b. 1639, m. 15 Oct. 1657, Nathaniel Coolidge, brother of Simon², whose dau. Mary³ married Nathaniel² Bright. [p *]. His dau. Beriah, youngest child, b. 22 Sept. 1651, m. 30 Nov. 1671, Isaac Fowle of Charlestown, b. 1648, (son of George) whose dau. Abigail m. Capt. Wm. Smith, and had Rev. William who m. Elizabeth Quincy; they had Abigail who m. Hon. John Adams, second President, and father of Hon. and President John Quincy Adams, sixth president of the United States.

Rev. William and Elizabeth (Quincy) Smith had also a daughter Elizabeth, who married Rev. John Shaw, parents of Abigail who married Rev. Joseph B. Felt, Ex-President of the New England Historic-Genealogical Society.

March 29, 1689, Nathaniel² Bright was witness to an acknowledgement of the heirs of William Shattuck, that they had received their full proportion of their father's estate from their father-in-law [step-father] Richard Norcross. He was one of the trustees for the management of the fund raised by the "piously-disposed inhabitants of Watertown" for the purchase of a parsonage "for the accomodation of Rev. Mr. Gibbs, who is their present minister, and such as shall succeed him in the work of the ministry."

The English ancestry of the American immigrant Henry¹ Bright, b. 1602, as given by Mr. Somerby, runs thus (according to our system of notation) : Henry^A, bap. 20

---
† See p. 77.

Dec. 1560, and wife Mary; Thomas², buried 1st Sept. 1587, and wife Margaret of Bury St. Edmund's; Walter², buried 25th Jan. 1551, and wife Margaret, of Bury St. Edmund's, and John of Parish of St. Mary's, Bury St. Edmund's, Co. Suffolk, England. Reign of Henry VII.

One of the great grandmothers of Mrs. Farwell, Jemima⁴ Bright, b. 19 July, 1712, m. 1734, [s*] will be seen to occupy a central position in the generations from the immigrant ancestor in the maternal line to Nancy⁷ her great grandaughter, and herself being great granddaughter of Dea. John¹ Jackson, (Abraham², Margaret³) She also introduces the family of Bright, occupying in her paternal line the same relative positions in the generations, viz.: (Henry², Nathaniel³, Henry³ Bright.)

The date of birth of her two gr. grandfathers occurred the same year 1602. The earlier three generations comprise a period of one hundred and ten years, while the latter three only eighty-six, making of the six generations a total of one hundred and ninety-six years, averaging thirty-three years and reaching the highest estimate for a generation. Thus Nancy⁷ unites not only the Brights and Jacksons in the line of Dea. John, but also those in the line of his younger brother Edward.

THE AVERAGE MEASURE OF A GENERATION.

The commonly accepted historical standard for the length of a generation is 33 1-3 years or one-third of a century, but twenty-five (25) years may be said to be the generation of primogeniture, by which crowns and titles descend. The true average is between these standards.

The length from one generation to the next may be said to be the difference between the average date of deaths of the fathers of the former and that of the latter.

In like manner calculating the corresponding differences successively through a series, we can readily obtain their average as the length of a generation. Let us apply this rule taking *births* as the points of estimate; [See chart]:

From the date of birth of

Joseph² Farwell, 1642, to that of Joseph³ Farwell, 1670, was 28 years;
Joseph³, 1670, to that of Daniel⁴, 1717, was 47 "
Daniel⁴, 1717, to that of Daniel⁵, 1740, " 23 "
Daniel⁵, 1740, to that of Simeon⁶, 1766, " 26 "
Simeon⁶, 1766, to that of Henry⁷, 1795, " 29 "
Henry⁷, 1795, to that of John-Villars⁸, 1825, was 30 "
John-Villars⁸, 1825, to that of Arthur-Lincoln⁹, 1863, was 38 "
    Total of the seven differences   221 "
    Average length of a generation in this series   31 4-7"

Let us examine a series taken from the grand radial chart terminating with serial number 611 of the FARWELL MEMORIAL, the chart found, also, at page 322, under serial number 3614 of the WINSLOW MEMORIAL :

It may be seen that from the birth of

William^5 Holton, 1771, to that of his 2d child Reuben-R^7., 1795, was 24 years ;
Reuben-R^7, 1795, to that of his 2d child, Linus-T^8, 1817, was   22   "
Linus-T^8, 1817, to that of his 2d child, Helen-R^9., 1851, was   34   "
Helen-Rebecca^9, 1851, to that of her 2d child, Centurius-Holton^{10}, 1871, 20   "

The sum total of the four differences,   100   "

Giving to this series of children (severally second in the order of birth in their respective families) 25 as the average of their generations, a number equal to that of primogeniture.

Again, on examination of the same chart, it will be seen that from the birth of Deacon William^1 Holton, 1611, through John^2, Wm^3, John^4, Joel^5 to the birth of William^6, 1771, first above mentioned, it was for the five generations a period of one hundred and sixty (160) years, giving 32 years as the average measure of a generation.

Uniting the three preceding averages [31 4-7+25+32—88 4-7] we obtain an average result very near 30, the measure which so well tallies with results otherwise variously obtained, that it is expedient to adopt thirty (30) as the number of years measuring an American generation.

748. HENRY-JACKSON^8, (*Henry^7*, [747] *Simeon^6, Daniel^5, Daniel^4, Joseph^3, Joseph^2, Henry^1*,) born 24 May, 1821, Campbelltown, Steuben Co., N.Y.; married at Mount Morris, Ill., 21 Sept. 1851, Mahala-Jane Raker, b. 29 Dec. 1825, in Mary land, dau. of George-W. and Elizabeth (Harrison) of Mount Morris, Ogle Co., Ill. Farmer.   Res. *Mount Morris, Ill.*

Children all born in Mount Morris, Ill.:

749. 1. CHARLES-HENRY^9, b. 28 Aug. 1856.
750. 2. WILLIAM-JACKSON^9, b. 3 March, 1858.
751. 3. GEORGE-VILLARS^9, b. 16 Apr. 1860.
752. 4. LILLIAN-LOUISA^9, b. 17 Oct. 1862.

753. HON. CHARLES-BENJAMIN^8,   (*Henry^7* [747] *Simeon^6, Daniel^5, Daniel^4, Joseph^3, Joseph^2, Henry^1*,) b. 1 July, 1823, Mead Creek, near Painted Post, Steuben Co., N.Y.; married, Williamstown, Mass., 11 Oct. 1852, Mary-Evaline Smith, b. 3 June, 1825, Ashford, Mass., dau. of Thomas and Phebe (Angell)

Mr. Farwell spent the first fifteen years of his life in the vicinity of his birth. He received his early education at the Elmira Academy, in which he took high rank, both for conduct and scholarship, and which he very reluctantly left to accompany his parents in their removal to Illinois in 1838.

Almost immediately after reaching his new home his mathematical attainments secured for him a position with a party of government surveyors, which he ably filled for three years. In this occupation, alternate with labor upon his father's farm, he passed his time until the winter of 1844, when with ten dollars in his pocket, and his parents blessing, he went to seek a new home in Chicago, then a small city of seven or eight thousand inhabitants. With this city he has since been identified in the closest possible manner. Making his way at first with difficulty, unknown and friendless, his first situation found he never *sought* another. He was at first employed as clerk in the County Court, then in a real estate office, and subsequently as teller in the principal bank of the city.

From the last named position he was elected, in 1853, clerk of the County Court, and by re-election held the office eight years. This position had a forming influence upon his life, as it threw him into the arena of politics where was developed his character as a politician.

His mind is of an intensely practical character, and he early saw that not the theoretical but *actual* state of affairs must be met if anything were to be done by way of reform in municipal affairs. His honest, manly and independent course, his fixed determination to use his influence for good administration may have made him enemies among the unscrupulous and dishonest, but among the honest and conscientious no man could desire warmer or truer friends than has the Hon. C-B. Farwell. He is most esteemed and best loved where he is best known.

No appeal for help is ever unregarded by him, and perhaps it would be difficult to find one whose practical life yields a more constant flow of noiseless charity.

It has been already stated that he is closely identified with Chicago. Not an interest has she that is not dear to him. No enterprise of a noble or philanthropic character is ever started that does not have his ready sympathy and aid to the extent of his ability.

Mr. Farwell was chairman of the Board of Supervisors of Cook Co. in 1868; was appointed National Bank Examiner in 1869, and in 1870 was elected to Congress, and by re-election represented Chicago three terms. During most of this time he occupied a prominent position on the Committee of Banking and Currency, for which position his tastes and previous experience well fitted him. This is eminently his specialty. The problems of finance which to many minds are troublesome and difficult, present no difficulties to him. From long experience and much study the whole subject seems to him plain and clear.

His term of office as County Clerk expired in 1861. For two years subsequent to this he was in a commission business with his younger brother [770]. At the end of that time he entered the firm of J-V. Farwell & Co., of which he has since been a member and which is now doing a business of $10,000,000 a year. See pp. 117-18-19. The New York branch of the firm at 115 Worth St., is ably represented by William-D.* Farwell [779]

Children, all born in Chicago, were:

754. 1. CHARLEY⁹, b. 3 June, 1853; died 23 June, 1853.
755. 2. MARY-NANCY⁹, b. 16 Aug. 1854; died 14 Mar. 1861.
756. 3. HENRY⁹, b. 29 Dec. 1856; died 7 Apr. 1861.
757. 4. EDWARD⁹, b. 30 Dec. 1858; died 20 Dec. 1864.
758. 5. ANNA⁹, b. 19 Nov. 1860.
759. 6. WALTER⁹, b. 23 June, 1863.
760. 7. GRACE⁹, b. 18 Apr. 1866.
761. 8. ⎰ ROBERT⁹, twin, was born 7 Mar. 1870; died at Lake Forest from the fall of a limb of a tree, 20 Aug. 1872.
762. 9. ⎱ ROSE⁹, twin of Robert was born 7 Mar. 1870.

763. JOHN-VILLARS⁸, [739ª] (*Henry⁷* [747], *Simeon⁶, Daniel⁵, Daniel⁴, Joseph³, Joseph², Henry¹,*) b. 29 July, 1825, Campbelltown, Steuben Co., N.Y.; married, Daysville, Ill., 16 Apr. 1849, Abigail-Gates Taylor, b. 9 Feb. 1828, Gilsum, N.H., dau. of John and Catherine of Dubuque, Iowa. She d. 9 May, 1851, Chicago, Ill. He married 2d, at Hartford, Conn., 8 March, 1854, Emerette Cooley, b. 25 Jan. 1826, Granville, Mass., dau. of Noah and Sophronia⁶ (Parsons) of Granville, Mass.

Until the age of sixteen, Mr. F. lived upon his father's farm, attending school during the winter months. At this time, although he possessed but limited means, he determined to have a more complete education, and accordingly entered Mount Morris Seminary, devoting himself earnestly to those branches essential to success in business. He gave special attention to mathematics, book-keeping and composition, and, for the sake of economy, boarded himself, continuing his studies until he had acquired a good business education.

In 1845 he went to Chicago, having in his pocket, upon his arrival, $3.25. He at once found employment in the City Clerk's office on a salary of $12 per month, with the privilege of reporting the proceedings of the Council at the rate of $2 per report. His accuracy and strict adherence to the truth gave offence to certain members of the council, and led to his withdrawal. He next entered the dry-goods house of Hamilton & White at a salary of $8 per month, and at the expiration of one year passed to the house of Hamlin & Day at an advanced salary of $250 per annum.

Later he became a book-keeper in the house of Messrs. Wadsworth & Phelps at a salary of $600, and, in 1851, was associated in the firm, which then conducted a business of $100,000 per annum. Forecasting the future destiny of Chicago as the Metropolis of the North-west, he early advocated the erection of a large building specially adapted to the wholesale business, and, notwithstanding the decided disapproval of the senior members of the firm, his efforts resulted in the erection of a large wholesale house in 1856. Nine years later he became the head of the firm, and by his marked executive and financial ability contributed no small amount to the success of that business, which, in 1868, reached the gigantic proportions of $10,000,000. Twice during the history of this house has it been entirely destroyed by fire; but as often there has risen from the ashes a structure more complete in all its apartments than the one preceding. The first fire occurred on Sunday afternoon—before the next Saturday night the store was in full operation, and goods to the amount of $275,000 had been sold and delivered. The fire of Oct. 9th, 1871, kept the firm out of a place of business for about two weeks, after which they occupied a temporary building, and commenced a permanent one of five stories, ninety by one hundred and ninety feet, on the 5th of Dec., and occupied it in February following. That building is part of their present store, the size now being one hundred and ninety by two hundred and twenty-seven feet, and six stories in height. It is located on the corner of Monroe and Market Streets, Chicago.

The present establishment fully sustains its former popularity, and is the oldest house, in its line, in Chicago.

From the *Chicago Tribune*, of Oct. 9th, 1875, we copy the following, showing not only the financial success of the firm, but its character, and the estimation in which it is held by the community:

JOHN V. FARWELL & CO.

A review of the position and condition of this great dry-goods house is particularly appropriate at the present time. To-day is the anniversary of Chicago's destruction. Elsewhere in this issue we notice the yearly work of progress since our last annual record of the course of reconstruction. The condition of the city four years ago requires no amplifying upon here, but this is a specially fitting place to chronicle a piece of interesting history.

An important incident of the early steps towards reconstruction evinced the confidence reposed in the business judgment of the firm of John V. Farwell & Co. The advice and counsel of the members of this house was then publicly sought and as publicly given. The fulfilment of their predictions is now a matter of common knowledge to all the world. While the ruins of Chicago were still smoking, and the sky at night still glowed with the lurid glare of the scarcely half-conquered embers, a meeting of merchants was called for mutual counsel.

Mr. C. B. Farwell, then and now Member of Congress from the Third Illinois District, was called to the chair, and John V. Farwell, senior member of the firm, was the first gentleman requested to express his views of the situation and prospects. His firm had lost very heavily, and his opinions were held to have a most practical weight.

He responded at once, declaring the situation to be critical but not hopeless, and expressing it as his fervent opinion that everything depended upon the action of the assembled representative merchants. Chicago, he tersely said, was "a living business fact." It had faced all varieties of opposition in the past from competitors, and had thrived under the treatment. He for one had no idea that the city could be materially hindered in its destined greatness by the fire. He considered that all that was wanted was a firm integrity of purpose to meet all obligations so far as their means would possibly permit. These obligations must be met without flinching. They must only ask such time as they needed to gather up the ashes of their business, and must begin anew; not discouraged by what had happened, but more determined than ever to make Chicago the centre of the whole North-western trade. They could do so if they would, and could do it soon. These earnest sentiments were received with hearty applause. There was but one dissenter to the honorable, manly views, and he was a liquor dealer who proceeded to advocate a universal and shameful repudiation, but was promptly hissed out of the meeting.

We can give no better individual illustration of how thoroughly Mr. Farwell's prophecy has been worked out than has been shown in the history of his own house

* * * * * * * *

Messrs. John V. Farwell & Co. are chiefly responsible for the starting of a new business centre, and for making what, in ante-fire days, seemed destined to be an eternally valueless portion of the city, into a thriving business quarter. They have seen their judgment in relation to the desirability of this section fully verified, dozens of leading firms having clustered within a few blocks of them inside of the past four years. They claim with justice, also, to have done the whole city a direct practical benefit by equalizing real estate values over a large district, and by lowering rents in the same generous ratio that the city has been enlarged. They have reclaimed what was formerly undesirable, and have aided most materially in changing Chicago's business area from a single focus of trade structures to the extent of a true metropolis.

The growth of the firm's business from what it was then to what it is now can be graphically illustrated. During the month of September last there were single days in which the sales were doubly larger than for a whole year in the earlier history of the firm. The sales one day last month reached the grand figure of $200,000, which tells the story of this firm's influence and magnitude of trade more eloquently than columns of elaborate description could ever do. Such figures speak for themselves.

The following is a brief history of the house, and the changes in connection with it, since Mr. Farwell became a member :

Cooley, Wadsworth & Co., from 1852 to 1859, [E-S. Wadsworth* and F-B. Cooley, both of Hartford, Conn.]; Cooley, Farwell & Co., from 1859 to 1864 [F-B. Cooley and M. Field]; Farwell, Field & Co., from Jan. 1st, 1864, to 1865 [I-Z. Leiter]; John-V. Farwell & Co., from 1865 [Char^les-B⁶. and William-D⁶. Farwell, S-N. Kellogg and J-K. Harmon] to 1869, when Mr. Samuel-N. Kellogg retired. In 1870 Simeon⁶ Farwell was admitted a partner, and the firm is now, 1879, composed of John-V⁶., Charles-B⁶., William-D⁶. and Sⁱmeon⁶ Farwell and J-K. Harmon.

During the late civil war, Mr. Farwell was marked for his philanthropy and devotion to the Union cause. He was active in raising the Board of Trade Regiment which was fully equipped by private contributions at an expense of $40,000. He was a constant friend of soldiers' families, and contributed liberally to the funds of the Sanitary and Christian Commissions. His special interest, however, centered in the Christian Commission, of which he was one of the executive committee, and to which he gave his time and money without stint.

The following clippings from papers published during the war of the rebellion, giving his utterances and exhibiting his sentiments and spirit during the great struggle for the integrity of the Union, though somewhat numerous and extended for the usual scope of a work like this, are believed, not only worthy of insertion, but it is

---

* E. S. Wadsworth is son of the late Tertius Wadsworth of Hartford, Conn., who married for 2d wife, Mrs. Eliza (Parsons) Miner, daughter of Capt. Joel⁵ Parsons of Granville, Mass., grandfather of Francis-Buell Cooley, and of his sister, Mrs. Emerette (Cooley), wife of J-V⁶. Farwell. [See Cornet-Joseph¹ Parsons Memorial.]

hoped may encourage a like patriotism and devotion to a just cause in the hearts of future generations who may be called to defend and protect the free institutions of this great republic.

PRESENTATION OF COLORS TO THE CHICAGO DRAGOONS.

The Young Men's Christian Association of this city, have prepared and presented to Capt. Charles W. Barker, of the Chicago Dragoons, a beautiful stand of colors for his company. The flag is of rich blue silk, five feet wide by six feet long, with a heavy silk fringe in "red, white and blue." On one side, in the centre of an oval, is a mounted dragoon in gold, on a cloud background. Above the figure appears the motto, "We will pray for you," surrounded by thirty-four stars. On the reverse side, in a similar oval, is an American eagle, with the motto, "In God is our trust."

The presentation was made by John V. Farwell, Esq., President of the Association, accompanied with the following address:

CAPT. BARKER: I need not tell you that history informs us, that in all ages of the world, emblems of nationality have commanded the homage, the purse, and heart's blood, if need be, of every true patriot; and in America, Sir, every insult to that *Magna Charta* of our blood-bought rights, brings to its rescue men who will peril their all to defend its honor. In every controversy, individual or national, there is a right and a wrong side, and "thrice is he armed who hath his quarrel just."

A heathen general once ordered his subordinates to number his army, before engaging a very much larger force in battle. The work being done, they reported a force of 10,000 men to go out against 40,000, and counseled a surrender. The general said they had made an egregious blunder in the numbering of his men.

After asserting that they had numbered them correctly, said he, "How many did you put me down for?"

"Only one, sir,"

"Bad mistake, gentlemen; you will let me number them over again. *Our cause is just.* You may therefore put me down for 20,000, and for each one of my soldiers you may count four, making in all 60,000 against 40,000 of the enemy, every man of whom is not over half a man, when fighting against the right. Now, will you fight them?"

"Aye, sir, and whip them too;" and they were as good as their word.

On behalf of the Young Men's Christian Association, many of whose number are under your command, I present you this flag, the emblem of our dearly-bought liberties, expecting that you will trust in God while under its folds, and be counted 20,000 against its enemies, and every man of your command, a host, to follow your lead in placing it in the record of national glory, second to none that waves in the free air of heaven.

Your commander-in-chief, the President of these United States, on taking leave of his home in Springfield to assume the guardianship of our National flag, said: I have a greater task before me than that which engaged the soul of a Washington, and without the assistance of the God of Nations, I cannot succeed; with it I cannot fail."

I believe, sir, that he will not fail, for I believe that the God of Washington is Lincoln's God, not for personal aggrandizement, but for our national weal, and the world's redemption from tyranny. And now, sir, while I hand you this stand of colors, permit me to propose this sentiment:

> "Down with the traitors' serpent flag!
> Death to the wretch o'er whom it waves
> And let our heaven born banner float
> O'er freemen's homes and traitor's graves."

Capt. Barker replied as follows:

Mr. Farwell—I accept this flag from the Young Men's Christian Association, and, through you, return them my sincere thanks. Could I find language to express my feelings, I should think this one of the proudest days of my life.

I am no speech-maker, but I am full of feeling. Little did I think when I commenced to raise my company, that I should have such men around me as I have, and when I bear this flag to those who have gone out from this Association, and they shall look upon it, I doubt not but that, though absent from you, they will be present with you, in thought and feeling.

I shall defend that flag with my life—(cheers)—I will protect it while life lasts, and if I live to bring it back, I shall bear it home with me as unsullied as I receive it. I see on each side of it the words "We will pray for you." Though I am not a man of prayers, I believe in the power of prayer, and therefore hope that you will ever remember this pledge, to pray for us. Again I thank you for this token of your Christian consideration."

The captain was indeed "full of feeling" in making this response, while many moist eyes attested a fellow feeling for him. Let traitors beware of the metal of Capt. Barker and his company.

DISCOUNTENANCING TREASON.
[From the editorial of the *Chicago Tribune*.]

The immense wholesale dry goods house of Cooley, Farwell & Co. has kicked the Chicago *Times* into the street on account of its treason. The following note, addressed to the proprietors of the *Times*, explains the matter:

COOLEY, FARWELL & Co., Wholesale Dry Goods,
42, 44 & 46 Wabash Avenue, Chicago, Jan. 1, 1863.

Messrs. Story & Worden:

GENTLEMEN: We wish to begin the new year *patriotically*, and know of no better way than to commence by excluding your paper from our counting room. Your vile sympathies with treason are too apparent, and now that a public example has been made of the manner in which such papers should be treated among honest men, we wish to be among the endorsers of the movement. You will therefore send your bill and keep your paper, and oblige,

Yours Respectfully,
COOLEY, FARWELL & Co.

On the receipt of this note, instead of quietly discontinuing the paper as directed to do, the Tory organ prints the note and flies into a huge passion, foams at the mouth, and commands "every Democrat to avoid their doors as he would the gates of h—ll."

Democratic merchants, we presume, suit themselves, and purchase their goods where they can buy to the best advantage. There are very few Democratic merchants that endorse the treasonable course of the *Times*, or sympathize with its purpose to produce civil war in Illinois, by arraying the Democratic party in armed hostility to the Federal government. If there be any such merchants in the West, Cooley, Farwell & Co. can well afford to do without their custom.

There are several hundred Republicans—ardent Union men—whom, we are sorry to say, still continue to take that infamous sheet, and contribute their $10 a piece for its support. Many of these persons complain of the weight of their taxes, but have not a word to say against paying a poll-tax of ten dollars for the support of Jeff. Davis' organ in their midst. If they want to take a Democratic paper, there is the *Post*, which is as bitterly partisan as can be desired, but is yet loyal to the Federal flag.

U. S. CHRISTIAN COMMISSION.

A Week at the Front.

From the Northwestern Christian Advocate.

If I recollect right the colored race were coming through the Red Sea, led by God's Abrahamic Moses into the Canaan of U. S. citizenship, when we parted company last week. This will probably cause copperheads speedy dissolution, while it enforces with another epoch of history, the proposition that God reigns, and has stirred up his strength to seal a great national wrong with his unqualified disapproval. After passing through the country at Point of Rocks, and partaking of a hasty supper at the rooms of the Christian Commission, the bugle sounded for Church, and we were conducted to a beautiful rustic chapel, constructed under the direction of Chaplain Williams, a field agent of the commission, holding over six hundred persons. It was filled to its utmost, while the soldiers took charge of the meeting with the manifest help of Him who said, "Lo, I am with you."

To realize what the meeting was, one must be there ; it cannot be put into type. A stalwart colored man, in blue uniform, who had lost both eyes in the service, rose to his feet, and with a calmness that bespoke the veteran, said: "Brudren, dough my body sight am failed, de eye of faith am clear and strong. I sees de reward of victory jus' afore me, and I'se going to grasp de prize mid the promises of my hebenly Fader." A very intelligent white soldier followed him with an account of his conversion only a few days before, and the assault Satan had made upon his faith. In the midst of the conflict, apparently overcome, he thought of the great Captain— went to him, and returned with the marching order, "Get thee behind me Satan," which was instantly obeyed, and then with the pathos of the "new creature" in Christ Jesus, and a mind quickened with the energy of this new birth, he called on his fellow soldiers to enlist under the blood-stained and victorious banner of King Jesus, whose kingdom is not of this world, but is set up within us.

An old sun-burnt Methodist from Indiana, said he had just received a letter from two of his little girls at home, in which they said "Papa, we have taken your advice, and given our hearts to Jesus." With his heart so full that he could scarcely speak, he said, "How this intelligence steals from my thoughts the hardships of a soldier's life who has dear ones at home. The thought that his house had determined to serve God buried all hardships and toil under its broad shield, and he was a happy man.

Drs. Scudder and Duryea could no longer retain their seats, and the other New York gentlemen were taken with the same symptoms. Such extemporaneous remarks from men accustomed to read sermons, I never heard before. Truly, God was in that place.

At the appointed hour Gen. Patrick's boat came to carry us to City Point, and the services had to be closed.

Our next march was to the extreme front, via Petersburg to Hatcher's Run, under the escort of Gen. Gwyn. who shared our hospitality at City Point, and insisted on our sharing his at the front.

Well, Doctor, I wish now that you could have dined at the general's head quarters. I was going to draw the general presiding at the table, and the dinner, but it's no use trying. I give it up.

The general won his stars by his gallantry in taking a rebel fort, and suffice it to say, that he *captured* us likewise upon the first charge, and if he ever comes West I propose to let you look upon every inch a man.

After dinner the general had his brigade drawn up in a hollow square, in front of his quarters, to hear from George H. Stuart and others of our party, who addressed them briefly, after which the camp rang with cheers for General Grant and President Lincoln.

An hour's ride brought us to a lookout station, from which through a glass, I could survey the streets of Petersburg and its defences, while a little out to the left a rebel brigade was drilling, whose bayonets glistened in the sun with a horrid glare. Only a few hours previous two men had been drawn up before them, shot and buried like dogs—probably for believing that to desert was more patriotic than to fight against the good old flag.

On our return we visited the headquarters of Gen. Crawford, where we found Gen. Davis, chief of cavalry, and Gen. Warren; all young men whose names will shine in history.

The next day was the Sabbath and our party were detailed for special service in several of the army chapels at different stations, of which there are one hundred and fifty now in the service.

At Warren Station there was a communion service, where, for some reason, I learned that nearly all the Methodist delegates of the Commission had been sent by our field agent. A heavenly Methodist revival has been in progress there for some weeks, and at this communion twenty-five were baptized, and two hundred communed, one hundred and thirty of whom were new converts.

Ministers of four denominations assisted in the service, and no one asked whether they were all Close-communion Baptists, or lineal descendants of the Apostolic Church, while they came forward with broken hearts to commemorate the suffering of him who prayed the Father that *they all might be one*, as He and the Father were one—and such they seemed to be, as full hearts and moistened eyes amply testified on this occasion. Such scenes are a foretaste as well as a symbol of heaven.

From all quarters of the globe almost, and from all denominations, did this company draw its numbers, and yet the religion of Jesus broke down all walls of national or sectarian partition, and placed them all at Jesus' feet, an exalted level of true nobility.

Monday morning Gen. Grant placed his private boat at our disposal for a visit to the army of the James, and telegraphed Gen. Ord to furnish us transportation on arriving at his headquarters for that purpose. It had been intimated to us that Gen. Ord was a Catholic and that we should not probably be very cordially treated. In this we were misled. Our transportation was duly furnished and in conversation with him in regard to the work of the Christian Commission in his department, he seemed to take a deep interest in it, saying that it was doing more good in proportion to its means *than any other agency in the army*, and that among his colored troops the schools were doing an immense amount of good. This is the universal testimony of all the officers of the army, with whom I conversed. God bless the Christian Commission, seems to resound all along the lines of these armies.

Riding along the lines of Gen. Ord's army, nothing but black soldiers met the eye. At one point Brother Stuart ordered a halt, when the soldiers were off from duty, and called a large number together in an incredible short space of time, and talked to them about Jesus and their duty to him, as well as to their country, after which they all joined heartily in singing a hymn. Before prayers, all who wished to be prayed for, were requested to raise their hands. A majority raised their hands in token of such desire, and one of the ministers led in an earnest prayer.

Passing on, we soon came to a regiment on dress parade. The Colonel requested another impromptu meeting with his regiment.

With a saddle for a pulpit, and a file of armed soldiers for an audience, Bro. Mingins officiated, and we passed on to other scenes, wondering the while at the *quiet order* and neatness of these colored soldiers in every department of their duty.

Fort Harrison in our lines is confronted by a rebel fort, the muzzle of whose guns are almost visible to the naked eye; while in plain sight, between the two, were federal and rebel lines of pickets, marching their tedious beats in talking distance of each other—ready at any moment upon word of command to open the red sepulchre of war, and bury each other out of sight.

Returning to the boat about 9 o'clock at night, the captain informed us that it was too foggy to go back to City Point, so we were booked for a night's lodging and a supper in the same rooms, and around the same table, where President Lincoln and Secretary Seward met the rebel peace commissioners but a few weeks before to discuss the terms of peace. About 4 o'clock in the morning, I was awakened from a comfortable sleep by the discharge of artillery which shook the boat, and the thought struck me that the rebel rams, whose smoke we had seen the day before from Dutch Gap Canal, had come down the river to retake a boat-load of our prisoners which lay just above in the river waiting to go down to City Point.

The journey home, the waiting on the boat with rebel deserters, would form another chapter, but I will only give one instance of a facetious rebel's leave-taking from his former companions.

He was a cavalryman, and told me that he had spent $4,500 since the war began for horses, and a short time before he left, an order was issued that any one found destroying rails, would be required to maul 300, as a punishment for the offense.

He had built a shelter for his horse, and had used two rails to keep the shakes (you know, doctor, what shakes are) on the roof, for which he was called up to the captain's quarters to answer.

He plead that the rails were not destroyed, but were *in the service*, protecting his horse. His plea was denied and sentence passed that he must split 300 rails. The captain lent him an ax without a helve, that had been "jumped" so often that there was scarcely anything left but an eye. While he was making the helve he remembered that he was to be on picket duty that night, and he had left word for the captain, that as he knew nothing about splitting rails, he had concluded to go and take a few lessons of Abraham, who, he was informed, understood the business; meanwhile he hoped he might be able to dispense with the rails until his return.

They will all take lessons of Abraham ere long. Thank God he is an apt teacher, who will soon convince the rebel crew that the way of the transgressor is hard, and that the rebellion can be split as well as rails.

CONTINUATION OF THE FOREGOING.

In my last I gave you some incidents on the way to the front. We will now take some observations together from the tusks of the "Elephant," commencing at Gen. Grant's headquarters, where we found ourselves a short time after our arrival at City Point. Mr. Stuart introduced the company to the General, consisting of Drs. Duryea, Scudder and Chambers, and Messrs. Jessup, James, Walis and Holden of New York —members and friends of the Commission, who were received cordially. While talking with us it was evident from his countenance that the chess-board of the conflict was uppermost in his mind, and when Sherman's name was mentioned, his face seemed to glow with mingled satisfaction and pride, as he pointed to Fayetteville on the map, saying, "he will be there in a few days." The papers were sending him off to Saulsbury after our prisoners, but it was evident that Grant had sent him to Fayetteville.

Grant says "Go, and he goeth"—*anywhere*. From here we proceeded to Gen. Patrick's headquarters, Provost Marshal of the armies of the James and Potomac, whose heart and soul seemed to be in sympathy with the work of the Christian Commission. After giving us some excellent advice, by way of suggestions, etc., he ordered his own private boat to convey us to Point of Rocks for an inspection of the large hospitals at that place, and accompanied us there. Would to God that all our generals were like him—Christian men, wearing the star of Bethlehem as prominently as the stars of their rank in the army. Passing through the hospitals, which wore an aspect of neatness and comfort, our attention was suddenly arrested by the sight of a colored man just being taken out for burial. Mr. Stuart called the little gathering to order and proposed a short burial service, consisting of singing, remarks and prayers, which were kindly received by the soldiers and nurses. A little further on, an old colored man, who seemed very intelligent, attracted my attention, and I said to him, "How do you like this phase of the war?" "Oh, sir," said he, "I shall never fight any more, am sixty years old ; I shall soon get my discharge and go up yonder." "Up where?" "Where Jesus is—I shall not live long."

Having taken a hasty look at the diet kitchen, in which are prepared by Christian women, such delicacies as a sick man can appreciate, we mounted ambulances and rode out to the front, and from a lookout station, elevated some one hundred and fifty feet, we took a bird's-eye view of the rebel pickets and their works. This done, Bro. Stuart asked the signal boys in attendance if they wouldn't like to have a prayer-meeting in the tower, to which they readily assented. After prayer by Dr. Scudder, and thanks from the boys, we were lowered away to terra firma again, wondering if ever a prayer-meeting was held in such a place before.

The next point of interest to us was the cemetery. It is laid out in circular form, with a vacant space in the centre for a monument, and ranged in alternate sections, with walks dividing them. Each state had her long line of wooden head boards, who dadcnngaih ti ithere laid down their lives for their country, and a prominent feature was the space allotted to the *colored troops*, of which there seemed to be a longer line of head-boards, than in any other section (the army of the James being largely colored troops). It taught me that colored men *have* some rights that white men are bound to respect—the right to lay down their lives for a government that has been an asylum for the oppressed of all nations except their own.

The spectacle is sublime—meeting a martyr's fate in the cause of their own former oppressors. From Deep Bottom on the James to Fort Harrison, and on to the extreme right, for miles and miles, these black men *without rights* stand behind breastworks of their own construction, and within forts built by their labor, carrying Uncle Sam's muskets and manning his loud-mouthed peacemakers, stamping the rebellion into the dust, and the memory of Roger B. Taney with eternal infamy, while white men in the Senate ask the nation to place a marble bust of this "chief justice" (chief anything but *justice*) in the Supreme court-room of the United States.

Thanks to the God of justice and Abraham Lincoln that the colored man's answer to a delegate's question, "What does U.S. mean?" as it stands on the badge of the U.S. Christian Commission, is prophetic of the coming position of his countrymen—said he, "It means us." Those breastworks made by colored soldiers, those muskets, and those cannon borne and manned by colored troops, and those graves filled by colored dead, speak to us of the rights of black men in tones that cannot be stifled by the cry of "Nigger worshippers" in the ears of the American people. They do mean *us* most surely.

Pardon me if I say more than I ought in this connection, and put it down to the account of a weakness of mine in being captured by these sights, around "the elephant." On the boat we saw a very intelligent contraband with whom we had the following conversation, "What is your name?" "Eli Brown." "Any relation to John Brown?" "No massa, but I have heard of him in Richmond. It cost Gov. Wise millions to hang him but 'his soul is marching on.'" "You are from Richmond, then, and of course you recognize Jeff. Davis and the Southern confederacy?" "No sar, I doesn't no how."

"Havn't you heard that Lincoln is going to do it?" With a look of astonishment he was speechless for a minute, and then gathering faith in the author of the proclamation, said he "Wal, sar, when Mister Lincoln does dat, den I will."

"How did you get here?" "I runned away, sar." "Did you consult your master about it?" "No, sar. Massa Allen didn't consult me when he sold my two childrens, so I no consult him when I leaved him."

"White people down South say that you black people cannot take care of yourselves when you are free, how is that?" "Wal, Massa, we takes care of them and us too, when we's slaves—can't we take care of us alone, when we's free?"

Another of the contrabands—servant of one of the generals, who had learned him to read—said, that before he left his master, they told him that the Yankees would shoot the black men, make breast-works of them, and drown their women and children—but he had concluded to try it on. We said to him, "Your masters tell us that you don't want your freedom; how is that?" "Dey try to shut your eyes same as they did us, about your shootin' us."

We attended a colored prayer-meeting at City Point, the attendants being a number of a regiment of whom two-thirds had been killed in the famous attempt to take Petersburg. Our New York D.D's, etc., were very much interested and shook hands heartily with the leader of the meeting, who, after some ten had come forward for prayers, could keep still no longer, and so shook hands with most every man in the house. This man spoke with such force and clearness, as to command the attention of those learned men. I took occasion to talk with him after the meeting was over, and found that he had been a slave in Louisville, Kentucky—was a preacher, and gave this account of his first sermon:

He was sixty years old. At the age of thirty, he had a vision in which the first chapter of Job and the second chapter of Acts were given to him word for word, and the next day being the Sabbath, he repeated the two chapters, and spoke to his brethren. After the services, a white man who knew him well, asked him where he had learned them, when he gave him the facts, and this friend took out his Bible and read them to him. He had never before known that there were such books in the Bible as the book of Job and the Acts. Job, bereft of all he had, and the disciples of Jesus endued with the Holy Ghost, and having all things common, was to him all the theology he needed to preach to the slave who was bereft of all, surely—yet the gift of the Holy Spirit was left within his grasp, which levels all distinctions and raises to a common level, in the regards of the great All, Father, every child of the dust. J. V. F.

After the close of the war, Mr. Farwell was appointed a member of the Board of Indian Commissioners by President Grant, and in the discharge of his duties in this office, has been characterized by the same devotion, zeal and benevolence that have marked his entire career. He has twice visited the Pacific coast, traveling about 12,000 miles in the discharge of these duties.

The following is a copy from the original letter of appointment:

DEPARTMENT OF THE INTERIOR.
Washington, D.C., 15 Apr. 1869.

Dear Sir: The President has directed me to invite you to become one of the Commission provided for by the late act of Congress to act as auxiliary to this Department in the supervision of the work of gathering the Indians upon reservations, etc.

The Commission will serve without pay, except for expenses actually incurred in traveling, and is expected to act both as a consulting board of advisers, and (through their sub-committees) as Inspectors of the Agencies, etc., in the Indian Country.

The design of those who suggested the Commission was that something like a Christian Commission should be established, having the civilization of the Indian in view, and laboring to stimulate public interest in this work, whilst also co-operating with the Department in the specific purpose mentioned.

The following gentlemen have been requested to become members of the Board with you:

William Welsh, Philadelphia; Geo. H. Stuart, James E. Tratman, St. Louis; Wm. E. Dodge, New York; E. S. Toby, Boston; and Felix R. Bruns of Pittsburg.

Perhaps two others will be added, and as soon as answers are received, a preliminary meeting will be called here.

Earnestly hoping you will consent to your own appointment, and that you will in any event withhold any refusal until the preliminary meeting has been held, and you have thus been enabled to discuss more fully the objects and the importance of the contemplated movement,

I am, very respectfully,

Your obedient servant,

J. D. Cox, etc.

Hon. John V. Farwell,
Chicago

Mr. Farwell has never taken any active part in politics except in 1864, when he allowed his name to be used as a Presidential Elector for Mr. Lincoln. He has been honored with various positions of public and private trust; was at one time Vice-President of the Board of Trade.

The following letter, copied from the "Northwestern Christian Advocate" gives no uncertain sound in relation to his political views in 1864:

ABOLITIONISM EXPOSED.

Letter from John V. Farwell, Esq., Presidential Elector for the First Congressional District.

Mr. Editors: Having had my name placed before the people for Presidential Elector without having sought the position, you will please allow me space in your columns to tell the people my views without their having asked for them, so that no one shall have it to say that he voted for an "Abolitionist" without knowing it. I always have been a *Democratic-Republican Abolitionist*, though I never voted an Abolition ticket. I have served as one of a jury in the U. S. Courts in indicting men for resisting the execution of the fugitive slave law, not because the law was just, but because *obedience to law is the only safety for free governments*. I have a great love for the U. S. Government, because, as it is democratic in principle, republican in form, and now proposes that every man, woman and child shall be free, from the bottom to the top of its population, I believe it to be the only true exponent of liberty and progress for the human race. Having this faith, I am for abolishing everything and everybody that would tarnish its honor or diminish its power.

Its Constitution, and the Union of the States under it, must be preserved at all hazards. Abraham Lincoln and the platform of principles he occupies are unequivocally pledged to this purpose; therefore, if the voice of the whole world were necessary to make him President, and I were empowered to cast the vote, I would cast it for this man, before all other good and true men who honor our times.

The rebellion was established because the essential principles of the Baltimore platform elected him four years since. Those principles, baptized with the blood of patriots, will elect him again, and abolish the rebellion at the point of the bayonet. Then will he be President of the whole territory over which he was first constitutionally elected, the nation's honor and integrity will be vindicated before the world, and the Constitution will be regarded everywhere a real and holy bond of inalienable rights, and not empty words wasted on worthless parchment.

This must be accomplished to secure permanent peace and prosperity to the nation, and hereby many things must necessarily be abolished which now hold high carnival in expectation of a different result in the November election.

The African "nigger" and his mixed descendants having been the authors of all the fusions and confusions which have made the fire and brimstone of the present war, and of our past political broils, must have *his* office abolished by abolishing his chains. The blood of thousands slain, and the peace of our children, demand this of the present Administration.

That freedom of speech and of the press which belittles the Government and pronounces the work of our victorious armies a failure, while it magnifies the rebellion and its agencies, must be abolished by serried battalions of free ballots.

Vallandigham, Woods, Seymour & Co., must have their pretensions to leadership and other aspirations to power abolished, with no freedom of speech left them, except upon penitential knees to implore "Father Abraham" to send some poor Abolitionist to bring them in out of the cold, where the coming elections will surely leave them.

The aspirations of all wicked and unprincipled men for places of power and trust in the administration of the Government, must be *abolished*, because "righteousness exalteth a nation, but sin is a reproach to any people." We want no more Buchanans in the White House, to allow his Secretaries to steal our guns, our ships, our forts and our money, as the price of his office.

Professional politicians, and office-seekers, and brokers, must be abolished. The people must learn to ask their best men to fill their offices, from justice of the peace to President of the Republic ; and not allow the Woods, Seymours, Voorheeses and Vallandighams to hoodwink them into the belief that they are the real conservators of the peace and prosperity of the nation—the only men capable of managing its affairs.

A bogus Democracy with such leaders, who proposed to *coax* the minority to yield to the majority, in the first election of Abraham to the Presidency, must be *abolished* beyond the hope of resurrection, or democratic governments must of necessity prove a disgraceful failure.

That partisan spirit which would revive such a miserable organization of dry bones by voting with a party which declares the war to be a failure, must be abolished by such a robust, living majority of intelligent, patriotic and independent Union votes, as will demonstrate that patriotism and genuine Democracy know no party as such.

British swagger and gentlemanly French insolence, breathing out sympathy for the rebels, must be abolished by the same host of genuine Democratic voters.

That political secession humbug, called "State rights" or "popular sovereignty," requiring the whole nation to make a bow to South Carolina, while she fires upon Sumter and sets up for herself, must be abolished, or our government is not worth the value of the plain white canvas which receives the stars and stripes as the emblem of its power and identity. Our flag is called a "dirty rag" by the rebels, and such it is, if the State can defy the Federal authority with impunity. "Let us rally round the flag, boys," until no head nor heart shall attempt to ride such a miserable hobby over the ruins of our national authority and greatness.

In short, the Chicago platform and its candidates must be abolished by a grand abolition charge. Without principles and without men, the American people must bury them out of sight, simply because the rebels want them to live and rule. Any other reason in addition to this would be insulting to the common sense of a free people.

After this general Abolition ticket has been stereotyped upon the Government, by the logic of the November elections, as it will be, then it will be comparatively an easy task for our boys in blue to abolish the rebel armies. Taking heart from such substantial moral reinforcements from home, their valor will be irresistible, and *Abolitionist* will then be the motto on the coat of arms for our regenerated Government; which shall commend it to the affectionate regard of mankind, and the approbation of Him who sits "as Governor among the nations," and commands them to "break every yoke."

If I am chosen as one of the Presidential Electors of the great State of Illinois, which has furnished the best President, and the best General, since the days of Washington, I herewith give notice to the voters who shall so elect me, that I shall vote to place them securely in Abraham's bosom, and not in the hearse of the grave-digger of the Chickahominy, for political burial in the graveyard of nations.

JOHN V. FARWELL.

The reader will have noticed that some of the foregoing articles were dated "U. S. Christian Commission." We are informed that the Commission grew out of the efforts of the Young Men's Christian Association of Chicago, of which Mr. Farwell was an active and efficient member.

At the age of fourteen years Mr. Farwell united with the M. E. Church, but is now a ruling Elder in the Presbyterian Church. Liberal in his sentiments, he favors unity of effort, and shrinks from that exclusiveness which would shut out from full fellowship any person heartily believing in a broad Christian platform upon which all may stand. Since first uniting with the church he has been proverbial for his liberality, and has been known to devote half his salary to charitable objects. Mr. Farwell was an active worker with Mr. Dwight L. Moody in organizing the "North Market Mission," designed especially for outcast boys and girls, and for several years was superintendent of the same; he contributed largely for current expenses, and, when it finally developed into the Illinois Street Church, gave $10,000 toward the erection of the building. The membership has numbered 600 persons under the pastoral charge of Mr. Moody, of whom Mr. Farwell has been a constant and liberal supporter and friend.

In the establishment of the Young Men's Christian Association of Chicago in 1857, Mr. Farwell was a prime mover, and to his constant zeal and earnest effort the prosperity of that institution is largely due. He sold the Association the ground upon which their building stands, taking his pay in stock, and when it had suffered a succession of losses by fire, and found itself involved in financial difficulty, he was among the number who donated their entire stock to relieve it from embarrassment. He has been connected with the Association as Trustee, Vice-President, and President for several years, participating actively in its labors, and contributing largely for current expenses. We here reproduce his last official report as President of the Association, given in a Chicago paper, April 1876:

EIGHTEENTH ANNUAL REPORT OF THE YOUNG MEN'S CHRISTIAN ASSOCIATION.

President's Report.

In presenting our Eighteenth Annual Report, all who are conversant with the history of our Association cannot but be impressed with one central fact, around which all others gather, like the rich, ripe clusters, clinging to the one vine, of which the Father is the husbandman—and that is, that the Husbandman has dug about and pruned this vine, until its fruitage is more than its most sanguine friends ever anticipated.

"Sweet are the uses of adversity" may be well said of this organization. While the material fire has twice reduced her local habitation to ashes, and the hot flames of opposition have shot out their forked tongues of hate, she has not forgotten her royal Master's earthly career. Nor has that Prince of the kings of the earth forgotten her. The reports of the several committees give ample proof of these facts. He would not be true to his precious promises, given during that wonderful career, if His blessing had not been with His Church (against which He has said the gates of hell shall not prevail) in this their united efforts to extend its usefulness.

All branches of the one Church can point to some of their individual members who have been greatly benefited by their connection with the work of the Young Men's Christian Association, and have been made more a blessing to their own church. Were this not the result, I, for one, would lose my interest in them.

Rounding out of Christian character should be the office of all appliances of the Church, and if there is any one point where, in the present age of scepticism and infidelity, it needs to be fully developed, it is in the cultivation of the spirit of union, to the fruit-bearing point. No amount of theoretical leaves in reference to this essential thing in Christ's body will satisfy Christ, "The Head," or a carping world.

This work the Young Men's Christian Association are doing. How well they are doing it may be traced, specially, in the wonderful revival of God's work in the hearts of men and women in the church, as seen in England and America the past three years; and also in the natural results of such a revival—the world believing that God has sent His Son to save them, and that by thousands. Revivals there have been, of wonderful power, in the past, but in these last times the Church has massed her forces, just when the Malakoffs of rationalism were defying the armies of Israel, and the Captain of the Lord's host, with the drawn sword of a united Church, has led on his one army to signal victory.

Let us learn wisdom from this one great fact of this age, and not spend our strength foolishly in trying to explain away one of God's mile-posts in the wilderness journey of Christ's blood-bought Church.

Let me say to one and all: Look calmly at the facts of history in connection with Association work among the churches. See for yourselves, not through the green goggles of sectarian jealousy, but through the crystal light of "the white stone," upon which is graven the name of each one "that overcometh," as individual members of the one Church, in the battle of life, and then close up the broken ranks, so closely wherever the church or the world may see any real points of separation, that none, from above or beneath, may justly charge God's people with folly in their visible relations with each other in the common work of saving souls.

This Association has only begun its career of usefulness, if the churches of Chicago shall continue to smile upon and second her efforts. The field is not Chicago alone. This great centre of human influence may not confine her light to the corporation map. It must extend far and wide, into the regions beyond.

How important, then, that our trumpet give no uncertain sound, either for the gathering or the moving of the Lord's hosts.

As there was only one tabernacle of old, into which all the tribes gathered, so now, there is only one true tabernacle, and the Lord pitched that on Calvary. "Look unto me, all ye ends of the earth, and be ye saved." A look at the crucified one should melt all hearts into one mould, for his work on earth, left in our hands from that central point in the world's history.

JOHN V. FARWELL,
President.

In 1858, with Mr. J. B. Stillson, he began his labors among the prisoners at Bridewell, and, by his earnest temperance appeals and religious services, has rescued some of the most obdurate, and saved several men of fine education and ability. He was one of the most liberal contributors to the fund for the erection of a chapel for prison worship.

Mr. Farwell's acquaintance and co-operation with Mr. Moody in the North Market Mission Sunday-School in Chicago led to a firm friendship from the first of their united labors in this direction. The result was the erection of a large hall for the Young Men's Christian Association, which, at its dedication, was named (at the suggestion of Mr. Moody) "FARWELL HALL." It contains, in addition to a fine auditorium, offices, reading, prayer, lecture and other rooms, and every appliance that can contribute to successful work.

In all of Mr. Moody's projects for the cultivation and spread of Christian union, Mr. Farwell took a lively interest.

The culmination of these projects was his trip to England to do evangelistic work in that land that may justly be called the mother of the churches in these last days. Mr. Farwell was with him in London three months, and accompanied him back to this country.

When he came to Chicago, Mr. Farwell built him a tabernacle that would hold 8,000 people, which, Mr. Moody said, was the best building that had ever been erected for him, and thus gave evidence of his confidence, not only in Moody, but in the cause, of which he is the most successful exponent that has lived since the days of Paul. Beginning in an unoccupied grocery-store, 20x40 feet, in the poorest part of Chicago, and coming back, after practically uniting the churches of England and Scotland, for Christian work, to unite the churches of Chicago in such a building, was certainly ample proof of the sagacity of Mr. Farwell in seconding his efforts when there were but few to do so, in so grand, though apparently at the first so insignificant a work.

The Tabernacle is now being changed into a block of five large wholesale stores, but the result of the meetings held there may never be changed—for God's work remains while man's may fade in a day—and yet Mr. Farwell may regard that as the grandest work of his life, and it was there that Mr. Moody more than vindicated his world-wide reputation as an evangelist, for the Lord's prophet was greatly honored in his own country.

If any apology were needed for the extended biography and quotations of correspondence and reports in the preceding pages (which need the compilers do not recognize) they would say it was their belief that in no way could they better portray the political and religious views entertained by Mr. F., or more briefly and graphically represent the work of the Christian Commission, the Y. M. C. Association and other patriotic and Christian agencies with which he was so thoroughly identified during the late struggle for national liberty and union. His earnest, Christian course and munificence in the cause of temperance and evangelization they desired to record for imitation by those who, though as highly endowed in intellectual and financial resources, yet fail to employ them, as he has done, for the welfare of humanity and the glory of God. May his bright example prompt many to go and do likewise.

Mrs. Emerette (Cooley) Farwell, dau. of Noah and Sophronia⁶ (Parsons) and gr. dau. of George Cooley is, in her maternal line, descended from Cornet Joseph¹ Parsons of Springfield and Northampton, Mass., and wife Mary Bliss, through Ensign Samuel² and his 2d wife Rhoda (Taylor) who removed from Northampton to Durham, Ct.; Ithamar³ and wife Sarah of Durham ; David⁴ and Rebecca (Robinson) who removed from D. to Granville, Mass.; Capt. Joel⁵ and Phebe (Robinson) of G. ; and Sophronia⁶ (Parsons) Cooley of Granville.

Children of John-Villars⁸ Farwell all born in Chicago :

764. 1. ABBIE⁹, b. 4 Apr. 1851 ; m. at Lake Forest, Ill. 12 Oct. 1875, William-Henry⁷ Ferry, b. 15 May, 1845, s. of William-Henry⁶ and Mary-Ann (Williams) of Lake Forest.*   Res. *Lake Forest, Ill.*

Children :

764ᵃ.   1. William¹⁰, b. 13 July, 1876, Lake Forest.
764ᵇ.   2. John-Farwell¹⁰, b. 12 Oct. 1877, Sterling, Ill.
764ᶜ.   3. Francis-Montague¹⁰, b. 25 Nov. 1878, Lake Forest.

765. 2. JOHN-VILLARS⁹, b. 16 Oct. 1858 ; 1879, is a senior in Yale College.
766. 3. FRANK-COOLEY⁹, b. 28 Dec. 1860 ; 1879, is a freshman in Yale College.
767. 4. ARTHUR-LINCOLN⁹, b. 17 Jan. 1863 ; 1879, preparing for Y. C. at Lake Forest.
768. 5. FANNIE⁹, b. 19 Nov. 1864; 1869, student in Lake Forest Seminary.

769. SIMEON⁸, (*Henry⁷*, [747] *Simeon⁶, Daniel⁵, Daniel⁴, Joseph³, Joseph², Henry¹,*) b. 28 Feb. 1828, Campbelltown, N.Y.; d. there, 22 Sept. 1829.

770. SIMEON⁸, (*Henry⁷* [747], *Simeon⁶, Daniel⁵, Daniel⁴, Joseph³, Joseph², Henry¹,*) born 22 Mar. 1831, Campbelltown, m. Sardinia, Erie Co., N. Y., 22 March, 1857,

---

*Mr. Ferry is a descendant of Charles⁵ of Springfield, who m. there, 29 Jan. 1661, Sarah, dau. of John¹ Harmon of S., through Charles⁶ Ferry, b. 1655, and Abigail Warner, dau. of Mark² and gr. dau. of John¹ and Abigail², dau. of Richard¹ Montague ; Noah³ Ferry, b. 1712, d. 4 Nov. 1798, and Experience (Allis) ; Noah⁴ Ferry, b. 18 Oct. 1748, Granby, Mass. and Hannah (Montague) dau. of Joseph and Sarah (Henry) who was dau. of James and Elisabeth (Hastings); Heman⁵ b. 4 Aug. 1786, Granby and Roxana⁷ Burchard, descendant of Thomas¹ of Norwich, Conn., and gr. gr. dau. of Capt. David¹ Barton from Devonshire, Eng.; and his parents, William-Henry⁶ Ferry, b. 10 April, 1809, Remsen, N.Y. and Mary-Ann Williams, descendant of Robert¹ of Roxbury, Mass. Mr. Ferry is also, acc. to his father Wm-Henry⁶, of the 9th generation from William Montague, Earl of Sandwich, who died in 1500.

Ebenette-Charlotte-Maria Smith, b. 16 Feb. 1837, Porter, Niagara Co., N.Y., dau. of Rev. Isaac-Bateman and Hannah (Ryan) of Scottsville, N.Y.

Mr. Farwell went to Chicago July, 1849, being then in his nineteenth year. He has been Deputy Clerk of the circuit court ; connected with the banking-house of George Smith & Co. ; book-keeper with the firm of Cooley, Wadsworth & Co., (the predecessors of the present firm of J. V. Farwell & Co.); in the grain commission business, firm of Farwell & Co., and Farwell, Hill & Knox of Chicago several years ; and, since 1870, has been one of the present firm of J. V. Farwell & Co.

Res. Campbelltown, N.Y., Stirling and *Evanston, Ill.*

Children :

771. 1. SIMEON-ALLEN⁹, b. 25 July, 1859, Chicago; d. 30 Oct. 1859, C.
772. 2. HENRY-SMITH⁹, b. 25 Nov. 1861, Chicago.
773. 3. ANNA-PEARL⁹, b. 24 March, 1868, Forest-Home, Noxubee co., Miss.
774. 4. RUTH-LOUISA⁹, b. 13 Sept. 1872, Chicago.

775. MARIA-LOUISE⁸, (*Henry⁷* [747], *Simeon⁶, Daniel⁵, Daniel⁴, Joseph³, Joseph², Henry¹*,) b. 28 Aug. 1837, Big Flats, Chemung co., N.Y.; m. Chicago, Ill., 8 Mar. 1863, Epaphras-Wadsworth **EDSON**, b. 31 Oct. 1833, Huntington, Pa., s. of Charles and Susanna (Stearns) of Huntington; afterwards of Shasta Valley, Cal.

Mrs. M. L. (Farwell) Edson graduated at Ingham University, Leroy, Genesee co., N.Y., 25 June, 1856.

Mr. Edson belongs to the Sturgis Rifles of Chicago, a picked company of eighty sharpshooters armed and equipped by Solomon Sturgis of Chicago at his own expense, and accepted by the War Department as an independent company ; were never attached to any regiment or brigade. General McClellan, when taking command in West Virginia, took this company as his special guard—the company so much advertised as his body-guard. When called to Washington after the first battle of Bull Run they accompanied him. When McClellan was relieved of his command they were mustered out of service. Never did any duty except at headquarters. During the peninsular campaign, Mr. Edson had charge of the mail from headquarters to White House Landing. All correspondence between the commanding general and President and War Department was put in his hands with instructions not to go out under any circumstances till delivered to proper persons—a pleasant but responsible position. Knew well Prince De Joinville, Count De Paris and Duc De Chartres and all the other staff officers. They left the service in Nov. 1862. After his marriage he engaged in business in San Francisco. While returning from a visit to his mother in Shasta Valley, the stage in which he was traveling was upset, and he was thrown so violently on his head as to disable him for business for two years. On recovery he returned to Illinois and settled in Stirling, where he has since resided.

Stirling, Ill.

Children :

776. 1. CHARLES-FARWELL⁹, b. 3 Apr. 1864, San Francisco, Cal.
777. 2. NANCY⁹, b. 30 June, 1867, Shasta Valley, Cal. ; died there 1 Aug. 1867.

778. BENJAMIN⁷, [560] (*Simeon⁶, Daniel⁵, Daniel⁴, Joseph³, Joseph², Henry¹*,) b. 25 May, 1798, Fitchburg, Mass.; married at Painted Post, Steuben Co., N.Y., 6 July, 1826, Hannah-Mary Knox, b. 9 Dec. 1806, Painted Post, dau. of John and Hannah (Douglas) of Stephentown, Rensselaer co., N.Y.

Mr. Farwell removed to P. P. about 1800. He has been supervisor of Campbelltown, Steuben co., four years, and is elder in the Presbyterian church. Merchant.

Res. *Painted Post, N.Y.*

Children:

779. 1. WILLIAM-DOUGLAS⁸, b. 31 May, 1827, Big Flats, Chemung Co., N.Y.; m. Olean, Cattaraugus Co., N.Y., 11 Apr. 1866, Hannah-Danelia Ripley, b. 5 Jan. 1843, Ackron, Erie Co., N.Y., dau. of Allen-P. and Cornelia (Smith) of Buffalo, N.Y. Merchant, firm of J. V. Farwell & Co., Chicago.

The New York branch of the house, at 115 Worth Street, is ably represented by William-D⁸, whose business talent, tact and probity, combined with his cordial spirit and manner, nobly maintain the prestige of this leading firm of the metropolis of the West.

Child:

780.   1. Hannah-Cornelia, b. 17 Jan. 1867, Buffalo, N.Y.

781. 2. JOHN-KNOX⁸, b. 5 Jan. 1829, Big Flats, N.Y.; married, Painted Post, 22 June, 1868, Harriet-Rose, b. 24 Feb. 1843, P. P., dau. of James and Catharine (Castleline) of Painted Post. She died 28 May, 1869, Chicago, Ill. He married 2d, 9 July, 1873, at Albany, N.Y., Charlotte Lawton. Merchant—with J. V. Farwell & Co.

Res. *Chicago, Ill.*

Child:

782.   1. Harriet⁹, b. 28 May, 1869; died 11 Aug. 1869.
783. 3. MARY-AURELIA⁸, b. 28 Jan. 1831, Big Flats; died 15 Aug. 1832.
784. 4. DEIDAMIA-KNOX⁸, b. 11 Feb. 1833, Campbelltown, Steuben co., N.Y.; m. Painted Post, 12 June, 1860, William-James Hotchkiss, b. 12 Mar. 1835, Chester, Warren Co., N.Y., s. of William and Elizabeth (Sherman) of Chester. She res. 1879, *Lake Forest, Chicago, Ill.*

Children

785.   1. Douglass-Farwell⁹, b. 26 May, 1861.
786.   2. William-Benjamin⁹, b. 13 May, 1864.
787. 5. MARY-AURELIA⁸, b. 16 June, 1835, Campbelltown, N.Y.; m. Painted Post, 8 Oct. 1862, Solomon-Cushing Campbell, b. 1836, Calhoun Co., Mich., son of Philo and Calista (Cushing) of Campbelltown. Merchant.

Res. 1879, *Corning, Steuben Co., N.Y.*

Child:

788.   1. Wallace-Farwell⁹, b. 8 Sept. 1863.

789. DEA. PETER⁷, [561] (*Simeon⁶, Daniel⁵, Daniel⁴, Joseph³, Joseph², Henry¹*,) b. 24 June, 1800, Fitchburg, Mass.; m. F. 21 Sept. 1828, Catharine Boutelle, b. 2

Oct. 1798, at Fitchburg, dau. of Nathaniel and Polly (Hills) of F. She d. there, 17 Sept. 1835.

He married 2d, at F., 20 Apr. 1837, Maria Patch, b. 5 June, 1804, Fitzwilliam, N.H., dau. of Samuel and Betsey (Mellen) of Fitzwilliam. She died at Leominster, Mass., 10 Feb. 1838. He married 3d, at L., 26 Nov. 1839, Elizabeth-Smith Burrage, b. 2 May, 1820, Leominster, dau. of Josiah and Ruth (Kilbourn) of L.

In 1835 he was deacon in the Evangelical church, Leominster.

Res. Leominster, Mass.; 1879, Chicago, Ill.

Children:

790. 1. HENRY-BOUTELLE⁸, b. 25 Jan. 1825, Greenwich, Hampshire co., Mass.; m. 31 Jan. 1850, at Brookline, Hillsborough Co., N.H., Emily-Augusta Harris, b. 1 Aug. 1828, dau. of David and Louisa (Marshall) of Brookline. Leather Dealer. s.p. <i>Res. Boston, Mass.</i>

791. 2. ARTEMAS-SIMONDS⁸, b. 29 July, 1835, Fitchburg. He enlisted for three months in Co. G of the 1st New Hampshire, Volunteer Regiment, 8 May, 1861; re-enlisted in Co. F, 25th Mass. Regt., in which he was corporal and orderly sergeant; was afterwards sergeant in a N. H. regt. He participated in the battles of Newbern and Roanoake, and died 23 Nov. 1862, of sickness, in hospital at Newbern, N.C.

792. 3. FRANCIS-WILLIAM⁸, b. 19 Mar. 1841, Leominster, Worcester co., Mass.

Mr. Farwell has been Secretary and Treasurer of Babcock's Manufacturing Co. of Chicago, and senior member of the firm of Farwell, Steele & Pratt, Fancy Groceries, 28 and 30 River Street, Chicago.

793. 4. CATHERINE-SMITH⁸, b. 4 Dec. 1842, Leominster, Mass.; married there 10 July, 1869, James-Nesmith Steele, who was born at Goffstown, N.H., on Sunday, 5 June, 1842, s. of David and Isabella-Abigail (Nesmith) of Goffstown, Hillsborough Co., N.H.

Mrs. Catharine-S. (Farwell) Steele was a graduate of Mount Holyoke Seminary in 1866. <i>Res. Chicago, Ill.</i>

Children:

794. 1. Isabella-Elizabeth⁹, b. 23 May, 1870, Michigan Avenue, Chicago, Ill.
795. 2. Ruth⁹, b. 6 Aug. 1873, Kenwood, (Hyde Park) Ill.
796. 5. CHARLES-EMORY⁸, b. 2 Mar. 1845, Leominster; died 14 Apr. 1846, at L.
797. 6. EMORY-BURRAGE⁸, b. 10 May, 1847, L.; d. L., 24 June, 1849.
798. 7. GEORGE-EDWARD⁸, b. 24 Feb. 1851, L. <i>Res. Chicago, Ill.</i>
799. 8. ARTHUR-BURRAGE⁸, b. 2 Oct. 1852, L. " "
800. 9. HELEN-GERTRUDE⁸, b. 28 Dec. 1858, Milford, Worcester Co., Mass.

801. MARY⁷, [562] (<i>Simeon⁶, Daniel⁵, Daniel⁴, Joseph³, Joseph², Henry¹,</i>) b. 28 Oct. 1802, Fitchburg, Worcester Co., Mass.; married at Big Flats, Chemung Co., N.Y., 6 Sept. 1835, Elias-Cooledge LANE, b. 30 Dec. 1809, Ashburnham, Mass.; s. of Elias and Nancy (Jones) of A. Proprietor of Saw and Grist Mills.

Res. New Gloucester, Me.

Children :

802. 1. MARY-HEPZIBAH⁸, b. 12 Sept. 1842.
803. 2. DAVID-ALLEN⁸, b. 26 May, 1845, New Gloucester; died there 12 Nov. 1857.

804. MIRIAM-THURSTON⁷, [563] (*Simeon⁶, Daniel⁵, Daniel⁴, Joseph³, Joseph², Henry¹,*) b. 14 July, 1806, Fitchburg, Mass. ; died 24 Jan. 1840, Daysville, Ill. ; married, 30 Apr. 1827, Stephen **BEMIS**, of Fitchburg, at the residence of Mr. David Allen [558]. He was born in 1804. They removed to New York State, and thence to Daysville, Ogle Co., Ill., where he resides, 1879.

Children all born in Fitchburg :

805. 1. STEPHEN-ALLEN⁸, b. 6 Feb. 1828, Fitchburg, Mass. ; married 31 May, 1854, at Chicago, Ill., Hannah-Jane Thomas, b. 27 Jan. 1835, in New York State. 1878, res. *St. Louis, Mo.*

Children :

806. 1. Fanny-Ann⁹, b. Sycamore, Ill., 11 Oct. 1855.
807. 2. Miriam-Farwell⁹, b. Sycamore, Ill., 27 Sept. 1857.
808. 3. Judson-Stephen⁹, b. San Francisco, Cal., 26 March, 1867.

809. 2. MARY-HEPSEY⁸, b. 21 Dec. 1830, Fitchburg, Mass. ; married 24 Dec., 1857, Nathan Lattin, b. 2 May, 1834, at Veteran, Chemung Co., N.Y., son of Ransom and Almy (Crawford), of Veteran.
1879, res. *Sycamore, Ill.*

Children :

810. 1. Sidney⁹, b. 18 Oct. 1858; died 22 Sept. 1859.
811. 2. Clarissa⁹, b. 20 Jan. 1860.
812. 3. Judson-Moss⁹, b. 27 Feb. 1863.
813. 4. Almy-Crawford⁹, b. 23 May, 1864 ; d. 7 Apr. 1865.
814. 5. Frederick⁹, b. 12 March, 1866.

815. 3. JUDSON-MOSS⁸, born 18 May, 1833, Fitchburg ; married at Cambridgeport, Mass., 21 Nov. 1866, Alice Cogswell, of C., who was born at Ipswich, Mass., 5 Jan. 1844. In 1874 was of the firm of Bemis & Brown, Boston, Mass. Res. St. Louis, Mo., and 1879, *Newton, Mass.*

Child :

816. 1. Judson-Cogswell⁹, b. St. Louis, Mo. 8 Dec. 1867.

817. SIMEON⁷ [564] (*Simeon⁶, Daniel⁵, Daniel⁴, Joseph³, Joseph², Henry¹,*) born 28 Feb. 1809, Fitchburg ; married in Fitchburg, by Rev. Mr. Van Arsdale, 10 June, 1831, Mary-Ann Downe of F. who was born at F., 22 March, 1810, dau. of Joseph and Polly (Thurls). He removed to Detroit in company with his son-in-law Mr. Burbank in 1858, where he has since resided. Chair manufacturer.

Children :

818. 1. SARAH-DOWNE⁸, b. 21 June, 1833, Big Flats, Tioga Co., N.Y.; married at Worcester, Mass., 20 May, 1851, Silas-David **Burbank**, born at Worces-

ter, in 1828. He removed in 1853 to Detroit, but returned to Worcester in 1859, at which place he was living in 1869. Machinist.

Res. Fitchburg, Detroit and *Worcester, Mass.*

Children :

819.   1. Frank-Farwell⁹, b. in 1853 at Worcester, Mass.
820.   2. Edgar-David⁹, b. Detroit, Michigan, 1855.
821.   3. Charles-Sumner⁹, b.   "   1857.
822.   4. Alfred-Allen⁹, b. Elsie, Michigan, 1859.
823.   5. Ethel-S⁹., b. Worcester, Mass., 1863.

824. 2. GEORGE-AUGUSTINE⁸, b. 3 June, 1835, Fitchburg ; m. at Detroit, Mich., 31 August, 1856, Helen Smith who was born at Fulton, N.Y., 17 May, 1835, He has been book-keeper in the office of the Detroit Gas Co. and in 1874, Superintendent of the Gas Co.'s works in Lawrence, Kansas.

825. 3. ALFRED-ALLEN⁸, born 7 May, 1838, Worcester, Mass. ; m. at Detroit, 21 May, 1861, Catharine-Isabel Morton. 1874, was superintendent of the Weber Furniture Co. at Detroit, Mich.

826. 4. ELIZABETH-TRUE⁸, b. 25 Dec. 1843, Worcester; died there, 20 July, 1844.

827. 5. ANNETTE-ELIZABETH⁸, b. 2 July, 1845, W.; married at Detroit, 23 Dec. 1872, Joseph-Comstock **Jones**, a teacher in Detroit Public School 1874;

[Since the above was in type we learn that Mr. Jones grad. Mich. Univ. June, 1872; became Supt. of the Pontiac Schools 15 July, 1872, and of the East Saginaw Schools, 20 July, 1877. He is s. of Eliphalet Jones, born Sandwich, Mass. 28 May, 1808; died at Raisin, Mich, 20 May, 1870; gr. son of Elisha whose ship was captured off Florida, 1812; d. on his way home at Havre de Grace. Md..was b. there.

Child :   *Res. Pontiac, Mich.*

Edward-Horton⁹, b. 20 Feb. 1877.   1879, Res. *East Saginaw, Mich.*

828. SOPHIA⁷, [556] (*Asa⁶, Daniel⁵, Daniel⁴, Joseph³, Joseph², Henry¹,*) b. 11 Nov. 1797, Fitchburg; m. there, 28 Nov. 1824, Micah-Lawrence Wheeler, b. 4 July, 1794, son of Joseph and Elizabeth (Lawrence). He died 14 Apr. 1867. She resided in 1874, at Ashby, Mass.

Children:

829.   1. EMELINE-SOPHIA⁸, b. 12 July, 1829, Fitchburg; m. 9 Jan. 1857, Lemuel-Porter **Martain**, born 22 July, 1824, s. of John, of Woburn, Mass. He died at Worcester, Mass., 29 June, 1869. She was m. 2d, at Stoneham, Mass., by Rev. E. B. Fairchild, 24 Oct. 1872, to Dexter Bucknam, Esq., of S., son of Albert and Sally (Wiley).

Child:

830.   1. Fannie-Sophia⁹, b. 16 Aug. 1857, Cleveland, O.

831.   2. MARY-ANNE⁸, b. 8 Jan. 1832, Fitchburg; m. 4 Sept. 1856, Elbridge-Gerry **Pierce**, b. 11 Mar. 1818, s. of Joseph and Jemima, of Amherst, Mass. He d. 14 Aug. 1865.

Children:

832.   1. Henry-Ernest⁹, b. 23 March, 1861.
833.   2. Franklin-Brown⁹, b. 14 Nov. 1863.

834.   3. RUFUS-WARREN⁸, b. 1 April, 1835, East Cambridge, Mass.; m. 16 Aug. 1856, Susan-Melissa Monroe, b. 11 Aug. 1838, dau. of John and Nancy-Whiting (Cushing), of Ashburnham, Mass.   *Res. Ashby, Mass.*

Children:

835.   1. Edward-Lawrence⁸, b. 6 Jan. 1861.
836.   2. Isabel-Farwell⁸, b. 7 Sept. 1865; d. 21 Aug. 1867.
837.   3. Etta-Davis⁸, (or Susie-Etta) b. 3 Nov. 1868.
838.   4. Hattie-Elizabeth⁸, b. 11 Sept. 1871.

839. JANE⁷, [568], (*Asa⁶, Daniel⁵, Daniel⁴, Joseph³, Joseph², Henry¹,*) born 21 Jan. 1802, Fitchburg; died 4 March, 1870, Boston, Mass.; married at F., 25 Dec. 1828, Benjamin BROWN, born 14 Jan. 1799, son of Benjamin and Jemima (Jackson) of Westminster Mass. He died 11 Jan. 1839. Housewright.   Res. *Boston, Mass.*

Children, all born in Boston, were:

840.   1. BENJAMIN-FRANKLIN⁸, b. 13 March, 1830 ; m. at Hampton, N.H., 13 Oct. 1870, by Rev. DeW-H-Clinton Durgin, Clara-Minerva Neal, b. 3 Sept. 1843, Hampton, N.H., dau. of John-Dearborn and Harriet (Piper) of Hampton, N.H. Oil merchant.
        Res. 1874, 41 *West Cedar St., Boston.*
   Child :

841.   1. Abbie-Farwell⁹. b. 21 Aug. 1871.

842.   2. EDWARD-JACKSON⁸, b. 26 June, 1833 ; m. Boston, 2 Dec. 1863, Mary-Eliza Brown, dau. of Charles, of Boston and Susan (Morehead) of Gloucester, Mass.
        Mr. Brown was named Jackson because he was born on the day of Andrew-Jackson's last visit to Boston.   Res. *Boston, Mass.*

Children:

843.   1. Charles-Farwell⁹, b. 20 Jan. 1865.
844.   2. Edward-Lyman⁹, b. 25 Mar. 1867.
845.   3. Walter-Jackson⁹, b. 5 Oct. 1870.
846.   4. Frederic-Hamilton⁹, b. 15 Mar. 1873

847.   3. FREDERIC-LYMAN⁸, born 3 Dec. 1837 ; m. 17 May, 1865, Elizabeth McFarland, daughter of Nelson of Charlestown and Lucinda (Durgan) of Limerick, Me.   Res. *Boston, Bunker Hill District.*
   Child :

848.   1. Jane-Farwell⁹, b. 31 Oct. 1869.

849. CHARLES⁷, [569] (*Asa⁶, Daniel⁵, Daniel⁴, Joseph³, Joseph², Henry¹,*) b. 21 Nov. 1803, Fitchburg, Mass.; died 27 Apr. 1868, of cancer on the tongue ; married at Lancaster, Mass., 18 Sept. 1832, Ann-Elmira Sanderson of L., b. 10 Oct. 1810, dau. of Elisha or Elijah and Mary (Dinsmore, who was dau. of Dr. Phineas of Lunenburg, Mass.) She died at Fitchburg, 25 Oct. 1834. He married 2d, at Shirley, Mass., 22 Sept. 1835, Hannah-Page Chaplain, b. 11 Nov. 1808, S., dau. of William and Hannah (Page) of Shirley. She died 3 May, 1866. He was a farmer.
    Res. 1867, *Boston, Mass.*

Children

850. 1. ANN-ELMIRA⁸, b. 25 May, 1831; died 9 July, 1837, Fitchburg.
851. 2. JANE⁸, b. 18 Apr. 1839; married, 8 Feb. 1863, Edwin-Augustus Goodrich, son of Alonzo and Eveline (Gilson), of Fitchburg, Mass.

  Child:

852.   1. Elmira-Hannah⁹, b. 13 Jan. 1864.

853. 3. ANN-ELIZA⁸, b. 11 Oct. 1840.
854. 4. HANNAH-ELVIRA⁸, b. 7 Jan. 1844; m. Fitchburg, 17 Jan. 1872, Howard Gilson, son of John and Mary (Howard), of Ashby, Mass.

855. MARY⁷, [573] (*Polly*⁶ (*Farwell*) Hartwell, *Daniel*⁵, *Daniel*⁴, *Joseph*³, *Joseph*², *Henry*¹,) b. 16 July, 1792, Lunenburg, Mass., where she died, 18 Sept. 1858; married at L., 4 Apr. 1811, Stephen GIBSON, b. 23 Dec. 1783, at Fitchburg, son of Thomas and Lucy (Martin) of F. He m. 2d, 8 Feb. 1855, Mary Billings, b. 8 Sept. 1799. He died, 18 Jan. 1864, at Lunenburg. Farmer. Res. *Lunenburg, Mass.*

Children:

856. 1. MARY-FAIRBANKS⁸, b. 5 Sept. 1812, Lunenburg, Mass.; married, L., 31 Dec. 1832, Stephen-Melvin Longley, b. 11 Aug. 1802, at Shirley, Mass., son of Stephen and Rhoda (Parker) of Shirley.

  Mr. Longley has held various town offices, such as selectman, overseer, assessor, etc. Occupation, farmer. Res. *Shirley, Mass.*

  Children, all born in Shirley, were:

857.   1. Charles-Albert⁹, b. 7 Aug. 1834; m. 5 May, 1855, at Worcester, Mass., Hannah-Elizabeth Powers, b. 8 June, 1835, Pepperell, Mass., dau. of Jonathan-Jackson and Priscilla-Emily (Read) of Shirley, Mass. Farmer and mechanic. Res. *Shirley, Mass.*

    Children, all born in Shirley:

858.   1. *Lilla-May*¹⁰, b. 18 June, 1858.
859.   2. *Charles-Chandler*¹⁰, b. 25 Dec. 1859.
860.   3. *Alice-Gertrude*¹⁰, b. 24 Feb. 1862.
861.   2. Lieut. Stephen-Webster⁹, b. 1 Aug. 1836; married, 1 Dec. 1867, Townsend, Mass., Sarah-Elizabeth Sylvester, b. 28 Dec. 1842, T., dau. of Quincy and Sallie (Wallace) of T. He served in the war of the rebellion as First Lieutenant in Co. D., 53d Regiment, Mass. Volunteers.
862.   3. Nelson-Parker⁹, b. 18 Jan. 1838; d. 24 Aug. 1838, at Shirley.
863.   4. Mary-Maria⁹, b. 9 Sept. 1839.
864.   5. Ellen-Eliza⁹, b. 10 Aug. 1842; d. 27 May, 1866, S.
865.   6. Clara-Melissa⁹, b. 31 Jan. 1845.
866.   7. Melvin-Whitmore⁹, b. 2 Feb. 1849.
867.   8. Mariette-Frances⁹, b. 17 June, 1853, S.

868. 2. JOHN-STEARNS⁶, b. 31 Oct. 1814, Lunenburg; d. 30 May, 1819, L.
869. 3. ELIZA-PUTNAM⁶, b. 10 June, 1816, Shirley, Mass; d. 13 Aug. 1818, S.
870. 4. HENRIETTA⁶, b. 3 June, 1818, S.; died 5 June, 1818, S.
871. 5. ELIZA-PUTNAM⁶, b. 15 July, 1819, Lunenburg; m. 3 July, 1848, L, George Elbridge Martin. She d. 7 Apr. 1853, Troy, N.Y. s.p.
   He res. 1872, *Hartford, Conn.*
872. 6. ABBY-MARTIN⁶, b. 10 May, 1821, Lunenburg; mar. 18 Oct. 1842, Shirley, George Page, b. 19 Oct. 1818, Boston, Mass, son of Dennis and Sarah (Jenerson) of Shirley. She died 13 July, 1868, at Boston. Farmer.
873. 7. MARRETTE⁶, born 20 Aug. 1824, Lunenburg; m. 16 Mar. 1843, L., James Arrington, b. 6 Oct. 1822, Lynn, Mass., son of Loadman and Elizabeth-Hemenway Alley of Lynn. Mechanic. Res. Leominster, Lunenburg and Shirley, Mass., and Brattleboro, Vt.   1870, *Lynn, Mass.*

Children:

874.   1. Mary-Catharine⁶, born 7 Aug. 1843, Lunenburg; died 15 Dec. 1848, Lynn, Mass.
875.   2. James⁶, b. 13 Nov. 1844, Lynn, Mass.
876.   3. Charles-Loadman⁶, b. 23 Sept. 1850, Leominster, Mass.
877.   4. Benjamin-Franklin⁶, b. 6 July, 1856,   "
878.   5. Stephen-Melvin⁶, b. 30 Mar. 1860, Lynn, Mass.

879. 8. CHARLES-EDWIN⁶, b. 29 May, 1826, Lunenburg; married, Pepperell, Mass. 22 Dec. 1853, Mary-Elizabeth Smith, born 6 Oct. 1831, Littleton, Mass., dau. of Samuel and Eunice (Hoar of Lincoln, Mass., see chart v.)
   1870, res. *Williamsport, Pa.*
880. 9. LUCY-ANN⁶, b. 12 Sept. 1828, Lunenburg; m. 30 Nov. 1852, at L., Albert Adams, b. 6 Mar. 1830, L., son of Edward-Gary and Martha (Spaulding) of L. Mechanic.   1872, res. *Shirley, Mass.*

Children:

881.   1. Mary-Eliza⁶, b. 28 Sept. 1853, Lunenburg.
882.   2. Edward-Gary⁶, b. 11 Aug. 1860, L.
883.   3. Charles-Albert⁶, b. 5 Oct. 1862, L.
884.   4. Nellie-Alberta⁶, b. 1 May, 1865, Shirley.
885.   5. Florence-Luella⁶, b. 25 July, 1869,

886. 10. JOSEPH-HARTWELL⁶, b. 21 Feb. 1831, Lunenburg, Mass.; married, but we have not the name of his wife. He is a piano forte maker.
   Res. 1872, *Boston, Mass.*

Children:

887.   1. Frank-L⁷.
888.   2. Arthur-D⁷.

889. NANCY⁷, [574] (*Polly⁶* (*Farwell*) Hartwell, *Daniel⁵*, *Daniel⁴*, *Joseph³*,

Joseph⁵, Henry¹,) b. about 1796, Lunenburg, Mass.; married Samuel **DAVIS**, of Holden, Mass.   Res. *Ware, Mass.*

Child :

890.   JOSEPH⁸.   1870, res. Brimfield, Mass.

891. JOSEPH⁷, [575], (*Polly⁶ (Farwell)* **Hartwell**, *Daniel⁵, Daniel⁴, Joseph³, Joseph², Henry¹*,) b. 19 Aug. 1798, Lunenburg, Mass.; married, 1821, Clarissa Read, of Boston, Mass., born, Weymouth, Mass., dau. of John and Rachel (Clark). She died 4 June, 1862, Ware. He married 2d, East Brookfield, Mass., 9 Dec. 1863, Martha-Maria (Bean) widow of John-N. Doan, b. Waldoboro, Me., dau. of Charles and Betsey (Monson).   Res. *Ware, Mass.*

Children :

892.   1. DR. JOHN⁸, b. 23 Jan. 1822, Bolton, Mass.; married Pamelia-C. Batchelor, of Readfield, Me., born there. He died 22 August, 1855, at Ware, Mass.

Children :

893.   1. Frederick-S⁹.
894.   2. Mary-B⁹.
895.   3. Pamelia-C⁹.

896.   2. JOSEPH-W.⁸, b. 21 Sept. 1823, Bolton, Mass.; married Alice-D. Clark, of Ware, Mass., b. Barnard, Vt. He died 27 June, 1859, South Bend, Ind. s.p.

897.   3. SILAS⁸, b. 15 Apr. 1825, Bolton; d. 4 Nov. 1826, Ware.
898.   4. SILAS-M.⁸, b. 30 July, 1827, Ware; d. 25 May, 1830.
899.   5. CLARA⁸, b. 10 Apr. 1830, Ware; married Dr. Ebenezer-Coolidge **Richardson**, of Ware, b. 25 Apr. 1820, Townsend, Mass., son of Samuel and Mary (Kidder) of Watertown, Mass., afterwards of Peterborough, N. H., and finally of Watertown. Dr. Richardson grad. H. U. in 1842; settled at Ware where he was residing in 1872. He was enrollment officer of Ninth Dist.

Children, all born in Ware, Mass.:

900.   1. Maria-Anita⁹, b. 4 Feb. 1849.
901.   2. Carrie-Virginia⁹, b. 19 Sept. 1852.
902.   3. Harriet-Gardner⁹, b. 3 Nov. 1854.
903.   4. Charlotte-Houghton⁹, b. 27 March, 1857.
904.   5. Martha-Reed⁹, b. 11 July, 1861.
905.   6. Edward-Coolidge⁹, b. 2 July, 1870.

906. DORCAS⁷, [581] (*Daniel⁶, Daniel⁵, Daniel⁴, Joseph³, Joseph², Henry¹*,) b. 13 Dec. 1804, Fitchburg, Mass.; married at Fitchburg, Mass., 26 Jan. 1826, Nathaniel-Seaver **BOUTELLE**, b. 6 Nov. 1800, F., s. of Nathaniel and Polly (Hill) of F. He died 26 Oct. 1868, at Fitchburg, Mass. Farmer.

She resides, 1878, *Ashby, Mass.*

Children all born in Fitchburg, except the first two :

907. 1. CHARLES-AUGUSTUS⁹, b. 26 Nov. 1826, Northfield, Mass.; died at St. Louis, Mo., 4 March, 1850.
908. 2. GEORGE-FARWELL⁹, b. 5 Feb. 1829, Northfield; died 22 Dec. 1831, Fitchburg, Mass.
909. 3. ABBY-MARSHALL⁹, b. 21 Dec. 1832 ; died 19 Jan. 1888, Fitchburg.
910. 4. NATHANIEL-GEORGE⁹, b. 15 July, 1836 ; d. 17 Jan. 1852, at Fitchburg.
911. 5. { MARY-HILL⁹, b. 27 Feb. 1840 ; died 16 Sept. 1840, F.
912. 6. } DORCAS-WETHERBEE⁹, b. 27 Feb. 1840 ; m. Fitchburg, 15 Apr. 1858, Joseph-Lorin Piper, b. 16 Nov. 1832, Greenland, N. H., s. of Mirrick and Abigail (Johnson) of Stratham, N. H. Mr. Piper is a member of the School Board. Printer. Res. Fitchburg, and 1878, *Ashby, Mass.*

Children born in Fitchburg, except the youngest :

913. 1. Charles-Boutelle⁹, b. 21 March, 1859 ; died 16 Nov. 1859, Fitchburg.
914. 2. Marcia-Farwell⁹, b. 13 Aug. 1860 ; d. 1 Dec. 1869, F.
915. 3. Nathaniel-Merrick⁹, b. 25 Sept. 1862 ; d. 5 Oct. 1862, F.
916. 4. Frederick-Joseph⁹, b. 13 Jan. 1864.
917. 5. Abbie-Dora⁹, b. 6 Nov. 1868.
918. 6. George-Maurice⁹, b. 28 Feb. 1871.
919. 7. John-Johnson⁹, b. 21 May, 1873.
920. 8. Sidney-Richard⁹, b. 24 May, 1878, Ashby, Mass.

921. 7. REBECCA-EMILY⁸, b. 4 May, 1842, Fitchburg, Mass.; m. Fitchburg, 3 Oct. 1868, Henry-Francis Piper, b. 25 March, 1843, son of Merrick and Abigail (Johnson) of Stratham, Rockingham Co., N. H. Printer. Has been editor of the *Fitchburg Reveille*.   1878, *Fitchburg, Mass.*

Children born in Fitchburg :

922. 1. Mary-Boutelle⁹, b. 17 July, 1871.
923. 2. Ruth-Marston⁹, b. 30 Nov. 1873.
924. 3. Henry-Lyman⁹, b. 12 June, 1877.

925. 8. FRANK-LYMAN⁸, b. 21 Jan. 1846, Fitchburg, Mass.; died 1 Feb. 1877, Fitchburg ; married Fitchburg, 9 Jan. 1873, Frances-Ellen Upton, b. at F. 16 Sept. 1846, dau. of Warren-C. and Ellen M. (———) of F. Printer.
    She res. 1878, *Fitchburg, Mass.*

Children :

926. 1. Ralph-Upton⁹, b. 16 Jan. 1875, Fitchburg.
927. 2. Amy-Farwell⁹, b. 2 Aug. 1876,   ""

928. LYMAN⁷, [583] (*Daniel⁶, Daniel⁵, Daniel⁴, Joseph³, Joseph², Henry¹,*) b. 7 Sept. 1811, Fitchburg, Mass.; m. Southboro, Mass. Elizabeth-Anna Adams, b. 1 Sept. 1815, S., dau. of Jasper and Jerusha (Sibley) of S.

Mr. Farwell entered the Deerfield Academy with a view of preparing for a college course; but, before he was 16 years of age, concluded that mercantile were more congenial to his tastes than literary pursuits and might be made more lucrative. His guardian therefore obtained for him a situation in the store of Dexter, Fay & Co., Southboro, Mass., where he remained until he was twenty years of age. He was next employed as clerk with Levi Bartlett & Co., Boston, a firm in which Mr. B. was principal for nearly 60 years, and whose daughter married A. G. Farwell [955].

From 1833 he was partner with Col. Francis B. Fay in commission business at Boston till 1835, when his cousin, A. G. Farwell, joined him at St. Louis in forming a branch of Fay & Farwell's, of Boston, under the name of L. & A-G. Farwell & Co., their business at Boston being commission, and at St. Louis, both commission and on their own account.

Jan. 1, 1838, Hon. Thos. G. Cary, then just going out of business in the house of Perkins & Co., China merchants, joined them as special partner, which gave the firm a good capital for those times, and enabled them largely to extend their business.

When, in 1837, all the banks suspended specie payments, the United States Bank having previously closed its business at the termination of its charter, Mr. Farwell's firm passed through the financial ordeal by an arrangement with the lead dealers of Galena. In the autumn of 1841, when the "fiat" money which had been used by St. Louis merchants showed great depreciation the firm converted all its collections into pig-lead until the close of navigation to Galena, and after that, exchanged its bills receivable into Boston and New York exchange and advances on shipments to their Boston firm, most of the exchange being four months' bills of their Galena friends, who advanced money to the smelters to be paid at the price of lead the following spring.

Their piles of lead could not be sold until May, 1842, when Messrs. William Appleton & Co. took the whole of it at 8 1-4 cents and shipped it to Canton. In this way and through their Boston connection they were able to continue their business while so many mercantile firms failed. The firm of Corwith & Co., Galena, with whom they transacted their lead business, was also sustained by means of its connection with the firm of C. H. Rogers & Co. of N. Y.

In 1842 the firm of L. & A. G. Farwell & Co. took the agency of the St. Louis Sugar Refinery which was owned and managed by William H. Belcher, and gave up the agency of the New Orleans Refinery, which they had held for several years.

In 1843 A. G. Farwell returned to Boston, leaving Mr. F. alone in St. Louis, and in 1846 left the firm and established that of A. G. Farwell & Co. of Boston, which continued till his death in 1864.

On the 1st of Jan. 1848, commenced a third term of special partnership of five years each, the business in St. Louis being under the name of Farwell & Co. The business of the Sugar Refinery had grown so much that large buildings had been erected and so much capital absorbed that the firm had quit all business except that and the lead traffic with the Galena firm of Corwith & Co. and advances on shipments to the Boston firm.

Jan. 1, 1851, Page & Bacon, Bankers, furnished bills of exchange at four months in exchange for Belcher & Brothers notes, at same term, to enable them to dispense with agents, and soon reduced the balance of Farwell & Co., so that by the 1st of July of that year, with proceeds of sales of sugar at different cities on the Ohio and lakes the firm was paid in full.

In the mean time Mr. Farwell had returned to Boston and the partnership was dissolved. His health failed, and for a time he appeared to be in a decline which his friends thought must terminate his life. He, however, accepted an easy position proffered him by his old friend, C. H. Rogers, 80 Wall St., N. Y., under power of attorney for Rogers & Co. during Mr. R's absence abroad; sold his house in Boston and purchased No. 24 West 37th St., N. Y., where he remained till a year after the dissolution of Rogers & Co., 1 Jan. 1859. His health, by removal from the "labrador" winds of Boston to the milder climate of New York, had been restored.

Having established his oldest son in the hardware business in company with T. F. Cheritree at St. Paul, Mr. F. returned to Boston and purchased a house near the one he formerly owned where he resided till after the marriage of his youngest child, Mrs. T. F. Cheritree, when he removed to 28 Lefferts Place, Brooklyn, where he resided till his death, Jan 22, 1879.

Mr. Farwell was one of the most earnest friends of the Union cause, and one of the most liberal contributors of Boston to the fund for the benefit of the soldiers families in Boston and vicinity.

Children all born in St. Louis :

929.   1. FRANCIS-BALL⁸, b. 25 May, 1837 ; m. Mystic, Conn., 22 Feb. 1864, Mary-Mason Farnham, b. 27 July, 1841, Mystic, dau. of Calvin-B. and Louisa (Fish) of Westerly, R. I.

Early in 1859 Mr. Farwell left his clerkship in New York, and, with a fellow clerk, T. F. Cheritree, entered into partnership in the hardware trade at St. Paul, Minn., under the name of Cheritree and Farwell. This company continued till 1874, when the present firm was formed, consisting of himself and brother, George-Lyman⁸ [933]. He has been a director in the 2d National Bank of St. Paul, and is proprietor of a ranch of seven hundred acres in Texas.

He has resided in St. Louis, Mo., St. Paul, Minn., and,
1879, at Waresville, *Uvalda Co., Texas.*

Children :

930.   1. Lyman⁹, b. 19 Dec. 1864.
931.   2. Frank-Mason⁹, b. 9 June, 1868.

932.   2. HELEN-MARIA⁸, b. 20 Aug. 1839 ; died 9 April, 1840, at St. Louis, Mo.
933.   3. GEORGE-LYMAN⁸, b. 20 Oct. 1841, St. Louis, Mo.; married at St. Paul, Minn. 15 Feb. 1869, Sara-Gardner Wyer, b. 1 Dec. 1845, Cambridge, Mass., dau. of James Ingersol and Hannah-Hastings (Ladd) of Red Wing, Goodhue Co., Minn.

Mr. F. left Boston in 1861, and commenced business in St. Paul as wholesale grocer, sugar being a specialty. In this he continued til 1866, when he entered the firm of Cheritree & Farwell, and on the dissolution of that partnership in 1874 united with his brother, Francis-Ball⁹, [929] in forming the present firm of "Farwell Brothers," and is now, 1879, in charge of the business of the company at St. Paul. He has been an officer in the Board of Education at St. Paul, and director in the St. Paul Fire and Marine Insurance Co. Hardware merchant. Res. St. Louis, Mo., Boston and Fitchburg, Mass., New York City, and,

            1879, *St. Paul, Ramsey Co., Minn.*

Children:

934. 1. Sidney-Emerson⁹, b. 14 Apr. 1870, St. Paul, Minn.
935. 2. Arthur-George⁹, b. 28 April, 1872,   " "
936. 4. THOMAS-CARY⁹, b. 4 Feb. 1845; died 5 Dec. 1855, New York City.
937. 5. ELLEN⁹, b. 9 July, 1846; died 17 Dec. 1847, St. Louis, Mo.
938. 6. ALMIRA⁹, b. 2 March, 1849; married, Boston, 14 Sept. 1869, Theodore-Frelinghuysen **Cheritree,** b. 20 July, 1835, Greenville, Greene Co., N.Y., son of Sheldon and Olive (Botsford) of Oakhill, Greene Co., N.Y. Mr. C. left a position as clerk in New York City in 1859 and formed, with Francis-Ball⁹ Farwell, [929] a copartnership in the hardware business at St. Paul, Minn., called "Cheritree & Farwell"; continued there till 1867, when he took up his residence in New York as local or New York partner of the St. Paul firm, and so remained till its dissolution in 1874. He has since been New York agent for his brothers, hardware manufacturers, Oak Hill, N.Y., his office being at 97 Chambers St., N.Y.

  Res. St. Paul, Minn., New York City, and, since 1870, 28 Lefferts Place, Brooklyn, N.Y.

Child:

939. 1. Paul-Theodore⁹, b. 16 Sept. 1873, Brooklyn, N.Y.

940. DANIEL-GEORGE⁷, [584] (*Daniel⁶, Daniel⁵, Daniel⁴, Joseph³, Joseph²,   Henry¹,*) b. 10 July, 1815, Fitchburg, Mass.; died 19 Sept. 1850, St. Louis, Mo.; m. 19 Jan. 1849, Charlotte Maynard, b. 1 Jan. 1823, New York City, dau. of Daniel and Sarah (Beckwith) of Waterford, Conn. He was by trade a printer; was captain of the steamer Champlain plying between St. Louis and New Orleans for a number of years.

  Mrs. Farwell married 2d Theodore Laveille and resided, 1878, *Chateau Avenue, St. Louis, Mo.*

Child:

941. 1. LOUISA-CHARLES⁸, b. 26 July, 1850, St. Louis, Mo.; married there, 9 Oct.

1878, Charles-Carroll **Soule**, b. 1842, Duxbury Mass.; is partner in the firm of Little, Brown & Co. of Boston, Mass.   Res. 1879, *Boston, Mass.*

942. BETSEY⁷, [587] (*Levi⁶, Daniel⁵, Daniel⁴, Joseph³, Joseph², Henry¹,*) b. 5 Apr. 1804, Fitchburg, Mass.; died 28 Dec. 1870; married, at Fitchburg, 4 June, 1825, Abel **Baldwin**, b. 9 Feb. 1799, F.; died 4 Feb. 1849, Stoneham, Mass.
Res. *Boston, Mass.*

Children all born in Boston :

943.   1. CAROLINE-FARWELL⁸, b. 6 Oct. 1826 ; died 20 Aug. 1828, Sudbury, Worcester Co., Mass.
944.   2. HENRY-JACKSON⁸, b. 11 June, 1829; m. Boston, Mass., 4 Jan. 1851, Mary-Jane Tothill, of Cambridgeport, Mass.

Children all born in Boston :

945.   1. William-Henry⁹, b. 25 June, 1853.
946.   } 2. George-Edward⁹, b. 9 Sept. 1856.
947.   } 3. Frank⁹, b. 9 Sept. 1856.

948.   3. OTIS-LINCOLN⁸, b. 12 May, 1831; married at Stoneham, Mass. 11 Nov. 1853, Lydia-Maria Thompson, b. 3 July, 1833, at Saugus, Mass.
Res. *Lynn, Mass.*

Children all born at Lynn :

949.   1. Frank-Otis⁹, b. 25 Aug. 1854.
950.   2. Frederic-William⁹, b. 4 Oct. 1857.
951.   3. Emma-Caroline⁹, b. 24 Jan. 1859.
952.   4. Hattie-Florence⁹, b. 19 Aug. 1863.
953.   5. Edward-Lincoln⁹, b. 22 May, 1867.
954.   6. Mary-Bartlett⁹, b. 17 Nov. 1869.

955. ABEL-GOODRICH⁷, [591] (*Levi⁶, Daniel⁵, Daniel⁴, Joseph³, Joseph², Henry¹,*) b. 6 Feb. 1813, Fitchburg, Mass.; died 26 Dec. 1868, at Boston, and was buried in Mount Auburn Cemetery; was married in Boston, 12 Dec. 1844, to Susan-Walker Bartlett, born 4 Aug. 1822, Boston, Mass., dau. of Levi and Clarissa (Walker) of Boston. Mr. Farwell was a merchant in West India goods. For additional mercantile interests see Serial No. 928. Mrs. Farwell resides, 1878, No. 16 Beacon St., Boston, Mass.

Children :

956.   1. CLARA-WALKER⁸, b. 16 Feb. 1846, Boston, Mass.; died there, 28 Aug. 1847.
957.   2. CHARLES-HALLET⁸, b. 26 Oct. 1849, Boston; died 30 March, 1850, Boston.

958. DEXTER⁷, [592] (*Levi⁶, Daniel⁵, Daniel⁴, Joseph³, Joseph², Henry¹,*) b. 27 Jan. 1815, Fitchburg ; married, Milford, N.H., 2 Sept. 1844, Olive Shaw, b. 6 June,

1814, Milford, dau. of William and Asenath (Hopkins) of Milford. Mrs. Farwell died in Fitchburg and was buried there. Farmer. Res. *Fitchburg, Mass.*

Children born in Fitchburg were :

959. 1. CLARA-ASENATH⁸, b. 14 Dec. 1847 ; married, in Worcester, Mass., 8 Dec. 1868, by Rev. R. R. Shippen, Oscar-Ferdinand **Woodbury**, of Fitchburg, Mass., born there, 14 Feb. 1842. Res. *Fitchburg, Mass.*
960. 2. LEVI-ASA⁸, b. 23 Sept. 1854, at Amherst, Hillsboro Co., N.H.
1874, Res. *Fitchburg, Mass.*

961. ASA⁷, [593] (*Levi⁶, Daniel⁵, Daniel⁴, Joseph³, Joseph², Henry¹,*) b. 29 March, 1817, Fitchburg; married, 6 March, 1860, Fitchburg, Mass., Marcia Piper, b. 7 Aug. 1840, Stratham, N.H., dau. of Merrick and Abigail (Johnson) of that place. 1874, commission merchant, 1 Pemberton Square, Boston.
Res. 42 *Worcester St., Boston, Mass.*

Children born in Boston :

962. 1. LOUISE-MARSTON⁸, b. 15 Jan. 1861.
963. 2. WALTER-MERRICK⁸, b. 22 Jan. 1863.
964. 3. EDITH-CARTER⁸, b. 11 Nov. 1866.

965. HENRY-NEWTON⁷, [594] (*Levi⁶, Daniel⁵, Daniel⁴, Joseph³, Joseph², Henry¹,*) b. 12 Jan. 1822, Fitchburg ; married 24 July, 1852, *Boston rec.*, Clara Richardson, of Cambridgeport, Mass. 1874, commission merchant, 1 Pemberton Square.
Res. 86 Mt. Vernon St., Boston, Mass.

Children :

966. 1. CHARLOTTE⁸.
967. 2. HENRY⁸, deceased.
968. 3. FRANK.
969. 4. FREDERIC.
969ᵃ. 5. Son, name not given.

970. SAMUEL⁷, [597] (*Anna⁶* (Farwell) **Carter,** (*Daniel⁵, Daniel⁴, Joseph³, Joseph², Henry¹,*) b. 1 Nov. 1804, Fitchburg, Mass.; where he died 27 Nov. 1876,; married there, 18 May, 1828, Martha Litch of F., dau. of Thomas and Hannah. She died at Fitchburg, 16 Feb. 1851, aged 41. He married 2d, 1 Sept. 1852, Elvira-A. Lancaster, of Boston, Mass.

Children :

971. 1. EDMUND-THOMAS⁸, b. 18 Jan. 1830, Fitchburg.
972. 2. HANNAH-ANN⁸, b. 12 Dec. 1831, F.; died at Burlington, Vt., 1 Apr. 1858, s.p.; married 2 Jan. 1856, John-J. Dadman, of Fitchburg.

973. ANNA-FARWELL⁷, [601] (*Anna⁶* (Farwell) Carter, *Daniel⁵, Daniel⁴, Joseph³, Joseph², Henry¹,*) b. 13 Sept. 1813, Fitchburg, Mass.; m. Leominster, Mass.,

2 May, 1836, Charles-Pinckney DEAN, of Fitchburg, b. 26 Jan. 1807, Westboro, Mass., son of Capt. Francis of Dedham, Mass., and Hannah (Morse) of Canton, Mass. Farmer.   Res. *Fitchburg, Mass.*

Children :

974.   1. MARTHA-LOUISA⁸, b. 11 June, 1837, Fitchburg; m. there 4 Feb. 1864, John Elmer Jones, of Keene, N. H., son of John-Elmer and Cynthia (Lincoln) of Leominster.

   Children all born in Keene, N.H. :

975.   1. Anna-Lincoln⁹, b. 27 Dec. 1864.
976.   2. Arthur-Dean⁹, b. 9 March, 1867.
977.   3. George-Laflin⁹, b. 3 Sept. 1871.

978.   2. SYBIL-AUGUSTA⁸, b. 3 Feb. 1839, F.; married Fitchburg, 30 Aug. 1866, Charles-Louis **Fairbanks**, of F., b. Ashburnham, Mass., 12 Dec. 1839, son of Seth-Phelps and Almira (——) of Jaffrey, N. H. Coal dealer.
                          Res. *Fitchburg, Mass.*

   Children of whom the two latter are regarded as their own and bear their name ;

979.   1. Hattie-Abbie⁹, b. in Fitchburg, Mass., 12 Sept. 1870; died 15 Jan. 1871.
979ᵃ.   Effie Dean, b. 15 Apr. 1873; died at Shelburn Falls while on a visit, 12 Aug. 1875.
979ᵇ.   Robert-Frank, b. 16 Jan. 1875.

980.   3. ABBY-ELIZA⁸, b. 26 Oct. 1840, Fitchburg; died 22 Sept. 1841.
981.   4. ABBY-CAROLINE⁸, b. 14 Apr. 1842; married as 2d wife, 9 Aug. 1865, at Fitchburg, James-W. **Laflin**, of New York City ; born Lee, Mass., 18 Feb. 1824, son of Winthrop and Fanny (Loomis). He died at Salenas, Cal., 27 Feb. 1877. Banker.

982.   5. NATHANIEL-CARTER⁸, b. 14 Sept. 1844; married at Williamsport, Penn., 16 July, 1872, Kate-Helen Klett, b. 18 Feb. 1850, Philadelphia, Penn., dau. of Andrew and Helen M. (Morton,) of Williamsport.

   Mr. Dean enlisted in Fitchburg as volunteer in the 27th Mass. Reg., 19 July, 1861; was wounded and discharged; "re-enlisted for another term." He was wounded at the battle of Roanoke in his right arm, and at the battle of Coal Harbor, 1 June, 1864, in left leg; was mustered out of service 30 Aug. 1864, having served his country three years.
                          Res. *Mansfield, Penn.*

   Children ;

983.   1. Kate-Marion⁹, b. 7 Sept. 1873, at Burgettstown, Washington Co., Penn.
984.   2. Effie-Augusta⁹ b. 23 Dec. 1875, Mansfield Alleghany Co., Penn. ; died 11 May, 1876.

985.   6. CHARLES-HENRY⁸, b. 5 Dec. 1846; died 16 May, 1848.

986. 7. GEORGE-MORSE⁸, b. 29 Nov. 1848; was killed by an accident on a railroad in Williamsport, Penn.
987. 8. ELVIRA-ANN⁸, b. 23 Aug. 1850; died 30 March, 1854.
988. 9. CHARLES-EDWARD⁸, b. 17 May, 1853.

989. THOMAS⁷, [602] (*Anna⁶* (Farwell) Carter, *Daniel⁵*, *Daniel⁴*, *Joseph³*, *Joseph²*, *Henry¹*,) b. 13 June, 1815, Fitchburg, Mass.; married 21 June, 1838, Mary Phelps, b. 14 Sept. 1813, Lancaster, Mass., dau. of Robert and Anna (Todd) of L. Farmer.

Children;

990. 1. MARY-ANN⁸, b. in Lancaster, 3 Apr. 1839; married in Fitchburg, 5 July, 1863, Lucius Carter, of Leominster, b. 8 July, 1841, son of Frank and Nancy (Chace) of L.

Children;

991.   1. Wilfred⁹, b. 22 Feb. 1865, Leominster.
992.   2. Herbert-Franklin⁹, b. 25 Feb. 1869, L.
993.   3. Carrie-Addele⁹, b. 4 Feb. 1871, L.
994. 2. CORNELIA⁸, b. 3 Sept. 1840.
995. 3. SYBIL-EUNICE⁸, b. 12 Nov. 1846; married, as 2d wife, in Leominster, 28 Nov. 1877, Wooster-Ferdinand Dodge, of L., b. 28 March, 1841, son of Stephen of L., and Elvira (Foster) of Ashburnham, Mass. Box maker.
996. 4. ELIZA-ADDELLE⁸, b. 28 Aug. 1849, died 27 Apr. 1859.
997. 5. IDA-ELIZABETH⁸, b. 12 June, 1853, died 7 March, 1855.
998. 6. SAMUEL-EDMUND⁸, b. 17 Feb. 1856, died Sept. 1856.

999. CHARLES-FARWELL⁷, [605] (*Anna⁶* Farwell) Carter. *Daniel⁵*, *Daniel⁴*, *Joseph³*, *Joseph²*, *Henry¹*,) b. 8 June, 1827, married in Leominster, Mass., 25 Apr. 1861, Harriet-May, daughter of William and Harriet (Derby) of L. Farmer.

Children:

1000. 1. FREDERIC⁸, b. 25 Jan. 1862, Leominster.
1001. 2. ALBERT-W⁸., b. 28 Oct. 1865,   "
1002. 3. GEORGE-DENNIS⁸, b. 8 Oct. 1867. "

1003. ERASTUS-ALEXANDER⁷, [607] (*Joel⁶*, *Bethiah⁵* (Farwell) Holton, *William⁴*, *Isaac³*, *Joseph²*, *Henry¹*,) b. at Westminster, Vt. 9 Sept. 1803; died there, 30 Aug. 1849; married at W., 2 Sept. 1834, Hannah-Brainerd May, b. 4 Aug. 1807, daughter of Huntington and Clarissa (Brainerd) of Putney, Vt.

Mrs. H. m. 2d, Hiram Phelps of Williston, Vt.

From an obituary by his pastor, Rev. W. H. Gilbert, we extract the following: Mr. Holton "possessed remarkable energy, a frank and generous disposition and unbounded integrity. His dwelling was the abode of hospitality. He was a host in support of every cause which he espoused. * * * Any delineation of his excellencies is not needed to render his memory precious to those who knew and loved him. It is for the honor of Divine grace that we would speak of what he was and what he did. In his decease, a bereaved family are made to mourn a most judicious and affectionate husband and father; the church and society, in which he was a pillar, weep, for 'a great man is fallen.' The friends of every noble enterprise in the town and county grieve for the loss of a most efficient helper. Though in the midst of many schemes of useful enterprise, he met death with composure, maintaining a humble reliance on the merits of Christ. * * * Perhaps there was no scheme of benevolence in which the deceased enlisted with greater energy than the temperance reform. In efforts to promote this cause, he has long stood among the first in our commonwealth, and has cheerfully allowed it to tax both his time and purse to an extent unsurpassed and perhaps unequaled in the county. * * * He has fallen at his post. 'He rests from his labors, and his works do follow him.'" [See Winslow Memorial, 3820.]

Children born in Westminster, Vt.:

1004. 1. Capt. EDWARD-ALEXANDER⁶, b. 28 Aug. 1835; married at Alburgh, Vt., 15 Sept. 1863, Kate-Matilda Chase, b. 12 July, 1841, Champlain, N. Y., dau. of Rev. John and Roxy (Shute) of Alburgh.

Capt. Holton volunteered for the maintenance of the Union 18 April, 1861; was mustered into service for three months, 2d May following, and assigned to Co. H, First Vermont Infantry; was discharged at Brattleboro, 16 Aug. 1861; reenlisted 28th of same month for three years; was appointed, 15th Oct. 1st Sergeant Co I, Sixth Vt. Vols.; distinguished himself at the battle of Lee's Mills, by rescuing, under most hazardous circumstances, the colors, after the bearer had been shot down, and received the highest commendations of his Brig. Gen. for his bravery, and was therefor promoted to the 2d Lieutenancy; promoted to 1st Lieutenant 15 June, 1863; and to Captaincy of Co. F, 16 May, 1864. He participated in seventeen battles; was wounded in the battle of the Wilderness, 5 May, 1864, about one hour after the death of his brother, David-May [1007]; and was honorably discharged, on report of Board of Surgeons, for disability, 17 Aug. 1864, and still carries the wounding bullet too near an important artery for safe extraction. The compilers of this book think he should apply for a pension. [Fuller interesting details in Winslow Memorial [3821]. Res. *Williston, Vt.*

Children born in Lee, Mass.:

1005. 1. Kate-May⁶, b. 4 May, 1865.
1006. 2. Charles-Edward⁶, b. 18 Dec. 1868.

1007. 2. Serg. DAVID-MAY⁶, b. 1 Oct. 1836, at Westminster, Vt.; was killed 5 May 1864, in the battle of the Wilderness; graduated at Williams' College in 1859; was classmate and friend of Rev. Stephen H. Tyng, Jr., and was intending to enter the Episcopal ministry, when the call to fight seemed for the time more imperative than the call to preach, and though nothing could be more foreign to his tastes and habits, he enlisted in the same regiment as his brother, Edward-Alexander [1004], Sixth Vermont Infantry, and bravely bore his part in its battles, receiving special commendations of his Colonel as having at the battle of Fredericksburg "behaved splendidly."

The evening before his death, he wrote to his mother, "I am blessed with such good health and strength that I can endure and suffer much, if need be. I wish you to dismiss all anxiety on my account, especially as I have none. I hope to live; but I trust I am not afraid to die; in any event I am determined to do my whole duty and leave the result to Him who doeth all things well."

He fell on the first day of the battle, being shot through the head with a percussion ball, and dying instantly. He was a man of fine abilities and excellent scholarship, his talents solid rather than showy. His amiable disposition, singularly modest demeanor, and agreeable manners, secured the affection of all who knew him; and though he sleeps in an unknown and nameless grave, there will be a lasting monument to his memory in the hearts of many who

"Knew him but to love him,
And named him but to praise."

ermont Record.]

1008.   3. CATHARINE-MAY⁵, b. 25 Feb. 1838; died 30 Aug. 1841, Westminster, Vt.
1009.   4. JOEL-HUNTINGTON⁵, b. 15 Nov. 1841; m. Westminster, 29 Oct. 1863, Emma-Jane Diggins, b. 26 Sept. 1839, dau. of Sylvester and Amanda-Malvina (Farnum) of W. He enlisted September 26, 1862, in 12th Vt. regiment for nine months, and was discharged at Brattleboro, July, 1863. In 1864 went into the silver plating and saddlery hardware business at Derby Line, Vt., where he remained till 1871, when he removed to Burlington, Vt., forming a co-partnership with Edwin-L. Ripley in the wholesale and retail builders and saddlery hardware business.

1879, *Burlington, Vt.*

Children:

1010.   1. Frank-Erastus⁶, b. July, 1864, Derby Line, Vt.; died there 27 March, 1865.
1011.   2. Harry-Sylvester⁶, b. 23 June, 1869, Derby Line.
1012.   3. Susie⁶, b. 11 Oct. 1875, Burlington, Vt.

1013. MINERVA⁵, [608] (*Joel⁴*, *Bethiah³* (Farwell) Holton, *William⁴*, *Joseph³*, *Joseph²*, *Henry¹*,) b. 18 Oct. 1805, Westminster, Vt.; died 30 June, 1875, at Hillsgrove, McDonough Co., Ill.; married at Westminster, 31 Dec. 1829, Charles-Grandison GILCHRIST, born Walpole, N. H., 27 May, 1802, son of Samuel of Lunenburg,

Mass., and Betsey (Allen) of Pomfret, Conn. They resided at Saxton's River till 1837, when they removed to Hillsgrove, which has since been the family residence.

Res. *Hillsgrove, McDonough Co., Ill.*

Children:

1014. 1. HELEN-MINERVA⁶, b. 23 Oct. 1831, Saxton's River, Vt.; m. Hillsgrove, Ill. 23 May, 1850, Leonard-Thompson **Ferris**, M. D., b. 4 Jan. 1817, N. Y., son of Stephen and Eunice (Beebe) of Fountain Green, Ill. Dr. Ferris has a large and lucrative practice at Fountain Green. where they have resided since their marriage.

Children all born at Fountain Green :

1015.   1. Fidelia-Miriam⁷, b. 17 Mar. 1851; died 10 Dec. 1853, at Fountain Green, Hancock Co., Ill.
1016.   2. Charles-Leonard⁷, b. 26 Dec. 1853 ; grad. at the Lutheran College, Carthage, Hancock Co., Ill., May, 1876, and at Rush Medical College, Chicago, 26 Feb. 1878. Is now in practice with his father at Fountain Green.
1017.   3. Lelia-Francina⁷, b. 14 July, 1856; has been a student in the college at Carthage three years.
1018.   4. Delia-Helen⁷, b. 21 Nov. 1858; died at F. G., 25 June, 1862.
1019.   5. Alice-Lavinia⁷, b. 13 Nov. 1862 ; 1879, student in Carthage College, Ill.
1020.   6. John-Milton⁷, b. 20 Apr. 1865; d. 7 Oct. 1866, F. G.
1021.   7. Ulysses-Stephen⁷, b. 5 Sept. 1868.
1022.   8. Ralph-Willie⁷, b. 14 Mar. 1871.
1023.   9. Mary-Helen⁷, b. 25 Sept. 1873.
1024.   10. Hiram-Gano⁷, b. 16 Aug. 1876.

1025. 2. Gen. CHARLES-ALLEN⁶, b. 13 Feb. 1834, Saxton's River, Vt. ; m. Fountain Green, Hancock Co. Ill., 1 Oct. 1857, Lucy-Ellen Walker, b. 30 March, 1835, McDonough Co., Ill., dau. of Joseph Gilmer, of Rockbridge Co., Va., and Susan-Pope (Bell) of Richmond Co., Va.

Gen. Gilchrist was educated at the College of the City of N. Y. ; pursued the business of civil engineer and surveyor in Illinois and Iowa till the breaking out of the war of the rebellion, when he enlisted in defense of the Union and rendered essential service in the army of the Tennessee.

By successive promotions he rose from the rank of private to that of Brev. Brig. General.

After the close of the war he resumed his old occupation, and was employed in laying out several of the Western railroads. In 1878 was engaged on a projected railroad running out from Fort Madison, Iowa. Since 1874, has also been in the lumber business, owning an extensive lumber yard in Carthage, Ill.

He is distinguished for zeal, energy and efficiency in all his enterprises.

For further details see Winslow Memorial [3841].

Res. *Carthage, Hancock Co., Ill.*

Children :

1026. 1. Joseph-Gilmer⁹, b. 17 Aug. 1858, Macomb, McDonough Co., Ill. ; 1878, was a junior in Carthage College.
1027. 2. Minerva-Frances⁹, b. 25 Nov. 1859, Hillsgrove, Ill. 1878, a junior in Carthage College.
1028. 3. Charles-Van Brugh⁹, b. 30 Dec. 1861, Hilsgrove, died there 21 Sept. 1864.
1029. 4. Magnolia-Vick⁹, b. 6 May, 1864, Vicksburg, Miss.
1030. 5. Ellen-Ferris⁹, b. 24 Aug. 1866, Fountain Green, Ill.
1031. 6. Robert-Allen⁹, b. 30 Oct. 1868, Carthage, Hancock Co., Ill.
1032. 7. Edward-Percy⁹, b. 3 June, 1872,   "   "   "
1033. 8. Anna-Mary⁹, b. 29 July, 1875,   "   "   "

1034. 3. DAVID-VAN BRUGH⁸, b. 11 Apr. 1836, Westminster, Vt.; m. Pulaski, Ill., 4 Dec. 1862, Sallie Robinson, b. 10 Feb. 1839, Oldtown, Green Co., Ohio, dau. of Henson and Sarah-Ann (Reed) of O. Farmer.

Res. *Hillsgrove, Tennessee Township, McDonough Co., Ill.*

Their children, all born at Hillsgrove, are :

1035. 1. Helen-Elva⁹, b. 4 Oct. 1863.
1036. 2. Grace-Gertrude⁹, b. 23 June, 1865.
1037. 3. Ivan-Erastus⁹, b. 7 July, 1867.
1038. 4. Charles-Van Brugh⁹, b. 1 Feb. 1869.

1039. 4. ERASTUS-HOLTON⁸, b. 8 Sept. 1839, Hillsgrove; died there, 24 Oct. 1851, from the kick of a horse.

1040. 5. Capt. EDWARD-MAY⁸, b. 18 Jan. 1846, Westminster; m. at St. Mary's, Ill., 25 Dec. 1866, Mary-Jane Botts, b. 10 Apr. 1846, St. Mary's, dau. of William-Oscar and Mary-Ann (Darnell) of St. Mary's.

Capt. Gilchrist enlisted in the 71st Ill. Vol. Inf. 16 July, 1862, for three months; was "high" private in the front rank, being only second in height, though only sixteen years of age.

March, 1864, he received an appointment from Adj't. Gen. Thomas as Second Lieutenant in the 12th La. Vol. Infantry, afterwards the 50th U. S. Col. Infantry, and was assigned to Co. H. In Feb. 1865, was promoted to First Lieutenant, and in Nov. 1865, to the Captaincy in the same Company, which position he held till 20 March, 1866.

When camped at Vicksburg on May 5, 1864*, he was taken sick with typhoid fever, and on the 7th was sent to the Marine Hospital. On the 9th he was laid out on a stretcher, his measure taken for a coffin, and word sent to his brother Charles-A. [1025], who was then Colonel of the

---

*The date of the death of his cousin, David-May⁸ Holton; see Nos. 1004 and 1007.

CHART XVIII.—MIRIAM⁴ WINSLOW—BENJAMIN⁵ PARSONS.
19 Apr. 1779.

MIRIAM⁴ WINSLOW, [3303] b. 6 May, 1758; d. 8 March, 1835; dau. of Thomas, of Harwich, Mass. —— BENJAMIN⁵ PARSONS, b. 5 Jan. 1753, at Palmer, Mass.; d. 8 Oct. 1812, at Moriah, N.Y., aged 59. Rem. from Swanzey to Westminster, thence to Bockingham, Vt., thence to Moriah, in 1810. Enl. for the one campaign with Arnold, 1775; was at the battle of Quebec. Suffered so much in the expedition from hunger, small-pox, etc. that his health was undermined, and he died of lockjaw 11 days after an accident.

1802.—Joel Holton.
See Holton Rs. Ch. 1
1. Benjamin, d. 1789.
2. David, b. at Swanzey; d. in infancy.

Phebe, [3814] b. 1780.

8. Miriam, [3302] b. 30 Dec. 1783; at Swanzey, N.H.; d. July, 1866, at Quitman, Miss.

28 Aug. 1810.—Isaac Stoddard, b. 29 Oct. 1776, at Westminster; d. 1846, at Stanstead, Q. W. Farmer. Res. Westminster, Vt.

2. Ruth-Emily, b. 1813–d. 1814.
3. Adelia-Parsons, [3909] b. 1811, Charles-Heman Swift, M.D., Pres. of Bank; 9 years Mayor of Sacramento City, Cal. 1863 to 1879.
4. John-Burnell, [3-99] b. 1816; d. 1844; m. 1841, Maria-F. Parkhill, b. 1820; had one child.
6. Jane-Miriam, [3899] b. 1821, Montreal; adopted nephew Francis-W. Paige, of St. Louis, b. 1830.
8. Jas-Monroe, [3994] Confederate officer; m. 1846, Christiana P. Blakeney, of Ala.
Francis-Paige, [3999] b. 1849; adopted by Jane-Miriam; m. 1870, Mary-E. Kellogg, d. 1852

1860.—Chas-Baker Durden, b. 1830; d. 1859.
1. Florence-Adelia, b. 1 Dec. 1859.
2. Minnie, [3872]; m. 18-71, Zachary-Taylor Therrell. Had 2 ch. Zoe & Chs-Baker.
3. Ellen-Baker, b. 1863.
4. Jennie-Paige, b. 1867.

5. David, b. Swanzey; d. m. 3 Aug. 1791; m. 1814, Sophia Lovell. [See Ch. XIX.]
6. Philander, [3901] m. 1814, Sophia Lovell. [See Ch. XIX.]
8. Abigail, [4005] m. 1819, Elijah Carpenter. [See Chart XIX.]

1827.——Alvin Fisher, [3908] of Bristol, Vt.; artist; deceased.
1. Martha, [3908] b. 1810.
1. Martha-Jane, [3908] b. 1828; m. 3. Emily-Augusta, [3-976] b. 1832, N.Y., 1843, in N.Y., John-Langford Smith, b. 1828, Residence, Brooklyn.
  1. Francis-Edgar, b. 1850.
  2. Henry-Lovell, b. 1853; d. 1857, of dropsy of the brain.
  3. Lillie-Mary, b. 1853.
  4. Ada-Granites, b. 9 Feb. 1860.
  5. Viva-Adela, b. 1870.

4. Chas-Young, b. 1841; d. 1858.
5. Margaret-McIver, [3894] m. Edgar Mills, b. 1827.
1. Wm-Carey, b. 1837; d. 1858.
3. Frances-Ella, [3870] b. 1839; m. 1865, Isaac Lohman, b. 1834, Bavaria.
  1. Jennie-Adelia, b. 5 May, 1864.
  2. Fannie-Swift, b. 1866.
  3. Edw-Hull, b. 68.

7. Phila, [3902] b. 18 Aug. 1791; d. Aug. 1791; d.
8. Aug. 1807.——Horace Lovell, of New Haven, Vermont, son of John; died Bartonville, Vermont.

1831.——Joel-B. Parsons.
3. Phila, [3905] b. 1814, m. Alvah Ward. Res. Little Falls, N.Y.

1. William-Edgar, b. 12 Nov. 1851, N.Y.
2. Emma-Frances, b. 13 Mar. 1853, N.Y.
3. Albert-Freeman, b. 22 Oct. 1854, N.Y.; d. 19 Jan. 1857, N.Y.
4. Frank, [3839] b. 1847; m. 1870, Martha McDonald. She d. 1874.
1. Jasper-McDonald, b. 18-71; d. 1874.
2. Florence-Martha, b. 18-74; d. 1874.

John Cordon.
2. Henry, d. N.Y.
3. Frances-Miriam, [3901] b. 1812, m. 2d, John Cordon.
2. Henry, d. N.Y.
3. Emily-Augusta, [3-976] b. 1832, N.Y., Rev. Gardiner-Spring Plumley.
1. David, b. 1857.
2. Chas-M., b. 1859.
b. 18-Henry, 69; d. 4 ms. b. 1859.

——David-Marie, [3-85] b. 1858; m. Albert-M. Magary.

4. Richard-Haight, b. 22 Sept. 1858, N.Y.; d. 3 June, 1860, N.J.
5. Elizabeth-Marriner, b. 1859, N.J.
6. Gardiner-Ladd, b. 14 Feb. 1862, N.J.
7. Alexander-Boisston, b. 21 Nov. 1863, N.J.
8. Emily-Louisa, b. 19 Aug. 1865, N.J.

1. Julius-Franklin, [3902] b. 1854, Albany; m. 1866, Anna Mattock, of St. Louis.
2. Frances-Eleanor, [3-923] b. 1857, Albany, N.Y.; m. 1854, Geo-Casey Kimbrough, b. 1830, in Ky. They res. St. Louis.
1. Frank-Parsons, b. 1856.
2. Emma-Katie, b. 1860.

9. Polly, [4050] b. 1797; d. 1876; m. 1819, Augustus Cook, 1792; d. 1874. [See Chart XIX.]
10. Elisha-Winslow, b. 1800; teacher.

5. Henry, [39-67] b. 1818; m. Caroline Turnbull
Solon-Winslow, [4005] b. 18-16; m. Susan d. Albert, 1818; b. 1862.
Res. Cal.
1. Harry.
2. Charles.
3. Frances.
4. Daughter.

3. Catherine-Augusta, [3998] b. 1840; m. 1880, at St. Louis, Henry-Lyman Foot, Res. St. Louis.
1. Maria-Laflin, b. 13 Feb. 1869.
2. Frances-Ellen, b. 18 June, 1865.
3. Geo-Berman, b. 1863.
All b. in St. Louis.

Two sons and one or two daughters. Their names and dates of birth are not known to us.

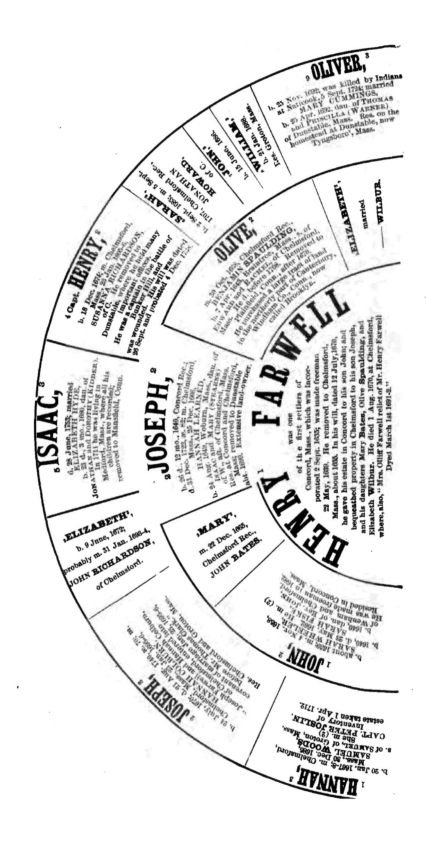

The Parsons Homestead.

In 1875, Dr. Holton visited the place where his grandfather Parsons lived before the breaking out of the Revolution, and after his return from service in that war. It is situated near the residence of his uncle, Aaron[4] Parsons, *i.e.*: forty-two rods directly north from Dea. Aaron's homestead, where are now depressions in the soil, showing the outline of the cellar and locating the house on a gentle rise sloping in every direction. When David[4] Parsons (1876 residing in Swanzey) was a boy, the remains of a tan-yard were to be seen a few rods distant, lying a little north of west of the homestead of Benjamin and Miriam[8] (Winslow) Parsons. A small stream, called "Parsons Rill," flowed past the tannery into Martin's brook, which empties into the south branch of the Ashuelot.

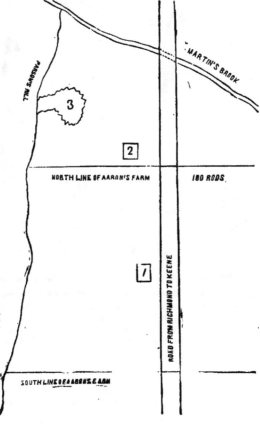

Map of the Homestead of Dea. Aaron[4] Parsons, Swanzey, N.H.

1. Residence of Dea. Aaron[4] Parsons, where died his father, Benjamin[3], of Kingston (alias The Elbows), now Palmer, Mass.; also of Josiah[3] and Josiah[4] Parsons; the birth-place of Amanda[6] (Parsons) **Stone** and of Marinda-Natalia[5] (Parsons) **Smith**, of Camden, N.Y.; of Silas[5] Parsons, a great mechanical genius; of Aaron[5], who removed to Williamstown, Vt., the father of Mrs. Norris and Mrs. Ellis, of the latter place.

   Here were born David[6] Parsons, of Swanzey, and Louisa-Ann[6] (Parsons) **Hammond**, whose daughter, Augusta-Louisa[7] (Hammond) **Chandler**, 1877, res. Tipton, Iowa.

2. The residence of Benjamin[5] Parsons, after his services in the Revolutionary war, till he removed to Chesterfield, N.H.

3. His tannery, by Parsons Rill, near Martin's Brook.

MAP OF A PART OF SCHOOL DISTRICTS 7 AND 8, OF
WESTMINSTER, WINDHAM CO., VERMONT.

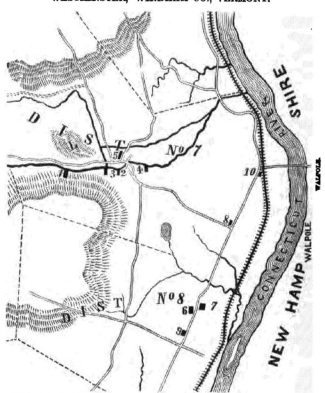

[*The Principal dwellings in the village are not indicated on this outline.*]

EXPLANATION OF THE FEW REFERENCE NUMBERS.

10. The Red School House, where HORACE WELLS, the discoverer of nitrous oxide as an anæsthetic, commenced, with the compiler of this book, his school studies. In grateful remembrance of this discovery it is proposed to make a public park, (S. E. corner) where the road turns toward Walpole, N. H.; and thereon erect a public library.
9. The first Meeting House in town.
8. Homestead of Joel⁶ Holton.
1. Location of his saw-mill, the first in Westminster.
2. His second saw-mill. 3. The saw-mill of his son Joel⁶.
4. Cloth-dressing establishment of Joel⁶ Holton, near which was his homestead and the birth-place of his children.
5. The Sawtelle Hill, through which a channel for the Averill brook was dug, uniting that water with the Holton brook.
6. The Old Cemetery, containing the monument to French and Houghton.
7. The site of the Court House.
L. Apple Oven Ledge [4033].

regiment. The Colonel went immediately and personally administered to the captain, whom the surgeons considered as then dying.

After unremitted watching and attendance day and night for one hundred and twenty hours, the elder brother had the happiness of seeing the patient regain consciousness. After thirty days he was able to return to his regiment.

For further interesting military history, etc., see Winslow Memoria [3855]. Farmer. *Res. Adrian, Hancock Co., Ill.*

Children :

1041.   1. Helen-Frances[8], b. 18 Nov. 1867, Hillsgrove, Ill.
1042.   2. Mary-Albertine[8], b. 12 Dec. 1876.

1043. MIRIAM[7], [609] (*Joel*[6], *Bethiah*[5] (Farwell) **Holton**, *William*[4], *Isaac*[3], *Joseph*[2], *Henry*[1],) born 31 Oct. 1807, Westminster, Vt.; died 8 Nov. 1865, at Le Claire, Scott Co., Iowa; m. Sumpterville, Sumpter Co., S. C., 10 March, 1855, Dr. Henry-Smith **BROWN**, born 26 Dec. 1809, Clarendon, Rutland Co., Vt., s. of William and Thankful (Smith) of Clarendon.

He married 2d, Rochester, N.Y., 27 August, 1868, Martha-Ann (Doney) Wood. b. 25 May, 1810; Ballston Spa, N.Y., dau. of James and Esther (Burton) of Saratoga Springs, N.Y.

Mrs. Miriam (Holton) Brown was a woman of very superior endowment, knowledge of human nature, great penetration of motives and character, and independent judgment ; and was very tenacious of her generally well-founded opinions. She held in abomination the institution of slavery, and being somewhat familiar with Southern character, predicted with unreserved assurance, years before its occurrence, the Rebellion which so deluged our land with the blood of its citizens.

She had a keen sense of the rights of the oppressed; and some of the most successful and remarkable proofs of her power in compassing her object were evinced when her sympathies were enlisted for some one whom she believed was suffering wrongfully. In such cases, borne on by sympathy and indignation combined, she seemed overpowering and irresistable, and the guilty would not soon desire another encounter with her.

The following, relating to a well-known event, will illustrate this trait in her character:

At the time Hon. Charles Sumner was smitten down by Brooks in the Senate chamber, Mrs. B. was occupying a position near the distinguished Senator. With characteristic fearlessness in emergencies she first sprang to the rescue.

Some time after, while seated at the dinner-table on board of a steamer for Europe, some of the Southern chivalry were speaking of the cowardice of the Northern people and instanced Charles Sumner as cowardly, submitting to a beating in the U. S. Senate. The sentiment seemed contagious and no voice was lifted in defence or disapproval. This was, of course, very distasteful to her, and there was a limit to her forbearance. When that point was reached she boldly and decidedly expressed her contempt for the *cowardice* of a *being* who could stealthily administer such a beating from *behind* the object of his hate, and for those who could entertain any sympathy for that kind of cowardice. Her scathing rebuke, so sudden and severe, silenced the conversation, the subject was never again broached in her presence and she received only the most respectful consideration.

Her business capacities were equalled by few of the sterner sex. With such capabilities and a laudable ambition to provide for herself and be useful to others, by energy, perseverance, and industry, she acquired a goodly fortune, considerable of which she bequeathed for educational interests and for the encouragement of family records and history.*

Mrs. B. spent a large portion of her active life as a teacher. In this employment she had the happy art of securing attention, awakening thought, and impressing the subject on the minds of her pupils, to a remarkable degree, as well as enlisting their confidence and affection. She died while on a visit to a beloved aunt. [For further details of her career as a teacher, see Winslow Memorial, Vol. 1, serial number 3857].

1044. DAVID-PARSONS⁷, A.M, M.D., [610] (*Joel⁶*, *Bethiah⁵* (Farwell) Holton, *William⁴*, *Isaac³*, *Joseph²*, *Henry¹*,) b. 18 June, 1812, Westminster, Vt.; m. by Rev. Albert Barnes, Philadelphia, Pa., 12 May, 1839, to Frances-Keturah Forward, b. 5 May, 1815, Southwick, Mass., dau. of Pliny and Fanny (Root) of S. [4274 Root Gen.]

Doctor Holton after leaving his district school in Westminster, was under the instruction of his uncle Isaac Holton, in the academies of South Berwick and Limerick, Maine, and Bellows Falls, Vermont. Leaving Bellows Falls in 1832, he was for two years preceptor of an academy in Southwick, Mass., and subsequently became a student in the University of the City of New York. In 1836 he commenced the study of medicine at the College of Physicians and Surgeons, then located in Barclay and subsequently in Crosby Street, graduating 9th March, 1839. Practiced mostly in N. Y. dispensaries and hospitals till 1843; when he removed to Westport, Essex Co., N. Y., and followed his profession there, till his return to the city, 1847. While in Essex Co. he accepted the office of County Superintendent of Schools and performed its duties two years. In 1853 went to Europe, and having attended lectures for four years at the universities and schools of Paris, Berlin and Vienna, returned to New York, 26 Nov. 1857.

Before going to Europe, he had in various forms advocated the establishment of Agricultural Colleges; while abroad, he strengthened his purpose to labor in this cause, and printed a pamphlet in this interest for gratuitous distribution there and in America; and on his return the Congressional grant for their establishment was

---

* The amount bequeathed for the collection and publication of records of her immediate ancestry and relatives, though supposed by her and also by the compilers at the inauguration of their work, to be ample for that purpose, proved, under the circumstances, very insufficient even for *her* limited portion of the large American families in the patronymic line of her grand parents.

During the groping search for the complete ancestral lines of these four names, extensive collections were made which eventually proved to be outside of the specified branch, and which of themselves would more than exhaust in payment of postage, fees to town and county clerks, abstracts, etc., the liberal amount bequeathed for her own pedigree.

This statement is made solely to correct misapprehensions on the part of some, outside of her immediate relatives, who suppose her gift to have been of a more general character.

perfected by the signature of the President, Abraham Lincoln, 2 July, 1862. [See Winslow Memorial, page 390.]

When the war commenced, 1861, his first impulse was to encourage enlistments and strengthen the Union cause by providing for the care of orphans of those who should fall in the country's service. He aided in organizing the society called Institute of Reward for Orphans of Patriots, of which he was, and has continued to be the Corresponding Secretary. He has lectured extensively in schools on the subject of Physiology and Hygiene. Through his direct exertions and at great personal sacrifice he secured the establishment of the first free baths of the City of New York; i.e., the first of the series of free baths on the Hudson and East rivers now successfully established for this city. In 1872 he was appointed Professor of Physiology in the New York Free Medical College for Women. He is a life member of the American Geographical and Statistical Society, the American Institute, New York, and the New England Historic-Genealogical Society, 18 Somerset Street, Boston; also a member of the New England Society in New York. He is secretary of the Pilgrim Record Society, whose regular sessions are (1879) at 20 Sutton Place, Eastern Boulevard, corner of East 59th Street, the second Tuesday evening of each month; and is Corresponding Secretary of the American Philological Society whose public meeting is at Room 36, Cooper Institute, the third Wednesday of each month.

The New York Genealogical and Biographical Society was formed through the instrumentality of Dr. Holton at his residence, 27 Feb. 1869, to which he has given much time and means. Its sessions for ten years have been held with great regularity at the Mott Memorial Hall, 64 Madison Avenue, the second and fourth Wednesday evenings of each month. [From this date, 26 March, 1879, Friday is substituted for Wednesday]. Its Quarterly appears without interruption and forms an annual volume of great value to the student of history.

For the past few years he has been mainly employed in the compilation of family records and genealogies of early settlers of New England. Manuscripts for twelve volumes are in a state of great forwardness for the press; one of which, an octavo of 656 pages of the "Winslow Memorial," was published 18 June, 1877. The manuscripts of other volumes are fully ready for the press, waiting only the requisite means for their publication.

Mrs. Holton is a descendant, in the seventh generation, of Samuel and Ann Forward of Windsor, Conn., in 1670; and on the maternal side is a descendant, in the eighth generation, of John, b. in Badby, Eng., and Mary (Kilbourn) Root, of Farmington, Conn.

On the paternal side she is descended from ancestors of the names Owen, Morton, Lawton, Moore, Griswold, Ellsworth; and on the maternal, from those of Root, Whitney, Nelson, Lamphier, Marshal, Loomis, Leonard, Spencer, Kilbourn.

---

*He has recently been hoping soon to see a very extensive public bath established in the waters of the East River, at East 59th Street, fronting Eastern Boulevard, from Sutton Place southward. This location calls for ample arrangements and multiplied accommodations, exceeding all previously built, it being convenient for visitors to the Central Park, and near the Belt railroad, and the stations of the Elevated railroads on Second and Third Avenues.

Children, all born in N. Y. City :

1045. 1. D-PLINY-FORWARD[9], b. 29 March, 1840; died at Southwick, Mass. 27 Sept. 1849. [Winslow Memorial 3859].
1046. 2. CHARLES-ALEXANDER[9], b. 8 Aug. 1842 ; died in Paris, France, 23 June, 1856. [Winslow Memorial 3860].
1047. 3. FANNIE-MIRIAM[9], b. 23 Oct. 1852; died in New York City, 20 May, 1859. [Winslow Memorial 3861.]

1048. REUBEN-ROCKWOOD[7], [614] *William[6]*, *Bethiah[5]* (Farwell) **Holton**, *William[4]*, *Isaac[3]*, *Joseph[2]*, *Henry[1]*,) b. 16 June, 1795, Westminster, Vt. ; m. Westminster, 20 Aug. 1815, Rebecca-Baker Tower, b. 20 July, 1797, W., dau. of Lines and Lucy (Gary) of W. She d. 4 Sept. 1845. He m. 2d, at Dorset, Vt. 13 Nov. 1847, Margaret-Albro (Whitehorn) Albee, (widow of William Albee) b. 31 Jan. 1808, Wallingford, Vt., dau. of John and Hannah (Carpenter) of Wallingford. Farmer. Res. Westminster, Wallingford, Vt., and *Plymouth, Ill.*

Children :

1049. 1. SABIA[8], b. 8 Jan. 1816, Westminster, Vt., m. Wallingford, Vt. 8 May, 1859, Oliver-Lewis **Allen**, b. 2 Nov. 1814, Wallingford, son of Oliver and Nancy (Sweetland). s.p. Res. *E. Wallingford, Vt.*
1050. 2. LINES-TOWER[8], b. 20 Feb. 1817, Westminster; died 26 Nov. 1866, Lemoine Township, Ill. ; m. Wallingford, Vt., 1 Jan. 1842, Lucinda Allen, b. 5 Oct. 1817, Wallingford, dau. of Oliver and Nancy (Sweetland).
Res. *Lemoine, near Plymouth, Hancock Co., Ill.*

Children born in Wallingford, Vt. :

1051. 1. Nancy-Emma[9], b. 4 Aug. and died 30 Aug. 1846, Wallingford.
1052. 2. Helen-Rebecca[9], b. 28 Oct. 1851 ; married at Quincy, Ill., 24 Sept. 1868, Josiah-Marshall **Ralston**, b. 8 Sept. 1847, Lemoine, Ill., s. of Josiah-Marshall and Roxanna (Smith) of Ravensburg, Hancock Co., Ill. Farmer. Res. *Lemoine, McDonough Co., P. O. address, Ravensburg, Hancock Co., Ill.*

Children :

1053. 1. *Minnie-Estelle[10]*, b. 2 Jan. 1870, Lemoine Ill.
1054. 2. *Centurius-Holton[10]*, b. 26 July, 1871, Lemoine—one hundred years from the date of birth of his gr. gr. grandfather William[6] Holton —hence his name. [See the grand radial chart of the descendants of Deacon William Holton.]
1055. 3. Wallace-Lines[9], b. 25 Feb. 1854 ; m. Vermont, Fulton Co., Ill., 29 Jan. 1873, Sylvia-Rosetta Parish, b. 30 July, 1854, Woodford or Waterford, ? Knox Co., Ohio, dau. of John-Nelson and Melissa (Baugh).
1056. 4. Charlotte-Emily[9], b. 26 April, 1860; 1878, was receiving her education in Vt.

1057.   3. NELSON-ALEXANDER⁶, b. 8 Dec. 1818, Wallingford, Vt.; married, Wallingford, 1 Jan. 1850, Sophia-Bigelow Earl, b. Mount Holly, Rutland Co., Vt., Apr. 1821, d. of Jacob and Betty (Whitney).

    In the spring of 1873, Mr. Holton bought eight hundred acres of land in Harvey Co., Kansas, broke, and planted with corn 30 or 40 acres, erected houses, etc.

Children :

1058.   1. Jason-Mercellus⁹, b. 8 Jan. 1851.
1059.   2. Eva-Adelaide⁹, b. 13 Nov. 1853 ; m. 13 Nov. 1872, Albert-Lyman Stillman.
1060.   3. Alice-Emogene⁹, b. 18 Aug. 1855; m. 11 Oct. 1873, Judson-Daniel Shattuck.   Res. *Mount Holly, Rutland Co., Vt.*
1061.   4. Martha-Jane⁹, b. 16 Feb. 1857.
1062.   5. Clark-Emmons⁹, b. 26 Sept. 1858.
1063.   6. Jay-Reubenᵃ, b. 6 Feb. 1863.

1064.   4. HARRIET-ANN⁸, b. 5 Aug. 1820, Wallingford, Vt.; married, 3 Nov. 1851, Kimball-D. Grimes, b. 9 Oct. 1818, Hancock, Hillsborough Co., N. H., son of William and Mary (Jones).   s. p.
    Res. *Proctorville, Windsor Co., Vt.*

1065.   WILLIAM⁷, [617] (*William⁶, Bethiah⁵* (Farwell) Holton, *William⁴, Isaac³, Joseph², Henry¹,*) b. 31 Oct. 1801, Westminster, Vt. ; married, Cavendish, Vt. 15 Aug. 1826, Betsey Mason, b. 11 Oct. 1800, dau. of Daniel and Betsey (Spaulding) of Cavendish. She died 21 May, 1841, Bethel, McDonough Co., Ill., to which place they removed from Westminster in 1835. He married 2d, at Bethel, 15 Sept. 1841, Sophia-Maria Waddell, b. 15 June, 1805, in Washington Co., Tenn., dau. of Charles and Margaret (King) of Hillsgrove, Ill. She died 4 June, 1854, Tennesee Township, Ill. He married 3d, Chalmers, McDonough Co., 8 Nov. 1854, Dorcas-Ford Hoyt, b. 11 July, 1817, Grafton, N. H., dau. of Jonathan and Jemima (Ford) of Chalmers. He is deceased. Farmer and clothier.   Res. Westminster, Vt., and *Bethel, Ill.*

Children :

1066.   1. WILLIAM-MASON⁸, M. D., b. 15 July, 1827, Westminster, Vt. ; married in New York City, 14 March, 1853, Caroline-Emily Cuyler, b. Essex, Essex Co., N. Y., 23 Dec. 1833, dau. of Col. E-S. and Emily (Parkhill) of Elizabethtown, Essex Co., N.Y. She died 8 March, 1873, at New Harmony, Ind. He m. 2d, 4 July, 1875, Mary Fretageot.

    Dr. Holton commenced the study of medicine with Dr. Leonard-T. Ferris [1014] 1 March, 1849; attended medical lectures at the College of Physicians and Surgeons of N. Y. City, as student of Prof. Willard Parker, graduating M. D. 11 March, 1852; practised in New York one year; returned to McDonough Co., Ill., in March, 1853, and removed to New Harmony, Ind., Nov. 1859.

He enlisted as private in his country's service 25 Oct. 1861; commissioned 18 Nov. 1861, as 2d Lieut. Co. B, 10th Reg. Ind. Vol. Inf.; was transferred to 25th Ind. Vol. Inf. as Assistant Surgeon, date of commission 25 Apr. 1862; joined the regiment at Pittsburg Landing, and was at the seige of Corinth, Miss. After the evacuation, he became ill and resigned 20 Aug. 1862.

Dr. H. is a member of the Tri-State Med. Society, and of the Indiana State and Posey Co. societies. 1879, res. *New Harmony, Posey Co., Ind.*

Children :

1067. 1. Emily-Elizabeth^9, b. 15 Sept. 1854, Middletown, [Young, now Fandon] McDonough Co., Ill; married, 4 July, 1873, Leopold **Kohn.**
1878, res. *Evansville, Ind.*
1068. 2. Frances-Caroline^9, b. 21 Feb. 1856. Middletown; m. 2 Jan. 1875, William-A. **Kight.** Res. 1878, *New Harmony, Ind.*

Child :

1069. 1. *Arthur*^{10}, b. Oct. 1875.

1070. 3. Mary-Alice^9, b. 21 Aug. 1857, Middletown, Ill.; died 4 Aug. 1875.
1071. 4. Charlotte-E^9, b. 16 Dec. 1859, Stewartsville, Posey Co., Ind.
1072. 5. William-Edward^9, b. 27 Nov. 1861, Stewartsville, Ind.
1073. 6. Kate-Cornelia^9, b. 22 Jan. 1864, New Harmony, Ind.
1074. 7. Frank-Cuyler^9, b. 29 July, 1866, " "
1075. 8. Minnie-Grace^9, b. 27 Aug. 1868, " "

1076. 2. HENRY-ALFRED^8, b. 15 March, 1829, Westminster, Vt.; married, Bethel, McDonough Co., Ill., 4 Feb. 1851, Rebecca-Scott, b. 4 Dec. 1826, in Ohio, dau. of John and Mary (Kendrickson) of Bethel. Farmer.
Res. *McDonough Co., Ill.*

Children :

1077. 1. William-Scott^9, b. 22 Dec. 1851, Bethel, Ill.; d. 20 Jan. 1852.
1078. 2. Mary^9, b. 24 March, 1853, Bethel township.
1079. 3. John^9, b. 31 Dec. 1854, Lemoine, Ill.
1080. 4. Jeremiah, b. 29 Dec. 1856, " "
1081. 5. Catharine^9, b. 13 Jan. 1859, " "
1082. 6. Emma^9, b. 24 Apr. 1861, " "
1083. 7. David^9, b. 16 Feb. 1863, " "
1084. 8. Amos^9, b. 28 Dec. 1864, " "
1085. 9. Isabella^9, b. 3 May, 1869, " "

1086. 3. CHARLES-ELIJAH^8, b. 7 Sept. 1830, Westminster, Vt.; m. Camden, Schuyler Co., Ill., 12 Nov. 1867, Ettie-Horton McKinley, b. 3 Jan. 1847, at Chester, Meigs Co., O., dau. of Byard and Catherine-Amelia (Young) of Camden. Farmer. Res. *Bethel, Ill.*

Children :

1087. 1. Ida-Blanch⁹, b. 28 Sept, 1868, Bethel, Ill.
1088. 2. Ada-Ford⁹, b. 5 Aug. 1872,   "   "

1089. 4. Infant⁸, b. and died 1832.
1090. 5. REUBEN-ALLEN⁸, b. 22 Jan. 1834, Westminster, Vt.; m. at Bethel, Ill., 25 Nov. 1851, Hannah-Seviah Albee, b. 1 Aug. 1842, Dorset, Vt., dau. of Willinm and Margaret (Whitehorn) of Lemoine, Ill. Farmer.
Res. *Bethel, Ill.*

Child :

1091. 1. Charles-Lindsey⁹, b. 26 Oct. 1863, Bethel.

1092. 6. ELIZA-JANE⁸, b. 4 July, 1837, Bethel, Ill.; m. at B. 22 July, 1855, James Toland, b. 19 Feb. 1829, Fox township, Carrol Co. O., son of William and Jane Hendrickson o. Bethel, Ill.; died 12 Dec. 1871, Bethel.
Res. *Lemoine* and *Bethel, Ill.*

Children :

1093. 1. John-Fremont⁹, b. 15 July, 1856, Lemoine, Ill.
1094. 2. Charles-William⁹, b. 6 Sept. 1858,   "   "
1095. 3. Alvah-Calvin⁹, b. 30 March, 1861, Bethel, Ill.
1096. 4. Clara-Annetta⁹, b. 24 Feb. 1863, B.; died at Bethel, 9 June, 1868.
1097. 5. Mary-Jane⁹, b. 2 Feb. 1965, Bethel, Ill.
1098. 6. Martha-Elizabeth⁹, b. 10 May, 1867, B.
1099. 7. Solomon-Henry⁹, b. 4 Aug. 1869, B.
1100. 8. James-Allen⁹, b. 6 Dec. 1871, B.

1101. 7. MARY-ELLEN⁸, b. 3 Nov. 1840, Bethel, Ill.; died there 6 Oct. 1867.
1102. 8. JOHN-WESLEY⁸, b. 12 Jan. 1844, Bethel ; married, B., 18 March, 1866, Harriet-Emily Polite, b. 2 May, 1846, dau. of Richard and Nancy (Brenington) of St. Mary's.

Children:

1103. 1. Richard⁹, b. 4 May, 1870, St. Mary's Township, Hancock Co., Ill.
1104. 2. Lillie-May⁹, b. 3 June, 1872,   "   "   "

1105. 9. ELIZABETH-RACHEL⁸, b. 9 Nov.1846, Bethel, Ill.; m. 19 Dec. 1864, Truman-Hobert Huff, b. 5 Jan. 1841, son of Jacob and Mary (Wilson) of St. Mary's. Farmer.   Res. Lemoine, Ill., and *Labette Co., Kansas.*

Children :

1106. 1. John-Francis⁹, b. 30 Dec. 1865, St. Mary's, Ill.
1107. 2. Mary-Bell⁹, b. 29 Dec. 1868,   "   "
1108. 3. Lizzie-Bell⁹, b. 20 Jan. 1873, Shelton's Grove, Schuyler Co., Ill.

1109. 10. CYRUS-FARWELL⁸, b. 29 Jan. 1856, Bethel, Ill.; died there, 15 Dec. 1857.
1110. 11. ELLA-ISABELL⁸, b. 21 Feb. 1858, Bethel.
1111. 12. LYMAN-HOYT⁸, b. 12 Jan. 1860, B.

1112. OLIVE⁷, [619] (*William⁶, Bethiah⁵* (Farwell) **Holton,** *William⁴, Isaac³, Joseph², Henry¹,*) b. 2 Apr. 1806, Westminster, Vt.; married, W. 26 Sept. 1830, Joshua **Ruggles,** b. 1 Dec. 1782, Hardwick, Mass. s. of Thomas and Hannah (Winslow) of Hardwick and Oakham, Mass. He died 3 Sept. 1852, in McDonough Co., Ill.

Res. 1878, *Shibley's Point, Adair Co., Kan.*

Joshua⁷ Ruggles descended from the immigrant Thomas¹ of Nazing, England, who came to Roxbury, Mass. 1627, and wife Mary, through Capt. Samuel² and Ann or Hannah Fowle who married for his 2d wife Ann Bright, dau. of Henry and Ann Goldstone of Watertown, Mass.*; Capt. Samuel³ and Martha Woodbridge†; Rev. Timothy⁴ and Mary White; Capt. Benjamin⁵ and Alice Merrick of Hardwick, Mass.; Thomas⁶ and Hannah⁶ (Winslow) [4075 of Winslow Memorial] of Hardwick and Oakham, whose son Joshua⁷ married Olive⁷ Holton as above.

Children:

1113. 1. HARRIET-ELIZABETH⁸, b. 5 Jan. 1832, Westminster, Vt.; died 22 Apr. 1873; married, near Vermont, Fulton Co., Ill. 11 Aug. 1851, Rev. Joseph-Warren **Arnold,** b. 3 Jan. 1832, near Oxford, Holmes Co., O., s. of Thomas and Electa (Purdy) of Oxford. He enlisted as a volunteer in 1861, and served three years. Farmer and minister of the United Brethren.   Res. *Iola, Allen Co., Kansas.*

Children:

1114. 1. John-Franklin⁹, b. 3 June, 1852, McDonough Co., Ill.
1115. 2. Charles-Lawrence⁹, b. 25 Dec. 1853,   "   "
1116. 3. Electa-Isabel⁹, b. 19 Nov. 1855,   "   "
1117. 4. Henry-Thomas⁹, b. 27 July, 1857,   "   "
1118. 5. Mary-Olive-Alvira⁹, b. 15 June, 1859,   "   "
1119. 6· Martin-Boehm⁹, b. Iola, 24 Dec. 1861; died there Oct. 1862.
1120. 7. Amy-Adeline⁹, b. 27 Nov. 1865, Iola, Kansas.
1121. 8. Asel-Edwin⁹, b. 18 Apr. 1868,   "   "
1122. 9. Frank-Dixon⁹, b. 7 Feb. 1870,   "   "

1123. 2. JULIA-ISABEL⁸, b. 21 Jan. 1834, Westminster, Vt.; m. Middletown, Mc Donough Co., Ill., 14 Dec. 1852, Rev. Merit **Husted,** b. 14 Sept. 1833· Oxford, Holmes Co., O., s. of Oliver and Laura (Smith) of Martinstown Putnam Co., Mo. Merchant and minister of the United Brethren.

Res. *Indian Territory; P. O. Chetopah, Labette Co, Kan.*

Children:

1124. 1. Joseph⁹, b. 18 July, 1854, in Illinois; d. there, 19 July, 1854.

*Chart IX page 76, and page 113 under serial number 747. See, also, Appendix, page 24, of Winslow Memorial, and serial number 1201 of this book.
†See Appendix of Winslow Memorial p. 25, also the Woodbridge Chart in Bulletin of the Pilgrim Record Society.

Descendants of Bethiah⁵ (Farwell) Holton.

1125. 2. Mary-Melissa⁹, b. 13 Jan. 1857, Ill.; d. 1 Feb. 1857.
1126. 3. Maria⁹, b. 24 Aug. 1859, Ill.; d. 24 Aug. 1859.
1127. 4. William-Otterbein⁹, b. 23 Aug. 1860, in Illinois; d. 23 Apr. 1861 or 2.
1128. 5. Lurena-Almira⁹, b. 11 Nov. 1862, in Kansas.
1129. 6. Stephen-Edward⁹, b. 27 May, 1864,   "
1130. 7. Laura-Olive⁹, b. 17 Jan. 1866,   "   and d. 28 Aug. 1873.
1131. 8. Charles-Thomas⁹, b. 17 Aug. 1867, Shibley's Point, Mo.
1132. 9. Hiram-Oliver⁹, b. 5 Oct. 1869, S. Point; d. 21 Oct. 1870.
1133. 10. Etta-Belle⁹, b. 2 Oct. 1871,   "
1134. 11. Sarah-Inis⁹, b. 15 Aug. 1873,   "
1135. 12. Clyde-Merit⁹, b. 15 Dec. 1876, in Schuyler Co., Ill.

1136. 3. HENRY-AUSTIN⁸, b. 12 June, 1836, Westminster, Vt.; married, Birmingham township, Schuyler Co., Ill., 25 May, 1858, Martha Haviland, b. 12 May, 1840, Kalida, O., dau. of Lewis and Martha (Barger) of Kalida, Putnam Co., O.   Farmer.   Res. *Shibley's Point, Adair Co., Mo.*

Children :

1137. 1. William-Henry⁹, b. 19 Nov. 1859, Birmingham, Schuyler Co., Ill.; died 7 Aug. 1862, Allen Co., Kan.
1138. 2. Julia-Ann⁹, b. 21 Sept. 1861, Kan.
1139. 3. Joseph-Lester⁹, b. 9 Dec. 1863, in Kansas; died there, 21 Sept. 1864.
1140. 4. James-Albert⁹, b. 5 Aug. 1865, Kan.
1141. 5. Eddie⁹, b. 17 Apr. 1867, near Leroy, Coffee Co., Kan.; d. there, 19 Sept. 1867.
1142. 6. George-Grant⁹, b. 24 Sept. 1868; d. 23 Aug. 1869.
1143. 7. Mary-Olive⁹, b. Sept. 1870; d. 23 Aug. 1871, near Martinstown, Putnam Co., Mo.
1144. 8. Sarah⁹, b. and d. 15 Feb. 1872, Elm township, Putnam Co., Mo.
1145. 9. Sarah-Ettie⁹, b. 5 May, 1873; d. 19 Jan. 1876.
1146. 10. Merrit-Solomon-Alfred⁹, b. 15 March, 1878.

1147. 4. CHARLES-AMBROSE⁸, b. 5 Sept. 1838, Bethel, Ill.; d. there 16 Feb. 1852.
1148. 5. THOMAS-EDWIN⁸, b. 13 Jan. 1841, Bethel ; d. 22 Apr. 1875 ; m. Leroy township, Coffee Co., Kansas, 3 March, 1864, Sarah-Roxana Briles, b. 31 Dec. 1841, Putnam Co. Mo., daughter of Alexander and Sarah (Rush) of Leroy. Farmer. Res. Martinstown, Putnam Co.
        P. O. address, *Shibley's Point, Adaire Co., Mo.*

Children :

1149. 1. Ida-May⁹, b. 24 Jan. 1865, near Leroy, Kansas
1150. 2. Annie-Louise⁹, b. 24 May, 1866,   "   "
1151. 3. Dora-Bell⁹, b. 22 Feb 1869,   "   "
1152. 4. Austin⁹, b. 3 Feb., d. 17 Feb. 1870, near Martinstown, Mo.
1153. 5. Charles Lester⁹, b. 3 June, 1872.
1154. 6. Henry-Thomas⁹, b. 29 March, 1875, Putnam Co., Mo.

1155. 6. HANNAH-MINERVA⁶, b. 16 Apr. 1843, Bethel, Ill.; d. 7 Apr. 1862, Iola, Allen Co., Kansas; m. Bethel, 12 June, 1858, John **Haviland**, b. 25 Apr. 1836, Kalida, O., s. of Lewis and Martha (Barger) of K.   Farmer.
                           Res. *Iola, Kan.*

   Children:

1156. 1. James-Ambrose⁸, b. 1 May, 1859, Middletown, McDonough Co., Ill.; died there, 12 May, 1859.
1157. 2. George-Washington⁸, b. 17 May. 1860, Iola, Kansas; d. 10 July. 1860.

1158. 7. REUBEN-WINSLOW⁶, b. 5 July, 1845, Bethel, Ill.; d. there, 20 July, 1845.

1159. 8. MARY-ANN⁶, b. 27 Oct. 1846, Bethel, Ill.; married, 13 Nov. 1864, Leroy, Kansas, John-Franklin **Briles**, b. 17 Dec. 1843, Salem, Randolph Co., N. C., son of Alexander and Sarah (Rush) of Leroy.   Farmer and blacksmith.   Res. *Leroy, Coffee Co., Kansas.*

   Children :

1160. 1. Effie-Jane⁸, b. 7 Oct. 1865, Leroy, Coffee Co., Kan.
1161. 2. Sarah-Olive⁸, b. 5 Sept. 1867, L.
1162. 3. Alice-Ettie⁸ b. Feb. 1870, L.
1163. 4. William-Alexander⁸, b. Putnam Co., Mo. 1 Apr. 1873 ; d. 1876, in Kansas.
1164. 5. Elisha⁸, b. 3 March, 1875, Leroy, Coffee Co., Kansas.
1165. 6. Elizabeth⁸, b. Jan. 1877, L.

1166. ISABEL⁷, [620] (*William⁶, Bethiah⁵* (Farwell) **Holton**, *William⁴, Isaac³, Joseph², Henry¹,*) b. 13 Aug. 1808, Westminster, Vt. ; died, 19 March, 1841, Hillsgrove, McDonough Co., Ill. ; m. at Mendon, Adams Co., Ill., 6 June, 1837, John-Calvin **CONANT**, b. 30 Jan. 1803, Hollis, N. H., s. of Abel and Lydia (Frideker) of Hardwick, Vt.   1872, he res. *Geneva, Allen Co., Kan.*

   Children:

1167. 1. WILLIAM-HOLTON⁸, b. 14 March, 1838, Quincy, Ill.; died 27 Feb. 1857, at Hillsgrove, Ill.; was a student at Knox College, Galesburg, Ill.

1168. 2. MARY-CELESTIA⁸, b. 20 July, 1839, Quincy; d. 29 July, 1839.

1169. 3. JOHN-EDWIN⁸, b. 19 March, 1841, Hillsgrove, Ill. ; enlisted in the Union army, 15 Nov. 1861, and was stationed at Iola, about twelve miles from his home, till April 27, when he was sent to Fort Leavenworth; visited his home 12 June, 1862, by leave of absence for a single night, and returned to the army; was stationed at Fort Scott where he was taken sick. His father removed him to his home at Geneva, reaching there the 25th Nov. He died 1 Dec. 1862.

Farwell Memorial.

1170. ISAAC-FARWELL[1], [622] (*Wm*[6], *Bethiah*[5] (Farwell) **Holton**, *Wm*[4], *Isaac*[3], *Joseph*[2], *Henry*[1],) b. 30 Aug. 1812, Westminster, Vt.; d. 25 Jan. 1874, Everett, Mass. He commenced classical studies in Maine at the academies of South Berwick and Limerick under the tuition of his uncle, Isaac Holton,[640] and completed his preparatory course under Rev. Simeon Colton at the Amherst Academy, Mass. He was a graduate of Amherst College in the class of 1836, with Rev. Dr. Roswell D. Hitchcock of New York, Ex-Governor Bullock of Massachusetts, and other eminent men. He was a graduate of the Union Theological Seminary in the City of New York, 1839.

From early life he was a student of natural history, and, under Dr. John Torrey, Professor in the College of Physicians and Surgeons, was a fellow student with Asa Gray, subsequently the eminent Cambridge Professor. The friendship of teacher and associate pupils was strong and interrupted only by death.

Soon after his graduation at the Union Theological Seminary, 1839, he became a teacher in the Mission Institute near Quincy, Ill., founded by Rev. David Nelson, D.D. Among his pupils there he counted, in after life, those bound to him by the strongest ties of friendship and Christian sympathy, of whom those dearest to him were Rev. John and Jane (Ballard) Rendall, missionaries in India, stationed at Battalagunda, about 33 miles from Madura.*

While in this Mission Institute, planting and cultivating in the young the seeds of successful mission work, he enjoyed long and frequent walks in quest of specimens of prairie growth, that he might cultivate and enlarge botanical science.

At the conclusion of his educational labors and botanical researches in the Mississippi Valley, he accepted a professorship in the College of Pharmacy in the City of New York.

From our scrap-book we take the following, clipped from a New York paper of that date:

CITY INTELLIGENCE.

On Monday evening Prof. Holton, of the College of Pharmacy, delivered at the the Hall of the College, 411 Broadway, the introductory to a course of lectures on that interesting branch of natural science whose ultimate aim is "the development of the boundless resources of the vegetable kingdom, for our sustenance, protection and enjoyment; for the healing of our diseases, and the alleviation of our wants and woes." Among the audience were noticed many of the professors of the College of Physicians, and other distinguished physicians and men of science. The following is the substance of the lecture very much condensed:

INTRODUCTORY LECTURE ON BOTANY, BY PROFESSOR HOLTON.

Matter is found in forms organic and inorganic—the former being made up of

---
See lines at the close of this article.

organs or parts formed for the service of the whole, and necessary to its completeness. Organic bodies have the power of originating others organized similar to themselves.—These are said to be of the same species. The whole number of species is supposed to be about three hundred thousand, about one half of which belong to the vegetable kingdom. So numerous then are the vegetable species that no man could become familiar with any large portion of them, and so local is the growth of most, that such general knowledge of them would be scarcely desirable. The impression that botany is but a knowledge of species of plants, has been highly injurious to the science as a subject of philosophical attention, particularly in this country, owing to the peculiar character of our text books, made rather by book makers than botanists. But there must be something more in botany—in some way a truth ascertained of one species must be applied to thousands, and those thousands must be recognized and the truth read in their very structure, by the botanist who sees them for the first time.

All this is accomplished by a *philosophical classification*. The first step in classification is to arrange species into *genera*. The oaks are a genus characterized by acorns. Why should a genus be made of trees bearing acorns, rather than of trees bearing similar leaves, or having some other resemblance? Because trees bearing acorns have a thousand points in common—flowers, wood, properties of bark, etc., while a genus made of plants of similar leaves would embrace a heterogeneous mass, having no other point of resemblance. The next step in classification is more difficult. It is to arrange the genera into *orders*. There are about two hundred and fifty of them, but more than half the plants of this state are contained in only *eleven*. Some of these orders are readily recognized, as one containing the Pea, Bean, Tare, Vetch-Locust, Honey-Locust, Acacia, Tamarind, Husks of the Prodigal Son, Clover, Lucerne, etc. Another contains the Parsnip, Carrot, Dill, Fennel, Hemlock and Assafœtida. Another may be known from the Mustard, Radish, Horseradish and Turnip. But when we come to the Pine, Cedar of Lebanon, our own Red Cedar, Cypress, Larch, Yew and Arbor Vitæ, a difficulty arises as to the fruit, some bearing large woody cones, and others what appears to be a one-seeded berry. *Our Cedar is a Pine cone in disguise.*

Without attempting to prove this, Professor Holton stated the three great principles on which all such reasoning is based—the basis in fact of the philosophy of natural history. These are best illustrated by examples from animal structure, as we are more familar with it than that of vegetables, which in reality, however, would furnish more numerous and striking examples, were we only familiar with them.

The first of these three principles is like an axiom ever present to the mind, but difficult to define or name. He called it the law of "coincidence of characteristics." One characteristic being found in an organized body, certain other particular characteristics will be sure to accompany it. Feathers are met with only in animals—in bipeds, furnished with a beak and having air cavities in the bones, etc. Scales are a characteristic of cold-blood animals with an imperfect heart and small brain.

Correspondence of Organs and Unity of Structure.

This law is best known by its exceptions. The whale and porpoise are not fishes, their fins to the contrary notwithstanding. The Australian Platypus is a quadruped, covered with fur, but lays eggs and feeds her young like birds. The operation of this law is to draw plants and animals into groups having many characteristics in common and among others their medical, poisonous or nutritive properties.

The second of these laws, that of "correspondence of organs," may best be understood by a comparison of the anterior extremities of the horse, a bird, and a bat. [Drawings of the bones of each were exhibited.] Each consists of an arm, fore-arm, wrist and hand, but modified according to the purpose they are to serve. The forearm in man consists of two bones capable of rotating the wrist; in birds, of two similar bones distinct but incapable of such a motion. In the horse, they are nearly soldered into one, and in bats, generally, one is wanting. The bat has five fingers as long as the whole arm, serving as a frame-work to the wing. Birds are furnished with a much stronger wing, made on quite another principle—the bone and sinew being all collected at one edge. The hand has but three fingers partially soldered together, being made of but five distinct pieces instead of nineteen as in man. The hand of the horse is but a single finger of four joints completely capped by an enormous finger-nail, the hoof.

The third of these three principles, the law of *Unity of Structure*, was discovered by the world-famous poet Gœthe, by the comparison of the bones of a stag found as he was hunting. The spine is made of vertebræ, having each a main part or *body*, two lateral processes and a bony *arch* under which the spinal marrow passes. The tail is composed of similar vertebræ, except that the arch is reduced to a mere process, as there is there no spinal marrow to be protected. The pelvis is evidently but the bodies of several vertebræ partially soldered together, and their lateral processes completely soldered together, enormously enlarged, distorted and brought round so as to meet each other, to make the whole into a complete ring. The ribs are lateral processes, elongated and articulated to the vertebræ. The skull is but a vertebræ, with its arch enormously enlarged to make room for the brain. The bones of the face are one or two more vertebræ very much enlarged; and, finally, the limbs are but lateral processes of vertebræ metamorphosed, as the poet terms it, and adapted to the wants of the animal.

Improbable and fanciful as this scheme *seems*, all nature is full of evidence of its truth, and the light which it throws on natural history is incalculable.—Probably the first two laws are but manifestations of this, or all the three may be but expressions of some deeper law yet undiscovered. Without these laws all nature would be in chaos. Every article of food for man or beast would then necessarily be sought by repeated experiments, always dangerous and often fatal, and the most inoffensive animal would be to us an object of terror, like an unknown species of reptile. Only imagine a world formed without regard to these three laws; a world of "centaurs, gorgons and chimeras dire," where in every created thing might be found mingled, characteristics of beast, bird, insect and reptile; where the next animal we encountered might assail us with the touch of the torpedo, or the fang of the rattlesnake. When, in short, there should be nothing of which we could say, this is animal, or this is vegetable. Such a world would teach what the fool now reads in the Book of Nature—there is no God.

In addition to his professional duties in the college he for several years gave courses of lectures on Botany in the leading schools for young ladies in New York; and was occasionally called by Professor Torrey, during temporary absences, to lecture for him on Chemistry and Botany at Princeton College, N. J., and in the College of Physicians and Surgeons of the University of the State of New York.

Subsequently he visited South America, and published a volume of over 600 pages, entitled, "Twenty Months on the Andes, by Rev. Isaac-F. Holton, Professor of Natural History in Middlebury College, Vermont."

For some years he was pastor of a Presbyterian Church, at Lawrence, Illinois ; and in 1864 was called east to aid in editing the *Boston Recorder*.

He wrote for other papers, and did a great amount of general literary and scientific work, occasionally supplying vacant pulpits in Boston and vicinity.

Those who knew him intimately and understood his somewhat hidden powers, had for him the highest regard and esteem, flavored by no little affection for him personally. Like many others in the world, he did a vast amount of labor hidden under the surface.

Crowned with gray hairs, he finished a life of useful and honorable toil, and died with the harness on.

The following incidents illustrate one of his striking characteristics—his passionate fondness for science in whatever department presented, sometimes turning him from the courtesies of life and from the continuity of his subject even while officiating in the professorial chair :

In the winter of 1854-5 he was lecturing before the medical students of the College of Physicians and Surgeons during the absence of Dr. Torrey, then Professor of Chemistry in that institution. His subject was "Mercury," and unexpectedly he needed to know, on the instant, whether a piece of crude chloride was corrosive sublimate or calomel. Without pausing he touched it with potassa; a black spot showed that it was *calomel*. Instantly occurred the solution of the old puzzle, the etymology of the word *kali-mel* is the mercurial chloride which *kali* (potassa) turns *black*;—in time out of mind some one who "knew too much" having corrected the well-constructed name into *calomel*.

Rejoicing in the recovery of the etymology of the word he left the chemical analysis in hand for a philological diversion, attributing former failures in pursuit of the origin of the word or of its elemental sources to an entanglement with error which for two centuries had turned inquiry astray, on the theory that the import of the word for the white substance calomel was in some way allied to that of *beautiful black*. One, in his fancies, suggested that the nomenclator had a black assistant who used to prepare it beautifully. In their perplexity chemists have resorted to the conjecture that the *mel* might mean honey—because calomel is sweeter than corrosive sublimate. Etymologists seem never to have doubted that *katos* (beautiful) was part of the name; but we now see that calomel comes from two words $\left\{ \begin{array}{l} \text{kali–potassa} \\ \text{mel–black} \end{array} \right\}$ a substance which on the application of potassa becomes black.

Thus far etymologically,—and he resumed the consideration of the chemical properties of mercury.

Another incident of the effect of a discovery upon him :

In his early school days he commenced to collect specimens from the animal and vegetable kingdoms for study and classification. Entering the house of a friend where for months he had been a stranger, his eye rested upon a plain, modest, native plant from the fields—a variety which he had sought, but had never before been able to find, and which caught his attention so fully that he forgot, for the moment, the courtesy due his friends.*

Let it not be inferred that his love for the study of the mysterious laws of nature lessened his devotion to relatives and friends; or that this love and devotion to the created in any degree diminished his worship of the Creator.

Rev. Professor Isaac-Farwell' Holton died at Everett, Mass., Sunday, 25 Jan. 1874, at thirty-five minutes past the hour of noon. For some three months he had under his ordinary labors been sensible of fatigue, to which he had previously been a stranger; yet during the past three weeks he had felt more of his former vigor; and in adition to the discharge of his duties in Boston, as clerk of the Senate Committee of Elections, he prepared three articles of great value and forwarded them for New York magazines or periodicals with which he was in correspondence.

He was uncommonly cheerful and vigorous his last Sunday morning, and, having attended worship at the Congregational Church in Everett, he expressed himself as highly interested in the discourse of the pastor, Rev. Mr. Bryant, upon the subjects embraced in the tenth chapter of Genesis. After morning service, he, facing the cold wind, walked three-fourths of a mile to his home. Four times he was seen to turn his back to the wind, allowing himself a short pause.

Reaching home, he seated himself in his arm-chair before taking off overcoat, hat or gloves. He gave two directions—one for warm tea and another for closing a door. These two orders in his usual voice—when his head inclined somewhat backward. His daughter Clara heard a sound as from one snoring. His wife at the moment coming from an adjoining room, hastened to his relief. He spoke not—he

---

*Prof. Holton's herbarium, including his valuable collection of botanical specimens from the New England States, the Mississippi Valley and South America, was by him with great care arranged and preserved.

Since his death Prof. Gray of Harvard University, Rev. Dr. Rosswell-D. Hitchcock of the Union Theological Seminary, City of New York, Dr. Nathan Allen of Lowell, Mass., and others, have united in a proposal "to do a double good ";—first to the family of Prof. Holton, deceased, and second to Amherst College, by procuring this herbarium for a donation to his Alma Mater.

The late President of Amherst College, W-A. Stearns, in reference to this proposal, wrote: "The present time would be opportune for such an act. There has been quite a revival of interest here in botanical studies during the past year. Mr. Jessup, an amateur botanist of reputation and ability, has been engaged, by volunteer efforts, in sorting out and scientifically arranging a chaotic mass of botanical material which the College already possessed. Prof. Tuckerman, who has a world wide reputation for pre-eminence in some departments of botanical study, has entered heartily into and spent considerable money in this enterprise, while the College has assigned room and has been putting up shelves for these collections. Prof. Harris is also teaching botany with success.

"If Professor Holton's herbarium could be sent to Amherst, it would be specially attended to and carefully preserved. It would furnish a pleasant monument to a remarkably deserving graduate, and the contributors would receive the thanks of the friends of the College.

Yours truly,
W-A. STEARNS."

breathed once—and, after some intermission, he breathed again. It was his last. . . . She sent to a neighbor for aid, and, thinking it a case of fainting, applied the usual remedies, including the sprinkling with water. But all made no impression —he was dead in his chair.

On leaving the church he had said to Mrs. Bryant, that he was glad he had had the opportunity of hearing that sermon. He told Deacon Burt that the minister had handled the subjects of the chapter with great ability and to his entire satisfaction.

After the expression of his happiness in the church exercises, it is not known that he uttered any words, except the two short directions as above said, during the two minutes subsequent to his entrance into his house.

His sudden and peaceful translation from the scenes of earth formed a fit close of his eventful life, devoted to the highest interests of humanity, in the love of God.

The burial services were very solemn. Never were utterances from a pulpit more *positive* and *full* in testimony of the high merits of a deceased man, than were those of the Malden and Everett clergymen at the funeral of Professor Isaac-Farwell' Holton.

He left for his widow and four children a comfortable home and very pleasant surroundings.

His valuable HERBARIUM was left systematically and conveniently arranged which it has been proposed by some of the Alumni of Amherst College to purchase and present to his Alma Mater.

Lines by Prof. Isaac-Farwell' Holton written, 1845, in the album of Jane Ballard, one of his beloved pupils in the Mission Institute, who died, the wife of Rev. John Rendall, 1867, on the Mediterranean, returning from India. Over them, in the album was a scroll containing the air of "Oft in the stilly night," adapted to the words— lines now appropriate, in memory of their author, our departed friend:

> Oh the music of the past!
>   How it lingers in my brain;
> Oh the voices I have heard,
>   But shall never hear again!
> In my memory still they live;
>   I can call them at my will,
> But in vain I bid them go,
>   They are present with me still.
>
> Oh the voices I have heard
>   But shall never hear again;
> They are silent in the dust,
>   Or are heard beyond the main,
> They are silent in the dust,
>   They are warbling now above;
> And I yet shall hear them sing,
>   Sing a Savior's dying love.
>
> With the music of the past,
>   Soon the present too shall go;
> And the sounds that soothe us now
>   Shall be heard no more below;
> But the glorious hope is ours
>   That to us will soon be given
> Songs of praise for evermore,
>   In the holy choir of Heaven.

Rev. Professor Holton married, Cornwall, Vt., 26 Apr. 1858, Mary-Susanne Warner, b. 24 Apr. 1827, dau. of Dan and Nancy Gates.

His family reside, 1879, at *Everett, Mass.*

Children :

1171.   1. CLARA⁶, b, 16 Jan. 1859, Lawrence, McHenry Co., Ill d,. 19 March, 1879.
1172.   2. NANCY-GATES⁶, b. 25 Aug. 1860, Cornwall, Vt.
1173.   3. EDWARD-PAYSON⁶, b. 24 Feb. 1864, Hillsgrove, Ill.
1174.   4. CHARLES-SUMNER⁶, b. 4 May, 1866, Medford, Mass.

1175. WEALTHY-ANN⁵, [623] (*William⁴, Bethiah⁵* (Farwell) **Holton,** *William⁴, Isaac³, Joseph², Henry¹,*) b. 24 Jan. 1815, Westminster, Vt. ; died 18 July, 1852, Keokuk, Iowa; m. Quincy, Ill. 24 Dec. 1843 Rev. Horace **Worden,** born in Mass. 9 Feb. 1812. Baptist clergyman. Res. *Quincy, Ill.*

Children :

1176.   1. SARAH-PEABODY⁶, died Nov. 1844, Barry, Ill.
1177.   2. EDWIN-BROWN⁶, b. 13 Feb. 1846, and died aged two weeks.
1178.   3. ANN-AUGUSTA⁶, b. 3 Feb. 1849, and died 10 July, same year.

1179. NOADIAH-LOOMIS⁵, [626] (*Zoheth⁴, Bethiah⁵* (Farwell) **Holton,** *William⁴, Isaac³, Joseph², Henry¹,*) b. 4 Dec. 1805, Westminster, Vt. ; died 5 Feb. 1859, Walpole. N. H. ; married by Joseph Hemphill, at Rockingham, Windham Co., Vt. 16 Aug. 1847, to Eliza Burroughs, b. 10 March, 1819, Winhall, Bennington Co., Vt., dau. of John and Anna (Slade) of Alstead, Cheshire Co., N. H. Farmer.

Res. *Westminster, Windham Co., Vt*

Children all born in Westminster :

1180.   1. IRA⁶, b. 30 Nov. 1849.
1181.   2. ANNA⁶, b. 2 Oct. 1851 ; married Brigham **Phelps.** Deputy Sheriff of Windham Co., Vt. Res. *Bellows Falls, Windham Co., Vt.*
1182.   3. ABBY⁶, b. 30 May, 1856.

1183. ELIHU-DWIGHT⁵, [627] (*Zoheth⁴, Bethiah⁵* (Farwell) **Holton,** *William⁴, Isaac³, Joseph², Henry¹,*) born 19 Feb. 1807, Westminster, Vt. ; was married there by Rev. Sylvester Sage, 31 Nov. 1831, to Nancy Grout, b. 24 Feb. 1812, W.; dau. of John and Elizabeth (Upham) of Westminster. Mrs. Holton is aunt of the missionary, Rev. Lewis Grout, and of the Revs. Edwin and Isaac Bliss, now in Turkey. Farmer.

Res. *Saxton's River, Rockingham Co., Vt.*

Children :

1184.   1. LUCEBA-GROUT⁶, b. 12 Jan. 1833, Westminster ; m. 10 March, 1853, Saxton's River, Leonard-Emerson **Butterfield,** son of Leonard and Almira-Ward (Randall) of Springfield, Vt. She m. 2d, Feb. 1863, Jonathan-

Erastus Smith, b. 18 Nov. 1825, son of Otis and Rebecca (Lane) of Rockingham, Vt. Farmer. Res. *Saxton's River, Vt.*

Children :

1185. 1. Henry-Lewis⁹, b. 2 July, 1855, Saxton's River; died at St. Johnsbury, 28 May, 1856.
1186. 2. Hattie⁹, b. 14 Jan. 1865, Saxton's River.
1187. 3. Henry-Erastus⁹, b. 24 Aug. 1871, S. R.

1188. 2. HENRY-DWIGHT⁸, M. D., b. 24 July, 1838, Saxton's River, Vt. ; married there, 19 Nov. 1862, Ellen-Jane Hoit, b. 28 Nov. 1839, Saxton's River, daughter of Theophilus and Mary-Dana (Chandler) of S. R. The early training of Dr. Holton was of the strictest New England kind, and much of his success in life is undoubtedly due to the principles thus early instilled into his mind by his parents. His boyhood was like that of the majority of boys brought up on a farm and is well described by David-Dudley Warner in his book entitled "Being a Boy." The following account of his life is from a book entitled "Physicians and Surgeons of America," and a sketch of his life in a work published by the Rocky Mountain Medical Association. He was fitted for college at the Saxton's River Seminary, and studied medicine two years with Dr. J-H. Warren of Boston, and two years with Professors Valentine and A-B. Mott of New York, attending lectures at the same time in the medical department of the University of New York, from wnich he graduated in March, 1860, settling successfully in Brooklyn, N. Y., (physician to Williamsburgh Dispensary, Brooklyn, 1860), Putney, Vt. and Brattleboro, Vt., his present residence. He has traveled extensively in Europe and this country. He is a member of the Conn. River Valley Med. Soc. of which he was secretary from 1862 to 1867 and president in 1868 ; the Vt. Med. Soc. of which he was a censor for several years and the president in 1868 the American Med. Asso. and the British Med. Asso., a corresponding member of the Boston Gynæcological Society and member of the Amer. Pub. Health Asso. and a delegate to the International Medical Congress at Brussels in 1875. He is also a member of the Rocky Mountain Medical Association. The Dr. has contributed some valuable papers to medical journals and to transactions of medical societies, and reported at one time "Mott's Cliniques" for the press. An article describing his apparatus for keeping in place sternal dislocations of the clavicle, and an article on diphtheria, are contributions which show research and ability. He was appointed by the Court, in 1873, Medical Examiner to the Vt. Asylum for the Insane ; and in the same year was elected by the Legislature one of the trustees of the University of Vt. He has been surgeon of the 12th regiment of Vt. Militia. He is now Professor of Materia Medica and General Pathology in the medical department of the University of Vt. The Dr. is a vigorous orator and a clear

thinker and well up in a knowledge of the most approved and latest methods of relieving human suffering.

Mrs. Holton is a descendant, in the eighth generation, of John^1 Hoit and his first wife Frances, who settled in Salisbury, Mass. before 1639, through their son John^2 and Mary (Barnes) ; Joseph^3 and Dorothy (Worthen); John^4 and Mary (Eastman); Eastman^5, who d. at Westmoreland, N. H. 27 Feb. 1825, æ 87, and Martha (Clough); Theophilus^6 and Sebrina (Shaw)*; Theophilus^7, b. 19 Feb. 1813, married 13 March, 1839, Mary-Dana Chandler; the parents of Ellen-Jane^8 Hoyt who married Dr. Henry-D. Holton as above [*Hoyt Family*].

Dr. Holton has lived at Saxton's River, Putney and *Brattleboro, Vt.*

Child :
    Edith, b. 3 Nov. 1868.

1189. JULIA-ANN^7, [628] (*Zoheth^6, Bethiah^5* (Farwell) **Holton**, *William^4, Isaac^3, Joseph^2, Henry^1,*) b. 3 Nov. 1809, Westminster, Vt. ; m. 30 Oct. 1832, W., Hiram **KING**, of Walpole, N. H., son of Daniel and Susanna (Wood). He died 19 Oct. 1840. She married 2d, on the 19th March, 1844, Darwin **WOOD**, son of Asa and Mary (Merick).   Res. *Ashburnham, Mass*·

Children :

1190.   1. JULIA-FRANCES^8, b. 24 Apr. 1834 ; m. 6 Sept. 1855, Alfred-Gilson **Woodward**, b. Fairlee, Vt., 14 Apr. 1826, son of Leonard and Malinda (Gilson).
    Res. *Lowell, Mass.*

Children :

1191.   1. James-Abbot^9, b 9 July, 1857; d. 16 July, 1857.
1192.   2. Carrie-Frances^9, b. 12 July, 1858.
1193.   3. Lizzie-Maria^9, b. 8 June, 1860.
1194.   4. Alfred-Gilson^9, b. 12 May, 1865.
1195. 2. MARY-AMANDA^8, b. 31 March, 1841 ; married, 1 Jan. 1862, John-Thomas **Kelly**, son of George Kelly of Boston. He died Oct. 1867. She m. 2d, James-A. **Merrill**   Res. *Boston, Mass*

Children :

1196.   1. George-John$_9$, b. 10 Nov. 1862; d. 7 June, 1866.
1197.   2. Lizzie-Jane^9, b. 14 Feb. 1864.
1198.   3. Edward-Everett^9, b. 12 Dec, 1865 ; died 15 June, 1866.
    By 2d marriage :
1198^a.   4. Eddie^9.

1199. HARRIET-ANN^7, [633] (*John^6, Bethiah^5* (Farwell) **Holton**, *William^4, Isaac^3, Joseph^2, Henry^1,*) b. 28 Nov. 1808, Springfield, Vt. ; married, 28 June, 1838,

---

* Theophilus^6 Hoyt was born 4 Feb. 1773, at South Hampton, N. H., and died 26 Sept. 1849, in Wisconsin. His wife Sebrina d. 26 Feb. 1818. He married 2d, Rebecca (Fish) Winslow, widow of Dr. Joseph Winslow of Windsor, Vt. [See Winslow Memorial [5451]].

John-Humphrey NOYES, b. 8 Sept. 1811, son of John and Polly (Hayes) of Brattleboro, and Dummerston, Vt. Mr. Noyes was a licentiate of Yale Theological School in 1833.

Child :

1200. 1. THEODORE-RICHARDS⁸, b. Putney, Vt. 26 July, 1841 ; commenced the study of medicine at Yale College, pursued his studies at Bellevue, N. Y. City and graduated at the medical department of Yale College 18 July, 1867.

1201. JONATHAN-WARNER⁷, [635] (*Alexander⁶*, *Bethiah⁵*, (Farwell) **Holton**, *William⁴*, *Isaac³*, *Joseph²*, *Henry¹*,) b. 30 July, 1807, Westminster, Vt. ; m. in Jennings Co., Ind., 17 Dec. 1829, Charlotte-Bailey Perry, b. 13 Feb. 1812, Blount Co., Tenn., daughter of Ransom and Catharine (Martin) of Tenn., and gr. dau. of Warner and —— Bailey, Crown Point, Lake Co., Ind.

At the organization of Lake Co. Ind. Mr. Holton was elected County Treasurer, and now, (1879), holds the office of post master. Farmer.

Res. Deep River, Ind., and, 1879, *Stevens Creek, White Co., Ark.*

[Since the record of his parents was in type on page 99, we learn that his aged mother, now in her ninety-seventh year, is living with her son William-Augustus-Warner⁷ Holton, at Crown Point, Lake Co., Ind., who writes of her that she "is slowly passing away. She has become entirely blind and hard of hearing, and only leaves her bed for her chair which she occupies, the most of the day, with continued rocking. Her mind is quite active and she talks of things long since past ; * * * sings with effort 'Old Hundred,' 'Be Thou O God exalted high,' and many other pieces." The compiler, who visited her a few years since, was struck with her stately, dignified appearance—tall, erect and strong she seemed to have inherited the best qualities of her renowned ancestry.

This venerable mother was the daughter of Gen. Jonathan Warner and Hannah (Mandell), and grand daughter of Paul Mandell and Susanna (Ruggles).

The following is her Ruggles pedigree : Thomas¹ Ruggles from Nazing, Essex Co., Eng. and of Roxbury, Mass., 1637, and wife Mary; Capt. Samuel² and wife Ann or Hannah (Fowle)*; Capt. Samuel³ and Martha (Woodbridge)†; Rev. Timothy⁴ and Mary (White) of Rochester, Mass.; Susanna⁵ Ruggles who married Paul Mandell of New Bedford and Hardwick, Mass. ; and Hannah⁶ Mandell who married Gen. Jonathan Warner, whose daughter Harriet⁷ Warner married Alexander⁶ Holton.

From the late Mrs. Jones, 12 Court St., Springfield, Mass., sister of the above Mrs. Harriet (Warner) Holton, we learn that Paul Mandell was a merchant of New Bedford, and left there because his aristocratic nature could not brook the idea that

*Capt. Samuel² m. 2d on the 26 May, 1670, Ann Bright, b. 17 March, 1644, dau. of Henry and Ann (Goldstone) and sister of Beriah who m. Isaac Fowle, uncle of his first wife. [See Chart IX, page 113, and serial number 1112.]

†Martha Woodbridge was dau. of Rev. John and Mercy (Dudley) who was dau. of Gov. Thomas Dudley, and sister of Ann, the poetess, wife of Gov. Simon Bradstreet, Patience, wife of Maj. Gen. Daniel Dennison, and of Gov. Joseph Dudley, whose son Paul was Chief Justice of Massachusetts. [See 1112 this book, also page 25 Appendix Winslow Memorial.]

his apprentice should presume to compete with him in trade in the same city—hence his removal to Hardwick, thereby placing his family where educational advantages were few, and throwing upon himself and wife the task of educating their children. For this duty, fortunately, they were both well qualified, Mrs. Mandell having been educated with her brothers, one of whom at least, Brig. Gen. Timothy Ruggles was a graduate of Harvard College; consequently, Mrs. Hannah (Mandell) Warner though highly educated was never a student at any school.]

[For fuller records of the Ruggles family and others allied to them by marriage see Appendix of Winslow Memorial.]

Children of Jonathan-Warner[7] and Charlotte-B. (Perry) Holton:

1202. 1. ELLEN-MARIA[8], b. 15 Nov. 1830, Jennings Co., Ind.; married at Valparaizo, Porter Co., Ind., 12 Sept. 1865, Lewis Mosier.

Child:

1203.   1. Catharine-Louisa[9], b. 15 Dec. 1866, Porter Co., Ind.

1204. 2. JOHN[8], b. 18 Feb. 1833, Jennings Co. Ind; d. 11 Apr. 1843, at Crown Point, Ind.
1205. 3. MARTHA[8], b. 23 Feb. 1839, Crown Point, Lake Co., Ind.; d. there 19 Jan. 1840.
1206. 4. ALEXANDER[8], b. 14 July, 1841, C. P.; d. there, 3 May, 1843.
1207. 5. CATHARINE[8], b. 12 Jan. 1845, C. P.; m. 7 Apr. 1863, Philip Louks, of Canada West, b. 23 Apr. 1837. He is of Dutch and English descent.
Res. 1879, *Stevens Creek, White Co., Ark.*

Children born at Wheeler, Porter Co., Ind.:

1208.   1. Warren-Lincoln[9], b. 27 Jan. 1864.
1209.   2. Jonathan-Wilber-Augustus[9], b. 2 Nov. 1868.
1210.   3. Perry-Holton[9], b. March, 1871.
1211. 6. CHARLOTTE[8], b. 2 May, 1849, Deep River, Lake Co., Ind.
1212. 7. PERRY[8], b. 24 Feb. 1852, Deep River; died there 18 Apr. 1855.

1213. WILLIAM-AUGUSTUS-WARNER[7], [636] (*Alexander[6], Bethiah[5]* (Farwell) Holton, *William[4], Isaac[3], Joseph[2], Henry[1]*,) b. 15 May, 1809, New Hardwick, Vt.; married, 8 Feb. 1846, Bernetta Vosburg, b. 1 Nov. 1828, dau. of Barnet and Sarah (Ballard) of Crown Point, Ind. Mr. Holton was the first Recorder of Lake Co., Ind. Farmer and fruit grower.   Res. Deep River and *Crown Point, Ind.*

Children all born in Crown Point, Ind.:

1214. 1. HARRIET-ANN[8], b. 14 Aug. 1847, Crown Point; d. 28 Aug. 1847.
1215. 2. CHARLES-AUGUSTUS-WARNER[8], b. 1 Aug. 1848; m. Apr. 1873, Elizabeth Dyke of McComb, Hancock Co., Ohio.
Res. 1879, *Linneus, Lynn Co., Mo.*
1216. 3. SARAH-FRANCES[8], b. 7 Feb. 1850; d. 24 Feb. 1853.

1217. 4. JOHN-DUMONT⁸, b. 25 Nov. 1851 ; died in Kansas, 17 Sept. 1875.
1218. 5. OLIVE⁸, b. 3 Feb. 1853, d. 23 Sept. 1853.
1219. 6. GEORGE⁸, b. 11 Aug. 1856, d. 9 July, 1858.
1220. 7. WILLIAM-AUGUSTUS-WARNER⁸, b. 3 July, 1859.
1221. 8. FRANCIS-ALEXANDER⁸, b. 13 Dec. 1868.

1222. HARRIET⁷, [637] (*Alexander⁶*, *Bethiah⁵* (Farwell) **Holton.** *William⁴, Isaac³, Joseph², Henry¹,*) b. at Vevay, Ind. 1 Nov. 1818; married, near Crown Point, Ind., 8 Jan. 1846, Asahel **ALBEE,** b. Barton Vt. 17 Dec. 1816, son of Benjamin and Sophia (Vance) of that place; later of Henry, Marshall Co., Ill. and Crown Point, Lake Co., Ind.*

Mr. Albee settled in Wheatland, Bureau Co., Illinois, where he has since resided.
Farmer   Address, *Tiskilwa, Bureau Co., Ill.*

Children :

1223. 1. MARIA⁸, b. 19 Nov. 1846 ; m. 22 Dec. 1863, Elisha-P. De Maranville, b. 1 July, 1825, in Thompkins Co., N. Y., son of Nehemiah and Phebe (Parish) originally of Massachusetts, subsequently of Milo, Ill. She d. Wheatland, 4 Jan. 1871.

Children :

1224. 1. Chloe⁹, b. 25 Dec. 1865, Tiskilwa, Bureau Co., Ill.
1224ᵃ. 2. Henry⁹, b. 11 Feb. 1870.

1225. 2. CHARLES⁸ b. 20 July, 1848.
1226. 3. ALMA⁸, b. 5 May, 1850 ; m. Princeton, Ill., 27 Oct. 1875, Alvin-Eugene **Willard,** b. 22 Dec. 1846, at Great Falls, N. H., s. of Fabens and Hannah (———.) Machinist in watch factory, Elgin, Ill.
1227. 4. SERAPH⁸, b. 30 July, 1852; d. 28 Aug, 1852.
1228. 5. MIRIAM⁸, b. 2 Aug. 1854 ; m. Princeton, Ill., 11 March, 1875, James-Byron **Swarthout,** b. 8 July, 1850, Barrington, Yates Co., N. Y., son of James-W. and Maria (Wright) of State of N. Y. Farmer.
                                   Res. *Milo, Bureau Co., Ill.*

Child :

1228ᵃ. Ada-Elizabeth⁹ b. 1 May, 1877, Milo.

1229. 6. ALEXANDER⁸, b. 1 Jan. 1858.

---

*Benjamin¹ Albee was in Braintree, Mass. 1641, was made a freeman there, 18 May, 1642. His son Benjamin² was b. at Medfield 1653. Mr. Savage names John of Braintree, 1640, and a John of Rehoboth who had a daughter Hannah, b. 10 Oct. 1673. We have partially traced several lines of this name, but have not as yet fully established the ancestral line of Asahel of Tiskilwa. This we hope to give in the HOLTON MEMORIAL VOLUME. It may be found to be in a line from John Albree, b. in the Island of New Providence in 1688, who came to Boston in 1700, where he m. in 1711 Elizabeth Green, a cousin of Gov. Belcher.

Yours truly
Pliny N. White.

Rev. Pliny H. [...]

Rev. PLINY HOLTON [...]
[...] Isaac, Joseph, Henry [...]
[...] at Coventry, Vt.
[...] left fatherless when a little more [...]
[...] upon his mother, a woman of great [...]
[...] acquired facility in reading [...]
[...] train his other relations [...]
[...] study and [...] at [...]
[...] and many of the elder [...]
[...] suggested. In a school [...]
[...] where he was a [...] from [...]
[...] a store for a few years [...]
[...] Vt., and was ad[...]
[...] first session of Court [...]
[...] at law in West Ward [...]
[...] from the latter date till [...] and [...]
[...]mber, 1852.

[...] 1851 [...] he was editor of the Brattleboro[...]
during the next year was [...] editor. From January, 1853 to
[...] as clerk in the [...] establishment of L. and T. Fair-
[...] St. Johnsbury, Vt. From [...] 1857 [...] 1858 was editor and
[...] of the [...] at Andover [...]. He pur-
sued a [...] course of study [...] of years [...]
[...], Vt. [...] A[...] 1858, [...] was licensed [...]
[...] Hampshire [...] Association. After preaching [...]
[...] Peru and Putney, Vt.; he removed to Coventry,
[...] pastor 8 [...] 1858. In a few [...]
[...] twenty were added to the church. He was [...]
[...] N. W[...] preached the sermon. He graduated in [...]
[...] York. 1[...]

[...] was interred at Westminster, Windham county, Vt. 27 A[...]
[...] his grand-parents Joel and Lethiah (Farwell) Holton, who [...]
[...] rest in the same cemetery.

[...] associations, with which he had long been connected [...]
[...] monument to his memory; a few rods from [...]
[...] legislature to commemorate an early step in the process [...]
[...] establishment of national independence.

[...] about twenty years of age he commenced writing for the [...]
[...] a contributor to the newspapers and magazines [...]
[...] At different times he wrote editorially for the Vermont [...]
Newport Express, Coaticook, and Orleans Independent [...]
[...] the Congregational Quarterly he contributed and [...]
[...] in these.

[...] he furnished some hundreds of articles [...]
Vermont history and biography. Among them was a [...]
[...] of Middlebury college, continued nearly every week [...]

Yours truly,
Thos. B. Reed.

Rev. Pliny-Holton⁷ White.

1230. REV. PLINY-HOLTON⁷, [631](*Bethiah⁶* (Holton) **White**, *Bethiah⁵* (*Farwell*) Holton, *William⁴, Isaac³, Joseph², Henry¹,*) b. 6 Oct. 1822, at Springfield, Vt.; d. 24 April, 1869, at Coventry, Vt.

He was left fatherless when a little more than three years old, and his education devolved upon his mother, a woman of great energy and force of character. His early *home* acquired facility in reading and memorizing became, in later times, a great aid to him in his official relations and pastoral duties, as he could in the pulpit or elsewhere accurately and *confidently* repeat all the psalms and most of the chapters of the New Testament and many of the other parts of the Bible, or any sections thereof, as occasion suggested. His school privileges were only those obtained at Limerick So. Berwick where he was a student from his eighth to his fifteenth year. He was clerk in a store for a few years, then studied law with Hon. Wm. C. Bradley of Westminster, Vt., and was admitted to the Windham County Bar, 24 Nov. 1843, it being the first session of Court after his arriving at the age of twenty-one.

He practised law in West Wardsboro from 15 Apr. 1844 till 31 March, 1848, in Londonderry from the latter date till 1 February, 1851; and in Brattleboro from that time till 25 December, 1852.

From 1 February, 1851 till the end of the year he was editor of the Brattleboro *Eagle*, and during the next year was assistant editor. From January, 1853 to August, 1857 was clerk in the manufacturing establishment of E. and T. Fairbanks & Co. St. Johnsbury. From 15 Aug. 1857 to 7 May, 1858 was editor and joint publisher of the Hampshire and Franklin *Express* at Amherst, Mass. He pursued theological studies privately for a number of years; preached his first sermon at Westminster, Vt. 18 Apr. 1858, and was licensed at Amherst, Mass. 11 May 1858, by the Hampshire East Association. After preaching a few sabbaths each at Barnardston, Mass. and Putney, Vt.; he removed to Coventry, Vt. and commenced his labors as acting pastor 8 August, 1858. In a few months a revival occurred by which about twenty were added to the church. He was ordained 15 February, 1859. Rev. George N. Webber preached the sermon. He remained in Coventry to the close of his life 24 April, 1869.

His body was interred at Westminster, Windham county, Vt. 27 Apr. near the graves of his grandparents Joel⁵ and Bethiah⁵ (Farwell) Holton, whose monument ancestral stands in the same cemetery.

Temperance associations, with which he had long been an active co-laborer, united in erecting a monument to his memory; a few rods from that placed by order of the Vermont legislature to commemorate an early step in the course of events which established our national independence.

When about twenty years of age he commenced writing for the periodical press and was a copious contributor to the newspapers and magazines during all the rest of his life. At different times he wrote editorially for the *Vermont Journal, Peoples Journal, Newport Express, Caledonian,* and *Orleans Independent Standard.* To the *Historical Magazine* and *Congregational Quarterly* he contributed numerous historical and biographical articles.

For the *Vermont Record* he furnished some hundreds of articles, most of them relating to Vermont history and biography. Among them was a series of biographical notices of Alumni of Middlebury college, continued nearly every week for several years; a series of biographies of Presidents of the University of Vermont, and a series of Memoirs of Governors of Vermont. He was the Vermont correspondent of the *Congregationalist* from 1852 till 1869. He wrote much for the New York *Observer*, The Rutland *Herald*, The Vermont *Chronicle*; and contributed occasionally to many other periodicals.

Among his published addresses and sermons were the following:

1. "The Golden Age of Agriculture," an address before the Windham county Agricultural Society, at its Annual Fair, 3 Oct. 1850.

2d, "Religious Lessons from the Atlantic Telegraph," a sermon preached at Coventry, Vt. 2 Aug. 1858.

3d, "The life and Services of Mathew Lyon," an address pronounced October 29th 1858, before the Vermont Historical Society, in the presence of the General assembly of Vermont. Published Burlington, 1858, pp. 26, 8vo.

4. "A History of Coventry, Orleans co. Vt." Irasburgh 1859, pp. 70, 8vo.

5. "Death in the Midst of Life," a sermon at the funeral of Henry-H. Frost.

6. "Methuselah," a sermon preached at Coventry February 12, 1860. Published in the *Herald of Truth*, Vol. II.

7. "Home Duties in Time of War," a sermon delivered in Coventry, Vt. on the occasion of the National Fast, Sept. 26, 1861.—Published in the *Orleans Independent Standard*, 11 Oct. 1861.

8. "Christian Patriotism," a sermon preached at North Troy, 25 May, 1862, in commemoration of Lt. Charles-F. Bailey, who died of a wound received in the skirmish at Lee's Mills, Va. 16 April. In the *Orleans Independent Standard*, 6 June, 1862.

9. A sermon preached at Coventry on occasion of the National Thanksgiving, August 9, 1863. In the *Orleans Ind. Standard*, 21 Aug. 1863.

10. A sermon occasioned by the assassination of President Lincoln. Preached at Coventry, 23 Apr. 1865. Brattleboro, 1865, pp. 20, 8vo.

11. "The Ecclesiastical History of Vt.," an Essay read before the General Convention of Vermont at Newbury, June, 1866.

12 "Jonas Galusha, the Fifth Governor of Vermont," a memoir read before the Vt. His. Society at Montpelier, Oct. 1866.

13. "Annals of Salem," 8vo., pp. 4.

14. A sermon preached at Westminster, Vt. June 11, 1867, on the one hundredth anniversary of the organization of the Cong. church. Bellows' Falls, 1867, pp. 27, 8vo.

15. "Manual of the Congregational church, Coventry, Vt." Montpelier, 1868, pp. 19, 8vo.

16. History of Newspapers in Orleans county, 1868.

17. History of Westminster church. 1869, p. 20.

18. History of Orleans county churches. 1868, pp. 61.

In 1851 he was an assistant clerk of the Vermont House of Representatives. In 1852-3, he was Secretary of civil and military affairs to Gov. Fairbanks, was the representative of Coventry in the Legislature of Vermont 1862 and 1863, and Chaplain of the Senate 1864 and 1865. In November, 1863, he was appointed Superintendent of Recruiting in Orleans county, and held the office till the close of the war; also held the same office in the Fifth Military District of Vermont, and superintended the recruiting of the regiment. In November, 1862, he was appointed a member of the Vermont Board of Education, and, by repeated appointments, held the office for six successive years, and was the author of the annual reports of the Board; was Superintendent of schools in St. Johnsbury one year, 1857, and in Coventry two years 1862-1864; was chaplain of the third reg't of Vermont militia.

He was an earnest worker in the Temperance cause all his life, and at the time of his death held the office of Grand Worthy Chief of the Independent Order of Good Templers in the State of Vermont.

Rev. Mr. White married at Belchertown, Mass., 11 May, 1847, Electa-Barber-DickinsonGates, b. 18 Dec. 1821, at Belchertown, dau. of Horace and Electa (Dickinson) of that town. She resides, 1879, *Amherst, Mass.*

Children·

1231. 1. MARGARET-ELIZABETH⁶, b. 21 Mar. 1849, Londonderry, Vt.; graduated at Tilden Ladies Seminary, West Lebanon, N. H.; married, Amherst, Mass. 13 July, 1870, Earle-Grey Baldwin, b. 9 Dec. 1848, Coventry, Vt., son of John and Emeline (Thrasher) of Bolton, P. Q. Principal of Coventry Academy, Vt.; Belchertown High School, Mass.; 1874, Norwalk, Ct.; 1876, High School, Palmer, Mass.; 1878, Principal of Pittsfield High School, Mass. Res. Londonderry, Brattleboro, St. Johnsbury and Coventry, Vt., Amherst, Belchertown and 1879, *Pittsfield, Mass.*

Children :

1232. 1. William-Earle⁶, b. 13 Dec. 1871, Belchertown, Mass.
1233. 2. Winifred-May⁶, b. 12 Dec. 1875.
1234. 2. JOHN-ALEXANDER⁶, b. 15 Feb. 1851, Brattleboro, Vt.; died there, 12 Aug. 1851.
1235. 3. WILLIAM-HOLTON⁶, (named for William¹, the first American ancestor) b. 1 Aug. 1855, St. Johnsbury, Vt. Dec. 1878, in junior class of Amherst College.

1236. SETH-ARNOLD⁷, [641] (*Isaac⁶, Bethiah⁵* (Farwell Holton, *William⁴, Isaac³, Joseph², Henry¹,*) b. Limerick, Me., 14 Nov. 1828; married, Fontanelle, Nebraska, 4 Nov. 1857, Elizabeth Roe, born in England, 4 Nov. 1826, and died at Hillsgrove, McDonough Co., Ill., 4 Jan. 1860. s.p. He married 2d, at 502 West 4th St., Washington, D. C., 19 June, 1866, Margaret-Farley Shedd, b. 4 Mar. 1835, Baltimore, Md., dau. of William-Poole and Catharine-Maria (Simms) of Washington.

Mr. Holton was a farmer till he enlisted, 15 Oct. 1862, in his country's service. Was immediately assigned to duty as Hospital Steward U. S. A., at Island Hall and Stanton Hospitals, Washington, D. C., and College Hospital, Georgetown, D. C., which position he held till July, 1863. From 1863, was Hospital Steward U. S. A. at Medical Purveyor's office, Washington, under Capt. Henry Johnson, Medical Store-keeper U.S.A., and Brev. Lieut. Col. Charles Sutherland, Asst. Med. Purveyor U. S. A. Since 1867, in 3d Auditor's office, Treasury Department, Washington.

Mr. H. has resided at Bellows Falls and Westminster, Vt., Hillsgrove and Galesburg, Ill., Fontanelle, Neb., Washington, D. C. and,
1878, *Bladensburg, Prince George's Co., Md.*

Child :

1237. 1. WILLIAM-ISAAC⁸, b. Hyattsville, Prince George Co., Md., 26 Oct. 1872; died there, 12 July, 1873.

1238. REBECCA-RANNEY⁷, [642] (*Isaac⁶, Bethiah⁵* (Farwell) Holton, *Wm⁴, Isaac³, Joseph², Henry¹,*) b. 8 Sept. 1830, Limerick, Me.; married, Hillsgrove, Ill., 7

March, 1849, Rev. Joseph **MASON**, b. 4 Jan. 1812, Granby, Mass., son of Joseph and Elizabeth (White) of Spencer, Mass.   Res. *Godfrey, Madison Co., Ill.*

1239.   1. EDWARD-AUGUSTUS⁶, b. Spencer, Worcester Co., Mass., 3 July, 1850.
1240.   2. ANNA-ELIZABETH⁶, b. at Alton, Ill., 10 Aug. 1856.
1241.   3. CLARA⁶, b. Hamilton, Ill., 31 March, 1862; died at Carthage, Ill., 22 May, 1864.

1242.   Dr. JOHN-AMBROSE⁷, [643] (*Isaac⁶, Bethiah⁵* (Farwell) **Holton**, *William⁴, Isaac³, Joseph², Henry¹*,) b. at Bellows Falls, Vt., 12 Apr. 1832; d. 7 May, 1873 at Argenta, Pulaski Co., near Little Rock, Ark.; married, Danbury, Fairfield Co. Conn., 25 Nov. 1855, Adelaide Taylor, b. there, 3 Dec. 1838, dau. of Joel and Linda (Adams) of Danbury.

Dr. Holton was a student at Knox College, Galesburg, Ill. from 1851 to 1853; at the Medical College, Keokuk, Iowa, where his cousin Edward Arnold was Professor, from 1853 to 1855, when he graduated M. D.; commenced practice of medicine and dentistry at Macomb, Ill., and followed his profession, there and at Hillsgrove, till the autumn of 1858, when he removed to Stamford, Ct., and there remained in the practice of dentistry till he enlisted as private at Hartford, Ct., 12 June, 1861, in Co. I, 4th Reg. Conn. Vols., which was afterward the 1st Artillery. After one month's service as private, he was detached as Acting Hospital Steward at Hagarstown and Baltimore, Md., in which capacity he continued till his discharge, 29 March, 1862. He immediately reenlisted as Hospital Steward in the regular army for three years; was soon detailed as clerk in the Medical Purveyor's office, which position he held in Washington, till from exposure in the discharge of his duties he had an attack of lung disease, attended by hemorrhage. It was therefore decided by the army officers in Washington that it was for his own and the best interests of the service that he should perform the duties of Hospital Steward and Assistant Surgeon in the milder climate of Alberquerque, New Mexico. Accordingly, in the winter of 1864, he left Washington and entered on his duties at that place. He remained in New Mexico, mostly at A., till the fall of 1866, when he returned north, and the following winter attended medical lectures at the Jefferson Med. Coll. Philadelphia. His lung difficulty returning, he again sought a milder climate, and took up his residence at Argenta, near Little Rock, Ark., where he died of consumption in the triumphs of the gospel faith and hope 7 March, 1873.

Children;

1243.   1. PLINY-WHITE-TAYLOR⁸, b. Stamford, Conn. 10 June, 1860.
1244.   2. LINDA⁸, b. Danbury, Conn. 17 Nov. 1864.
1245.   3. JOEL-HERBERT⁸, b. Vineland, N.J., 7 Sept. 1867.

1246.   Rev. CHARLES-AUGUSTUS⁷, A. B., [644] (*Isaac⁶, Bethiah⁵* (Farwell) **Holton**, *William⁴, Isaac³, Joseph², Henry¹*,) b. Bellows Falls, Vt., 8 March, 1834; married, Prospect Grove, Scotland Co., Mo., 10 Aug. 1868, Mary-Elinor Yeager, b. 6 March, 1842, Phillippa, Barbour Co., West Va., dau. of Daniel and **Lucretia**

(Holder) of Prospect Grove. Mrs. Holton died at the United Brethren Parsonage, Five Mile Grove, Livingstone Co., Ill., 10 Sept. 1870. "She bade her husband and friends farewell with calm and cheerful words, and left the additional testimony of an earnest Christian life" [from Obit.]

He married 2d, on the 4th of May, 1873, Mary-Elizabeth Hopper, b. 1 Feb. 1852, dau. of Abraham and Elizabeth (Hayden, d. of Clement, brother of Luther of Huntington, L. I.) of Ozark, Christian Co., Mo.

Mr. Holton graduated at Knox College, Galesburg, Ill., in the summer of 1858. He enlisted for three years on the 28th anniversary of his birth (8 Mar. 1862) "as a true soldier to do battle for my country and her glory." His enlistment oath was taken at Macomb, Ill. He was sent to Chicago and remained in Camp Douglas till June 24, when his regiment, the 65th Ill., was ordered to report in Virginia and was stationed at Martinsburg till 11th Sept., when it fell back to Harper's Ferry, and four days later surrendered as prisoners of war ; exchanged 10 Jan. 1863, and 22 Apr was en route for Kentucky; remained in camp in Lexington, partly on account of small-pox among the soldiers, six weeks ; and in June proceeded up the Ohio to Catlettsburg, thence up the Big Sandy to Beaver River, doing duty in that region till August, when the regiment returned to Lexington, and thence to Camp Nelson, and there remained till Gen. Burnside began his march across the Cumberland Mountains. Reaching Knoxville September 5th, they participated in besieging that city. About Christmas, the army, or that portion of it to which Mr. H. belonged, was put on short rations. subsisting on parched corn and "marching at that."

At the expiration of his three years service he reenlisted as a veteran and was mustered in at Lanesville, 7 Apr. 1864. After a furlough of thirty days rejoined his regiment at Kingston, Ga., in which remained till after the fall of Atlanta ; subsequently reported to Gen. Thomas and marching from place to place watched the movements of Hood till that General was "outeroded." He was discharged 13 July, 1865; visited his friends, and proceeded to Chicago where he spent a few months in studying telegraphy; returned to Carthage where he was express agent, studying meanwhile for the ministry.

In the fall of 1867 he was licensed to preach by the M.E. Central Ill. Conference, and sent to Blandersville; in the fall of 1868, was stationed at New Michigan, Livingston Co., Ill.; 1869 took a dismissal from the M. E. Church and joined the United Brethren, but preached one year after for the Central Ill. Conference at Fairbury, Livingston Co.; he received ordination 14 Sept. 1877, at Arrowsmith, McLean Co., Ill., at the hands of Rev. J. Weaver, Bishop; settled in Blackstone, Livingstone Co., where he has since resided.

Rev. C. A. Holton has been postmanster in B. since 1871, and justice of the peace from 1875 to 1877. Though in deviation from genealogical practice we give the name with serial number of his adopted son.

Children :

1247. 1. WALTER-FAY^4, b. Five Mile Grove, Livingston Co., Ill., 8 May, 1870.
1248. 2. HARRY-LORENZO (adopted by decree of Court) b. 25 Nov. 1869, and died 1 Nov. 1876.

1249. JULIA-ESTHER[7], [645] (*Isaac[6], Bethiah[5]* (Farwell) **Holton**, *William[4] Isaac[3], Joseph[2], Henry[1]*,) b. 28 March, 1836, Hillsgrove, McDonough Co., Ill.; married there, 20 Aug. 1857, Hiram-Gano **FERRIS**, born at Howard, Steuben Co., N. Y., 13 May, 1822, son of Stephen and Eunice (Beebe) of Fountain Green, Ill. Lawyer.
Res. *Carthage, Hancock Co., Ill.*

Children all born at Carthage:

1250. 1. JUNIUS-HOLTON[8], b. 24 June, 1858; grad. A.B., at Carthage College, May, 1878, and was spending the following summer visiting points of interest in California.
1251. 2. ESTA-MAUD[8], b. 31 Aug. 1860; 1878, Student in Carthage Coll.
1252. 3. STEPHEN-HOLTON[8], b. 13 Sept. 1862 · 1878,   "
1253. 4. JULIA[8], b. 17 June, 1865.
1254. 5. ELLEN[8], b. 4 Sept. 1867.
1255. 6. PHEBE[8], b. 15 Dec. 1869.
1256. 7. HIRAM-BURNS[8], b. 25 Jan. 1872.
1257. 8. JOEL-EDWARD[8], b. 2 Jan. 1874.

1258. EDWIN-PARKER[7], [649] (*Orra-West[6]* (Parker) **Whitmore**, *Elisabeth[5]* (Farwell) **Parker**, *William[4], Isaac[3], Joseph[2], Henry[1]*,) b. 22 Jan. 1808, Lebanon, N. H.; married, 16 Nov. 1837, at Springfield, Vt., Mary-Elizabeth Chase, b. 10 Dec. 1820, S., dau. of Jonathan and Susan (Fisher) of S. She died at Springfield, 12 July, 1841.

Mr. Whitmore, after attaining his majority, remained a few years on the farm in North Charlestown, N. H., before entering on his career as a merchant in Springfield, Vt. After several years of success in mercantile pursuits in that place, he removed to New York City and became editor and one of the proprietors of the "Farmer and Mechanic"; held an interest and an editorial position in "The Artizan," and was also connected with other papers and magazines; subsequently, he furnished collections of books to town and Sunday-school libraries.

Many years since he spent considerable time and money in the collection of records of the Whitmore, Parker and Farwell families, which he has generously furnished to the compilers of this volume, and in various ways contributed to the progress of their genealogical and patriot orphan work, being from the organization of the Institute of Reward an efficient co-laborer and vice-president of the society. [See Winslow Memorial, page 390.]

In 1870 he was called as an executor of the estate of his brother, Horace-M., to California, the settlement of which has since required his attention and residence in San Francisco.

His unostentatious, orderly and efficient habits of life and business are worthy of imitation.

Children born in Springfield:

1259. 1. SUSAN-ELIZABETH[8], b. 25 May, 1839; married at Springfield, 4 Aug. 1864, William-Augustus **Wilcox**, born 4 Sept. 1839, Middlebury, Vt., son of

Augustus-Benjamin and Clarissa (Jewett) of Middlebury. [Augustus-B. was b. 12 Aug. 1795, Madison, Ct. ; d. there, 19 May, 1844 ; Clarissa Jewett b. in New Haven, Vt., 9 Sept. 1806. They were married at Middlebury, 22 June, 1829.] Res. Alton, Ill., Rockport, Mass., Middlebury, and, 1879, *Springfield, Vt.*
    Children :

1260.   1. Maie-Lizzie^9, b. 2 July, 1866, Alton, Madison Co. Ill.
1261.   2. Carrie-Emma^9, b. 1 Apr. 1869, Rockport, Essex Co., Mass.
1262.   2. MARIAN-PARKER^8, b. 16 Feb. 1841 ; married, 10 Jan. 1865, at Weathersfield, Vt,. Daniel-Augustus Wheeler, b. 3 July, 1839, Weathersfield, son of Artemas and Sarah (Harlow) of W.
                    Res. Rockport, Mass., and *Perkinsville, Windsor Co., Vt.*
    Child :

1263.   1. Edwin-Whitmore^9, b. 28 July, 1868, Rockport, Mass.

1264 HAMLIN^7, [650] (*Ora-West^6* (Parker) Whitmore, *Elizabeth^5* (Farwell) Parker, *William^4, Isaac^3, Joseph^2, Henry^1*,) b. 5 March, 1809, Lebanon, N. H. ; married, at Springfield, Vt., 16 Nov. 1837, Seloma-Whiting Sawyer, b. 10 July, 1818, Reading, Vt., dau. of Benjamin-H. and Maranda (Whiting) of Reading. She died 4 Sept. 1877, at Springfield.

[Benjamin Sawyer was born 22 May, 1793 ; Maranda Whiting, b. 6 May, 1792, d. 12 Jan. 1867. They were married, 19 June, 1817.]

Mr. Whitmore is an amateur farmer and a manufacturer, being the chief proprietor of a woolen factory in Springfield, Vt. Res. *Springfield, Vt.*

    Children born in Springfield, Vt.:

1265.   1. OSCAR-HAMLIN^8, b. 18 Jan. 1839; d. same day.
1266.   2. BENJAMIN-FRANKLIN^8, b. 28 Aug. 1840; d. 7 Oct. 1840, Springfield.
1267   3. ADIN-HAMLIN^8, b. 31 March, 1843; enlisted in the army, and having been educated in a military college, became drill master to the regiment, and was acknowledged to be the best tactician and drill officer in the brigade; was Acting Sergt. Major and Major. His regiment was held for the defence of Washington ; was on guard and picket duty from 23 Oct. 1863, to the time of mustering out in Sept. 1864, and participated in the battle of Gettysburg in common with other Vermont troops, fighting "like old soldiers." He became ill with camp fever and was discharged for disability.

        Mr. W. has been engaged with his father in the manufacturing of woolen goods.

1268.   4. NOEL-MOTT^8, b. 7 Sept. 1845 ; died, 24 Nov. 1872, Springfield, Vt. He completed his school education at Bishop Hopkin's school, Burlington, Vt.; commenced business in 1865 in the shawl department of H. B. Claflin & Co., New York City, remaining there five years. Upon leaving that firm he connected himself with a commission house in N.Y. (Wisner & Townsend), taking charge of the shawl account, and spending a part of his time at the mills in Walden, N.Y., and doing the designing for the same. In this he was remarkably successful. The head of the wholesale department of A. T. Stewart & Co. informed the writer that Mr. Whitmore's designs the year previous to his death were the best in domestic goods which the American market afforded.

While in the employ of Claflin & Co., he contracted a disease, which became chronic, and finally terminated his brief but efficient career 24 Nov. 1872.

1269.   5. AGNES-SELOMA⁶, b. 4 Aug. 1851; married 1876, George-Washington Prichards. Lawyer.   1878, *Hot Springs, Ark.*
1270.   6. JERVIS-JOHN⁶, b. 28 Mar. 1856. He was residing, 1878, *Jacksonville, Fla.*

1271. JOSEPH-FLAGG⁷, [652] (*Orra-West⁶* (*Parker*) Whitmore, *Elizabeth⁵* (*Farwell*) Parker, *William⁴, Isaac³, Joseph², Henry¹,*) b. 22 Dec. 1811, Lebanon, N.H:; d. a few years since; m. at Hartford, O., 15 Mar. 1837, Maria Hayes, b. 13 Dec. 1817, H., dau. of Judge Richard, b. 6 Jan. 1771, d. 5 Nov. 1837, and Mary (Lane), b. 15 Apr. 1773, d. 3 Aug. 1840. Mrs. Whitmore married, 2d, Benjamin Carpenter, and 1878, resided at Crystal Lake, Ill. Farmer.   Res. Cleveland and *Painesville O.*

Children:

1272.   1. ELLEN-LOUISA⁸, b. 17 Apr. 1838; died at West Andover, O, 6 Sept. 1857.
1273.   2. LUCIA-ESTELLA⁸, b. 24 July, 1839; m. George-B. Stone, of Painesville, Lake Co., O. Mr. Stone holds some responsible position on the Lake Shore railroad, with which he has been connected for twelve years.
1274.   3. HAYES-GIDDINGS⁸, b. 23 Aug. 1844; died at West Andover, 19 Jan. 1866.
1275.   4. MARY-JOSEPHINE⁸, b. 24 Dec. 1848; m. at Andover, O., 18 Dec. 1867, Osman-Smith King, of Sheriden, N.Y.; b. 10 Sept. 1844, son of Alexander and Louisa (Francisco) of Vineland, N. J.
Res. Painesville and *Zanesville, O.*

Child :

1276.   1. Hayes-Giddings⁹, b. 24 Dec. 1868, Painesville, O.

1277. HENRY-SYLVESTER⁷, [654] (*Orra-West* (Parker) Whitmore, *Elizabeth⁵*, (Farwell) Parker, *Wm.⁴, Isaac³, Joseph², Henry¹,*) b. 28 Oct. 1818, at Charlestown, N.H., m. 25 Nov. 1847, Charlestown, Mass., Mary-Ann Varney, b. 16 June, 1826, C. only child of Shadrack and Mary-Ann (Rice, b. Boston, 12 Nov. 1799) of Ch'town.

Mr. Whitmore was formerly engaged in mercantile pursuits but has retired from business, enjoying the fruits of his active life in a convenient and tasteful home, whose grounds have been laid out and ornamented chiefly in accordance with his own tastes and the labor of his own hands.   Res. *Everett, Middlesex Co., Mass.*

Children :

1278.   1. GEORGE-HORACE⁸, b. 8 March, 1850, Newton Corners, Middlesex Co., Mass.   Res. *Everett, Mass.*
1279.   2. ELLA-GERTRUDE⁸, b. 1 Sept. 1854. Newton Corners.
1280.   3. EDWIN-HENRY⁸, b. 4 Nov. 1856, Chelsea, Essex Co., Mass,
1281.   4. ADELAIDE-FRANCES⁸, b. 2 June, 1858, Chelsea.

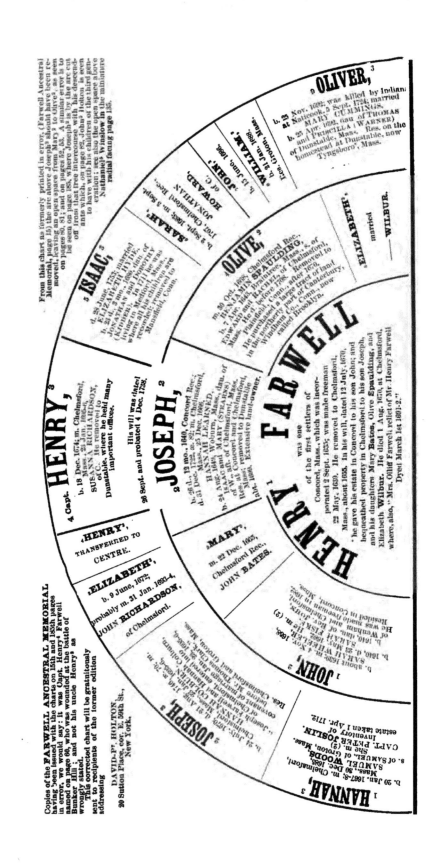

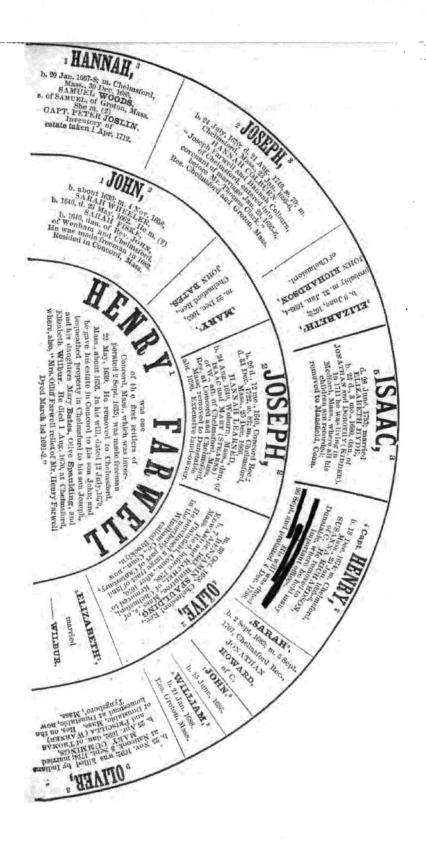

INDEX TO CHARTS.

Charts.		Page.
I.	English Farwell Families,	viii[a].
II.	Simeon[6] Farwell,	viii.
III.	Henry[1], Joseph[2], Joseph[3], his five brothers and three sisters,	15.
IV.	Daniel[4] Farwell,	80, 81.
V.	Hoar Family, a Parallel Chart,	22[a].
VI.	Elizabeth[6] (Farwell) Parker,	52, 53.
VII.	Holton, Dea. William[1], John[2], Wm[3], a Radial Chart,	82.
VIII.	Henry[7] Farwell, Sieze-quartiers Chart,	75.
IX.	Nancy[7] (Jackson) Farwell, "	76.
X.	Ancestral and Descendental Groupings,	134[a].
XI.	Whitmore Ancestral, a Parallel Chart,	102.
XII.	Farwell, Henry[1], Joseph[2], Isaac[3],	185.
XVI.	Dea. Benjamin[1] Parsons,	95.
XVII.	Ancestry of Descendants of Elizabeth[6] Farwell,	96.
XVIII.	Stoddard & Lovell, a parallel chart,	154[a].
XIX.	Cook, Carpenter & Parsons, "	154[a].

OTHER PAGES :

Explanation of Charts,	35, 36, 51, 72, 73, 74, 77, 78, 79.
Ancestral Monument,	58.
Map of a Section of Swanzey, N. H.	154[c].
Map of a part of Westminster, Vt.	154[d].
General Index.	from 187 to 206.
Supplemental Index of Topics and Places.	240.

INDEX.

1. Arabic figures immediately following names refer to serial numbers.
2. Figures preceded by p. or pp. refer to page or pages.
3. Ch. followed by Roman notation refers to chart or charts, and, to find their page reference see the Table of Charts on page 186.
4. G. R. C. refers to the grand radial chart of Henry Farwell's descendants, through Elizabeth[8] (Farwell) Parker—one of the grand folio in preparation for the bi-centennial 1976. [See page 36.]*

Abbot, Olive p. 45.
Abbott, Amos p. 83.
Adames, John p. 4.
Adams, Judge p. 70.
  Abigail[8] (Smith) p. 113.
  Albert 880.
  Alice[8] 269.
  Charles-Albert[9] 883.
  Edward-Gary p. 141.
  Edward-Gary[9] 882.
  Elizabeth-Anna 928.
  Florence-Luella[9] 885
  Jasper p. 142.
  Hon. and Pres. John p. 113.
  Hon. and Pres. John-Q[7]. pp. 76, 113, ch. IX.
  Jonathan 267.
  Jonathan[8] 27, 627.
  Linda p. 180.
  Mary 91.
  Mary-Eliza[8] 881.
  Nellie-Alberta[9] 884.
  Submit[8] 268.
Albee, Alexander[8] 1229.
  Alma[9] 1226.
  Asahel 1222.
  Benjamin p. 176.
  Charles[9] 1225.
  Hannah-Seviah 1090.
  Margaret-Albro[9] (Whitehorn) 1048.
  Maria[9] 1223.
  Miriam[9] 1228.
  William p. 158, 161.

Albrough, John p. 103.
Alexander, Mehetabel, pp. 50, 84.
Allen, Abigail 435.
  Benjamin pp. 31, 51, 54.
  Betsey p. 153.
  David 558, pp. 74, 137.
  James p. 90.
  Lucinda 1050.
  Mindwell p. 98.
  Oliver p. 158.
  Oliver-Lewis 1049.
  Prudence 433.
  Rachel 266.
Alley, Elizabeth-Hemenway p. 141.
Allis, Experience p. 134.
Andrews 436.
Angell, Phebe p. 115.
Appleton, William p. 144.
Arnold, Amy-Adeline[9] 1120.
  Asel-Edwin[9] 1121.
  Charles-Lawrence[9] 1115.
  Prof. Edward p. 180.
  Electa-Isabel[9] 1116.
  Frank-Dixon[9] 1122.
  Henry-Thomas[9] 1117.
  John-Franklin[9] 1114.
  Joseph-Warren 1113.
  Mary-Olive-Alvira[9] 1118.
  Phebe 640.
  Seth p. 100.
  Thomas p. 162.

Arrington, Benjamin-Franklin[9] 877.
  Charles-Loadman[9] 876.
  James 873.
  James[9] 875.
  Loadman p. 141.
  Mary-Catherine[9] 874.
  Stephen-Melvin[9] 878.
Arsdale, Rev. p. 137.
Atherton, Maj.General pp. 112, 113.
  Margaret p. 112.
Averill, John p. 55.
  Mary p. 97.
Bacon p. 145.
  John 97.
  Polly p. 70.
Bagg, Thankful p. 97.
Bailey, Charles-F. p. 178.
Baker, George-W. p. 115.
  Capt. Joseph p. 38.
  Mahala-Jane 748.
  Sarah[9] p. 110, ch. IX.
Balcom, Susan p. 98.
Baldwin, Abel 942.
  Dorothy 41, p. 49.
  Earle-Grey 1231.
  Edward-Lincoln[9] 953.
  Emma-Caroline[9] 951.
  Frank[9] 947.
  Frank-Otis[9] 949.
  Frederick-William[9] 950.
  George-Edward[9] 946.
  HattieFlorence[9] 952.
  Henry-Jackson[9] 944.

Samples of the pages of this grand folio, suitable for framing as parlor ornaments, may be purchased of the publisher.

Baldwin, John p. 179.
  Mary-Bartlett⁵ 954.
  Otis-Lincoln⁵ 948.
  William-Earle⁵ 1232.
  William-Henry⁵ 945.
  Winifred-May⁵ 1233.
Ballard, Jane pp. 165, 170.
  Sarah p. 175.
Bancroft, Capt. p. 26.
  Col. p. 40.
  Abigail³ 370.
  Chloe⁵ 378ᵉ.
  Ebenezer 378, pp. 38, 39.
  Ebenezer² p. 41.
  Ebenezer³ 378, pp. 41, 42.
  Ebenezer⁵ 378g.
  Elizabeth⁵ 368.
  Elizabeth⁵ 378ᵃ.
  Hepzibah⁵ 375.
  James⁵ 372.
  John¹ p. 41.
  Jonathan⁵. 374.
  Jonathan⁷ p. 41.
  Joseph-Farwell⁵ 378ʰ.
  Lois⁵ 373.
  Lucy⁵ 378ᶜ.
  Mary-Dandridge⁵ 378ᶠ.
  Rachel p. 41.
  Rachel⁵ 376.
  Rebecca⁵ 378ᵈ, 378ⁱ, p. 44.
  Sarah⁵ 371.
  Susannah⁵ 378ᵇ.
  Thomas¹ p. 41.
  Timothy p. 18.
  Timothy² 366.
  Timothy³ 367.
Banks, Gen. p. 67.
Barber 543.
Barger, Martha p. 163.
Barker, Charles-W. pp. 120, 121.
Barnes p. 72.
  Rev. Albert p. 156.
  Mary p. 173.
Barney p. 55.
Barret, Rebecca p. 44.
Barron, Jonathan 378ℓ.
  Oliver p. 43.
Bartlett p. 144.
  Caleb p. 59.
  Levi p. 147.
  Susan-Walker 955.
Barton, Capt. David¹ p. 134.
Batchelor, Pamelia-C. 892.
Bateman, Rebecca p. 45.
Bates, Elizabeth³. 12.

Bates, John 9.
  John³ 11.
  Lydia³ 13.
  Mary³ 10.
  Rebecca³ 14.
Baugh, Melissa p. 158.
Beach, Isaac p. 111.
Bean, Charles p. 142.
  Martha-Maria 891.
Beard, Andrew p. 62.
Beebe, Eunice pp. 153, 182.
Beers, Richard¹ p. 44.
  Sarah² p. 44.
Beckwith, Sarah p. 146.
Belcher, William-H. p. 144, 145.
Belding, Jonathan p. 84.
Bell, Susan-Pope p. 153.
Bellows, Benj. pp. 61, 62, 87.
Bemis, Fanny-Ann⁹ 806.
  George-Luke⁹ 689.
  Judson-Cogswell⁹ 816.
  Judson-Moss⁹ 815.
  Judson-Stephen⁹ 808.
  Luke 688.
  Miriam-Farwell⁹ 807.
  Stephen 804, pp. 74, 108.
  Stephen-Allen⁹ 805.
Bennett, Elizabeth p. 61.
  Moses p. 59.
Bigelow, James p. 25.
  Patience 124.
Billings, Mary p. 140.
Bixby p. 74, ch. VIII.
  Rebecca p. 60.
  Sarah; pp. 74, 89, ch. VIII.
Blanchard, Esther 349, p. 39.
  Jonathan⁵, 466.
  Capt. Joseph pp. 37, 39.
  Joseph 466. pp. 17, 62.
  Joseph⁴ p. 62.
  Rebecca pp. 61, 62.
  Susannah 355, p. 40.
  Thomas p. 20.
Bliss Rev. Edwin p. 171.
  Rev. Isaac p. 171.
  Mary p. 133.
Blodget William p. 41.
Blood, p. 74, ch. VIII.
  Abel⁵ 228ᵈ.
  Ann⁵ 189, 228g.
  Benjamin⁵ 182.
  Benjamin⁵ 184.
  Catharine 185.

Blood, Deborah⁵ 186.
  Edmund⁵ 185.
  Elizabeth⁵ 228ᵃ.
  Eunice⁵ 183.
  Hannah pp. 73, 74, 83, 101, ch. VIII.
  Hannah⁵ 228ᵉ.
  John p. 30.
  Joshua⁵ 187.
  Mary⁵ 228ⱼ.
  Moses 228.
  Moses⁵ 228ᶜ.
  Nathaniel p. 28.
  Nathaniel⁵ 228ʰ.
  Rachel⁵ 188, 228ᶠ.
  Sarah⁵ 228ᵇ.
  Sewall⁵ 228ᵢ.
  Simon p. 28.
Bolton, Rebecca 492.
Bonny, Elijah p. 100.
  Sarah⁵ (Root) p. 100.
Bostocke, Thos. p. 109.
Bosworth, Jemima p. 68.
Botsford, Olive p. 146.
Botts, Mary-Jane 1040.
  Wm. Oscar p. 154.
Boutelle, Abby-Marshall⁵ 909.
  Amy-Farwell⁹ 297.
  Catharine 789, p. 74.
  Charles-Augustus⁵ 907.
  Dorcas-Wetherbee⁵ 912.
  Frank-Lyman⁵ 925.
  George-Farwell⁵ 908.
  Mary-Hill⁵ 911.
  Nathaniel pp. 136, 142.
  Nathaniel-George⁵ 910.
  Nathaniel Seaver 906.
  Ralph-Upton⁹ 926.
  Rebecca-Emily⁵ 921.
Bowers, Jesse p. 63.
Boynton, Mary p. 44.
  Nathaniel p. 44.
Bradley, Gen. Stephen-Rowe p. 99.
  Hon. William-C. pp. 100, 177.
Bradstreet, Ann (Dudley) p. 174.
  Gov. Simon pp. 110, 174.
Brainerd, Clarissa p. 150.
Brazer, James 462.
Brenington, Nancy p. 161.
Bridges, Col. p. 42.
Brigham, Asa p. 35.
  Thankful 339.

Bright, Ann² p. 174.
  Beriah³ 839, pp. 113, 174.
  Henry⁵ p. 113.
  Henry¹ pp. 79, 113, 114, 174, ch. IX.
  Henry³ p. 114, ch. IX.
  Jemima⁴ pp. 113, 114, ch. IX.
  John⁴ p. 114.
  Margaret² (Jackson) p. 114, ch. IX.
  Mary² p. 113.
  Nathaniel² pp. 113, 114, ch. IX.
  Thomas p. 113.
  Thomasᵇ p. 114.
  Walterᶜ p. 114.
Briles, Alexander p. 163.
  Alice-Ettie⁹ 1162.
  Effie-Jane⁹ 1160.
  Elisha⁹ 1164.
  Elizabeth⁹ 1165.
  John-Franklin 1159.
  Sarah-Olive⁹ 1161.
  Sarah-Roxana 1148.
Brooke, Thomas p. 4.
Brooks, Gov. p. 42.
Brooks, p. 155.
  Anna 110, p. 45.
  Benjamin p. 43.
  Daniel p. 24.
  Joshua p. 24.
  Thomas p. 24.
Brown, 137, 147, 193.
  Abbie-Farwell⁹ 841.
  Abigail 100.
  Anna 388.
  Benjamin 58, 839, pp. 90, 189.
  Benjamin-Franklin⁸ 840.
  Charles p. 139.
  Charles-Farwell⁹ 843.
  Edward-Jackson⁹ 842.
  Edward-Lyman⁹ 844.
  Eli p. 126.
  Francis, D. D. p. 99.
  Frederick-Lyman⁸ 847.
  Frederick-Hamilton⁹ 846.
  Harriet 378ᵏ.
  Henry-Smith 1043.
  Jane-Farwell⁹ 848.
  John p. 126.
  Josiah 139.
  Mary-Eliza 842.
  Patience p. 25.
  Rebecca p. 61.

Brown, William, p. 155.
Bruns, Felix-R. p. 127.
Brush, Addie-Frances¹⁰ 382.
  Walter-Franklin 382.
Bryans, Mary-T. p. 44.
Bryant, Rev. p. 169.
  Mrs. p, 170.
Buchanan, p. 129.
Bucknam, Albert p. 138.
  Dexter 829.
Bulkley, Peter p. 3.
Bullard, Abigail 484.
Bullock, Ex-Gov. p. 165.
Burbank, Alfred-Allen, 822.
  Charles-Sumner, 821.
  Edgar-David⁹ 820.
  Ethel-S. 823.
  Frank-Farwell⁹ 819.
  Silas-David 818.
Burchard, Roxana p. 134.
  Thomas¹ p. 134.
Burge, John p. 11.
Burks, Capt. John p. 84.
Burnside, Gen. p. 181.
Burrage, Elizabeth-Smith 789.
  Josiah p 136.
Burridge, Elizabeth-Smith p. 74.
Burroughs, Eliza 1179.
  John p. 171.
Burt, Judge p. 100.
  Dea. p. 170.
  Elizabeth⁸ (Root) p. 100.
  Phineas p. 59.
Burton, Esther p. 155.
Busse, William p. 3.
Butler, Gen. p. 67.
Butterfield, John p. 42.
  Joseph 378ᵃ, p. 42.
  Leonard p. 171.
  Leonard-Emerson 1184.
Butters, James p. 107.
  James-Lawrence 733.
  Sarah-Ida⁹ 734.
Buttrick, Amos p. 105.
  Amos-Warren 690.
  Helen-Viora⁹ 692.
Byshop, Enoch p. 93.
Cady, Daniel p. 70.
  Mary 71, p. 69.
Campbell, Philo p. 135.
  Solomon-Cushing 787.
  Wallace-Farwell⁹ 788.
Capen, Hepzibah ch. VIII.
Caper, Hepzibah ch. VIII.

Caper or Capen, Mary⁸, p. 89, ch. VIII.
Carpenter, Benjamin, p. Hannah p. 158.
  Polly 430.
Carr, John ch. XI.
Carter, Albert-W⁸. 1001.
  Anna-Farwell⁷ 973.
  Beatrix 585.
  Betsey 585.
  Carrie-Adele⁹ 993.
  Charles-Farwell⁷ 999.
  Cornelia⁸ 994.
  Edmund-Thomas⁸ 971.
  Elijah pp. 90, 92.
  Eliza-Addelle⁸ 996.
  Eunice-Lincoln⁷ 603.
  Frank p. 150.
  Frederick⁸ 1000.
  George-Dennis⁸ 1002.
  Hannah-Ann⁸ 972.
  Herbert-Franklin⁹ 992.
  Ida-Elizabeth⁸ 997.
  John p. 93.
  Lucius 990.
  Mary-Anne⁸ 990.
  Nathaniel 596, p. 93.
  Samuel⁷, 970.
  Samuel-Edmund⁸ 998.
  Sybil⁷ 600.
  Sybil-Eunice⁸ 995.
  Thomas 596, ch. XI.
  Thomas⁷ 989.
  Vashti 565.
  Wilfred⁹ 991.
Cary, Lucy p. 158.
  Rebecca 114.
  Thomas-G. p. 144.
Castleline, Catharine p. 135.
Chace, Mary-Elizabeth 1258.
  Nancy p. 150.
Chaffee, Lydia 510.
Chamberlain, John 354.
Chambers, Rev. Dr. p. 125
Chandler p. 97.
  Mary-Dana, pp. 172, 173.
Chaplain, Hannah-Page 849.
  William p. 139.
Chaplin, Rev. Daniel p. 26.
Chapman, Rev. George-T. p. 99.
Charles II. p. 38.
Chase, Rev. John p. 151.

Chase, Jonathan p. 182.
   Kate-Matilda 1004.
Cheeney, J-B. p. 39.
Cheney, John 146.
Cheevers Ames p. 11.
Cheritree, Paul-Theodore⁹ 989.
   Sheldon p. 146.
   Theodore-Frelinghuysen 938, p. 145.
Child, Elizabeth p. 25.
Claflin, H. B. & Co. p. 183.
Clapp, Mark-Richards 629.
Clark, Alice-D. 896.
   Rachel p. 142.
   Thomas pp. 14, 16.
Clough, Martha p. 178.
Cobb, Albert⁷ 711.
   Alvin⁸ 712.
   Charles-Frederick⁹ 702.
   Davis⁹ 707.
   Emma-Jane⁹ 705.
   Farwell-Osborne⁸ 700.
   Frank-Eugene⁹ 704.
   George-Wallace⁸ 703.
   Hannah-Maria⁹ 717.
   Henry⁹ 714.
   Henry-Albert⁹ 701.
   Leonard 699.
   Leonard-Davis 713.
   Lizzie-Jane⁹ 719.
   Lizzie-Maria⁹ 706.
   Morgan p. 55.
   Sybil⁸ 708.
   Timothy⁹ 715.
Coburn, Mary p. 111.
Cogswell, Alice 815.
Coitt, Samuel 104.
Colburn p. 17.
   Edward pp. 13, 14.
   Hannah 45, pp. 74, 89, ch. VIII.
Colburn, John 59.
   Thomas pp. 10, 14.
Coley, Nathaniel p. 108.
   Sarah-Clapp 736.
Collier, Lucy 848.
Colman, Henry p. 99.
Conant 438.
   Abel p. 164.
   John-Calvin 1166.
   John-Edwin⁸ 1169.
   William-Holton⁸ 1167.
Conaway, Peter p. 22.
Cone, Lemuel 586.
Cook, Samuel 875.

Cooksey p. 22.
Cooley, Emerette 763, pp. 119, 133.
   Francis-Buell pp. 119, 134.
   George p. 133.
   Noah pp. 117, 133.
Coolidge, Elizabeth 106, ch. V.
   Mary³, p. 113, ch. IX.
   Nathaniel² p. 113.
   Simon² p. 113, ch. IX.
Corwith & Co. p. 143.
Cowden, Abel⁷ p. 85.
Cox, J-D. p. 128.
Cragin, Mrs. p. 46.
Crane, William-Nevins 382.
Crarey, Rachel 474.
   John p. 64.
Crawford, Almy p. 137.
   Gen. p. 123.
Crispe, p. 74, ch. VIII.
   Benjamin pp. 73, 74, ch. VIII.
   Elizabeth p. 73, ch. VIII.
Cromwell, Oliver, p. 38.
Crosby 192.
   Phebe 426.
Cross, Nathan p. 20.
Cummings, Sergt. p. 17.
   Betty⁵ 396.
   Catharine⁵ 389.
   Elizabeth⁶ 398.
   Hannah⁵ 386.
   Hannah⁶ 401.
   Rev. Henry⁵ 387.
   Jeramael 385 p. 18.
   John p. 21.
   Jonathan⁵ 407ᶜ.
   Jotham⁵ 388.
   Lois⁵ 407ᵈ.
   Mary 86.
   Nancy⁶ 400.
   Noah⁵ 407ᵇ.
   Noah⁶ 406.
   Polly⁶ 405.
   Rebecca⁵ 407ᵃ.
   Sarah⁶ 404.
   Samuel p. 48.
   Samuel-Gibson⁶ 407.
   Stephen⁵ 397.
   Stephen⁵ 399.
   Thomas p. 20.
   William-P.⁶ 403.
Cushing, Calista p. 135.
   Nancy-Whiting p. 138.

Cutler, Ebenezer³ p. 44.
   Ebenezer⁵ p. 44.
   James¹ p. 44.
   John² p. 44.
   Sally p. 46.
   Samuel⁵ p. 44.
   Sarah⁴ pp. 43, 44.
Cutting, Mr. John p. 84.
Cuyler, Caroline-Emily 1066.
   E-S. p. 159.
Dadman, John-J. 972.
Dana, Samuel p. 26.
   Rev. Samuel p. 82.
Dane, Thomas p. 4.
Danforth, Abigail 467.
Darbe, William 93.
Darnell, Mary-Ann p. 154.
Davis, Gen. p. 123.
   Jeff. p. 126.
   Joseph⁸ 890.
   Samuel 889.
   Sarah 143.
Day, p. 117.
Dean, Abby-Caroline⁹ 981.
   Abby-Eliza⁹ 980.
   Charles-Edward⁹ 988.
   Charles-Henry⁹ 985.
   Charles-Pinckney 973.
   Effie-Augusta⁹ 984.
   Elvira-Ann⁹ 987.
   Capt. Francis p. 149.
   George-Morse⁹ 986.
   Kate-Marion⁹ 983.
   Martha-Louisa⁹ 974.
   Mary p. 16.
   Nathaniel-Carter² 982.
   Sybil-Augusta⁹ 978.
De Chartres, Duc p. 124.
De Joinville, Prince p. 134.
Dell, Elizabeth (Bright) p. 113.
De Maranville, Chloe⁹ 1224.
   Elisha-P. 1223.
   Henry⁹ 1224ᵃ.
   Nehemiah p. 17.
Denison, Maj. Gen. Daniel p. 174.
   Patience (Dudley) p. 174.
De Paris, Count p. 134.
Derby, Harriet p. 150.
Dexter, p. 144.
Dickinson, Electa p. 179.
Diggins, Emma-Jane 1009.
   Sylvester p. 152.
Dimmick, Esther 419.

Dimmick, Shubael p. 50.
Dinsmore, Mary p. 139.
  Dr. Phineas p. 139.
Divol, Ephraim 125.
Doan, John-N. p. 142.
Dodge, Joseph p. 59.
  Stephen p. 150.
  William-E. p. 127.
  Wooster-Ferdinand 995.
Doney, James p. 155.
Dorr, Anna (Ruggles) p. 99.
  Joseph p. 99.
Doublet, Tom p. 22.
Douglas, Benaijah 98.
  Hannah p. 135.
Downe, Harriet-Augusta* 665
  Joseph p. 137.
  Joseph, Jr. pp. 72, 92.
  Louisa-Frances* 668.
  Mary-Ann 817, p. 74.
  Mary-Emeline* 672.
  Sumner* 674.
  Susan* 660.
  Sybil-Ann* 673.
  William 659.
  William-Narramore* 675.
  William-Stillman* 664.
Dresser, John¹ p. 89.
  Mary p. 89.
Dudley, Gov. Joseph p. 174.
  Mercy p. 174.
  Paul, Ch. Justice p. 174.
  Gov. Thomas p. 174.
Dunster p. 74, ch. VIII.
  Faith pp. 72, 73, 74, ch. VIII.
  Henry p. 73.
Durgan, Lucinda p. 139.
Durgin, Rev. De W-H-Clinton p. 139.
Duryea, Dr. pp. 122, 125.
Dyer, James p. 106.
  Leonard-Farwell' 710
  Louisa p. 106.
  Myra 711.
  Theodore-Jones 708.
  Walter-Alvin* 709.
Dyke, Elizabeth 1215.
Earle, Jacob p. 159.
  Sophia-Bigelow 1057.
Eastman, Mary p. 173.
Eaton, Abigail p. 41.
  Betsey 664.
  Naomi⁵ (Root) p. 100.
Eddy, Joseph p. 55.

Edson, Charles p. 134.
  Charles-Farwell* 776.
  Epaphras-Wadsworth 775.
  Nancy* 777.
Edwards, Abigail pp. 57, 94.
Eldridge, 423, p. 50, G. R. C.*
  Elisha p. 50.
Ellsworth p. 157.
Emerson, Alfred p. 104.
  Rev. Joseph p 27.
Emery, Sidney-Patterson 741.
Endecott, [Endicott] Gov. Jo. p. 4.
Esterbrook, Lephe p. 92.
Fairbanks, Charles-L. 978.
  Effie-Dean 979ᵃ.
  Gov. pp. 177, 178.
  Hattie-Abbie* 979.
  Jabez p. 40.
  Robert-Frank 979ᵇ.
  Seth-Phelps p. 149.
  T. p. 177.
Fairchild, Rev. E-B. p. 138.
Farnham, Calvin-B. p. 145.
  Mary-Mason 929.
Farnsworth, Dea. p. 26.
  Ebenezer pp. 40, 88.
  Isaac p. 40.
  Lydia 361 p. 60.
  Phila 547, G. R. C.*
  Sarah 429.
  Stephen p. 83.
Farnum, Amanda-M. p. 15
Farrington, Thirzah p. 87.

Farwell, Abby' 764.
  Abel-Goodrich'955, p. 144.
  Abel-Wetherbee' 582.
  Abigail* 364, 450, 469.
  Abigail* 570, p. 90.
  Abraham* 333, pp. 74, 88, 89, ch. VIII.
  Abraham* p. 34.
  Alfred Allen* 825.
  Almira* 938.
  Anna⁵ 139, 342.
  Anna* 519, 596.
  Anna* 758.
  Anna-Pearl* 773.
  Ann-Eliza* 853.
  Ann-Elmira* 850.
  Annette-Elizabeth 827.
  Artemus-Simonds* 791.

Farwell, Arthur-B*. 799.
  Arthur-George* 935.
  Arthur-Lincoln* 767, p. 114.
  Asa⁵ 422.
  Asa⁶ 565.
  Asa' 567, 961.
  Asenath' 578.
  Benjamin⁴ 89.
  Benjamin⁵ 848.
  Benjamin⁶ 517.
  Benjamin' 778, p. 74.
  Bethiah* 425, pp. 55, 56, 57, 72, 94, ch. VI.
  Betsey' 942.
  Bunker* 363, p. 37.
  Calvin* 456.
  Caroline' 589.
  Catharine-Smith* 793.
  Charles' 849, p. 90.
  Charles-Benjamin* 753, p. 116, 118, 119.
  Charles-Emory* 796.
  Charles-Hallet* 957.
  Charles-Henry* 749.
  Charley* 754.
  Charlotte* 966.
  Clara-Asenath* 959.
  Clara-Walker* 956.
  Daniel⁴ 340, pp. 29, 36, 72, 77, 89, 114, ch. VIII.
  Daniel⁵ 511, pp. 36, 73, 74, 77, 83, 114, ch. VIII.
  Daniel⁶ 577 pp. 72, 92.
  Daniel-George' 940.
  David* 434* p. 56.
  Deidamia-Knox* 784.
  Dexter' 958.
  Dorcas' 906.
  Dorothy⁴ 78.
  Dorothy* 432.
  Edith-Carter* 964.
  Edmund* 346.
  Edward⁴ 265.
  Edward⁵ 266.
  Edward' 757.
  Eldridge* 436.
  Eleazer* 350, p. 37.
  Elijah-Carter' 588.
  Elisha*, 429, p. 54.
  Elisha* p. 54.
  Elizabeth¹ 6, pp. 5, 36.
  Elizabeth³ 56, p. 36.
  Elizabeth⁴ 74, 80, 220, 866, p. 44.

*See notes on pages 36, 72, and 187.

Farwell, Elizabeth⁵ 331, 360, 438, 439, 455, 584, pp. 72, 101, ch. VI.
Elizabeth-True⁶ 826.
Emory-Burrage⁶ 797.
Esther⁴ 351.
Eunice⁵ 332.
Fannie⁷ 768.
Francis-Ball⁶ 929, p. 146.
Francis-C⁵. p. 51.
Francis-William⁶ 792.
Frank⁶ 968.
Frank-Cooley⁶ 766.
Frank-Mason⁶ 931.
Frederick⁶ 969.
George p. 1.
George-Augustine⁶ 824.
George-Edward⁶ 798.
George-Lyman⁶ 933.
George-Villars⁶ 751.
Grace⁶ 760.
Hannah³ 36, p. 25.
Hannah⁴ 147, 385, pp. 18, 19.
Hannah⁵ 354. p. 18.
Hannah-Cornelia⁶ 780.
Hannah-Elvira⁶ 854.
Harriet⁶ 782.
Helen-Gertrude⁶ 800.
Henry¹ 1, pp. 36, 44, 55, 74, 77, ch. VI, VIII.
Henry⁴ 64, pp. 14, 36.
Henry⁴ 349, 457, p. 18.
Henry⁵ 440, p. 59.
Henry⁷ 747, pp. 74, 77, 79, 114, ch. VIII.
Henry⁸ 967.
Henry⁶ 756.
Henry-Boutelle⁶ 790.
Henry-Jackson⁴ 748.
Henry-Newton⁶ 965.
Henry-Smith⁶ 772.
Hepzibah⁶ 557, pp. 74, 77, 88, 89, ch. VIII.
Hepzibah⁷ 558, p. 74, ch. VIII.
Isaac³ 73, p. 36, ch. VI.
Isaac⁴, 359, p. 18.
Isaac⁵ 140, 343, 365, 420, 433, 448, p. 54.
Isaac-Moors 339, p. 34.
James⁶ p. 34.
James-Brazier⁶ p. 60.
Jane⁷ 839.
Jane⁸ 851.
Jesse⁴ 435.

Farwell, John², 7, pp. 4, 5, 6, 7, 36, 45.
John³ 22, p. 36.
John⁴ 52, 82, 417, p. 49.
John⁵ 334, 419, 431, 472, pp. 43, 54.
John⁶ p. 34.
John-Knox⁸ 781.
John-Villars⁷ 763, pp. 79, 114, 118, 119, 120, 127, 128, 130, 132, 133, 134, 135.
John-Villars⁸ 765.
Jonathan⁴ 355, p. 18.
Jonathan⁵ 142, 358, 449, 464, pp. 18, 37, 39.
Joseph² 15, pp. 5, 6, 7, 14, 15, 36, 61, 114. ch. VI.
Joseph³ 45, pp. 45, 74, 79, 89. 114, ch. VIII.
Joseph⁴ 138.
Joseph⁵ 141, 338, 436.
Joseph⁶ p. 34.
Joseph⁷ 579.
Joseph-Rast⁷ p. 20.
Josiah⁵ 353, 361, pp. 18, 21, 59, 85.
Levi⁴ 453.
Levi⁵ 585, p. 89.
Levi⁶ 595.
Levi-Lincoln⁷ 590.
Levi-Asa⁶ 960.
Lillian-Louisa⁶ 752.
Louisa-Charless⁶ 941.
Louisa-Marston⁶ 962.
Lydia⁵ 336, 463, p. 34.
Lyman⁶ 928.
Lyman⁸ 930.
Maria⁷ 580.
Maria-Louise⁶ 775.
Mary³ 9, pp. 5, 36.
Mary⁴ 271, 408, p. 81.
Mary⁵ 145, 345, 468.
Mary⁶ p. 40.
Mary⁷ 801, pp. 74, 89, ch. VIII.
Mary-Aurelia⁶ 783, 787.
Mary-Hepsey⁶ 809.
Mary-Nancy⁶ 755.
Miriam⁷ p. 89.
Miriam-Thurston⁷ 804, pp. 74, 89, ch. VIII.
Moses⁶ p. 34.
Nancy⁵ 454.
Olive² 25, p. 5.

Farwell, Olive⁵ 352, 418, 437.
Oliver³ 86, pp. 17, 36, 61.
Oliver⁴ 366, 446, 465, pp. 18, 59.
Oliver⁵ 144, 467.
Oliver-P⁵, p. 20.
Peter⁷ 561, 789, pp. 35, 74.
Phineas⁵ 445, p. 59.
Polly⁵ 572.
Polly-Osborne⁷ 571.
Rachel⁵ 357, p. 18.
Rachel⁴ 358 pp. 39, 40.
Rebecca⁵ 466.
Relief⁵ 362.
Robert⁷ or Roland⁸ 761.
Rose⁶ 762.
Ruth-Louisa⁶ 774.
Samuel⁴ 329, pp. 74, 77, 89, ch. VIII.
Samuel⁵ 330.
Sarah³ 21, 31, pp. 8, 36, 45.
Sarah⁴ 55, 70, p. 18.
Sarah⁵ 335. 441, 471.
Sarah⁶ p. 35.
Sarah-Downe⁶ 818.
Sarah-Tyng⁶ 378ʰ.
Sidney-Emerson⁶ 934.
Simeon⁵ 557, pp. 74, 77, 114, ch. VIII.
Simeon⁷ 817, pp. 74, 89, ch. VIII.
Simeon⁸ 769, 770, p. 119.
Simeon-Allen⁶ 771.
Sophia⁷ 828, p. 90.
Submit⁶ 267.
Susan⁷ 659.
Susannah⁴ 68, p. 18.
Susannah⁵ 146, 337, 356, 442, p. 18, ch. VIII.
Sybil⁵ 443, p. 73.
Sybil⁶ 549.
Thomas⁴ 47.
Thomas⁵ 47, 143, 421.
Timothy⁶ 844.
Walter⁷ 759.
Walter-Merrick⁶ 963.
William³ 79, pp. 36, 59.
William⁴ 423, 437, pp. 54, 56, G. R. C.
William⁶ 426, 444. 447, 460, p. 59.
William-Douglas⁶ 779, p. 119.
William-Jackson⁶ 750.

Index. 193

Farwell, Zaccheus⁵ 215, 347.
Fasset, Josiah p. 69.
  Mary 500.
Fay p. 144.
  Col. Francis-B. p. 144.
Felt, Abigail⁶ (Shaw) p. 113.
  Rev. Joseph-B. p. 113.
Fenton, Dorothy p. 50.
Ferris, Alice-Lavinia⁹ 1019.
  Charles-Leonard⁹ 1016.
  Delia-Helen⁹ 1018.
  Ellen⁸ 1254.
  Esta-Maud⁹ 1251.
  Fidelia-Miriam⁸ 1015.
  Hiram-Burns⁸ 1256.
  Hiram-Gano 1249.
  Hiram-Gano⁹ 1024.
  Joel-Edward⁹ 1257.
  John-Milton⁹ 1020.
  Julia⁸ 1253.
  Junius-Colton⁸ 1250.
  Lelia-Francina⁹ 1017.
  Leonard-Thompson, M.D 1014, p. 159.
  Mary-Helen⁹ 1023.
  Phebe⁸ 1255.
  Ralph-Willie⁹ 1022.
  Stephen pp. 153, 182.
  Stephen-Holton⁸· 1252.
  Ulysses-Stephen⁹ 1021.
Ferry, Charles¹ p. 133.
  Charles² p. 133, 134.
  Frank-Montague¹⁰ 764ᶜ.
  Heman⁴ p. 133, 134.
  John-Farwell¹⁰ 764ᵇ.
  Noah³ p. 133, 134.
  Noah⁴ p. 133, 134.
  William¹⁰ 764ᵃ.
  William H⁶ pp. 133,134.
  William-Henry⁷ 764.
Field, M. p. 119.
Finn, Elizabeth 728.
Finney, Widow p. 103.
Fish, Louisa p. 145.
Fisher, Susan p. 182.
Fisk, Josiah p. 29.
  Sarah 7, 202.
Fiske, John p. 6.
  Sarah G.R.C.
Flagg, Elizabeth p. 101, ch. XI.
  Sarah p. 45.
Fletcher, Joseph p. 42.
  Susannah 378.
  Robert p. 3.
  William pp. 5, 7.

Flint, Rev. Henry ch. V.
Forbes, Jo. p. 83.
Ford, Jemima p. 165.
Forresttall, Czarina 678.
  Joseph p. 105.
Forward, Frances-Keturah⁸ 1044
  Pliny p. 156.
  Samuel p. 157.
Foster, Francis p. 108.
  Elvira p. 150.
  Susan-Maria 738.
Fowle, Abigail⁸ p. 113.
  Ann p. 174.
  Beriah³ (Bright) p. 113.
  George¹ p. 113.
  Hannah p. 174.
  Isaac² pp. 113, 174.
Fowler, James-H. p. 66.
Fox, Charles-J. pp. 6, 7, 10, 14, 17, 38, 39.
Foxe, Thomas p. 3.
Francisco, Louisa p. 184.
Freeman, Abigail 412.
  Edmund p. 49.
  Keziah 422.
  Mary 420.
  Skiff p. 50.
French, Alice p. 21.
  Lieut. p. 20.
  Mary p. 19.
  William p. 19.
Fretageot, Mary 1066.
Frideker, Lydia p. 164.
Frost, Henry-H. p. 178.
Furlong ch. XI.
Gage, Gen. p. 23.
Gale, Eunice p. 31.
Galusha, Jonas p. 178.
Garfield, Alvis p. 107.
  Susan-Eveline 731.
Garnett, Emily-Maria p. 98.
Gates, Electa-Barber-Dickinson 1230.
  Horace p. 179.
  Jonathan 80.
  Nancy p. 171.
Gaus, Deliverance p. 88, G. R. C.
Gibbons, Henry p. 112.
  Maj. p. 74.
Gibbs, Rev. Mr. p. 113.
Gibson, Abby-Martin⁸ 872.
  Arthur-D.⁹ 888.
  Charles-Edwin⁸ 879.
  Eliza-Putnam⁸ 871.

Gibson, Frank-L⁸ 887.
  Henrietta⁹ 870.
  John-Stearns⁸ 868.
  Joseph-Hartwell⁸ 886.
  Lucy-Ann⁸ 880.
  Marrette⁸ 873.
  Mary-Fairbanks⁸ 856.
  Stephen 855.
  Thomas p. 140.
Giddings, Lydia p. 101, ch. XI.
Gilbert, Mary 409.
  Rev. W-H. p. 150.
Gilchrist, Anna-Mary⁹ 1033.
  Charles-Allen⁸ 1025, p. 154.
  Charles-Grandison 1013.
  Charles-Van Brugh⁹ 1028, 1038.
  David-Van Brugh⁹ 1034.
  Edward-May⁹ 1040.
  Edward-Percy⁹ 1032.
  Ellen-Ferris⁹ 1030.
  Erastus-Holton⁸ 1039.
  Grace-Gertrude⁹ 1036.
  Helen-Elva⁹ 1035.
  Helen-Frances⁹ 1041.
  Helen-Minerva⁹ 1014.
  Ivan-Erastus⁹ 1037.
  Joseph-Gilmer⁹ 1026.
  Magnolia-Vick⁹ 1029.
  Mary-Albertina⁹ 1042.
  Minerva-Frances⁹ 1027.
  Robert-Allen⁸ 1031.
  Samuel p. 152.
Giles, James p. 61.
Gilman, Col. p. 63.
  Constantine p. 100.
Gilson, Alice⁶ 198.
  Anna⁶ 160.
  Catherine⁶ 150.
  David⁶ 209.
  Eleazer 147.
  Eleazer⁵ 148.
  Eleazer⁶ 152.
  Elizabeth⁵ pp. 32, 34, 89, ch. VIII.
  Elizabeth⁶ 154, 192.
  Esther⁶ 180.
  Eunice⁶ 182.
  Eunice⁶ 203.
  Eveline p. 140,
  Hannah⁵ 161.
  Hannah⁶ 158, 196, 206.
  Howard 854.

Gilson, James⁸ 156.
  Joel⁶ 197.
  John⁶ 195, p. 140.
  Joseph p. 26.
  Joseph¹ p 89, ch. VIII.
  Joseph² p. 89, ch. VIII.
  Joseph⁶ 201.
  Lydia 347.
  Lydia³ 216.
  Lydia⁴ 151, 215.
  Malinda p. 173.
  Mary 138.
  Mary⁶ 149, 199.
  Nathaniel⁶ 153.
  Peter⁵ 213.
  Peter⁶ 155.
  Rachel⁶ 194.
  Rebecca⁶ 200.
  Samuel⁵ 190.
  Samuel⁶ 191.
  Sarah⁵ 193.
  Simon⁴ 202.
  Simon⁵ 212.
  Submit⁵ 210.
  Susannah 159.
  Sybil⁵ 157, 214.
Granger, Eldad p. 97.
  Maria 618.
Grant, Gen. pp. 69, 123, 125, 127.
  Pamelia p. 69.
Graves, Benjamin ch. V.
  John p. 8, ch. V.
Gray, Prof. p. 165.
Green, Catharine 535.
  Isaac p. 41.
  Martha 874.
  Mary p. 82.
Griffin, Richard p. 3.
Grimes, Kimball-D. 1064.
  William p. 159.
Griswold p. 157.
Goethe p. 167.
Goldstone, Ann² p. 113,174, ch. IX.
  Henry¹ p. 113, ch. IX.
Goodell, Jerusha p. 98.
Goodrich, Alonzo p. 140.
  Edwin-Augustus 851.
  Elmira-Hannah⁵ 852.
  Jane pp. 90, 92.
Goodridge, Eunice 338.
Gordon, Timothy ch. XI.
Gould 439.
  David p. 59.
  Jonathan p. 59.

Grout, John p. 171.
  Rev. Lewis p. 171.
  Nancy 1183.
Grover, Elizabeth ch. XI.
Gwyn, Gen. p. 122.
Hagar, Hannah p. 97.
Hair, William p. 83.
Hale, Thomas p. 89.
Hall, Frances-Augusta 384.
  Mary 148.
  Capt. Samuel 491.
Hamilton p. 117.
Hamlin p. 117.
Hammond, Col. Charles-G. p. 110.
  Elijah⁴ 110.
  Isaac⁴ p. 110.
Hancock, John p. 61.
  Pres. John p. 42.
Hanscomb, Henry 722.
Harding, Alpheus p. 99.
Harlakenden p. 19.
Harlow, Sarah p. 183.
Harmon, John p. 133.
  J-K. p. 119.
  Sarah p. 133.
Harris, David p. 136.
  Emily-Augusta 790.
  Francis p. 59.
  Rachel p. 39.
Harrison, Elizabeth p. 115.
Hartwell, Clara⁶ 899.
  Frederick-S⁹ 893.
  John 572.
  Dr. John⁵ 892.
  Joseph-W. 896.
  Joseph⁷ 891.
  Mary⁷ 855.
  Mary-B⁹, 894.
  Nancy⁷ 889.
  Pamelia-C⁹. 897.
  William-Bascomb⁷ 576.
Harty, Margaret p. 101, ch. XI.
Harvey, John p. 55.
Hassell, Abiah pp. 87, 39.
Hastings, Elizabeth p. 134.
Haviland, John 1155.
  Lewis p. 163.
  Martha 1136.
Hawkes, John 876, p. 41.
Hayden, Clement p. 181.
  Elizabeth p. 181.
  Luther p. 181.
Hayes, Maria 1271, G.R.C.
  Polly p. 174.

Hayes, Judge Richard p.184
Hayward, Mary 681.
Heaward, Georg p. 4.
Hemphill, Joseph p. 171.
Hendrickson, Jane p. 161.
Henrick, Elijah p. 110.
Henry p. 59.
  James p. 134.
  Louisa 664.
  Sarah p. 134.
  Henry VII. p. 114.
Heldreth, James p. 5.
Hildrike, James pp. 8, 12.
Hill, p. 134.
  Abigail-Jones⁸ 380.
  Abraham p. 44.
  Adeliza⁸ 382.
  Charles-Ebenezer⁸ 378ˡ.
  Charles-Walter-Houghton⁹ p. 46.
  Ebenezer 378ˡ, p. 44.
  Rev. Ebenezer⁸ 378ᵈ, pp. 44, 45, 46.
  Ebenezer-Bancroft⁹ p.46.
  Edward-Stearns⁹ 379.
  Henry-Edward⁹ 384.
  Isaac-Parker⁸ 378ᵖ.
  John-Boynton⁸,⁷ 378ᵒ, pp. 4, 6, 8, 16, 19, 21, 38, 40, 42, 44, 61.
  John-Boynton⁹ 384.
  Joseph-Adna⁸ 378ⁿ.
  Rev. Joseph-Bancroft⁷ 378ᵏ.
  Lucy-Sylvania 381.
  Maria⁸ 381.
  Martha⁸ 383.
  Polly⁶ p. 44.
  Polly⁷ p. 44.
  Rebecca⁷ 378d and j,
  Rebecca-Howard⁸ 379ᵃ.
  Sally⁶ p. 44.
  Samuel⁵ p. 43.
  Samuel⁶, p. 44.
  Rev. Timothy⁸ 384.
  Timothy-Jones⁸ 381ᵃ.
  William-Bancroft⁸ 378ᵐ.
Hills, Mrs. Esther (Arnold) p. 100.
  Polly p. 136, 142.
Hitchcock, Roswell-D. p. 165.
Hoar, —, ch. V.
  Benjamin⁴ ch V.
  Daniel³ Sen. p. 22, ch. V.
  Daniel⁵ 105, ch. V.

Hoar, Daniel⁴ 105, ch. V.
  Daniel⁵ 107, ch. V.
  Ebenezer-Rockwood⁸ ch. V.
  Elizabeth³ ch. V.
  Elizabeth⁴ ch. V.
  Eunice p. 141, ch. V.
  Hezekiah² ch. V.
  Isaac⁴ ch. V.
  Joanna² ch. V.
  John¹ pp. 22, 23, ch. V.
  John² ch. V.
  John⁴ ch. V.
  John⁵ 106, ch. V.
  Jonathan⁴ ch. V.
  Jonathan⁵ 108, ch. V.
  Joseph⁴, ch. V.
  Leonard² ch. V.
  Leonard⁴ ch. V.
  Leonard⁶ ch. V.
  Margery² ch. V.
  Mary⁴ ch. V.
  Mrs. ch. V.
  Nathaniel-Pierce⁷ ch. V.
  Samuel⁴ ch. V.
  Hon. Samuel⁶ ch. V.
  Hon. Samuel⁷ ch. V.
  Timothy³ 109, ch. V.
Hobart, David ch. V.
  Deborah ch. V.
  Jael ch. V.
  James 386.
  Judith ch. V.
  Rebecca ch. V.
  Peter ch. V.
Hobbs, Capt. p. 83.
Hodgeman, Rev. Edwin-Ruthven 383.
  Edwin-Rutherford-Hill⁹ p. 48.
  Harriet-Mehetabel⁹ 383.
  Martha⁹ 383.
Hoit, Eastman⁵ p. 173.
  Ellen-Jane 1188, p. 173.
Hoit, John¹ p. 173.
  John² p. 173.
  Joseph⁴ p. 173.
  Rebecca (Fish) Winslow p. 173.
  Theophilus⁶ p. 173.
  Theophilus⁷ pp. 172, 173.
Holden p. 125.
  Anne p. 88.
  Caleb p. 59.
  Eunice 304.
  Isaac p. 59.

Holden, Philemon p. 59.
  Stephen p. 59.
Holder, Lucretia p. 181.
Holman, Edward p. 108.
  Eliza 736.
Holmes, Susanna p. 97.
Holton, Abby² 1182.
  Ada-Ford⁹ 1088.
  Alexander⁶ 634, pp. 64, 174.
  Alice-Emogene⁸ 1060.
  Anna⁶ 1181.
  Anna-Phebe⁷ 646.
  Ann-Jenette⁷ 631.
  Amos⁹ 1084.
  Bethiah⁴ (Farwell) 521, p. 177.
  Bethiah⁵ 638, pp. 54, 56, 57.
  Catharine⁸ 1207.
  Catharine⁹ 1081.
  Catharine-May⁸ 1008.
  Charles-Alexander⁸ 1046.
  Charles-Augustus⁷ 1246.
  Charles-Augustus-Warner² 1215.
  Charles-Edward⁹ 1006.
  Charles-Elijah⁸ 1086.
  Charles-Lindsey⁸ 1091.
  Charles-Sumner⁸ 1174.
  Charlotte⁸ 1211.
  Charlotte-E⁹ 1071.
  Charlotte-Emily 1056.
  Clara⁸ 1171.
  Clark-Emmons⁹ 1062.
  Cyrus-Farwell⁶ 1109.
  David⁹ 1083.
  David-May⁸ 1007.
  David-Parsons⁷ 1044, pp. 36, 56, 57, 77, 78, G. R. C.
  D-Pliny-Forward⁸ 1045.
  Ebenezer⁵ p. 98.
  Edith p. 173.
  Capt. Edward-Alexander⁷ 1004, p. 152.
  Edward-Payson⁸ 1173.
  Ella-Isabell⁸ 1110.
  Elihu-Dwight⁷ 1183.
  Elisha⁶ 532.
  Elisha⁷ 618.
  Elizabeth⁷ 615.
  Elizabeth-Rachel⁸ 1105.
  Eliza-Jane 1092.
  Ellen-Maria⁸ 1202.
  Emily-Elizabeth⁹ 1067.

Holton, Emma⁹ 1082.
  Erastus⁶ 528, 530.
  Erastus-Alexander⁷ 1003.
  Eva-Adelaide⁹ 1059.
  Fanny-Miriam⁸ 1047.
  Francis-Alexander⁸ 1221.
  Frances-Caroline⁹ 1058.
  Frank-Cuyler⁹ 1074.
  Frank-Erastus⁹ 1010.
  Harriet⁷ 1222.
  Harriet-Ann⁷ 1199.
  Harriet-Ann⁸ 1064.
  Harry-Lorenzo 1248.
  Harry-Sylvester⁹ 1011.
  Helen-Rebecca⁹ 1052, p. 115.
  Henry-Alfred⁸ 1076.
  Henry-Dwight⁸ 1188, p. 56.
  Ida-Blanche⁹ 1087.
  Ira⁸ 1180.
  Isaac⁶ 640, pp. 84, 101, 156, 165.
  Isaac-Farwell⁷ 1170.
  Isabel⁷ 1166.
  Isabella⁹ 1085.
  Jason-Marcellus⁹ 1058.
  Jay-Reuben⁹ 1063.
  Jemima⁶ 531.
  Jemima⁶ 525.
  Jeremiah⁹ 1080.
  Joel⁵ 425, 521, pp. 55, 56, 57, 84, 94, 115, 177, G. R. C.
  Joel⁶ 606, G. R. C.
  Joel-Alexander⁷ 647.
  Joel-Herbert⁸ 1245.
  Joel-Huntington⁸ 1009.
  Jonathan-Warner⁷ 1201.
  John² pp. 94, 98.
  John³ pp. 50, 84, 94, 115.
  John⁴ 632, p. 84.
  John⁷ 624.
  John⁹ 1079.
  John-Ambrose⁷ 1242.
  John-Dumont⁸ 1217.
  John-Wesley⁸ 1102.
  Joshua⁴ p. 98.
  Julia-Ann 1189.
  Julia-Esther⁷ 1249.
  Kate-Cornelia⁸ 1073.
  Kate-May⁹ 1005.
  Laura-Wolcott⁷ 630.
  Lillie-May⁹ 1104.
  Lines-Tower⁸ 1050, p.115.
  Linda⁸ 1244.

Holton, Luceba-Grout⁸ 1184.
Lyman-Hoyt 1111.
Mary⁷ 613, p. 98.
Mary⁸ 1078.
Mary-Alice⁸ 1070.
Mary-Ellen⁸ 1101
Martha-Jane⁸ 1061.
Minerva⁷ 1013, ch. XVI.
Minnie-Grace⁸ 1075.
Miriam⁷ 1043, ch. XVI.
Nancy-Gates⁸ 1172.
Nelson-Alexander⁸ 1057.
Noadiah-Loomis⁷ 1179.
Olive⁷ 1112.
Olivia-Arnold⁷ 629.
Phebe-Helen 611, ch.XVI.
Pliny-White-Taylor⁸ 1243.
Rebecca-Ranney⁷ 1238.
Reuben-Allen⁸ 1090.
Reuben-Rockwood⁷ 1048, p. 115.
Richard⁸ 1103.
Sabra⁸ 1049.
Seth-Arnold⁷ 1236.
Susie⁸ 1012.
Thomas² p. 98.
Wallace-Lines⁸ 1055.
Walter-Fay⁸ 1247.
Wealthy-Ann⁷ 1175.
Dea. William¹ pp. 56, 57, 85, 94, 98, 115, 158.
William³ p. 94.
William⁶ 612, pp. 57, 115.
William⁷ 1065.
William-Augustus⁸ 1220.
William-Augustus-Warner⁷ 1213, p. 175.
William-Edward⁸ 1072.
William-Mason⁸ 1066.
Worthington⁶ p. 98.
Zoheth⁶ 625.
Holton, pp. 58, 78, 95, 96, ch. XVI, XVII.
Hood, Gen. p. 181.
Hopkins, Rev. Dr. p. 99.
Asenath p. 148.
Bishop 183.
Huldah p. 99.
Lucy p. 43.
Hopper, Abraham p. 181.
Mary-Elizabeth 1246.
Horn, Mary 365.
Horton, Maj. Gideon p. 87.
Sarah 539.
Hosmer, Hannah 115.

Hosmer, James p. 3.
Hotchkiss, Douglas-Farwell⁷ 785.
William p. 135.
William-Benjamin⁸ 786.
William-James 784.
Houghton, Catharine 379.
Hovey, Aaron⁸ 412, 418.
Amos p. 49.
Ann p. 49.
Dorcas p. 91.
Edmund 408, G. R. C.
Edmund⁶ 409. p. 50.
Elizabeth⁵ 416, p. 49.
Isaac⁵ 410.
James p. 49.
Mary p. 49.
Mary⁶ 411.
Priscilla pp. 49, 50.
Sarah 334.
William p. 49.
How, Elizabeth p. 13.
Howard, Abigail 130.
Frank p. 69.
John p. 7.
Jonathan p. 10, G. R. C.
Mary p. 140.
Samuel 378ᵈ, 378ⁱ.
Howlet, Sarah p. 21.
Thomas p. 21.
Hoyt, Dorcas-Ford 1065.
Jonathan p. 165.
Hubbard, Abigail 465.
Edward 89.
Jonathan pp. 61, 62.
Rebecca p. 62.
Huff, Jacob p. 161.
John-Francis⁸ 1106.
Lizzie-Bell⁸ 1108.
Mary-Bell⁸ 1107.
Truman-Hobert 1105.
Huntington, Ann 408, p.50.
Gov. Samuel p. 70.
Thomas p. 49.
Huntoon, Nathan 546, G. R. C.
Patrick-Henry p. 88.
Huse, John ch. XI.
Husted, Charles-Thos⁸.1181
Clyde-Merit⁹ 1185.
Etta-Belle⁹ 1133.
Lurena-Almira⁹ 1128.
Merit 1123.
Oliver p. 162.
Sarah-Inis⁹ 1134.
Stephen-Edward⁹ 1129.

Hyde, Elizabeth ch. VI, G. R. C.
Elizabeth⁵ 73.
Jonathan p. 19.
Jonathan¹ p. 19.
Joseph p. 19.
Samuel² p. 19.
Ireland, p. 35.
Ives, Miles p. 109.
Jackson, Abraham² pp. 109, 110, 114, ch. IX, X.
Pres. Andrew pp. 71, 139.
Christopher⁶ p. 109, 134ᵃ, ch. IX.
Christopher⁷ p. 79.
Dolly p. 104.
Edward¹ pp. 109, 110, 111, ch. IX, X.
Dea. Edward² p. 110.
Edward³ p. 111, ch. IX.
Edward⁴ p. 110.
Edward⁵ p. 111, ch. IX.
Elisha⁸ p. 111.
Elizabeth³ p. 110.
Hannah⁵ p. 110, ch. IX.
Hannah⁶ p. 110.
Isaac⁴ p. 111, ch. IX.
Jemima p. 139, ch X
Dea. John,¹ pp. 109, 110, 113, 114, 134ᵃ, ch. IX.
John² p. 111.
John⁵ p. 108, ch. IX, X.
Jonathan² p. 110.
Jonathan³ pp. 110, 111.
Jonathan⁴ pp. 110, 11 .
Joseph³ p. 111.
Josiah⁵ p. 111.
Margaret⁴ p. 114, ch. IX.
Michael⁴ p. 111.
Col. Michael⁵ pp. 111, 112.
Nancy⁷ 747, pp. 74, 79, 110, 111, 112, 113, 114, ch. IX.
Pomp p. 111.
Sebas² pp. 110, 111, 112, 134ᵃ, ch. IX, X.
Timothy⁴ p. 111.
Timothy⁵ p. 111.
William⁶ p. 111.
William⁵, Esq. p. 111.
James p. 125.
Jeffries, Searg. Thomas p. 112.
Jefts, George-H. p. 34.
Jenerson, Sarah p. 141.

F *Index.* 197

Jennison, Mary p. 62.
Jessup p. 125.
Jewett, Clarissa p. 183.
　Stephen 385.
　Stephens 397.
Jones, Mrs. p. 174.
　Abigail[2] p. 44.
　Amos p. 92.
　Andrew p. 139.
　Anna-Lincoln[9] 975.
　Arthur-Dean[9] 976.
　Bartholomew[4] 116.
　Carrie-Josephine[9] 725.
　Daniel[5] 114.
　Ebenezer[3] 113.
　Edward-Horton 827[a].
　Maj. Ezra p. 87.
　Fanny 541, p. 88, G.R.C.
　Farwell 115.
　George-Laflin[9] 977.
　Henry-D. p. 66.
　John[1] pp. 3, 13, 45.
　John[2] 31, p. 45.
　John[3] 110, p. 45.
　John[4] 111 p. 45.
　John-Elmer 974, p. 149.
　Joseph-Comstock 827.
　Lizzie-Edna[9] 724.
　Lydia 588.
　Lydia[3] 121.
　Mary p. 159.
　Mary[3] 120.
　Nancy p. 136.
　Olive[5] 112.
　Orra-Louisa[9] 722.
　Polly[7] p. 44.
　Rebecca[3] 122.
　Rosina-Tuttle[9] 723.
　Ruth[5] 118.
　Sarah[4] 105, ch. V.
　Sarah[5] 119.
　Silas p. 107.
　Silence[6] 123.
　Thomas-Green-Fessenden 721.
　Timothy[4] 31.
　Timothy[5] 117.
　Col. Timothy[6] p. 45.
　William 248, 303.
Johnson, Abigail pp. 143, 148.
　Capt. Henry p. 179.
　Mercy 358.
　Noah pp. 39, 40.
Joslin, Dorothy p. 93.
　Nathaniel[2] p. 13.

Joslin, Peter[3] 36, G.R.C.
　Thomas p. 13.
Kellogg, Samuel-N. p. 119.
Kelly, Edward-Everett 1198.
　George p. 173.
　John-Thomas 1195.
　Lizzie-Jane[9] 1197.
Kelsey, John p. 59.
Kendall, Mary p. 101, ch. XI.
　Thomas ch. XI.
Kendrick, Ann[2] p. 110.
Kendrickson, Mary p. 160.
Keys, Edward ch. XI.
Kidder, Dorothy[3] pp. 19, 20, G.R.C.
　James[1] p. 20.
　James[2] p. 20.
　Mary p. 142.
Kight, Arthur[10] 1069.
　William-A. 1068.
Kilbourn, Mary p. 157.
　Ruth p. 136.
Kimball, Abgiail-Hill p. 46.
　Charles-Edward p. 46.
　Eliza-Jane p. 46.
　Isaac p. 46.
　John 380.
　John-Edward[9] 380.
　John-Richardson p. 46.
　Maria-Frances[9] 380.
　Martha 495.
King, Alexander p. 184.
　Mary-Amanda[3] 1195.
　Daniel p. 173.
　Hayes-Giddings-Whitmore[9] 1276.
　Hiram 1189.
　Julia-Frances[6] 1190.
　Margaret p. 159.
　Osman-Smith 1275.
　Sarah p. 13.
　Thomas p. 13.
Kingsbury, Rev. Ebenezer, p. 43.
Klett, Andrew p. 149.
　Kate-Helen 982.
Knowlton, Margaret 409.
Knox, p. 134.
　Hannah-Mary 778, p. 74.
　John p. 135.
Kohn, Leopold 1067.
Ladd, Hannah-Hastings p. 145.

Laflin, James-W. 981.
　Winthrop p. 149.
Lafayette, Gen. p. 64.
Lakin, Oliver p. 29.
　Sybil 148.
　William p. 29.
Lamphier p. 157.
Lane, David-Allen[9] 803.
　Elias p. 136.
　Elias-Cooledge 801, p. 74.
　Mary p.
　Mary-Hepzibah[6] 802.
　Rebecca p. 172.
Lancaster, Elvira-A. 970.
Larrabee, John 493.
Lattin, Almy-Crawford[9] 813
　Clarissa[3] 811.
　Frederick[9] 814.
　Judson-Moss[9] 812.
　Nathan 809.
　Ransom p. 137.
　Sidney[9] 810.
Laughton, Thomas p. 59.
Lawrence, p. 74, ch. VIII.
　Amos p. 26.
　Elizabeth p. 138.
　George[4] p. 73, ch. VIII.
　Hannah pp. 73, 74, ch. 8
　Jonathan pp. 26, 32.
　Samuel p. 83.
　Sarah p. 29.
　Hon. William p. 71.
Laveille, Theodore p. 146.
Lawton, p. 157.
　Charlotte 781.
Learned, Benoni[3] p. 11.
　Hannah 15, p. 6, 79, ch. VI, VIII, G.R.C.
　Isaac[2] 74, pp. 11, 12, ch. VIII.
　Isaac[3] p. 11.
　Mary pp. 11, 12.
　William p. 11, ch. VIII.
　William[3] p. 11.
Lee, John p. 54.
　Submit 436.
Leiter, I-Z. p. 119.
Length of generations p 114
Leonard pp. 95, 157, ch.
　Eliphalet p. 55.
Lincoln, Cynthia p. 149.
　President, pp. 123, 124, 125, 157, 178.
Lines (measure of) p 79
Litch, Martha 970.
　Thomas. p. 148.

Litchfield, Edward p. 108.
  Flora-Georgiana⁹ 744.
  George-E. 743.
Little p. 147.
  Joseph-Rodney p. 68.
Livingston, Dr. p. 94.
Locke, William ch. XI.
Longley, Alice-Gertrude¹⁰ 860.
  Charles-Albert⁹ 857.
  Charles-Chandler¹⁰ 859.
  Clara-Melissa⁹ 865.
  Ellen-Eliza⁹ 864.
  Joanna p. 74.
  Jonas p. 59.
  Lillie-May¹⁰ 858.
  Mariette-Frances 867.
  Mary-Maria⁹ 863.
  Melvin-Whitmore⁹ 866.
  Gelson-Parker⁹ 862.
  Stephen p. 140.
  Stephen-Melvin 856.
  Stephen-Webster⁹ 861.
  William p. 74.
Loomis p. 157.
  Amanda 625.
  Fanny p. 149.
  John³ p. 97.
  John⁴ p. 97.
  Jonathan⁵ p. 97.
  Joseph¹ p. 97.
  Noadiah² p. 97.
  Thomas² p. 97.
Loring, Hannah⁵ p. 110.
  Joshua³ p. 110.
  Commodore Joshua⁴ p. 110.
Loudon, Earl of, p. 83.
Louks, Jonathan-Wilbur-Augustus⁹ 1209.
  Perry-Holton⁹ 1210.
  Philip 1207.
  Warren-Lincoln⁹ 1208.
Lovell pp. 95, 96, chs. XVI, XVII.
Lovell, Martha, p. 96
Lovewell, Hannah 853.
  John¹, pp. 38, 63.
  Capt. John² p. 87, 89, 63.
  Nehemiah³ 357.
  Noah 468.
  Zaccheus³ p. 63.
Lyman, Job p. 99.
Lyon, Matthew p. 178.
  Hannah p. 99.

Mandell, Hannah⁴ pp. 174, 175.
  Paul 174.
Markham, Daniel ch. XI.
Marshfield p. 95, ch. XVI.
Marshall p. 157.
  Louisa p. 136.
Martain, Fannie-S.⁹ 830.
  John p. 138.
  Lemuel-Porter, 829.
Martin, Ambrose p. 3.
  Catharine p. 174.
  George-Elbridge 871.
  Lucy p. 140.
Mason, Anna-Elizabeth⁹ 1240.
  Betsey 1065.
  Daniel p. 159.
  Edward-Augustus 1239.
  Hannah p. 24.
  Capt. Hugh p. 24.
  Rev. Joseph 1238.
  Joseph p. 180.
May, Hannah-Brainerd 1003, p. 95, ch. XVII.
  Harriet 999.
  Huntington p. 150.
  William p. 150.
Mayhew, Thomas p. 110.
Maynard, Charlotte 940.
  Daniel p. 146.
  Samuel p. 107.
  Sarah-Noyes 727.
McClellan, General p. 134.
McCreary, Rachel 474.
McFarland, Elizabeth 847.
  Nelson p. 139.
McKinley, Byard p. 160.
  Ettie-Horton 1086.
McMaster p. 95, ch. XVI.
Measures (notation of) p.79.
Mellen, Betsey p. 136.
Merick, Mary pp. 95, 173, ch. XVI.
Merriam p. 44.
  Abbie-Caroline⁹ 882.
  Adams-Brooks p. 47.
  Adeliza-Frances⁹ 882.
  Ann p. 24.
  Annie-Louise⁹ 882.
  Benjamin-Wheeler 882.
  Emma-Rebecca⁹ 882.
  George p. 4.
  Harriet-Wheeler⁹ 882.
  Henry-Everett⁹ 882.
  John⁹ p. 11.

Merriam, Josiah p. 44.
  Maria-Hill⁹ 382.
  Robert pp. 3, 4.
  Ruth p. 24.
  Samuel p. 47.
  Sarah-Wheeler⁹ 882.
Merrill, Eddie⁹ 1198ᵃ.
  James-A. 1195.
Messenger, Elias p. 92.
Messerve, Colonel p. 83.
Metcalf, Elizabeth p. 41.
Method in Genealogy p. 78.
Miller p. 96, XVII.
Miner, Eliza (Parsons) p.119.
Mingins, Bro. p. 124.
Miriam, John 26.
Monson, Betsey p. 142.
Monroe, John p. 138.
  Susan-Melissa 834.
Montague, Abigail p. 134.
  Hannah p. 134.
  Joseph p. 134.
  Richard¹ p. 134.
  William p. 134.
Morehead, Susan p. 139.
Moody, Dwight-L. pp. 130, 132, 133.
  Samuel p. 11.
Moore, p. 157.
  Ann p. 20.
  Francis p. 20, G. R. C.
  Isaac p. 100.
Moors, Abraham p. 32, 34, 74, 77, 89, ch. VIII.
  Elizabeth 162, 329, pp. 77, 89, ch. VIII.
  Susan 281.
  Susannah 281.
  Timothy p. 27.
More p. 95, ch. XVI.
Morgan, Isaac 30, 488.
  Sarah 489.
Morse ch. XI.
  Eliza 588.
  Hannah p. 149.
Morton p. 157.
  Catharine-Isabel 825.
  Helen-M. 149.
Mosier, Catharine-Louisa⁹ 1203.
  Lewis 1202.
Mott, Prof. A-B. p. 172.
  Prof. Valentine p. 172.
Mudge, Alfred p. 12.
Mulford, ch. VI.
Munn p. 95, ch. XVI.

Index. 199

Narramore, Sara-A 674.
Neal, Clara-Minerva 840.
  John-Dearborn p. 139.
Nelson p. 157.
  Rev. David p. 165.
Nesmith, Isabella-Abigail p. 136.
Newgate, Elizabeth p. 110.
Newhall, Mary p. 41.
  Horace p. 92.
  Mary p. 35.
N. Y. Gen. and Biogr. Society, pp. 78, 157.
Norcross, Richard p. 113.
Notation (Genealogical) pp. 78, 79.
Noyes, John p. 174.
  Rev. John-Humphrey 1199.
  Theodore-Richards, M. D. 1200.
  William p. 111.
Nutting, Deborah 272.
  Joanna p. 30.
  Jonathan p. 32.
  Lydia p. 27.
  Sarah pp. 29, 32.
Oliver, Rev. John p. 110.
Ollyver p. 96, ch. XVII.
Onderdonk, Bishop. p. 68.
Ord, Gen. p. 124.
Osborne, Abram 660.
  Arvilla-Frances⁹ 663.
  Charles-Pierson-Johnson⁹ 732.
  Cynthia-Eliza⁸ 741.
  Daniel-Farwell⁷ 727.
  Daniel-Farwell⁸ 728.
  Elizabeth-Maria⁹ 739.
  Frank-Maynard⁹ 730.
  George-Warren⁸ 731.
  George-Warren⁹ 729.
  Hattie-Elizabeth⁹ 661.
  Helen-Georgiana⁹ 743.
  Jacob 549.
  Leonard⁷ 736.
  Leonard-Warren⁸ 738.
  Louisa⁷ ⁷720.
  Mary-Elizabeth⁸ 745.
  Polly⁷ 656.
  Nancy⁷ 699.
  Sarah-Eveline⁸ 733.
  Sarah-Frances⁸ 746.
  Susan⁷ 659.
  Sybil⁷ 676.

Osgood, Samuel, D. D. p. 99.
Otis, Martha p. 49.
Owen p. 157.
Packard, Susan p. 108.
Page p. 145.
  Abel⁶ 175.
  Augustus-Dole⁶ 317.
  Benjamin 656.
  Betsey⁶ 178.
  Betty⁶ 174.
  Daniel p. 159.
  Dennis p. 141.
  Ede⁶ 314.
  Edmund⁶ 312.
  Eli⁶ 315.
  Elizabeth⁷ 165, p. 73.
  Eunice⁶ 177.
  Eunice⁷ 163.
  George 872.
  Hannah p. 139.
  Hannah⁶ 171ᵃ.
  Hannah⁷ 168.
  James⁶ 171.
  Joel⁷ 170.
  John p. 33.
  John¹ pp. 44, 73, ch. VIII.
  John³ p. 73, 74, ch. VIII.
  John⁴ p. 72, ch. VIII.
  Jonas⁶ 173.
  Jonathan³ p. 73, ch. VI.I
  Joseph p. 33.
  Levi⁶ 312.
  Lucy 843.
  Lydia⁶ 172.
  Lydia⁷ 167.
  Mary p. 73.
  Oliver⁶ 179.
  Peter⁶ 176.
  Phebe p. 44.
  Phineas 308.
  Phineas⁶ 311.
  Roxalana 658.
  Samuel p. 73.
  Samuel-Dana 657.
  Sarah 344, p. 40.
  Simon 161.
  Simon⁶ 162.
  Simon⁷ 169.
  Susan⁷ 166.
  Susannah 306.
  Sybil⁵ 511 pp. 36, 73, 74, 77, ch. VIII.
  Sybil⁷ 164.
  Theophilus⁶ 309.
  Walter⁶ 316.

Paine p. 74, ch. VIII.
  David p. 71.
  Judge N. p. 88.
  Lydia 509.
  Priscilla 488.
Parish, John-Nelson p. 158.
  Phebe p. 176.
  Sylvia-Rosetta 1055.
Park, James p. 19.
Parke, Isabella ch. XI.
  Richard ch. XI.
Parker p. 74, ch. VIII.
  Acsah 388°.
  Col. David 541, 548, p. 88, G. R. C.
  Dolly⁵ 536.
  Elijah⁵ 534, pp. 83, 101, ch. VI, G. R. C.
Parker, Elijah⁶ 539.
  Elizabeth⁶ 537.
  Enos⁶ 543.
  Fanny-Jones 548, pp. 87, 88, G. R. C.
  Henry 70.
  Isaac p. 40, 45.
  Lieut. Isaac³ pp. 83, 86, 101.
  Isaac⁴ pp. 85, 86, 101.
  Isaac⁵ 535, G. R. C.
  Jacob⁶ 538.
  Capt. James¹ pp. 73, 83, 86.
  John⁶ 547.
  Joseph¹ pp. 73, 77, 83, 86, 101, ch. VIII.
  Joseph² pp. 73, 77, 83, 86, 101, ch. VIII.
  Joseph³ p. 73, ch. VIII.
  Margaret pp. 79, 101.
  Martha⁶ 544.
  Mary 330, p. 33.
  Mary³ p. 73.
  Mary⁴ pp. 72, 73, 77, 79, ch. VIII.
  Nathaniel⁴ p. 83.
  Obadiah p. 26.
  Orra-West⁶ 648, ch. XI, G. R. C.
  Phineas 545, p. 59.
  Polly⁶ 542.
  Rhoda p. 140.
  Sarah 437, 548.
  Sophia⁶ 546.
  Willard p. 159.
  William p. 83.
Parkhill, Emily p. 159.

Parallel charts, pp. 95, 96.
Parkhurst, Ebenezer p. 65.
   Polly p. 93.
Parris, Robert p. 9.
Parsons, pp. 58, 95, 96, chs. XVI, XVII.
   Dea. Benjamin[1] pp. 78, 93.
   Benjamin[2] p. 93, ch. XVI.
   Benjamin[3] p. 93, ch. XVI.
   David[4] pp. 93, 133.
      ch. XVI.
   Eben[4] p. 78.
   Ebenezer[2] p. 93, ch. XVI.
   Dr. Edward-Field[6] p. 78.
   Ithamar[3] p. 133.
   Joel[5] pp. 119, 133.
   Joseph[5] pp. 119, 133.
   Nathaniel[5] p. 78.
   Phebe[6] 606, ch. XVI.
   Philip[5] p. 78.
   Samuel[2] p. 133.
   Shubael[6] p. 78.
   Sophronia[4] pp. 117, 133.
Patch, Maria p 789, p. 74.
   Samuel p. 136.
Patrick, Gen. p. 122.
Patterson, Esther p. 20.
   James p. 59.
Payne, Molly p. 70.
   Phebe p. 73, ch. VIII.
   Solomon p. 70.
   William p. 73, ch. VIII.
Payson, Hannah[5] p. 42.
   Rev. John p. 88.
Peabody, Nathaniel p. 62.
Pearson, Samuel 373.
Pedigradation p. 78.
Pell p. 74, ch. VIII.
   Ann p. 89.
Pellet p. 16.
Perkins, Francis p. 92.
Perry, Charlotte-Baily 1201.
   Ransom p. 174.
   Warner p. 174.
Phelps, pp. 95, 117, ch. XVI.
   Brigham 1181.
   Hiram p. 150.
   Mary 989.
   Robert p. 150.
Philological Society p. 157.
Phinney p. 96, ch. XVII.
Pierce, Elbridge-Gerry 831.
   Elizabeth 47.
   Ephraim 254, p. 14.
   Franklin-Brown[9] 833.
   Henry-Ernest[9] 832.

Pierce, Henry-Willard 692.
   Joseph p. 138.
   Mary 487.
   Rachel p. 29.
   Samuel-Willard p. 105.
   Timothy p. 65.
Pierpont P. p. 10
Pierson, Nancy-Sargeant p. 71.
   Dr. William-S. p. 71.
Pilgrim Record Soc'y p. 157
Piper, Abbie-Dora[9] 917.
   Frederick-Joseph[9] 916.
   George-Maurice[9] 918.
   Harriet p. 139.
   Henry-Francis 921.
   Henry-Lyman[9] 924.
   John-Johnson[9] 919.
   Joseph-Lorin 912.
   Marcia 961.
   Mary-Boutelle[9] 922.
   Merrick pp. 143, 148.
   Rebecca p. 104.
   Ruth-Marston[9] 923.
   Sidney-Richard[9] 920.
Polite, Harriet-Emily 1102.
   Richard p. 161.
Pool, Elizabeth 397.
Porter, Almira[8] 688.
   Asa-G. 676.
   Charles-Henry[8] 680.
   Dorothy 472.
   Emma-Louisa[9] 684.
   Frederick-Leonard[9] 686.
   Henrietta-Jane[9] 679.
   Henry-Abbott[8] 678.
   Jacob-Osborne[8] 677.
   Leonard-Warner[8] 681.
   Lorinda[8] 690.
   Louisa[8] 694.
   Nellie-Maria[9] 687.
Potter, Luke pp. 3, 4.
Powers, Hannah-Elizabeth 857.
   Jerahmael p. 59.
   Jonathan-Jackson p. 140.
Pratt[5] p. 136.
   Anna 221.
   Betty[7] 394.
   Caty[6] 391.
   David[6] 390.
   Ebenezer-Hill[8] 381.
   Hannah[6] 392.
   Jeramiel[7] 393.
   John 375.
   Lydia 229.

Pratt, Molly[6] 395.
   Oliver-Hosmer 381.
   Thomas 389.
Prescott, Col. 457.
   Jonathan ch. V.
   Mary p. 30.
Preston, Dr. p. 35.
   Rejoice 446.
   William p. 59.
Prichard, George-W. 1269.
Proctor ch. XI.
Purdy, Electa p. 162.
Purrington, Lucinda-Clapp p. 108.
Putnam, Gen. Israel p. 70.
   William p. 70.
Quincy, Dorothy p. 110.
   Elizabeth p. 113.
   Joanna[2] ch. V.
   Col. Edmond ch. V.
Radcliff, ch. XI.
Radials pp. 36, 80, 185.
Ralston, Centurius-Holton[10] 1054, pp. 57, 115.
   Josiah-Marshall 1052.
   Minnie-Estelle[10] 1053.
Rand, Silas p. 35.
Randall, Almira-W. p. 171.
Rendall, Rev. John pp. 165, 170.
Ranney, Esther p. 100.
   Phebe (Phelps) p. 98.
Read, Clarissa 891.
   Priscilla-Emily p. 140.
Redlat, John p. 19.
   Mary p. 19.
Reed, John p. 142.
   Rebecca p. 73.
   Ruth p. 97.
   Sarah-Ann p. 154.
Relationship noted p. 79.
Reward, Institute of, p. 157.
Rice, Esther p. 87.
   Frederick-William p. 98.
   Joseph p. 98.
   Joseph-Parker 630.
   Mary-Ann
   Newbern p. 98.
   Richard p. 4.
Richards, p. 95, ch. XVI.
Richards, Abijah p. 99.
   Harriet 632.
   Hon. Mark p. 99.
Richardson, Carrie-Virginia[9] 901.
   Charlotte-Houghton[9] 903.

Richardson, Dr. Ebenezer-
    Coolidge 899.
  Edward-Coolidge⁹ 905.
  Ezekiel pp. 14, 16.
  Harriet-Gardner⁹ 902.
  Henry⁴ 58.
  Jane-Sophronia p. 46.
  John G. R. C.
  John³ 56, p. 16.
  John⁴ 57.
  Josiah² pp. 14, 16.
  Maria-Anita⁹ 900.
  Martha-Reed⁹ 904.
  Oliver 878⁶.
  Polly 436.
  Samuel p. 142.
  Samuel¹ p. 16.
  Sarah G. R. C.
  Susannah 64, p.40,G.R.C.
  Susannah³ 64, p. 14
  Susannah⁴ 60.
  Sarah⁴ 59.
  Thomas¹ p. 16.
Rigdon, Sidney p. 67.
Ripley, Allen-P. p. 185.
  Edwin-L. p. 152.
  Hannah-Danelia 779.
Robert, Henry p. 59.
  Israel p. 26.
Robertson, James 371.
Robinson, Henson p. 154.
  Phebe p. 133.
  Rebecca p. 133.
  Sallie 1034.
  Sally p. 103.
Rockwood, Olive 612.
  William p. 97.
Roe, Elizabeth 1236.
Rogers, C-H. & Co. pp. 144,
    145.
  Robert p. 37.
Root, Erastus, M.D. p. 100.
  Fanny p. 156.
  Gideon¹ p. 100.
  John p. 157.
  John² p. 100.
  John¹ p. 100.
  John³ p. 100.
  Samuel⁴ p. 100.
  Thomas² p. 100.
  Timothy⁵ p. 100.
Rose, Harriet 781.
  James p. 135.
Rowland, David-S. 480.
  Grace 478.
  Henry-Augustus p. 64.

Rowland, Samuel p. 64.
  William-Frederick⁶ p.64.
Rowlandson p. 23.
Ruggles, p. 96, ch. XVII.
  Anna p. 99.
  Annie-Louise⁹ 1150.
  Charles-Ambrose⁶ 1147.
  Charles-Lester⁹ 1153.
  Dora-Bell⁹ 1151.
  Hannah-Minerva⁹ 1155.
  Harriet-Elizabeth⁸ 1118.
  Henry-Austin⁶ 1136.
  Henry-Thomas⁹ 1154.
  Ida-May⁹ 1149.
  James-Albert⁹ 1140.
  Joseph p. 99.
  Joshua 1112.
  Julia-Ann⁶ 1138.
  Julia-Isabel⁶ 1123.
  Mary-Ann⁶ 1159.
  Merit-Solomon-A⁶. 1146.
  Capt. Samuel² p. 174.
  Capt. Samuel³ p. 174.
  Susanna⁴ p. 174.
  Thomas p. 162.
  Thomas¹ p. 174.
  Thomas-Edwin⁸ p. 162.
  Col. & Brig. Gen. Tim-
    othy⁵ pp.84, 174.
  Rev. Timothy p. 174.
Rush, Sarah p. 163.
Russell, John p. 59.
  Mary 346.
Ryan, Hannah p. 134.
Sabin, Matilda p. 67.
Sackett p. 83.
Sage, Rev. Sylvester pp. 97,
    171.
Sahler, Rev. Daniel-D. 382.
  Emma-Frances¹⁰ 382.
  Florence-Louise¹⁰ 382.
Saltonstall, Gov. Richard
    pp. 11, 44.
Sanderson, Ann-Elmira 849.
  Elijah p. 139.
  Elisha p. 139.
Sandwich, Earl of p. 134.
Sanger, Elizabeth 485.
Savage, James pp. 6, 7, 13,
    14, 16, 21, 24, 73.
Sawtell, Abigail⁴ pp. 73,77
    ch. VIII.
  Abigail⁶ 295.
  Bethiah⁶ 300.
  Eli⁶ 299.
  Elnathan 277.

Sawtell, Elnathan⁶ 278.
  Ephraim 147, 294.
  Ephraim⁶ 301.
  Hezekiah, pp. 32, 33, 59.
  Joseph⁶ 279.
  Josiah⁶ 300.
  Lucy⁶ 296.
  Molly⁶ 280, 298.
  Obadiah² pp. 74, 79, ch.
    VIII.
  Obadiah³ pp. 73, 74, ch.
    VIII.
  Richard¹ pp. 61, 74, 77,
    ch. VIII.
  Sarah 52, p. 82.
  Sarah⁶ 302.
  Sybil 464.
Sawyer, p. 134⁶ ch. X.
  Benjamin-H. p. 183.
  Jonathan p. 76, ch. IX.
  Seloma-Whiting 1264.
Scott, Elijah p. 20.
  John p. 160.
  Rebecca 1076.
Scudder, Dr. pp. 122, 125.
Sears, p. 96, ch. XVII.
Seize Quartiers, pp. 75, 76,
    134ᵃ.
Seward, Secretary p. 124.
Seymour p. 129.
Shae, Elizabeth p. 106.
  Mary-Ann 713.
  Timothy p. 106.
Shattuck pp. 78, 86.
  Anne p. 28.
  Hannah p. 28.
  Judson-Daniel 1060.
  Lemuel p. 4, 6, 24, 73, 86.
  Sybil p. 61.
  William p. 113.
Shaw, Abigail⁶ p. 113.
  Elizabeth⁶ (Smith) p. 113.
  Rev. John p. 113.
  Mrs. Keziah 612.
  Olive 958.
  Sebrina p. 173.
  William p. 148.
Shed, Abigail p. 88.
  Daniel p. 28.
  Elizabeth 190.
  G-H. p. 38.
Shedd, Margaret-F. 1236.
  William-Poole p. 179.
Sherman, Elizabeth p. 135.
  Genl. p. 125.
Sherwin, Henry-H. 653.

Shipman, Lydia p. 70.
Shippen, Rev. R. R. p. 148.
Shirley p. 83.
Shurtliff, Roswell-S. p. 99.
Shute, Roxy p. 151.
Sibley, Jerusha p. 142.
Simms, Catharine-Maria p. 179.
Simonds, Joseph p. 89.
  William p. 59.
Slade, Anna p. 171.
Slafter, Rev. Edmund-Farwell⁷, G. R. C.
  John 416, p. 49, G.R.C.
  Samuel p. 50.
Small p. 96, ch. XVII.
Smallwood, Edwin p. 109.
Smith p. 134ᵃ ch. X.
  Abigail³ (Fowle) p. 113.
  Abigail⁵ p. 113.
  Albert 698.
  Charles-Henry⁹ 695.
  Cornelia p. 135.
  Ebenette-Charlotte-Maria 770.
  Elizabeth⁵ p. 113.
  Elizabeth-Hunt 472, p. 43.
  Elizabeth (Quincy) p. 113.
  Ella-Frances⁹ 697.
  George p. 134.
  Hattie⁹ 1186.
  Helen 824.
  Henry-Erastus⁹ 1187.
  Rev Isaac-Bateman p. 134
  Jonathan-Erastus 1184.
  Josiah p. 105.
  Laura p. 162.
  Mary-Elizabeth 879.
  Mary-Eveline 753, p. 134ᵃ, ch. X.
  Nathan p. 60.
  Oliver-Henry 694.
  Otis p. 172.
  Priscilla 449.
  Roxanna p. 158.
  Samuel p. 141.
  Thankful p. 155.
  Thomas p. 115.
  Capt. William p. 113.
  Rev. William⁴ p. 113.
Snow, Esther 494.
  Silas 342.
Solendine 442.

Somerby, Mr. p. 113.
  H.-G. 134ᵃ, ch. X.
Soule, Charles-Carroll 941.
Spaulding, Judge p. 71.
  Abigail⁴ 98.
  Abigail⁵ 475, 491.
  Alexander⁶ p. 69.
  Alexander-Hamilton⁷ p. 69
  Alice⁵ 488.
  Alva⁷ p. 69.
  Amasa⁶ p. 65.
  Asa⁵ 478, pp. 70, 72.
  Asa-Blodgett⁶ p. 68.
  Azel⁶ p. 65.
  Azel⁷ p. 66.
  Azel-Wainwright⁶ p. 66.
  Bela-Payne⁶ p. 70.
  Benjamin 25, G. R. C.
  Dr. Benjamin-Bacon⁷ p. 70.
  Benjamin⁴ 102.
  Benjamin⁵ 473.
  Benjamin⁵ 474, p. 64.
  Betsey p. 159.
  Charles⁶ p. 72.
  Charles⁷ p. 66.
  Charles-Carrol⁵ p. 65.
  Rev. Prof. Charles-Nelson p. 68.
  David⁵ 482.
  David⁶ p. 64.
  David-C⁶. p. 64.
  Delos⁶ p. 69.
  Ebenezer p. 12.
  Ebenezer⁴ 500.
  Ebenezer⁶ p. 70.
  Ebenezer⁷ p. 70.
  Edith⁶ 95.
  Edmund⁶ p. 69.
  Edward¹ p. 12.
  Edward³ 91, pp. 70.
  Dea. Edward-Bigelow p. 68.
  Edward–Reynolds⁵ p. 66.
  Elisha-Abbott⁶ p. 68.
  Rev. Elisha⁵ p. 68.
  Elizabeth³ 29.
  Elizabeth⁴ 93.
  Elizabeth⁵ 497.
  Enos–Wilder⁷ p. 64.
  Ephraim⁴ 484.
  Ephraim⁵ 494.
  Ephraim⁶ p. 69.
  Ephraim-Hall⁷ p. 69.

Spaulding, Erastus⁶ p. 69.
  Rev. Erastus⁷ p. 68.
  Erastus-Holmes⁷ p. 69.
  Rev. Erastus-Wooster, p. 68.
  Ezekiel⁴ 495.
  Ezekiel⁵ 489.
  Frederick⁶ p. 69.
  Frederick⁶ p. 66.
  Frederick-Austin⁷ p. 69.
  George⁶ p. 72.
  Rev. George-Burley⁶ p. 66.
  George-Swift⁷ p. 72.
  Henry 60.
  Rev. Henry-George⁶ p. 66.
  Rev. Henry Whitehouse⁶ p. 68.
  Herbert-Eustis⁶ p. 65.
  Horace⁷ p. 64.
  Israel-Putnam⁶ p. 69.
  James⁷, M.D. p. 65.
  James-Franklin⁶ p. 69.
  James-Reid⁶ p. 66.
  Jason⁷ p. 65.
  Dr. Jason-Carpenter⁷ p. 66.
  John⁴ 101.
  John⁵ 485.
  John⁷ p. 65.
  John⁶ p. 65.
  Jonathan⁴ 95.
  Josiah⁵ 488, p. 68.
  Josiah⁶ pp. 67, 68.
  Josiah⁷ pp. 65, 68.
  Rev. Josiah⁷ p. 68.
  Josiah-Sawyer⁶ p. 68.
  Justus⁷ p. 64.
  Levi⁷ p. 64
  Levi⁷ p. 66.
  Luther⁵ 510.
  Dr. Luther⁶ p. 70.
  Dr. Luther⁷ p. 68.
  Luther-Paine⁶ p. 72.
  Lydia⁶ p. 70.
  Lyman-Austin⁷ p. 69.
  Maria-Elizabeth⁶ p. 70.
  Mary³ 30.
  Mary⁵ 480, 493, p. 70.
  Mary⁶ p. 65.
  Martha p. 141.
  Mehetabel⁵ 496.
  Nathan-Benton⁷ p. 64.
  Nathaniel-Goodell⁶ p. 65.
  Newall-Stevens⁷ 64.
  Olive⁴ 103.

Spaulding, Olive⁶ 476.
  Oliver⁵ 492.
  Parley⁶ p. 68.
  Dr. Parley-Joslyn⁷ p. 68.
  Peletiah⁵ 490.
  Phineas⁵ 486.
  Dr. Phineas⁷ p. 66.
  Pierce⁷ p. 66.
  Polly⁶ p. 70.
  Priscilla p. 16.
  Reuben⁵ 487.
  Dea. Reuben⁶ pp. 65, 66, 68.
  Reuben⁷ p. 68.
  Dr. Reuben⁷ p. 66.
  Robert⁷ p. 69.
  Royal⁶ p. 64.
  Dr. Rufus⁵ 509.
  Hon. Rufus⁶ pp. 71, 72.
  Rufus-Claghorn⁷ p. 72.
  Ruth⁴ 97.
  Samuel-J. p. 12.
  Sarah³ 26.
  Sarah⁴ 104.
  Sarah⁵ 481, p. 70.
  Solomon⁶ pp. 67, 68.
  Solomon⁷ p. 68.
  Stephen-Foster⁷ p. 66.
  Thomas⁴ 100.
  Dr. Volney⁷ p. 69.
  Dr. William-Cooper⁸ p. 66.
  Capt. William-Lawton⁸ p. 68.
  William-Wallace⁸ p. 69.
  William-Witter⁸ p. 69.
  Wright⁶ p. 64.
  Zephaniah-Swift⁷ p. 71.
Spencer 157.
Spafford, Peggy pp. 51, 54.
  Phebe 431.
Spofford, p. 74, ch. VIII.
  John¹ p. 89, ch. VIII.
  Lydia² p. 89, ch. VIII.
  Samuel² p. 89, ch. VIII.
Sperry, Nelly 543.
Stannard, Harriet 624.
  William p. 97.
Stark, Gen. John p. 97.
Stearns, Pres't of Amherst College p. 169.
  Rev. David p. 62.
  Edward p. 44.
  Isaac¹ pp. 11, 44, ch. VIII.
  Isaac² pp. 11, 44, ch. VIII.

Stearns, Mary pp. 11, 12, 74, ch VIII, G. R. C.
  Ruth pp. 61, 62
  Susanna p. 134.
  Rev. William-A. p. 169.
Stebbins p. 95, ch. XVI.
  Mary p. 98.
Steele p. 136.
  David p. 136.
  Isabella-Elizabeth⁹ 794.
  James-Nesmith 793.
  Ruth⁹ 795.
Stephens, Phineas pp. 83, 86.
Sterling, p. 134ᵃ, ch. X.
Stevens, Bill-Wright 135.
  John⁴ 217.
  Peter⁴ 216, 218.
  Capt. Phineas pp. 83, 87
  Simon⁴ 219.
  Hon. Thaddeus p. 72.
Stewart & Co. p. 183.
Stillman, Albert Lyman 1059.
Stillson, J-B. p. 132.
Stoddard, pp. 95, 96, ch. XVI, XVII.
Sylvester-Sage 631, pp. 56, 99, 100.
  Ezra p. 98.
Stone, Abel⁵ 250.
  Abel⁶ 252.
  Abigail⁵ 294.
  Abraham⁶ 222.
  Anna⁶ 227.
  Asa⁵ 255.
  Asa⁶ 256.
  Benjamin p. 26.
  Betsey⁶ 324.
  Betty⁵ 250.
  David⁵ 229.
  Elizabeth⁵ 228.
  Emma⁶ 258.
  Esther⁶ 254.
  Eunice⁵ 276, 284.
  George-B. 1273, G. R. C.
  Hannah⁵ 308.
  Hannah⁶ 241.
  Horace-Bradshaw p. 98.
  Isaac⁵ 246.
  Israel⁵ 224.
  James 271, p. 26.
  James⁵ 272.
  James⁶ 273, 325.
  Joel⁵ 304.
  Joel⁶ 305.

Stone, John 220, pp. 29, 32.
  John⁵ 221.
  John⁶ 223.
  Jonathan⁵ 281.
  Jonathan⁶ 274, 283.
  Joseph⁶ 247, p. 30.
  Lemuel⁶ 275.
  Levi⁵ 318.
  Levi⁹ 323.
  Lucy⁶ 253, 322.
  Lydia⁶ 230, 320.
  Mary⁵ 277.
  Mindwell⁵ 233.
  Molly⁶ 245, 288.
  Moses⁵ 287.
  Nathaniel⁵ 238.
  Nathaniel⁶ 225, 239.
  Olive⁵ 242.
  Oliver⁵ 292.
  Rachel⁵ 264.
  Rhoda⁵ 243.
  Sally⁶ 289, 319.
  Salmon⁵ 306.
  Samuel⁵ 328.
  Sarah⁵ 248, 303.
  Solomon⁵ 286.
  Sukey⁶ 262.
  Susannah⁵ 282.
  Sybil 238.
  Sybil⁶ 240.
  Thomas⁶ 249.
  William⁵ 260.
Storrs, Rev. Richard-Salter p. 43.
Stow p. 65.
  Joseph 112.
  Nathaniel p. 24.
  Ruth 116.
Stowe, Mrs. Harriet (Beecher) p. 99.
Stowell, Hannah 494.
Strafford, Earl of, p. 47.
Stratton, Mary p. 22, ch. V.
  Samuel ch. V.
Strong, Rev. Joseph p. 70
Stuart, George-H. pp. 123 124, 125, 127.
Sturgis, Solomon p. 134.
Sumner, Hon. Charles p. 155.
  Samuel p. 55.
Sutherland, Col. Charles p. 179.
Sutton Place p. 157.
Swarthout, Ada-Elizabeth⁹ 1238ᵃ.

Swarthout, James-Byron 1228.
James-W. p. 176.
Sweetland, Nancy p. 158.
Swift, Lucinda-A. p. 71.
  Judge Zephaniah pp. 67, 71.
Sylvester, Quincy p. 140.
  Sarah-Elizabeth 861.
Symbols of degree, p. 79.
System (American) p. 78.
Table of charts p. 186.
Taney, Roger-B. p. 127.
Tarbell, Lydia 457.
  Samuel pp. 26, 60.
  Thomas p. 59.
Taylor, pp. 39, 134ª, ch. X.
  Abigail 877, p. 41.
  Abigail-Gates 763.
  Adelaide 1242.
  Joel p. 180.
  John p. 117.
  Rhoda p. 133.
  Sarah 457.
Thatcher, Peter p. 63.
Thomas, Adj't Gen. p. 154.
  Hannah-Jane 805.
  Gen. p. 181.
Thompson, Charles (Sec'y) p. 42.
  Ezra 368.
  Jonathan ch. XI.
  Lydia-Maria 948.
  Silas 370.
Thrasher, Emeline p. 179.
Thurls, Polly p. 137.
Thurston, Daniel¹ pp. 74, 89, ch. VIII.
  Daniel² pp. 74, 89.
  John p. 84.
  John¹ p. 89.
  John⁴ p. 89, ch. VIII.
  Jonathan³ p. 89, cn. VIII.
  Priscilla⁴ 333, pp. 74, 88, 89, ch. VIII.
Titcomb ch. XI.
Toby, E-S. p. 127.
Todd 441.
  Anna p. 150.
  Rebecca-Baker 1048.
Toland, Alvah-Calvin³ 1095.
  Charles-William⁵ 1094.
  James 1092.
  James-Allen³ 1100.
  John-Fremont 1093.
  Martha-Elizabeth⁶ 1098.

Toland, Mary-Jane 1097.
  Solomon-Henry⁸ 1099.
  William p. 161.
Topliff, Calvin p. 50.
  Hannah 421.
Torrey, Prof. John pp. 165, 168.
Tothill, Mary-Jane 944.
Tower, Lines p. 158.
  Rebecca-Baker p. 158.
Towne, Dorcas p. 68.
  Gardner 378₆.
  Hannah 378₈.
  Israel p. 48.
Tratman, James-E. p. 127.
Trowbridge p. 134ª ch. X.
  Dea. James² pp. 112, 113, ch. IX.
  John³ p. 113, ch. IX.
  Jonathan⁴ pp. 112, 113, ch. IX.
  Thomas¹ pp. 112, 113, ch. IX.
  Thomas² p. 112.
  William³ p. 112.
Tryon, Governor p. 64.
Turner, George 558, p. 74.
Tuttle-Albert-Austin⁸ 726.
  Jedediah 720.
  Louisa-Osborne⁸ 721.
Tyng, Eleazer p. 10.
  Rev. Dr. Stephen-H, Jr. p. 151.
  William p. 9.
Underwood, Elizabeth p. 42.
  Remembrance pp. 14, 16.
  William p. 16.
Upham, Elizabeth p. 171.
Upton, Frances-Ellen 925.
  Warren-C. p. 142.
Vallandingham p. 129.
Vance, Sophia p. 176.
Varney, Mary-Ann 1277, G. R. C.
  Shadrach p. 184.
Vincent p. 96, ch. XVII.
Voorhees p. 129.
Vore p. 95, ch. XVI.
Vosburg, Barnet p. 175.
  Bernatta 1218.
Wade, Benjamin p. 72.
Waddell, Charles p. 159.
  Sophia-Maria 1065.
Wadsworth, p. 134ª, ch. X.
  E-S· pp. 117, 119, 184.

Wadsworth, Tertius p. 119.
Walis p. 125.
Walker, Clarissa p. 147.
  Joseph-Gilmer p. 153.
  Lucy-Ellen 1025.
Wallace, Sally p. 140.
Ward, p. 134ª, ch. X.
  John p. 110, ch. IX.
Warner, Abigail³ p. 133.
  Almon p. 100.
  Dan p. 171.
  David-Dudley p. 172.
  Harriet 634, p. 174.
  John¹ p. 133.
  Gen. Jonathan pp. 99, 174.
  Mark² p. 133.
  Mary-Susanne 1170.
  Priscilla p. 20, G. R. C.
Warren, Dr. J-H. p. 172.
  Gen. p. 123
  Gen. Joseph p. 42.
  Levi p. 43.
  Micah p. 92.
Washington, Gen. George pp. 35, 42.
  Martha p. 48.
Weaver, Rev. J. p. 181.
Webb p. 96, ch. XVII.
Webber, Rev. George-N. p. 177.
Weld p. 17.
Welsh, William p. 127.
Wendall, Elizabeth p. 63.
Wentworth, Edward p. 47.
  Elizabeth⁶ 234.
  Eunice⁶ 235.
  Gov. p. 83.
  Hannah-Matilda² p. 47.
  Maud p. 47.
  Moses 233.
  Oliver⁶ 237.
  Phebe⁶ 236.
  Thomas-Handford p. 47.
Wesson, Abigail 111.
Wetherbee, Dorcas 577.
  Lucinda p. 107.
  Paul p. 91.
Wheat, Sarah p. 54.
Wheeler, Artemas p. 183.
  Daniel-Augustus 1262, G. R C.
  Deborah 473.
  Edwin-Whitmore⁶ 1263.
  Edward-Lawrence⁶ 835.
  Emelina-Sophia⁸ 829.

Wheeler, Ephraim 29.
  Etta-Davis⁹(or Susie-Etta) 837.
  Hattie-Elizabeth⁹ 838.
  George p. 8, 7.
  Joseph p. 138.
  Joshua p. 35.
  Lucy p. 47.
  Mary-Ann⁸ 831.
  Oliver 128.
  Micah-Lawrence 828, p. 90
  Rufus–Warren⁸ 834.
  Sarah 7, G. R. C.
  Thomas p. 3.
  Timothy pp. 7, 44.
Whitcomb, p. 95, ch. XVI.
White pp. 96, 117.
  David p. 100.
  Elizabeth p. 180.
  John 544, 838, p. 61.
  Margaret-Elizabeth⁸ 1231.
  Mary p. 174.
  Peregrine p. 57.
  Peter p. 100.
  Rev. Pliny-Holton⁷ 1230, p. 56
  William-Holton⁸, 1235.
Whitehorn, John p. 158.
Whitehouse, Rev. H-B., D.D · p. 68.
Whiting p. 13.
  Maranda p. 183.
Whitman, Nathaniel p. 48.
Whitmore, Abigail⁸ ch. XI.
  Abigail⁴ ch. XI.
  Adelaide-Frances⁸ 1281.
  Adin-Hamlin⁸ 1267.
  Agnes-Seloma⁸ 1269.
  Albert⁷ 651, ch. VI, XI, G. R. C.
  Amos⁹ ch. XI.
  David p. 101.
  David⁴ ch. XI.
  David⁵ ch. XI.
  Dorothy⁴ ch. XI.
  Ebenezer⁴ 61, XI.
  Ebenezer⁵ ch. XI.
  Edwin-Henry⁸ 1280.
  Edwin-Parker⁷ 1258, p. 103, chs. VI, XI, G.R.C.
  Elizabeth³ ch. XI.
  Elizabeth⁴ ch. "
  Elizabeth⁵ ch. "
  Ella–Gertrude⁸ 1279.
  Ellen-Louisa⁸ 1272.
  Francis¹ p. 101, ch. XI.

Whitmore, Francis² ch. XI.
  George, Sr. p. 109.
  George–Horace⁹ 1278.
  Giddings, 648, chs. VI, XI, G. R. C.
  Hamlin⁷ 1264, chs. VI, XI, G. R. C.
  Hannah⁴ ch. XI.
  Hannah⁵ ch. Xs.
  Hayes-Giddings⁸, 1274.
  Henry-Sylvester⁷ 1277, chs. VI, XI, G. R. C.
  Horace-Metcalf⁸ 665, p. 182, chs. VI, XI, G.R.C.
  Jacob⁵ ch. XI.
  Jervis-John⁸ 1270.
  John³ ch. XI.
  Jonathan⁴ ch. XI.
  Joseph³ p. 101, ch. XI.
  Joseph⁴ p. 101, ch. XI.
  Joseph⁴ ch. XI.
  Joseph-Flagg⁷ 1271, chs. VI, XI, G. R. C.
  Lucia-Estelle⁸ 1273.
  Lydia⁵ ch. XI.
  Margaret² ch. XI.
  Marian-Parker⁸ 1262, G. R. C.
  Martha⁷ 653, chs. VI, XI, G. R. C.
  Mary⁴ ch. XI.
  Mary⁵ ch. XI.
  Mary-Josephine⁸ 1275.
  Nathan⁴ ch. XI.
  Noel-Mott⁸ 1268.
  Phebe⁴ ch. "
  Ruth⁴ ch. "
  Samuel³ ch. "
  Sarah³ ch. "
  Sarah⁵ ch. "
  Susan-Elizabeth⁸ 1259.
  Thomas³ ch. XI.
  William-H. pp. 77, 78, 102.
Whitney p. 157.
  Professor p. 43.
  Ann⁴ p. 44.
  Petty p. 159.
  Daisy-Christabel¹⁰ 671.
  Edith-Louisa¹⁰ 669.
  Elizabeth p. 40.
  Franklin-Miller 668.
  Herbert-Prescott¹⁰ 666.
  James p. 41.
  John p. 59.
  John⁶ p. 44.
  Jonas-Prescott p. 104.

Whitney, Jonathan² p. 44.
  Jonathan³ p. 44.
  Joseph-M. p. 104.
  Julius 665.
  Lucy 872.
  Mary p. 14.
  Ray-Elliot¹⁰ 670.
  Sybil 213.
  Timothy p. 29.
Whittaker p. 49.
  Lydia 250.
Whittemore pp. 44, 46.
  Charles 380.
  Charles-Irving¹⁰ 380.
  Dexter p. 46.
  Josiah p. 46.
  William-John¹⁰ 380.
Wilbur, Elizabeth 6, p. 5, G. R. C.
Wilcox ch. XI.
  Carrie–Emma⁹ 1261.
  Maie-Lizzie 1260.
  William-Augustus 1259, p. 183, G. R. C.
Wilder, Elisha p. 93.
  Shepherd-Clark 600.
Wiley, Sally p. 138.
Wilkins, Daniel p. 63.
  Samuel 469.
Will of Miriam⁷ (Holton) Brown, p. 156.
Willard, Alvin-Eugene 1226.
  Fabens p. 176.
  Josiah pp. 55, 61, 62.
  Samuel p. 26.
  Simon p. 3.
Williams College p. 134ª, ch. 10.
  Chaplain p. 122.
  Col. Ephraim p. 110.
  Mary-Ann p. 133, 134.
  Jacob p. 59.
  James p. 55.
  John p. 59.
  Robert¹ p. 134.
  William p. 59.
Williston, p. 95, ch. 16.
  Rev. David-Howe⁸ 378ᵇ
  Hannah⁶ p. 48.
  Noah⁴ p. 42.
  Payson⁸ p. 43.
  Hon. Samuel p. 43.
  Sarah⁵ p. 43.
Wilson, p. 134ª ch. 10.
  Joanna pp. 32, 33.

Wilson, Joseph pp. 59, 88.
Mary p. 161.
Samuel 548, G. R. C.
Sarah³ p. 113, ch. IX.
Wing, p. 96, ch. XVII.
Winslow, p. 58, 95, 96, chs. XVI, XVII.
Maj. Gen. p. 23.
Capt. Edward² p. 110.
Edward³ p. 110.
Hanna p. 162.
John¹ p. 110.
Dr. Joseph p. 173.
Joshua⁴ p. 110.
Joshua⁵ p. 110.
Kenelm¹ p. 93.
Kenelm² p. 93.
Kenelm³ p. 93.
Miriam⁴ p. 93.
Rebecca (Fish) p. 173.
Rev. Seth p. 106.
Susannah⁵ p. 47.
Thomas⁴ p. 93.
Thomas⁴ p. 93.
Winthrop p. 113.
Gov. p. 21.
John p. 21, 44.
Witter, Mary 492.
Wood, Asa p. 173.
Darwin 1189.
Martha-Ann (Doney) p. 155.
Michael p. 4.
Nathaniel p. 92.

Wood, Susanna p. 173.
Woods, p. 129.
Abigail⁴ 41.
Abigail⁵ 128.
Abigail⁶ 134.
Alice⁴ 40.
Elizabeth⁵ 125.
Esther⁴ 42.
Eunice⁵ 129.
Hannah⁵ 127.
Isaac p. 26.
James⁵ 130.
James⁶ 131.
Jerusha 221.
John p. 26.
Jonathan p. 29.
Joseph⁴ 43.
Jotham⁶ 133.
Levi 214.
Martha⁴ 44.
Mary⁵ 137.
Nahum 132.
Rachel⁵ 39.
Rachel⁵ 135.
Samuel 36, G. R. C.
Samuel⁴ 124.
Samuel⁵ 126.
Susanna⁴ 38.
William⁵ 136.
Woodbridge, Martha 174.
Rev. John p. 174.
Woodbury, Oscar-Ferdinand 959.

Woodward, Alfred-Gilson 1199.
Alfred-Gilson³ 1194.
Carrie-Frances⁹ 1192.
David p. 22.
Eunice 95.
Franklin p. 106.
Leonard p. 173.
Lizzie-Maria³ 1193.
Louisa-Maria 700.
Wooster, Laura-Maria p. 68.
Worcester, Hannah p. 61.
Worden, Rev. Horace 1175.
Worder, p. 96, ch. XVII.
Worthen, Dorothy p. 173.
Worthington, p. 95, ch. XVI.
Mary p. 98.
Wright, Abigail 473.
Betsey p. 46.
Ebenezer p. 63.
Maria p. 17.
Mary-Ann 618.
Salmon p. 97.
Wyer, James-Ingersol p. 145.
Sara-Gardner 933.
Young, Catharine-Amelia p. 160.
Yeager, Daniel p. 130.
Mary-Elinor 1256.

The abbreviations used in this INDEX are explained on page 187.

A SUPPLEMENTAL INDEX

INCLUDING

———o TOPICS AND PLACES o———

May be found on page 241 at the conclusion of the REMINISCENCES hereto subjoined.

ABBREVIATIONS.

abbrev.	abbreviated	Hist.	History.
abt.	about.	hist.	historian.
acc.	according to.	hon.	honorable.
adm.	admitted, administered or administration.	inf.	infant, infancy, informed or information.
æ.	aged.	inhab.	inhabitant or inhabited.
aft.	afterward.	ins.	insert or inserted.
alleg.	allegiance.	inst.	institute or instituted.
art.	artillery.	intest.	intestate.
b.	born or was born.	inv.	inventory.
bap.	baptized, was baptized or baptism.	jud.	judicial.
bef.	before.	k.	killed.
bet.	between.	kn.	known.
br.	brother.	ld.	land.
bur.	buried, was buried or burial.	lieut.	lieutenant or lieutenancy.
capt.	captain or captaincy.	liv.	lived or living.
ch.	child, children, church or chart.	m.	married, was married, month or months.
chap.	chapter.		
co.	county or company.	maj.	major.
col.	colonel, colony or colonial.	ment.	mentioned.
col^d.	colored.	mil.	military or militia.
coll.	college or collections.	min.	minister or ministerial.
comb.	combined.	N. E.	New England.
comp.	compared.	N. S.	New Style.
cons.	constitute or constituted.	nam.	named.
cont.	continued or continuation.	No.	number.
corp.	corporal.	num.	numerous.
couns.	counsellor.	O. S.	Old Style.
cov.	covenant.	ord.	ordained.
ct.	court.	orig.	original.
d.	day, days, died or daughter.	p.	page.
Dart.	Dartmouth.	pp.	pages.
daus.	daughters.	petit.	petitioners or petitioned.
dea.	deacon.	prob.	probate or probably.
deg.	degree.	prop.	proprietor or proprietors.
div.	divided or division.	prov.	proved.
drd.	drowned or was drowned.	pub.	publish, publishment, published or was published.
educ.	educated.		
emp.	employed.	rad.	radial.
Eng.	England.	rec.	record, records, recorded or received.
eng.	engaged or engineer.		
enl.	enlisted.	rem.	remained or removed.
ens.	ensign.	rep.	representative or represented.
esq.	esquire.	res.	resided.
est.	estate.	ret.	returned.
exc.	except.	s.	son.
f.	father.	s.p.	no descendants.
fam.	family.	serg.	sergeant.
fidel.	fidelity.	sett.	settlers or settled.
fol.	folio, following or followed.	sev.	several.
freem.	freeman or freemen.	trans.	transferred.
Gen.	Genealogy.	unm.	unmarried.
gen.	genealogical.	vol.	volume or volunteer.
gr.	grant, granted or great.	w.	wife.
gr. f.	grandfather.	wid.	widow.
gr. mo.	grandmother.	wks.	weeks.
gr. s.	grandson.	yr.	year or years.
grad.	graduate, graduated or was graduated.	+	indicates descendants when names are unknown or unmentioned.
H. C.	Harvard College.		

GENEALOGICAL QUERY.

In the *Gentleman's Magazine*, 1766, among the deaths of aged people that year, is the following:

"August 2nd, COL. THOMAS WINSLOW, at Tipperary, in Ireland, aged 146 years. He was a captain in the reign of King Charles I, and went over to Ireland with Oliver Cromwell in the rank of Lieutenant-colonel."

Rev. Dr. Octavius[4] Winslow, of Brighton, England, Jan. 5, 1878, writes that the foregoing is a "well authenticated fact."

We wish to ascertain, if possible, what relationship existed between Gov. Edward[1] Winslow and Col. Thomas Winslow; and whether the Winslows in Roscommon, Sligo, Fermanagh, and Herbertstown, are descendants of the said Col. Thomas.

—— WINSLOW, of Herbertstown, County West Meath, Ireland, in 1770.

```
                                        |
        ┌───────────────────────────────┼───────────────────────────────┐
        1                                                               2
   Ellis, = Charles, b. 1725, prob Carick, in Co Meath, near         Daniel, born 1728, Herbertstown; died 1825; mar.
   daughter   Castlepollard; d. 1815;                                1775, in Carrick, Co. Meath, Dorothea Tyghe.
   of Capt.   He m. 3d, ——Nesbitt, of Loughhill, Co. Donegal,
   Ellis.     who died s.p. He took a lease forever of the
              land of Tullyhrin, on part of Lisruddy,
              now Mount Prospect, from Mr. Tyghe, and settled
              there, in County Fermanagh.
```

Daniel, d. Jan. 1887; m. Eliza-Catherine Nesbitt, of Woodhill, niece of his father's third wife, and settled in Co. Fermanagh. He had one son who died at sea, and four daughters, all of whom were married, and among whom the property was divided.

Blaney, d. 5 June 1827, Mt. Prospect; m. Elizabeth Winslow, his cousin, and had a large family, all of whom died young, except those here given. She d. in 1847. He was an officer in the Fermanagh Militia Res. Mt. Prospect.

Samuel, d. ab. 1820, at Cootehill; m. —— Davison, of C. s.p.

Daniel-Tyghe, d. 18—55; was an officer in the Fermanagh Militia and afterward Sub-Inspector of Police.

Mary Madden, of Wexford.

George, m. Mary-Anne Winslow, his cousin of Cloughin, and settled in Little Dristernan.

Allota, m. Greeson.

John, settled in Herbertstown, Co. West Meath, Ireland.

Blaney, P.O. add. Mt. Prospect, Derrylin, —— County Fermanagh, Ireland.

Leslie, of Holybrook, near Lisnaskea, County Fermanagh.

Dr. Wm-Wade, m. —— Justin, of Co. Cork. He is a practising physician in Co. Cavan.

Daughter m. Dr. Cottingham, of Cootehill, County Cavan.

Henry, was also in Canada, 1872.

George, emigrated to Canada.

George Leslie, in 1879 was unmarried in Australia.

Mary-Eliza, m. —— Karr, and emigrated to Hamilton, Canada.

Frances-Jane, m. —— Evans, and emigrated to Ottawa, Canada.

George-Nesbitt.

Dorothea, m. 1st, —— Adams; m. 2d, —— Berry.

Elizabeth, m. her cousin Blaney Winslow.

Maria, m. 1st, —— Quigly; m. 2d, —— Finlay.

Anne, d. unmarried.

Blaney-Thomas, m. —— Rutherford, of Dublin. He is Captain in Fermanagh militia.

Daniel-Tyghe, m. —— +

George-Blaney, was unmarried in 1872.

Edmond-Skelton, m. —— Fitzpatrick, of Belturbet.

Louisa-Dorothea, died unmarried.

Anne-Maria, married Maguire, of Aughcashel, County Leitrim.

Ellen-Caroline.

William-Frederick, m. —— Poe. He is a Police Officer.

Henry-Madden, m. his cousin —— Latimer.

Julia, d. unmarried.

Maria, died unmarried.

Georgina, died young.

Elizabeth-Catherine.

NEW YORK, Feb. 20, 1878.

DAVID P. HOLTON, M.D., *Secretary of the Pilgrim Record Society,* Eastern Boulevard, cor. 59th St., N.Y.

BIRTHS.

FULL NAME.	YEAR.	MONTH.	DAY.	REMARKS.

DEATHS.

FULL NAME.	YEAR.	MONTH.	DAY.	REMARKS.

REMINISCENCES.

By DAVID-PARSONS' HOLTON, M.D.

Read before the New York Genealogical and Biographical Society, 27 May, 1874. The regular sessions of this society are held the second and fourth Fridays of each month at 64 Madison avenue in the MOTT MEMORIAL Hall.

ABOUT 8 o'clock Saturday morning, May 10, 1834, I called at the American Bible House, 115 Nassau street, New York, to see Rev. John C. Brigham, the Corresponding Secretary of the American Bible Society, whose nephew had been for the two years preceding a pupil of mine in the Academy at Southwick, Hampden Co., Mass. The man in charge informed me that I was some two hours in advance of the time to find the reverend Secretary.

This led me to feel for my watch, which I soon remembered to have left under the pillow, at Holt's Hotel, where I had taken lodgings on my arrival by the Connecticut River steamboat, the night previous. Hastening to my sleeping-room, I found that the bed was made and that the watch had disappeared. The erection of this house (now, 1874, known as the United States Hotel), on Fulton, Pearl and Water streets, had, throughout the Union, been counted the great event of 1832–3.

The Astor House was commenced a few weeks after my arrival. Well do I remember how my previous notions of economy were all at sea, in view of the demolition of large brick stores on the west-side of Broadway from Vesey to Barclay street. However, learning that John Jacob Astor was then and there about to erect a house to eclipse Holt's Hotel, as a gift to his son, William B., my financial views were somewhat modified.*

Returning from my failure to find the watch, the Rev. John C. Brigham graciously showed to the Preceptor of his nephew, the extensive printing and binding establishments of the Bible Society, which subsequently in their new location on Fourth avenue and Eighth street were much enlarged.

For many years, and until his death, I occasionally counseled with this reverend gentleman, as with a father.

The second call made was at the temperance rooms in the Mercantile Library building, known as Clinton Hall, corner of Nassau and Beekman streets. There I found Mr. R. M. Hartley, the efficient Secretary in the temperance cause, with whom I formed a friendship which has continued vigorous and edifying these forty years.

This building was during many years the principal center of numerous

---

* Reference is here made to my visit in New York the previous year, at the time of the commencement of *preparations* for the building.

literary and benevolent associations and was the place for scientific and popular lectures; for Mr. Hale, proprietor of the *Journal of Commerce*, Mr. William Green and their associates, had not then erected, near Leonard street, the celebrated Broadway Tabernacle.

In Clinton Hall were commenced the instructions of the University of the City of New York, Rev. Dr. J. M. Mathews being Chancellor. At a later date, the building of the Mechanics' Institute on Chambers street between Centre and Chatham streets, was occupied for these instructions till the University on Washington square was completed.

To this University my attention had been somewhat turned as my future Alma Mater; and at my first visit to Clinton Hall, some conversation was had with Mr. Hartley about my purpose to complete my collegiate course in that Institution.

Subsequently I called upon Rev. Dr. Mathews at his residence in Liberty street. The Chancellor welcomed the new comer, as a Green Mountain candidate for University honors, and with words of encouragement spoke of the various ways by which a young man of sound principles and correct habits, with industry and perseverance, could pursue collegiate studies and financially sustain himself in the great metropolis.

At that time, the locations most sought for private homes, were in the neighborhood of the Battery, on Broadway to Eighth street and westward to include St. John's Park, on East Broadway and southward to Monroe street extending eastward to the Rutger's mansion, on Bond street, St. Mark's place, Leroy place, La Fayette place and Washington square, of which last only about one-fourth was bordered by dwelling houses.

It was subsequent to this, if my memory serves me right, that the first two houses on Fifth avenue were built by the Misses Green for their School for Young Ladies—No. 1 being the present residence of the Comptroller, Andrew H. Green.

At the interview of which I was speaking, Chancellor Mathews spoke of the fact, that many wealthy citizens of New York had given, each, fifteen hundred dollars towards founding the University, they, severally, becoming thereby perpetually entitled to place and keep one student in the occupancy of a scholarship, *i. e.* in the regular University course, without the additional payment of tuition fees. These facts and conditions I reported to Rev. Mr. Brigham, who subsequently saw Rev. Elihu W. Baldwin, pastor of the Seventh Presbyterian Church, Broome street, corner of Ridge, who had, through the gift of one of his parishioners, the disposal of one scholarship, and he assured Mr. Brigham that it should be at the service of the Vermonter.

After my interview with Mr. Hartley as aforesaid, I met Rev. Jeremiah Bridges, Elder of the Baptist Church in Southwick, the place which I had left the Thursday previous, the 8th of May, 1834. He introduced me to Rev. Jonathan Going, D. D., Editor of the principal Baptist paper in America, whose office was also in Clinton Hall. To him I told the story of my lost watch, and solicited that he would favor me by becoming my banker—for at this time I possessed just thirty-six dollars, and whatever goods and chattels were contained in my trunk and valise, the same being only ordinary wearing apparel.

My available assets, the said thirty-six dollars, I divided into two portions, handing to my banker twenty-four, and retaining in my wallet twelve; promising myself and Rev. Dr. Going, that I would find some remunerative employment, before I should have exhausted the latter portion. After this I met, in Broadway, Mr. Charles Jessup, of Mass., who had married a sister of one of my Southwick pupils. He invited me to accompany him the next day to the Sunday-school exercises at the House of Refuge, he having previously taken into his employ, at Westfield, one of the inmates of that Institution. The next day, my first Sunday in New York city, at the appointed hour, Mr. Jessup introduced me to Mr. N. C. Hart, Superintendent of the House of Refuge, then located *far out of town*, some distance north of Mr. Hogg's garden, on the Bloomingdale road.

In a geographical review, it is difficult to believe that remote place to be identical with our present *Madison Square*.

Mr. Hart loved his work, and devoted himself to the boys and girls entrusted to his charge. He loved to see the working of means to an end, and labored in faith with the hardest cases. After this introductory visit, I was kindly permitted to call during the school hours of any day; and of this privilege I subsequently availed myself for many years. His interest in any youth once under his charge, continued, like that of a parent, when the child had left for a new home. His book of letters showed, in those who had left the institution, a filial affection toward him, which to me seemed wonderful, nor have I seen the like in any other instance.

The character of Mr. Hart has ever since those years appeared to me a living force, elevating my purposes as a teacher.

On Monday, the third day of my New York residence, true to my purpose to find employment before spending the twelve dollars, I resolved to offer myself as a teacher in some department of any school in the city. With this in view I bought a small guide-book entitled, "NEW YORK AS IT IS IN 1833," containing a map of the city, and a list of all its public and private schools.

With this book and map, and a pocket full of testimonials from places where I had kept school, in Westminster and Bellows Falls, Vt., Cornish and Limerick in York county, Me., Effingham, Carroll county, N. H., and for the last two years at Southwick, Mass., I commenced at the Battery, and thence in geographical order presented my application at every private school. Many teachers assured me that they knew of no opening; others encouragingly said, it being May, they could make no changes in my favor before the fall term.

In parting, I assured each one that some opening for me would, surely, soon be found.

During that week I visited all the schools in the city, known through the printed page and through all channels of personal inquiry open to me. No vacancy was found. Then I spent Monday of the second week in Pearl street, in applications as a clerk or salesman. All responses were negatives. The most hopeful answers for the future were from Arthur Tappan and from Messrs. Bailey, Keeler & Remson.

Next, I passed a day among the law offices; but found no olive-leaves. The very numerous acquaintances formed during these two days among merchants and lawyers, proved a source of happiness and benefit in after years. The Wednesday of the second week I resolved to *revisit* every school which I had previously found—sure that I should gain an opening.

Near the close of the first day of this repetition of my applications, I found that in the Lafayette Institute on Broadway, corner of Ninth street, near the limit of the city built in that direction (a section which then had recently been occupied as the Sailors' Snug Harbor), the sickness of one of the teachers had providentially opened for me a situation, yielding me, besides a good home, $80 up to the approaching vacation.

Having settled my board bill at 68 Dey street, I had remaining from the $12, seventy-five cents, exactly the sum necessary to pay a coachman for taking me and my baggage to my newly-found home, the Lafayette Institute, Thursday, 22d May, at the same hour of the day on which, fourteen days before, I had left Southwick, Mass.

At that time the region northwestward from the corner of Broadway and Ninth street was unbuilt upon, and Eighth street was the northern terminus of the omnibus route—Brower's line having precedence over any others in the city.

At the close of the summer vacation, I entered as a student in the University, then located, as already said, in Chambers street, near Chatham, occupying the scholarship placed temporarily to my credit by the Rev. Elihu W. Baldwin, who soon left New York as President of Wabash College, Indiana. He was succeeded in the pastorate of the Seventh Presbyterian Church by Rev. Edwin F. Hatfield, then recently from his field of eminent success in St. Louis, Mo.

During my first week in New York, in the course of my applications, I met, in Mr. Sherwood's school in Albion place, which was a part of Fourth street, eastward from the Bowery, Mr. J. J. Greenough, recently a student in Andover Theological Seminary, with whom I formed an acquaintance which ripened into strongest friendship.

Having completed my engagement at the Lafayette Institute, I matriculated as student in the University, and subsequently shared with Mr. Greenough a lodging-room in the Fifth Ward, at 42 Hudson street, where he had, at the special solicitation of A. R. Wetmore, A. P. Halsey, B.

Strong, and a few other associate patrons, opened a private school for boys.

Here I pursued my University studies, and by uniting with several benevolent and reformatory associations already at work, learned of the personal labors and liberal contributions of citizens of New York for various objects of charity. I was profoundly impressed with the personal sacrifices and devotion of Mr. A. R. Wetmore in meeting the physical and moral needs of the city, and particularly in the Fifth Ward—for then my estimate of the gifts of people in their lifetime was upon a small scale compared with what the munificence of later years has established. Girard in his will had provided millions for the endowment of an asylum; but no Peter Cooper had then taught the beauty of one's personal administration on hundreds of thousands of dollars of his own estate for the general good of humanity.

With Mr. Greenough, I had the pleasure to unite with the Committee for tract distribution and visitations of charity, under Mr. Wetmore, in the Fifth Ward. Mr. Wetmore still lives, and I have yet to learn that he wearies in well doing. Mr. Greenough for many years, and till his death, continued his excellent school for boys.

After a few months in my University course, having in the meantime nearly exhausted the $24 left with my banker, the Rev. Dr. Going, and the $80 which I received as teacher of mathematics in the Lafayette Institute, I read in the New York *Observer*, some five days after publication, that a private tutor was wanted in a family residing in the vicinity of the city, applicants being referred to Anthony P. Halsey, Esq., cashier of the Bank of New York.

I called upon Mr. Halsey at his residence, 16 Jay street. He said I was the forty-ninth applicant, and that among the number were graduates from colleges and some graduates of Theological Seminaries, and although he read from my pile of New England testimonials, he gave me no encouragement. I reported matters to Mr. Brigham, who hastened to the Bank in Wall street, corner of William, and spoke good words for the preceptor of his nephew, immediately turning the scale in my favor.

The teacher sought was for the family of P. Van Brugh Livingston, at Dobbs Ferry, on the east bank of the Hudson, north of Yonkers, with whom I remained one year, receiving as salary $500.

During this time I occasionally visited the University, as I was endeavoring to pursue alone the regular studies of my class. After the close of this engagement I returned to the city, and, with much hesitation, reluctantly resigned my scholarship in the University, and as student of medicine entered the office of Dr. Ansel W. Ives, 367 Broadway, opposite the residence of Dr. John Kearny Rodgers, the students of the two offices being united for recitation, interchangeably, before each of the two doctors. With what remained of my $500, received from Mr. Livingston, I entered upon a course of medical lectures in the College of Physicians and Surgeons, Nos. 1 and 3 Barclay street.

On the death of my preceptor, Dr. Ives, I entered the office of Dr. Alfred C. Post, No. 4 Leroy place, the College having been removed from Barclay to 67 Crosby street, where, on the 9th of March, 1839, I was graduated as Doctor of Medicine.

Previous to my study of medicine in the office of Dr. Ansel W. Ives, I had read medical books and had attended some lectures on medical subjects, chiefly with a view to understanding the effects of alcoholic drinks on the human system. The scientific study of these effects was not necessary to convince me of the inexpediency of using intoxicating beverages, as my convictions were strong, resting upon my observations from early youth. Before I could intelligently read, my mother impressed me with the truth that strong drink is raging, and that he who is deceived thereby is not wise. Her words were confirmed by what I could almost daily see; and from that seeing and hearing I knew, as well as I could know anything, that total abstinence from all intoxicating drinks was the only safe and wise course.

Having this conviction, on my tenth anniversary birthday, the 18th June, 1822, I invited some boys to accompany me to the top of a hill on my father's farm in Westminster, Vt., where we pledged to each other never more to use the destroying drinks. I did not then know of any temperance society, and I have not yet learned that any *total abstinence* society had been formed previous to this date, 18th June, 1822.

The first two days of my being a medical student in the office of Dr. Ives were wholly devoted to the writing of twelve letters to as many friends in different places in New England, announcing my determination, and bespeaking, *in advance*, their charitable interpretation of my probable future course, when, having obtained my diploma as doctor of medicine, and having some knowledge of practice, my energies, my experience, and my acquirements should all be turned to the practical solution of problems for the prevention of the evils of intemperance.

In these twelve letters I also bespoke a charitable construction upon my future probable course in abandoning the medical practice, trusting that by the appropriate use of manikins, skeletons, and prepared specimens of human and comparative anatomy, I should be enabled to be a better teacher, thus being furnished with apparatus and natural means for *object teaching*, in which I had been indoctrinated by reading the publications of Josiah Holbrook, of Boston, about the time of my first essay at school-teaching, when fifteen years of age (1827), in my native town, where I had the honor to introduce the blackboard—doubtless the first in any district school in the State of Vermont.

Subsequently I read the scientific tracts and other publications upon the same subject, by Dr. J. V. C. Smith, afterward Mayor of Boston, and now,

1874, Professor of Anatomy in the New York Free Medical College for Women, 51 St. Mark's place, New York city; in which college I have the honor to occupy the chair of Comparative Physiology, a chair closely allied to that of my former Boston friend.

In 1833, by special permission of the Trustees of the Southwick Academy, I prolonged a vacation in order to pass a few weeks in Boston in witnessing the practical object-teaching system, as developed by Mr. Holbrook, aided by Drs. Alcott and Smith; and in attending the sessions of the American Institute of Instruction, in which W. C. Woodbridge, S. R. Hall and others, whose names are cherished as promoters of progressive steps in improved methods of teaching and discipline, were then active members.

I came to New York fully persuaded that, as means in educational developments, a *little* of ACTUALITY was better than *much* of ARTIFICIALITY.

These twelve letters were also apologetic in view of my anticipated turning aside from the practice of the medical profession in order to combat a false prejudice against the colored race, grounded upon peculiarities in the formation of their skeleton, their hair, their skin, and other tissues of the body. I do not remember the time when I first realized the great wrong of stealing, buying, selling, or holding a human being in slavery; but an incident, in 1826, gave character, form, and expression to my most positive convictions on this subject.

My brother, nine years my senior, had occasion to visit Montreal, Canada. After one week of his absence, my sister Miriam came running to the sawmill, to inform my father that the chest of the absent brother had been rifled of a new suit of clothes, and two rolls of valuable cloth.

We all hastened to the house to learn the details, and to consult as to the probabilities relating to the theft. Suspicion soon rested upon one William Williams, a traveling laborer, who, after having worked two weeks on the farm, had some four days previous left for parts unknown. Having myself worked with him in the field, and having heard him speak much of Old Springfield, Mass., and of his intention to go there on some raft of lumber moving down the Connecticut River, it seemed probable that he had gone in that direction. I plead with my parents to allow me, then fourteen years of age, to go in pursuit of the thief—at least in search of the stolen goods. With much reluctance they consented.

With ten or twelve dollars in my pocket, and unincumbered with luggage, I started, saying that if Williams went a-foot, I would walk; if he rode, I would take the stage; if he went by raft, I would do the same. Of course, I commenced on foot, southward bound, inquiring of every man, woman, and child whom I met on the road, or in the houses by the wayside, describing minutely the man whom I was seeking.

After having gone about five miles, I heard of his having passed three days before, empty-handed, or with a *small* package, southward; and that on the following morning the same man was seen, walking in the same direction with a *large* package on his back. Having learned this I walked with increased speed, making inquiries of every person whom I met.

Soon I heard that, at the next house the man had sold some undergarments. Going to the house, I recognized the articles as belonging to my brother. I promptly declared that they belonged to him, Mr. Erastus A. Holton, son of Joel Holton, the clothier and sawyer of Westminster, Vermont; that in the absence of my brother, Mr. Williams, the hired man, had stolen the articles. The purchaser of the stolen goods believed my story, and, recognizing that his claim to stolen property was void, notwithstanding he had paid money for the same, readily surrendered the garments. Passing onward another mile, I found under similar circumstances other of the missing garments. Near by, in like manner, I received all the remainder of the goods, except the two rolls of cloth; and of the sale of these I heard as being to a trader on the river bank in Putney, Vt. The man who last surrendered the stolen property, finding this just act had strengthened his moral powers, befriended the boy, and proffered his personal aid in a visit to said store. Entering, he inquired for cloth, as though contemplating a purchase, and one of the missing rolls was shown to him. My sympathizer then asked for some of a different color, when both of the stolen rolls were opened upon the counter, and were seen and identified by me. . . . An explanation followed, which resulted, after considerable delay and hesitation, in the delivery of the cloth.

All the lost goods thus recovered were taken to the hotel in Putney, where I remained till the northward going stage, the next morning, carried me towards Westminster, where at the post-office was gathered an unusual crowd, planning what should be done to find and restore, not the thief and the missing goods, but the presumptuous boy for whose safety great anxiety began to be felt through the village and neighboring districts. To their surprise, this boy, about whom they were wondering and conjecturing, stepped down from the open stage-door with his great pack.—Never since have I been lionized as then.

The quick surrender of the stolen goods, notwithstanding the holders had in good faith paid cash for the same, impressed me anew with a wholesome doctrine, that the negro, stolen in the place of his nativity or his home, and sold by the slave-dealer, does not become the property of any purchaser.

While in bed at the hotel in Putney, this truth took possession of all that could be called myself; and, if subsequently it acquired no new force, it is certain its hold upon me has never changed—has never diminished.

Though, in my sleeping apartment then and there, I may have rejoiced over the success in recovering the stolen articles; yet I chiefly valued the new light, and the new conviction which was forced upon me as a living actuality, that it was my duty to do my best for restoring the slave to freedom. This impression came to me in this form:

If a person buying clothes stolen from my brother has no right in them, notwithstanding he paid money for the same; then, the negro stolen from himself does not become the property of the thief or purchaser.

During the first two days in the office of Dr. Ives, while writing the twelve letters as stated, I recognized my obligations to work in either or all of these three directions—in the interest of temperance, education, and freedom. These duties were present in my vision as having, or as probably being about to have upon me, greater claims than the practice of medicine; nevertheless it appeared to me expedient to obtain a medical education, as a means to one or more of these ends.

Up to that date I had been firmly convinced that no person had a right to select a profession, a trade, or any kind of business or employment, chiefly in view of its financial remuneration to him or herself [himerself].* I most firmly believed it to be the duty of every one to do that, and that only, which would add most to the happiness of mankind; trusting that of the many and various fields of usefulness, one might be found suited to each person, in which individual and public benefits would harmonize. My views on this subject have not since changed.

While a student in the office of Dr. Ives, at my earnest solicitation, my sister Miriam, who had for some years been a school-teacher in Vermont, Massachusetts, and Connecticut, left New England to open a school in New York.

As a preliminary step to success in a city establishment, she taught awhile, in 1836, at Mrs. Starr's school for young ladies, 96 Madison street, and the next spring, without special patronage or promise from any one, she opened a school at 18 Amity street, beginning with one pupil. At the close of the first week she had six, and the number rapidly increased, until at the August vacation she had about thirty.

On commencing her fall term, she found her rooms too small, and one morning she and her brother were gratified to see, diagonally across the way, a bill on No. 11 Amity street, "To Let." Thither her school was forthwith removed to more ample quarters, and there, for six years, were accommodated from 60 to 125 boarding and day scholars.

During these years I gave my attention about equally to the medical profession and school-teaching, at all times co-operating with my sister in providing for the varied requirements of the school, sustaining a regular and progressive course of lectures in the natural sciences, especially in human and comparative physiology.

Selected topics in anatomy and physiology had been the subjects of my lectures, by the kind permission of Mr. N. C. Hart, at the House of Refuge before named; also, in the public schools and orphan asylums, in sundry private schools and other educational institutions, including the Deaf and

---

* A new pronoun for the English language; one word being used as equivalent to three. Nominative, hesh (he or she); Possessive, hizer (his or her); Objective, himer (him or her). Let the e in hesh be pronounced long, as in he.

Dumb Institution, favored by the presence and interpretation of Mr. Peet, or some one of the professors.

These subjects had not previously been introduced into the schools of New York, for the senior Dr. Griscom, father of Dr. John H. Griscom, had not then commenced his lectures upon them in the schools of the city.

My sister and myself had great cause of gratitude to Mr. Thomas Hastings, for his efficient aid in sustaining, in our Amity street school, the department of vocal music. His published works have comforted and edified millions of persons and thousands of congregations. At the commencement of our school Mr. Hastings was chorister in the Dutch Reformed Church, of which Chancellor Mathews and Rev. M. S. Hutton were pastors, worshiping in the newly-erected University on Washington square. Before the great fire, their house of worship had been on Garden street, near the Battery. Perhaps no person in America did more than Mr. Hastings to popularize music in schools, and to convince parents and teachers that all youth, with a few exceptions, may be trained to sing, beneficially to themselves and acceptably to others.

During the last year of my pupilage as a medical student, I was most of the time an assistant at Bellevue Hospital, having for my associate assistant P. W. Ellsworth, of Hartford, Conn.

After my graduation, 9th March, 1839, I immediately became one of the physicians of the Eastern Dispensary, located on Essex street; and my district embraced the region around the Seventh Presbyterian Church, which locality I selected in proof of my gratitude for the University scholarship formerly given me by its pastor, Rev. Elihu W. Baldwin, whose pulpit was then occupied by Rev. Edwin F. Hatfield, who for many years addressed crowded audiences, from which multitudes were forced to turn away for want of seats or even standing places.

This house, for years continuously overcrowded, was relieved only by the several colonists sent forth, as organized churches, into the eastern half of the city. Prominent among the off-shoots were the Memorial Presbyterian Church, at first located at the corner of Avenue C and Fourth street, then removed to Fifty-fifth street, near Lexington avenue, and now occupying the noble edifice on the corner of Madison avenue and Fifty-third street, of which Rev. C. S. Robinson, D. D., is pastor.

In this section of the city was the Brainard Church, Rivington street, to whose pastorate Rev. Asa D. Smith was called. The same was subsequently transplanted to Second avenue, corner of Fourteenth street, whence the reverend pastor was invited to the presidency of Dartmouth College, his *alma mater*.

It was while Mr. Smith was preceptor of the Academy at Limerick, Me., that my sister Miriam there completed her studies, preparatory to teaching ; and in this fact was found an additional cause of my selecting, as the field of my labors for two years, the dispensary district named—thus rendering a compliment to the preceptor of my beloved sister.

Soon after the commencement of my duties as a physician, I received one of New England's greatest gifts, confirmed at Philadelphia, Sunday, 12th May, 1839, by Rev. Albert Barnes, in my marriage to Miss Frances K. Forward, of Southwick, Mass., who seven years before had been one of my pupils in the academy of her native town, and who has proved to be a helpmeet in word and in deed.

During the course of my medical studies, in addition to my labors in connection with my sister's school at 11 Amity street, I found many opportunities to join with others in pushing forward the objects named in the twelve letters written during my first two days in the office of Dr. Ansel W. Ives. I particularly enjoyed my labors to advance the temperance cause, being honored with the presidency of the temperance society organized in the College of Physicians and Surgeons in Barclay street, which is believed to be the first medical temperance society anywhere formed.

While memory lasts, it will never cease to be a cause of gratitude, that, with the able speakers invited at sundry times to address the College Medical Temperance Society, the Rev. Dr. James M. Mathews, the then Chancellor of the University, was ever ready to render hearty co-operation.

After my graduation at the College of Physicians and Surgeons of the State of New York, then located at 67 Crosby street, I was for four years very active in the practice of the medical profession, appropriating time to my part of the duties connected with the Eastern Dispensary and the Marion street Lying-in-Asylum, and to the calls of a small private practice.

In 1843, being in correspondence with a friend, Dr. Evander W. Ranney, son of Dr. Waitstill Ranney, of Townsend, in my native county, Windham, Vt., who had at that time an extensive practice at Westport, Essex county, N. Y., I made an arrangement with him for an exchange of property.

He removed to New York, and soon invited one of his brothers to locate in the same city, then another and another, till the metropolis was favored with the active services of six live physicians of the name—a respectable delegation from the Green Mountain State. Surely no one can accuse me of deserting my post unsupplied.

In the exchange I received a neat brick house, with garden, orchard and outbuildings, pleasantly located on the western shore of Lake Champlain, nearly westward from Vergennes. The ride included Westport and portions of Moriah, Elizabethtown, Essex, and Lewis. In a visit to me, my father was gratified at seeing my location and success in practice; but in paternal kindness expressed his fears that my interest in the Academy and in the public schools—for he found me active as town Superintendent of Public Schools—would occupy my attention too much for eminent success in medical practice.

Subsequently, I was surprised one morning by finding a beautiful, fleet, and strong horse, saddled and bridled, standing at the post in front of my house, labeled "For DR. HOLTON, WESTPORT, ESSEX CO., N. Y." To the saddle was attached a letter from my brother, Mr. Erastus A. Holton, of Westminster, Vt., containing a condition, that said horse should be used by Dr. Holton in the practice of his profession—eating, not post-meat at the school-houses, but hay and oats in his own barn. And here I trust a confession may relieve a conscience not fully at ease; for it did happen that the doctor, as by instinct—or the horse in obedience to an instinct of the master—would, in his tour, sometimes halt before a school-house, when in an undertone the horse was told that he must not eat "post-meat," but might have free range over the grass on the school grounds, while a short visit was being made to the school. This matter was finally settled to the mutual satisfaction of all concerned, by the act of the Board of Supervisors, appointing me to the office of County Superintendent of Common Schools, and by the subsequent consent of my father and brother, that the horse might carry his master to the house of the sick, or officially leave him at any of the one hundred and sixty-nine schools of Essex County. Thus accredited in full faith, and with no compunctions, the horse and his master enjoyed new liberty, and for two years left no school district unvisited in their semi-annual tour.

Having arranged with a young physician to attend to my medical duties, I devoted myself fully to work for the improvement of schools, laboring not only during the usual school-hours, but inviting parents, teachers, and pupils to assemble in the evening. I held extra sessions alternately in the several school-houses of the entire county, averaging more than five evenings a week for the two years; and the length of the sessions often exceeded *three hours an evening*. I made very free use of a globe and some select charts, diagrams, and apparatus, which I usually transported with me for the illustration of various departments of school studies, making frequent use of the blackboard, then found in most of the schools.

Referring to my diary of that period, I find that in every school-house in the county, I thus lectured at least once, in many from two to four times, and in each of thirty-nine districts five times. All of this extra labor was entirely gratuitous to the recipients and to the county.

Among the exercises which occupied me during a part of these evening sessions, was that of analyzing and classifying the sounds of spoken language, and practicing in concert the pronunciation of the vocal elements, thus enunciating the several steps of progression in the speaking of a word or of a sentence. This *exercise* of the voice, as a help to clear enunciation in reading, was, before this, unheard of in the schools of the county. We also paid some attention to the phonetic letters which might be used in ordinary script and print to symbolize unmistakably to the reader these elemental movements of the voice. From about that date, 1843–47, these exercises have gradually increased in the schools of the Union.

These vocal elements thus enunciated by the youth of this generation, and through their agency recognized, individualized, and practiced upon by the masses of the people, will create a demand for the phonetic letters of *some* form, having uses analogous to the ends sought by Pitman, Comstock, Leigh, and others engaged in this department of progress.

In celebrating the seventy-first anniversary of American Independence, Saturday, 3d of July, 1847, it was my privilege to accompany several school-teachers to the top of Whiteface, a mountain in the western section of Essex Co., N. Y., and there to engrave the symbols of these elementary sounds, giving on that occasion an address upon the "Aid which PHONOTYPES will be in translating the BIBLE into the languages of the heathen." A copy of this address may be seen, commencing on page 34 of the PHONETIC MAGAZINE, printed that year in Philadelphia.

One month later, August 3d, similar exercises were had at the school district of the *Adirondack Iron Works*, and on Tahawus (Mount Marcy), August 4th and 5th; and on the thirty-first anniversary of that occasion, August 5th, 1878, I hope to meet some teachers and promoters of educational progress on the same Tahawian heights. I here reproduce a copy from the Westport paper of September 9th, 1847, of my last official circular. It may be suggestive of some of the many topics which will be before us at the proposed thirty-first anniversary commencing the first Monday evening of August, 1878, and continuing the remainder of that week.

ESSEX COUNTY TEACHERS' INSTITUTE.

THE Teachers' Institute will be in session in the Court House at Elizabethtown, on Monday, 18th October, and continue two weeks.

The organization and exercises will be after the plan adopted last session; though I hope to secure an order admitting a more extended course on Physiology.

Those Teachers in the county who have executed District Maps, Histories of School Districts, Historical Trees, Books of Grammar Trees, or Books of Diagrams, illustrating arithmetical and geometrical principles, are invited to bring them for practical use, for exchange, or for gratuitous distribution. Teachers will also bring such minerals as they may wish to exhibit or exchange; also samples of all kinds of school-books they may have, either in the *new* or *old* type. Slates, Dictionaries and Bibles are indispensable.

Board, exclusive of washing and lights, $1.50 per week. There is no charge to the members for tuition.

All persons who have taught or who design to teach are invited to attend.

As my professional arrangements lead me to decline being a candidate for reappointment, I shall be happy to have a full attendance of Teachers of Essex County, who generally manifest a laudable zeal in adopting the best modes for developing, transplanting, and cultivating living TRUTH.

DAVID P. HOLTON.
County Superintendent of Common Schools.

Westport, Essex Co., N. Y., September 9th, 1847.

At the close of this session of the Teachers' Institute, I sold out my interest at Westport, and returned to New York city, continuing my educational reformatory and medical labors there; and making lecture tours in New England and other States, including Wisconsin and Minnesota, till 1853, thus realizing to my friends the purposes announced in the twelve letters written fourteen years before, during the first two days of my studies in the office of my medical preceptor, Dr. Ansel W. Ives.

During the fall of 1849, the dysentery prevailed very extensively in the valley of the Connecticut, with which my brother, Erastus Alexander, died at Westminster, Vermont; a sister of my wife at Southampton, Mass.; and my first-born son at Southwick, Mass., where he had been visiting his grandmother.

In 1853, in compliance with my sister Miriam's advice, I left for a visit to Europe, accompanied by my son, then a lad of eleven years, leaving my daughter with her mother in New York, where they remained until the ensuing summer, when the family were reunited in France.

For over three years I attended the best lectures in Paris, Berlin, and Vienna, being much of the time accompanied by my wife and son to the public courses given in the College of France, at the Garden of Plants, and at other institutions in Paris . . . . . . This son, born in New York, August 8th, 1842, to our great affliction died in Paris, the 23d of June, 1856. His body was embalmed, and, at the cemetery of Mont Martre, placed in the family vault of Professor Lenormant of the College of France, who had manifested great interest in the young American, his proficient student in archæological investigations as pursued in the College course. In the Roman Catholic professor's vault remained the body of his favorite Protestant pupil, till it was removed, on our return some sixteen months later, to Southwick, Massachusetts.

In connection with his memory and that of my sister and her Amity street school, stands associated that of Mr. Josiah Holbrook and Mr. Alexander Vattemare, whose labors were analogous and reciprocal. About the time of the last visit of the Marquis, the General La Fayette, to America, now fifty years since, Mr. Holbrook, in Massachusetts, commenced a system of school exchanges of specimens of nature and art. Many collections, now large, in America and in foreign lands, date their origin from the miniature cabinets of minerals, plants, insects or handiwork of children, presented by the pupils of some primary school, incited by Mr. Holbrook to give to others of such specimens as they found in their locality, or made by their industry. These cabinets were sent not only throughout our Union, but also to Canada, Mexico, and other places on this continent and beyond the Atlantic, meeting the concurrent approbation of educationists on both hemispheres.

Having prosecuted his system of exchanges for fourteen years in Boston, Mr. Holbrook visited New York, and one morning, having read of his arrival at the Astor House, I hastened to see him, as one whose system of labors was highly appreciated, one with whom it had been my privilege to work in Boston, during a prolonged vacation in the Southwick Academy in 1833. This interview gave me great joy, and at the urgent solicitations of sister and myself, he remained our guest at 11 Amity street for two years; while he prosecuted in New York his educational plans, as, aforetime, he had done in Boston.

Mr. Vattemare, who had long been distinguished on both sides of the Atlantic as an eminent ventriloquist, appreciated the labors of Mr. Holbrook. They became frequent correspondents and Mr. Vattemare devoted the remaining portion of his life to amplifying and developing his system. Thus they labored harmoniously: Mr. Holbrook chiefly with educational institutions; Mr. Vattemare with municipal corporations, republics, kingdoms, and empires; the one in exchanging specimens, forming small cabinets; the other in exchanging books, forming libraries. The American Library in the spacious alcoves of the Hotel de Ville, Paris, free to the reading public, was the result of Mr. Vattemare's labors.

During our stay in Paris, it was often my privilege to visit his rooms on Rue Clichy, with my son. His habit was to labor, from 4 A.M. till noon, in correspondence, in receiving and forwarding books between near and remote nationalities. The numerous boxes of various sizes, containing books, recently received or about to be sent away, often gave to his depository an appearance like that of a wholesale mercantile house. These eight hours of work daily, with the duties of social life, might be counted sufficient; but he was also active in organizing and visiting evening schools for the LABORING CLASSES IN PARIS. In this respect his character resembled that of his friend Josiah Holbrook, who was very efficient in evening schools, particularly in those for the education of the colored youth of Boston, in which it was my privilege to be an humble participant. It was in 1855, that I read, in Paris, the announcement of the death of Josiah Holbrook, who, with hammer in hand, gathering geological specimens at Lynchburg, Va., slipped from a ledge and was drowned in the James River. I hastened to Rue Clichy to communicate the intelligence. Mr. Vattemare was deeply affected, and taking his file of American letters, read one recently received from Mr. Holbrook, containing the utterance of grateful emotions in view of the multiplication of school apparatuses and cabinets, and State geological surveys, for which he had been striving; a letter full of hope for the triumph of the principles which they had been mutually seeking to advance nearly twenty years before, while guests in Amity street.

The earthly labors of Holbrook and Vattemare, as also those of my sister, are terminated, but living, acting principles remain; and, as in the vegetable and animal kingdoms, vital forces—themselves created and continued by the omnipotent God—developed in material elements, give forms adhering to types, modified by external agencies, resulting in great diversity, yet in harmony with the eternal purposes of the Creator and upholder of the universe; so may we hope that the principle of benevolent reciprocities manifest in the life of these co-workers, may assume such modified forms of manifestation as will best secure the true progress of mankind; and that the spirits of these philanthropists may be found in Heaven under circumstances securing their perfect development.

Let us cherish their associated memories and imitate their virtues.

At a stated meeting of the American Institute, held 5th May, 1864, at the Cooper Institute, New York, the President, William Hall, Esq., having announced the death of an honorary member, M. Alexandre Vattemare, the following preamble and resolution were offered by Thomas McElrath, Esq.:

Whereas, Since our last regular meeting, information has been received of the death of Monsieur Alexandre Vattemare, a distinguished philanthropist, and an honorary member of this Institute; and,

Whereas, The labors of our deceased member were for many years directed to the extension and improvement of the Public Libraries of the United States, many of which were enriched by the valuable contributions effected through his instrumentality; and,

Whereas, The Library of the American Institute contains several hundred volumes, embracing a wide range of literature, and many of them particularly rich in statistics and the practical sciences, which were contributed mainly through his system of international exchanges and without expense to the Institute; therefore,

Resolved, That, as a testimony of the appreciation of the enlightened and eminently useful services of this noble-hearted and generous-minded French citizen, the Trustees of this Institute are directed to procure a portrait of the late Alexandre Vattemare, and that the same be suitably framed and hung in the rooms of the Library.

DAVID-P. HOLTON, M. D., in seconding the motion said: "To those acquainted with the earlier career of Alexandre Vattemare, and with the circumstances which established his character, will belong the duty of presenting the biography of an active philanthropist, whose benefactions reached most of the nations of the earth, through a system of

INTERNATIONAL RECIPROCITIES.

We now speak of his labors for the *last thirty years* of his life; during which period the system of international exchanges has been so happily developed. For a quarter of a century the American Institute has participated in the benefits of this system in connection with works of literature, science, and art.

As the tourist, having reached an eminence, delights to look back and trace the course of his route accomplished, and that which is before him; so in contemplating the life of Alexandre Vattemare, we may select a prominent point for retrospective and prospective views.

The stand-point best presenting my personal knowledge of the labors of M. Vattemare, is the period, when, after twenty years of strong faith, ardent zeal, and indefatigable works, he had the pleasure to receive from the Institute of France, nine years ago, the high commendations of his system.

In the center of the hall of the Institute of France, Feb. 22, 1855, were arranged series of tables on which were piled numerous publications, as contributions, through the offices of M. Vattemare, to the city of Paris.

To M. Guizot was assigned the privilege of stating, to members and invited guests, the principles of the system, and the development it had assumed among the various nations entering into co-operation. It was a day of triumph—a triumph in the peaceful walks of social and national progress—one in which I was deeply interested.

As M. Guizot presented the principle, the system and the results, I noticed the noble and benign countenance of M. Vattemare, bespeaking a high and pure joy of which croakers and misers are ignorant. The commendations of M. Guizot were followed by those of MM. Dupin, Naudet, Michel Chevalier, Cousin, and Villemé.

The occasion was highly complimentary to America, as holding, in the estimation of the learned historian of "Civilization," a high rank, not only in material progress, but also in the department of literature.

It was characteristic of M. Vattemare that, on this occasion, he chose Washington's Birthday Anniversary for the crowning of his system, and presented to the Institute chiefly American books. A Frenchman, true to his native country, he had the magnanimity to credit the paternity of his system to the United States, which he was ever pleased to count as the land of his adoption. The portraits of Washington and Lafayette, with the Declaration of the American Independence, formed the central ornaments of his studio in Rue Clichy.

On the 18th June, 1857, we met at London, by appointment, my sister and her husband, Dr. Henry-Smith Brown, they having been married at Sumpterville, S. C., 10th March, 1855, and having planned to make the tour of Europe with us, commencing on my forty-fifth anniversary birthday.

From London we visited Scotland and Ireland, and then the Continent. In Switzerland, at Altorf (Altdorf), a village celebrated as the place where, five hundred years before, in the time of William Tell, the rights of man were boldly declared and vindicated, my wife and daughter left the others of the party for rest and quiet study in Italy. By stage she passed over the Alps at St. Gothard, and down the valley of the Ticino to Bellinzona and Magadino, and thence by steamer on Lake Maggiore to Locano, where, finding a temporary home, she added to her formerly acquired knowledge of the Italian, a sufficient familiarity with the language to enable herself and friends, about to make the tour of Italy, to do so with the freedom which those speaking the language of the country visited can alone enjoy.

The others of the party went by the way of the Danube, and after visiting the Carpathian Mountains in Hungary, returned by way of Vienna, and crossed the Illyrian Alps to Trieste on the Adriatic, thence by steamer to Venice. This division of the tourists, having also visited lakes Como and Lugano, and the regions thereabout, arrived at Locano on Lake Maggiore, where meeting the Italian students, the said mother and daughter, the company was reunited.

After visiting Milan, Genoa, Pisa, Lucca, Florence, Leghorn, and other places in the north of Italy, we reached Rome, October 18th. On the 23d, in celebrating the fifth anniversary birthday of our daughter, we ascended to the highest accessible point in the ball above the lantern and dome of St. Peter's for a view of the city, the surrounding Campagna, and the distant hills and mountains of this classic region.

Our subsequent tour included Naples, and other places in the south of Italy. We made the ascent of Mount Vesuvius 31st October, thus celebrating the fiftieth anniversary birthday of my sister Miriam, Mrs. Dr. Brown.

One week had been passed in examining the antiquities and modern structures of Rome, when on Sunday, 25th October, 1857, my sister Miriam, accompanied by her husband, her brother, and his wife and daughter, sought the silence and seclusion of the Protestant burial ground, situated near the Gate of St. Paul (Porta di S. Paolo), close to the Pyramid of Caius Cestius. The inscriptions in this cemetery tell the English and American travelers, in their native tongue, of those who have found their last resting-place beneath the bright Italian skies. The place has an air of romantic beauty, which forms a striking contrast with the tombs of the ancients, and with the massive city walls and towers which overlook it.

Among those who are buried here are the poets Shelley and Keats, Richard Wyatt the sculptor, and John Bell the celebrated surgeon. By far the greater number of monuments bear the names of Englishmen; the other Protestants interred here are chiefly Americans, Germans and Swiss.

It was a melancholy interest which drew us, especially my sister, to this spot, where had been interred the body of one of the beloved pupils of her Amity street school in New York city, one of the *first three*, who was the youngest of the girls in the first months of the school, which circumstance may have additionally contributed to secure for her an abiding place in the affections of her teacher. This visit in Rome to the burial-place of Mary (Ludlum) Cass, who twenty years before had been her affectionate pupil in America, gave rise to stirring reflections and deep emotions, and the broad waters ceased for a time to separate the Tiber and the Hudson.

She was a daughter of Nicholas Ludlum, of New York, and her husband, the son of General Lewis Cass, at the time of her death was representing at Rome the Government of the United States. Her death was very sudden, occurring while in the act of taking an ordinary bath. She was interred at Rome, but her remains were subsequently transported to New York. Mary commenced her school studies with my sister. All her words and acts fully secured the affection of those about her, and being for some time the youngest member of the school, it was very pardonable in her teacher that ties of unusual force and endurance should be formed.

Mrs. Ludlum and Mrs. R. W. Martin, of Fourth street, and Mrs. Thomas McKie of Mercer street, all residing on the same block where my sister's school was located, were its first three patrons; and their enduring friendship tended to increase her prosperity and usefulness.

To the three patrons above named were soon added Mr. Thomas Lawrence, an honored Alderman of the Fifteenth Ward, Mr. S. V. S. Wilder and Mr. Thomas Denny, eminent bankers; Mr. Gideon Lee, then the late Mayor of the city; Mr. Henry Starkweather, whose daughter is the wife of Governor Hoffman; Drs. Ansel W. Ives, J. W. Francis and Alfred C. Post; Chancellor Mathews, Messrs. Frederick W. Steinbrenner, Jacob Brandegee, T. B. Bleecker, J. H. Ransom, Elisha Bloomer, Cornelius Bogert, Rev. John Lindsey, John Bodine, Augustine Averill, E. H. Herrick, Benjamin D. Breck, George H. Homan, James Van Norden, Lavielle Duberceau, Anthony

Civill, A. Brower, Edward McLean, Frederick A. Gay, William Popham, Tiletson Cushing, Myron Beardsley, Henry Greenwood, Elias H. Kimball, Cyrus Price, Nathaniel Thurston, William R. Allen, Peter See, Wm. Blacket, Nathaniel Gray, Morgan L. Livingston, William Constable, James Connor, and other honorable citizens.

The friendly co-operation of the above added much to the happiness of my sister, and the success of her school.

Having returned to America, I resumed my lectures on Physiology until the commencement of the war of the rebellion; these being addressed chiefly to the children of orphan asylums in New England, also in New York, Wisconsin, and Minnesota, including places *en route*.

Having in my own right, and also in company with my sister, some real estate at Waterville, in Waukesha county, Wisconsin, I there devoted some of my time to farming and to the erection of buildings, purposing to employ the remainder in lecturing in schools and orphan asylums east and west, and in places between the Connecticut and the Mississippi.

During these years I sought to apply some of the principles previously suggested in the series of articles under the title of "*Caen Stone Dreams*," written in 1853, with the *compound* purpose of advancing the cause of Agriculture, and the welfare of Orphans.

In 1859, at the Wisconsin State Fair, I was favored in hearing a very valuable discourse by Hon. Abraham Lincoln, of Springfield, Illinois.

His theme was the dignity of labor, the high order and variety of talent brought into requisition in agricultural pursuits and mechanic arts of the present day. He dwelt particularly on recent improvements in the implements and machinery of the farm, and the workshops.

In this address the practical workings of his powerful genius were distinctly shown.

His comprehensive view of the relations of the laboring classes, as connected with the elevated and progressive interests of our republic, established in the minds of his hearers the importance of institutions where should be combined the science and practice of agricultural and mechanical occupations. It was his clear perception, and his lucid presentation of the right, that gained for him the respect and confidence of his fellow-citizens.

The practical good sense exhibited in this address did much to prepare the way for his election to the Presidency.

In the meantime my energies were chiefly devoted to the orphan cause, and the following letters show the tenacity with which the compound purpose, manifest in the Caen Stone series of former years, was sought to be realized.

From the 18th April, 1861, some four days after the bombardment of Fort Sumter, till the 18th June, 1862, letters were repeatedly sent to every Senator and Representative in Congress, and many of them were personally addressed in the spirit manifest in the following:

To Hon. ―――――

DEAR SIR :—Assuming you appreciate the importance of donating lands for Agricultural Colleges in the several States of the Union, I respectfully invite your attention to the objects of the Institute of Reward, as stated in the accompanying Circular, dated June 18th, 1861.

Can you aid us in securing an appropriation of land to sustain, in the several States, an "AGRICULTURAL COLLEGE," and an "EXPERIMENTAL FARM," associated with which shall be the HOME OF THE PATRIOT ORPHAN ?

I am dear sir,
Very respectfully yours.

At the rooms of the New York Young Men's Christian Association, 31 Bible House, June 18, 1862, on occasion of the first anniversary meeting of the "INSTITUTE OF REWARD," it was a cause of great satisfaction to read in the *Tribune* of that morning, the telegraphic announcement of the passage, through both Houses of Congress, of the bill for which we had labored so hopefully, then wanting only the approval of the President to become a law ; and while, from the precedents of Mr. Lincoln, no doubts were entertained of his approval, the following letter was the next day written both as an acknowledgment of the President's interest and influence in what had already been accomplished, and as an exponent of the progressive series toward the realization of which his past favors were counted as an earnest of future aid.

NEW YORK, *June* 19th, 1862.

To the President of the United States :

HONORED AND BELOVED SIR :—By the accompanying Report of the First Anniversary of the Institute of Reward, it is seen that thus far its efforts have been directed to awaken public sentiment to the necessity and justice of establishing "HOMES FOR PATRIOT ORPHANS," and particularly in connection with "EXPERIMENTAL FARMS" and "AGRICULTURAL SCHOOLS."

The Government has generously given farms to its Patriots' Orphans, and surely is wise enough to train them rightly to cultivate the same.

At the Agricultural State Fair in Wisconsin, it was my privilege to profit from the advocacy of the application of science to farming in an address from one, wise to choose the proper means and times to effect the best ends, as has been demonstrated since he has been called to preside over our nation, whose sore trials prove a means of strength and progress.

The Senate Bill for Agricultural Colleges, which passed the House on the 17th inst., being an echo of his views spoken in Milwaukee, is assumed to be sure of the President's approval; and thus will be nationalized one of the objects in the series contemplated by the Institute of Reward.

Now, there presents a distinct line of progressive action, embracing—*First.* Application to each State Legislature to utilize this national bounty, by attaching to its Agricultural College an EXPERIMENTAL FARM, which, in addition to the practical solution of ordinary problems of culture, shall become the field for acclimating foreign plants and animals, in order to develop by progressive experimentation the valuable treasures in reserve for this nation, and reciprocally for others. [Plants and animals, both native and exotic, heretofore unused, being modified by unaccustomed influences on the experimental farm, there may be returned to the place of their origin, new varieties of species as valued contributions, amplifying the resources of human progress.]

Second. Application to State Legislatures to establish ORPHAN HOMES on the experimental farms, Homes whose scope and spirit, harmonizing with philanthropic deeds, may be developed in modes of REWARD rather than those of Almsgiving; thus testifying a grateful appreciation of the defenders of our nation, and thus rearing a monument to their memory; also, through the scientific and practical knowledge thus imparted to their orphans, greatly increasing the resources and wealth of the country.

I have the honor to be,
Very respectfully, yours.

To His Excellency,
ABRAHAM LINCOLN, *President.*

The signature of the President to this bill, July 2, 1862, assured our success, and concluded the first division of our labors.

THE SECOND DIVISION

embraced our labors with the several State Legislatures, together with the circulation and presentation of a petition, of which soon after the grant was obtained, six thousand impressions were furnished by the liberality of the *Chicago Tribune*, as captions to rolls for signatures in the loyal States.

The grant from Congress to the several States was land, in quantity equal to thirty thousand acres for each Senator and each Representative in the National Government, making for New York thirty-three times thirty thousand, or nine hundred and ninety thousand acres of said lands, worth to this State over one million dollars.

On the basis of the funds arising from this Congressional grant, it is with gratitude we refer to the patriot orphan privileges secured at Ithaca, in Tompkins county, New York, through the munificent co-operation of Hon. Ezra Cornell of that place, and to those secured in several other of the Agricultural Colleges of the Union.

We invite special attention to the ninth section of the Act of Incorporation of the Cornell University, which is the Agricultural College of the State of New York, in which provision is made for one hundred and twenty-eight "State Students;" and in the annual selection of these one hundred and twenty-eight occupants of the State Scholarships, it is made imperative that preference shall be given to patriot orphans, where other qualifications are equal.

The State Students presenting themselves at the Cornell University, with a certificate of selection in due form, will be admitted to any department or course for which they are fitted, and continue four years, or as long as they shall profitably employ their time in the University, *free from all matriculation fees, term taxes,* or any other payment for tuition.

It is contemplated that our patriot orphan State Students will labor on the Experimental Farm, and in the workshops of the University, to defray the larger part of their expenses for board and clothes. What remains for this Institute now to supplement, is to aid each of these orphans there admitted to meet the said excess of bills for board and clothes, above their earnings from this manual labor.

The circumstances and conditions above recited are essentially the same as those applicable to our patriot orphan students in the Sheffield Scientific School, a department of Yale College; in the Industrial University at Urbana, in Champaign county, Illinois; in Brown University, Rhode Island; in the State University at Madison, Wisconsin; and in the other Agricultural Colleges, in which the patriot orphan claim has been recognized, as contemplated by this Institute of Reward, in its labors with Congress, before the grant was obtained as the basis of our memorial work in all future time.*

In the Literary and Scientific Colleges and other institutions, in which we have scholarships, a supplementary work analogous to that for our students in the Agricultural colleges is requisite.

A comparatively small amount of additional aid remains to be provided; and it is earnestly hoped that the requisite contributions of board and money will be abundantly supplied from the wealth of those who dwell in peace and prosperity, purchased by the sacrifice of the fathers of these orphans.

Only in connection with the Experimental farms based on the grant from Congress, did we originally propose to found new homes for orphans; except when the necessity for their formation was very apparent.

It may not be amiss here to add that my personal expenses in the many visitations to Congress, and to State Legislatures, were principally met by money derived from the sale or mortgage of some portions of my real estate. In this way I gradually encroached upon my lands; commencing by a mortgage upon the northern *forty* acres of my Waterville farm in Waukesha Co., Wisconsin; subsequently selling the northern eighty, then the eighty southward, and so on, till all but forty acres of that large and excellent farm are sold.

Only a small portion of my time was passed at either my New York or Waterville residence.

The most of my library was removed to my farm house, some rods from which, under the shade of three oaks, I erected a square structure, for retirement or for social gatherings. It was supported by cedar posts, and below the upper platform was a room, walled by narrow, perpendicular slats, between each of which was an open space about the width of one.

This open room I designed for my daughter and for the children of the school located on the Waukesha road, about twenty rods eastward, at the cornering of four towns—Summit, Ottawa, Genesee, and Delafield. Into this open room, it was my purpose to invite the school children to bring specimens of whatever stones were to be found near their several homes, and in their more distant walks, and here they were to have full freedom to hammer the same to sizes suited to small cabinets, such as Josiah Holbrook had formerly prepared in Boston and New York for exchange with schools near and distant. Here, also, I hoped the youth would arrange their school herbariums,

---
See Note on Page 239.

and here, with wooden blocks of various forms, sizes and proportions (prepared with geometrical exactness), construct their little castles, each according to their several models or devices.

This structure I named the Minerva study, in compliment to my eldest sister Minerva, who loved me and guided me in my infancy, and with whom, afterwards, were passed many hours in South Berwick, Maine, which I count among the happiest of my life. She was there, attending a young ladies' school, while I was a pupil in the Academy. Though we boarded about a mile apart, I sought every available opportunity to be with her; and now look back to those delightful visits with unalloyed satisfaction. She married, 31st December, 1829, Charles-Grandison Gilchrist; and they now reside, 1874, at Hillsgrove, McDonough county, Illinois, having in that and in an adjoining county numerous descendants honored and prosperous.

. . . . A few months after this study was completed, before my daughter had seen it, she died of diphtheria at our residence in New York City, 20th May, 1859, aged six years, six months and seven days. . . . . The charm of the Minerva study vanished. The father and mother, thus bereft of children, concluded henceforth to work for others.

For my acts subsequent to 14th April, 1861, reference is here made to the serial numbers of the *Journal of the Institute of Reward for Orphans of Patriots*, of which the last number was printed March, 1874, containing the Twelfth Annual Report of the Board of Directors, dated 31st December, 1873. To give, from one of the standpoints, a bird's-eye view of *a part* of the workings of the Institute, an extract is made from said report:

"GENEALOGIES AND BIOGRAPHIES OF OUR PATRIOT DEAD.

"At a session of the Executive Committee of the I. R. O. P., held January 16, 1871, attention was drawn to the fact that in the formation of the Institute, the primary purpose was the organization of Historic Committees in the loyal towns and villages of the nation, to secure and perpetuate biographical sketches of those fathers who might die in the service of our Union, hoping thereby to incite American citizens gratefully to provide for the orphan children of such fathers, in a liberal spirit of REWARD, in place of almsgiving.

"The prominence given to this Historic Department may be seen in the early circulars of the Society, in its former annual reports, and in the *results obtained* in the legislative acts of many States.

"In keeping with this primary purpose and past practice of the Institute, the various Historic and other Societies in the land formed at our instance, are now invited to forward to the Corresponding Secretary the desired genealogical and biographical records of parents and ancestors of our patriot orphan protegés, including the full names of said orphans, the date and place of their birth; full name and last residence of their parents; when and where the patriot father enlisted, with name of company and regiment; where stationed during the war; in what battles he took part; when and where mustered out; date and place of his death, etc. If wounded, state particulars, and also any personal anecdotes or incidents that will prove of value to the children thus early removed from parental narrative, counsel, and direction.

"The ancestral line of the deceased patriot father is desired, as far back as correspondents may be able to give it.

"Ample arrangements are made for tabulating all such genealogical and biographical records, for their preservation, and for convenient reference thereto; not only in honor of ancestors, but for the sake of posterity.*

"All persons interested in this important department of the Institute, or in the demonstration of the GRATITUDE OF REPUBLICS, are respectfully invited to call and examine the system of records adopted at the studio of the Corresponding Secretary, David-Parsons' Holton, M. D., 19 Great Jones street, New York."

In said last number of the *Journal* may also be found additional statements concerning the life and death of my sister Miriam', especially of her acts in the interest of instruction by popular lectures. There, also, may be found a copy of her last will and testament.

The following letter was written at the time of her death:

LE CLAIRE, SCOTT COUNTY, IOWA.
November 9th, 1865.

To Horace Webster, LL.D., President of the Free Academy, New York City, and President of the Institute of Reward for Orphans of Patriots:

DEAR SIR:—My dear sister Miriam, afflicted with a disease of the heart, intensified by malarious influences prevailing in this region, died at this place, Wednesday, November 8th, aged 58 years and 8 days.

For some weeks she had been accompanying me on a tour of visitation, in the interest of our Patriot Orphans, for whom she had liberally given of her means and personal forces.

From the initiatory steps in the organization of the Institute, her sympathies were warmly enlisted in its objects. She assisted in the issue of our first Circular, April 18th, 1861, and since then has co-operated in the generalization of the principles of the Society and their practical application through individual, associate, and voluntary agencies, and through legislative action in Congress, and in the several States of the Union.

Recently she sought an enlargement of their application in sympathy with the proposition to establish at Fort Gibson, or some other suitable place, an INDIAN PATRIOT ORPHAN HOME, for the children of those loyal Indians who fell in the defense of our country.

Will her noble resolves, her personal sacrifices, and benevolent labors prove a failure? I trust not.

The Lord, in dealing with our nation, has shown that the means and agencies for effecting His wise purposes are varied, and not in the order of man's device.

The Lord has a unity of plan in accomplishing his purposes; though the agencies He employs are diverse in form and degree.

My precious sister has left me. We who had been for so many years associated in purpose and works, are now separated.

The Lord's chain is not bisected in the removal of an elemental link. He maintains the continuity by substitutions of his own election. Let us, therefore, work while our day lasts, trusting in the Lord at all times.

Her body will, to-morrow, be interred in Fairview cemetery, on the prairies of Iowa, some three miles west of the Mississippi. We trust her spirit has passed to a higher sphere of action.

With kind regards to your associate members of the Executive Committee, and Board of Directors of the Institute,

I remain, Dear Sir, yours truly.

---

* Correspondents and students in this work of family records may derive aid from the suggestions found on pages 30 and 31, where the *references* are to "Dr. Holton's METHOD in Genealogy;" and *not* to parts of *this* book.

Arrangements have been made for the removal of her body to the cemetery at Westminster, Vermont; where are interred the remains of her parents and grand-parents.

About the time when the memorial volume, relating to her four grandparents, now in course of preparation, is ready for distribution to their descendants, in accordance with her last will and testament, a cenotaph at Le Claire, and a monument at Westminster, are to be erected. The latter is being prepared at the marble works of Homer M. Phelps, of Burlington, Vermont.

EXTRACTS FROM THE DISCOURSE OF
REV. E. MILLER,

AT THE FUNERAL SOLEMNITIES OF MRS. MIRIAM (HOLTON) BROWN, LE CLAIRE, SCOTT COUNTY, IOWA, NOV. 10TH, 1865.

"MY friends, although the circumstances that convene us to-day are very sad, yet they exhibit one of the happiest phases of human life, as, also, the marked kindness of the great Creator.

"That a stranger, to most of us unknown, should not only receive every kind office while suffering, but the most delicate attentions in death and burial, is an exhibit of human sympathy that goes far to relieve the turmoil of life, as well as to give a striking comment upon the character of Him who has placed us in the midst of social relations.

"But in the present instance these kindnesses are peculiarly well placed in being bestowed upon one, the fruits of whose life toil and sacrifices are mainly consecrated to the benefit of the rising generation and the cause of helpless orphanage. * * * * * * * * * * *
*   *   These facts remind me of the expression of Balaam: 'Let me die the death of the righteous, and let my last end be like his.' But the striking *contrast* in these two characters constitutes the force of this suggestion. The false prophet of Mesopotamia sighed for the *end* of the righteous, though he ran greedily after gain and loved the lascivious pleasures of idolatry. He desired an effect without the cause—the harvest that had never been sown. In the present instance, we are told of the diligent sowing, the faithful tilling, the earnest devotion to a life of labor and love. Shall we doubt, dare we *ask* as to the harvest? If these causes modeled her character, no power contravenes the glorious effect. If *we* would have a peaceful and happy end, let us live lives of righteousness.

"While it is true that whatsoever we sow shall we also reap, there are other than spiritual fields and future harvests.

"The social field in which the deceased so faithfully labored furnishes in *this* world the fruits that the indifferent and selfish cannot have. Her harvests wave in the many hearts her munificence has gladdened.

"The Association, 'The Institute of Reward for Orphans of Patriots,' in which she labored, records her faithfulness and cherishes her memory. And the character of her enterprise, here and now, warms the hearts of strangers with its sanctity, and calls about her senseless clay their most delicate attentions.

"But as we commit this body to the grave, by one side of which a soldier's orphan sleeps, by the other a dear and cherished friend, we cannot but think of the rigid exactness with which God honors his servants.

"We are reminded of Moses, whom, having resigned the crown of 'Old Egypt' and the pompous burial of her kings, because of devotion to his one great enterprise, God did not permit to be buried by the gross Israelites; but himself selected the burial spot:

> "'And the angels of God upturned the sod,
> And laid the dead man there.'

"So, also, she who sought homes for the stranger receives at the hands of strangers the last sad offices of this world. She, who resigns society of friends, here in this strange land finds the grave and ashes of an early and dear friend with whom to lie down in the last, long sleep. She, who leaves her home, that the soldier's orphan may have a 'Home,' here mingles her ashes with the soldier's child in its last earthly home. And here this lover of culture and life-long educator shall sleep, asking no prouder monument than this prairie school-house, at once the exponent of her life and the fittest emblem of Christian civilization.

"Let us live the life of the righteous, that our last end may be like theirs."

Mrs. Brown had arranged her business in Wisconsin and elsewhere with a view to a long absence, intending to establish a Patriot Orphan Home in the Indian Territory. She had prepared a memorial to Congress which she had with her on her death bed; and which she was about to send to the Institute in New York, for their co-operation in obtaining a grant for this purpose.*

---

* *To the Honorable, the Senate and House of Representatives of the United States of America:*

Your memorialists, the officers and members of the "Institute of Reward for Orphans of Patriots," would most respectfully show to your Honorable Bodies, that we have well and faithfully, according to our articles of incorporation, and according to our ability, put in operation and carried forward the plans to aid the orphans of patriots fallen in the service of our country in the war for the suppression of the late rebellion.

We have secured from nearly all the loyal States legislation in aid of our general purposes, and have co-operated with other agencies in providing ways and means for supporting and educating such orphans; more especially have we endeavored to furnish increased facilities for instructing these youth, now the pledges of a nation's gratitude, into a practical knowledge of agriculture and the mechanic arts.

Our original design has been faithfully pursued, which was to extend the benefits of our organization to every orphan of a deceased patriot throughout the Union—all of which, by reference to the record of our Act of Incorporation [page 4, of the Journal of the Institute], and our proceedings and labors herewith most respectfully submitted to your Honorable Bodies, will more fully and at large appear.

AND NOW YOUR MEMORIALISTS would most respectfully further show to your Honorable Bodies, that, in our investigations in the pursuit of our objects, it has come to our knowledge that there are many orphans

After the death of Mrs. Brown the foregoing memorial was presented to Congress; but the absence of the prime mover in the work caused its postponement. It is hoped some philanthropists may yet feel impressed with a sense of their duty to go forward in this work.

Since her death I have been much occupied in my duties as Secretary and General Agent of the Institute of Reward for Orphans of Patriots. In the meantime my attention has been turned towards the completion of the work of gathering and arranging genealogical items and biographical records of her four grandparents, their ancestors and their descendants, a work commenced by my wife, on occasion of her first visit to the homes of my relatives during our wedding tour in 1839.

This labor has led us to collect similar records of all in America, bearing the patronymics of my four grandparents; and thus we have been brought to feel an interest in every Parsons, Winslow, Farwell, and Holton of whom we have any knowledge, and in *their* descendants, even when bearing other names.

Other objects have, also, claimed my attention and co-operation, among which may be counted the one set forth in the following letter:

To the Trustees of the New York Free Medical College for Women.

51 St. Mark's Place, New York.

Through appointment by your Honorable Board, I am charged with the duties of presenting to the students of the New York Free Medical College for Women the facts and principles of Physiology and Hygiène; also, with the duties of the chair of Experimental Physiology.

Allow me to present, that in the early days of the College I consented to give annually some twelve lectures on General Physiology. In the progress of their delivery, my interest in this work increased, and I cheerfully assumed a greater charge. This I still should enjoy, if other duties did not press upon me so heavily. In justice to myself and sundry other parties, and in harmony with my own predilections, I now solicit a modification of the terms

---

of loyal and patriotic Indians, who gave up their lives by the side of their white brethren, in the same glorious cause, and in the same great and successful war.

And your memorialists pray that your Honorable Bodies may enact a law, granting tracts of land or lands to the Society that your memorialists represent, for the purposes of carrying forward the same good work for the patriot *Indian orphan*, that we are now doing for the *white*.

And your memorialists pray for such other enactments for the securing of any further aid, gift, subsidy, or endowments, as in the wisdom of your Honorable Bodies may seem reasonable and just; so that the establishment of schools, the education, support, and instruction in agriculture and the mechanic or other arts, trades, or vocations may be secured to all such Patriot Indian Orphans.

And your memorialists further represent that we will enter upon our duties and labors in the prosecution of all the objects of our Institute toward such Indian orphans, immediately upon the reception of such grants or aids as your Honorable Bodies may by enactment give—that homes and schools, and all the advantages proposed by our Society, may speedily be secured for the said patriot Indian orphans, and also for such other Indian orphans as may absolutely need such aid.

And your memorialists would ever pray, etc.

of my appointment. . . . . . . The Department of Physiology may advantageously be divided among the three chairs, viz.:

1. Physiology. This may embrace all that is essential to graduation.
2. Experimental Physiology and Hygiène.
3. Comparative Physiology.

The two divisions last named embrace subjects of study, interesting and important, which may profitably be pursued by undergraduates, and by physicians in the practice of their profession.

Last year, at my solicitation, you appointed an Adjunct to the chair of Physiology. Now, I respectfully solicit that you transfer me to the charge of the duties of Professor of Comparative Physiology, leaving the first and the second chairs above-named to be filled by others at your discretion.

I have the honor to remain,
February 18, 1873.   Yours truly.

In the principal works alluded to, it has been and still continues to be my good fortune to be aided by the kind, discreet, and valuable co-operation of my wife.

We may not always act wisely or efficiently; but of the principles forming the basis of our action, and of the motives which we propose to have govern us during the balance of life, I cannot better make a succinct statement, than by here copying from a Waukesha paper a report of my address at a public meeting, Sunday evening, 2 Nov., 1873—a union meeting of all the churches for the purpose of raising funds for the relief of those in Memphis and Shreveport, suffering from the ravages of yellow fever:

It has pleased our Heavenly Father in His revealed word to enlighten human beings on certain subjects of vital interest to man. The highest human wisdom consists in, or is shown in, appreciating and applying the TRUTHS, precepts, rules or laws thus revealed in words adapted to human intellect.

In God's revealed word we learn that suffering is a means of checking pride, and notions of self-sufficiency—a means of leading us to acknowledge a power higher than ourselves. Man, thus brought to reflection, finds in the Holy Scriptures evidence that law—even violated law—becomes a schoolmaster to bring us to God. Suffering is designed as a *blessing;* not *alone* to the sufferer, but as a means of exercising co-dwellers on earth in its relief. Human sympathy, which exercises itself in the relief of suffering, is thereby strengthened.

Selfish man, unexercised in relieving afflicted humanity, becomes casehardened, hide-bound, and degenerated. His stony heart becomes petrified. The man himself becomes a walking petrifaction. Or, rather, the wicked elements of his being thrive to the suffocation of his higher nature.

The greater the distance of suffering relieved, the greater is the blessing which comes from sympathy so exercised. To relieve suffering in our very presence may be an unmixed good to the sufferer; and the giving of the needed relief, in very presence, may strengthen the better powers of the giver; but not to so great a degree as would a similar or equal amount of sympathy for the sufferer more distant in space or in social ties. Suffering at home, and in our presence, impels us to give relief, if possible.

Acting thus under a force almost allied to an instinct of our natures, we do not receive that high order of benefit to ourselves which comes from active sympathy for the sufferer far removed in location or consanguinity. Again: when a well-tried, true, and devoted friend is suffering, our sympathy and aid may, to the recipient, be of benefit equal to corresponding aid rendered to an enemy. That is, the friend may thus be benefited as much as the enemy; while, in the latter case, the development of our moral and religious nature is much greater than in the former.

To any present who have personal friends or relations in Memphis, Shreveport, or other places in the valley of the Mississippi or Red Rivers, where the fatal malady has so alarmingly prevailed, and also to any who look upon those places as near by, we say, give for their relief, as·from the instinct of your natures, and from a sense of duty; while, to any present who remember these afflicted people as lately in hostile array against our beloved nation, and as even now harboring bitter feelings against us, we say most confidently, give for the relief of suffering so located; give for the greater reflex good to yourselves, sure to return to you from this higher sphere of charity. Nay, verily, Waukesha is of the Mississippi Valley; its waters mingle with the Great River.

When first I saw your flowing stream, now twenty-one years ago, I raised my hands and my voice in gratitude that I had seen—yes, was veritably seeing a stream, a flowing stream, which was to be part of the mighty Mississippi, that from infancy I had almost venerated, as I also had the great valley and its inhabitants.

Citizens of Waukesha, even did your waters not mingle directly with those which flow near by your suffering fellow-beings; yea, if your waters flowed into the great chain of lakes which through the St. Lawrence empty into the Atlantic, even then, under the rule of our Heavenly Father, the commingling of waters from the rising mists of near and distant oceans, distilling alike on the just and the unjust, would teach us to exercise our sympathies, our charities, for the suffering of our common humanity.

---

* In their acceptance of the congressional grant, some States, in the hour of danger to the Republic, primarily acknowledging the Patriot Orphan Claim, may in subsequent legislation, in the hour of their prosperity, have ceased to be thus reconnoissant. [Brought from page 232.]

INDEX,

SUPPLEMENTAL TO THAT COMMENCING ON PAGE 187.

Absolution 128.
Ackron 185.
Adirondack M't's 223, 251.
Adrian 155.
Agricultural Colleges 156, 230, 231, 232.
Alps at St Gothard 227.
Am. Geo. Society 157.
Amherst College 169.
Amplitude 108.
Analysis of vocal sounds 222
Ancestral removes 79.
An early move in the temperance cause 82, 85.
An evangelist 133.
Annual Report 131, 233.
An unusual crowd 218.
Apple Oven Ledge 57, 251.
Ashford 115.
Ayle, 74, 75, 76, 77.
Baldwin, Rev. Dr. Elihu W. 214, 220.
Barnes, Rev. Albert 220.
Bellows Falls 55, 62, 100 156, 180, 213.
Berlin, University of, 156, 224.
Bethel 159, 160, 161.
Big Flats 108.
Biographies 233.
Boston 139, 141, 147.
Brattleboro 152, 173.
Brigham, Rev. John-C. 211, 215.
Brown, Dr. Henry-S. 227
Bunker Hill 42, 60.
Burlington, Vt. 99, 152, 172.
Business centre 119.
Calendar for 6000 years 250, 251. See preface
Cambridge Village 19, 109, 112.
Campbelltown 117.
Captives p. 13, 38, 39, 86.
Carpathian Mts. 227.
Carthage 153, 182.
Champlain, N. Y. 151.
Charlestown, Mass. 184.

Charlestown, N. H. 50, 86, 104.
Charts, explanation of, 36, 73, 74, 77, 78, 79, 95.
Charts, Table of, 186.
Chattanooga, p. 45.
Chelmsford 4, 8.
Chemung Co. 108.
Chesterfield Academy 99.
Chicago 116, 135, 136.
Choosing a business 219, 229, 232.
Christian Commission 122.
Chronology 263.
Clarendon 155.
Collateral branches.
College of France 224.
College of Pharmacy 165.
Col. of Physicians and Surgeons, 156, 221.
Concord, Mass. 1, 2, 23.
Consistency 111.
Containing a condition 221.
Co-operation 25, 35, 51.
Corning 135.
Coventry, Vt. 177.
Cowardice 155.
" Cruised about."
Danube 227.
Dartmouth College 99.
Daysville 108, 187.
Deerfield 100.
Derby Line 152.
Design of suffering 238.
Detroit 137.
Dunstable 7, 9, 37, 40, 61.
East River 157.
Effingham Academy 213.
Elizabethtown 94, 159.
Engraving 223.
Essex 94, 156.
Evanston 134.
Everett, 171, 184.
Experimental farms 232.
Explanations 73, 74, 77, 78, 79.
Extremes expressed 79.
Farmer and Mechanic 182.

Ferry Ancestry 133.
Filial Measures 79.
First Houses on Fifth Avenue 212.
First Med. Temp. Society 221.
Fitchburg 34, 103, 135, 148, 149.
Forefathers Monument 84.
Forefathers' Landing 251.
Fort Dummer 55,
Forward, Frances-K.' 221, 238.
Fountain Green 153.
Fredericksburg 152.
Free baths 157.
Garden of Plants 224.
Garrison Houses 10.
Genealogical Staff 79.
Genealogies 233.
Generations' length 114.
Genetic Space 79.
Going, Rev. Dr. Jonathan 212.
Granby 133.
Granville 133.
Great Fire 117, 118.
Greenough, J.-J. 215.
Griscom, Dr. John-H. 220.
Groton 14, 59.
Halsey, Anthony-P. 215.
Hampshire grants 56.
Hardwick, Mass. 99.
Hartford 57, 119, 141.
Hartley, Robert-M. 211.
Hatfield, Rev. Dr. 220.
Hastings, Thomas 220.
Herbarium 169.
Hillsgrove 100, 153, 154.
Historic Committees 157, 233.
Historical Novel 67.
Holbrook, Josiah 217, 224, 225.
House of Refuge 218, 219.
Index 187.
Indian Patriot Orphan Home 234.

Preliminary pp. 8
Succeeding 240 } 248   *Supplement*   { *248 preceding, this becomes* } 249

Indian Commission 127.
Inscriptions 58.
Institute of Reward 157.
Italy 227.
Ives, Dr. Ansel-W. 215.
Jessup, Charles of Westfield 213.
Journal of the Institute 233.
Knox College 180, 181.
La Fayette Institute 214.
Lake Forest 133, 185.
Lake Maggiore 227.
Lancaster 13.
Le Claire, Scott Co., Iowa 155, 234, 235.
Leap Year 251.
Lefferts Place 145.
Lenormant, Professor 224.
Letters apologetic 217, 229.
Limerick 100, 156, 165, 213.
Little except sacrifice.
Livingston 215.
Locarno 227.
Lunenburg 140.
Madison Square 213.
Map of New York 213.
Mason, N. H. 46.
Mathews, Rev. Dr. 212.
Memorial Gift 156.
Memorial Volumes 25, 35, 36, 51, 56, 72, 156, 233.
Memphis and Shreveport 239.
Merrimac 61.
Milwaukee 257.
Minerva Studio 233.
Mission Institute 165, 170.
Mont Matre 224.
Montpelier, Vt. 65.
Monument to French 56.
Col. C-T-J. Moore of Frempton Hall, Eng., ch. I, p. 8ᵃ.
Mormon Bible 67.
Mott Memorial 157.
Mount Auburn Cemetery 147.
Mt. Morris 115.
Newbern 98.
N. E. His. Gen. Soc. 157.
New Harmony 160.
New pronoun 219.
N. Y. Free Med. College for Women 157, 217.
Northampton 57, 85, 133.
Northfield, 57, 84.

North Market Mission 130, 132.
Not Preparing.
Number one 55.
Oak Hill 146.
"Old and New style" 251.
Old people's party 94.
Olean 134.
Oye 74, 75, 76, 77.
Painted Post 135.
Paris, University of, 156, 224.
Personal responsibilities 80.
Philadelphia 156.
Philological Soc. 157, 256, 257.
Philosophical classification 167.
Phonetic Alphabet 223.
Phonotypes on Tahawia 232
Physiology 157, 217, 219, 229, 237.
Pioneers 84, 108.
Piquaket 38.
Pittsfield 179.
Plymouth 93.
Post, Dr. Alfred-C. 228.
Powderhorn 60.
Profitable Amusement, 251.
Putney 150, 218.
Radial charts 52, 80, 82.
Rangers, 37, 60.
Ratio 57.
Reciprocal facilities 81.
Relationship measured 98.
Robinson, Rev. Dr. 220.
Rodgers, Dr. John-Kearney 218.
Rules for Practice 255-6.
Rome, Naples, etc. 227.
Russia, suggestion for, 250.
Sailors' Snug Harbor 214.
St. Gothard 227.
St. Johnsbury 177.
St. Louis 137.
St. Paul 145, 146.
San Francisco, 103, 182.
Sanitary provisions 157.
Saxton's River 171.
Scale of Consanguinity 79.
Search for stolen goods 217
Second purchase 56.
Senate Chamber 155.
Sessions (times of) 157, 258.
Seyffarth, Prof. Gustavus 256.*

Shasta Valley 134.
Shirley 59, 140.
Six live physicians 221.
Sixtieth Anniversary 251.
Smith, Prof. J V-C. 216.
South Berwick 100, 101, 165.
Southboro 143.
Southwick 156, 211, 214, 221.
Southwick Academy 211, 213, 221.
Springfield, Mass. 93, 133, 217.
Springfield, Vt. 99, 100, 183.
Stanstead 54.
Steuben Co. 108, 115, 116.
Stirling 108, 134.
Sumpterville 155.
Tahawian Heights 223.
Tarnished at his link.
Temperance Pledge 57, 216, 221.
Thirty-fifth Anivers'y 251.
Ticonderoga 62.
Transatlantic Notations.
Twenty Months on the Andes 168.
University of Vt. 100, 172.
Uvalda 145.
Vattemere, Alexander 224, 225, 226, 227.
Vevay, Ind. 99.
Wabash College 214.
Walking petrifaction 238.
Washington, D. C. 179.
Waterville 232.
Waukesha Co., Wis. 232, 239.
Weisse, Dr. John-A. 256.
Westminster, Mass. 111.
Westminster, Vt. 50, 55, 251.
Westport 94, 156.
Wetmore, A. R. 215.
Whiteface 223.
Whitesides 108.
Whole duty 152.
Wilderness, battle of p. 151.
Williston 150.
Winlsow Pedigree, 96.
Wisconsin University 232.
With new force 218.
Withholding 90.
Worth Street, N.Y. 135.
Y. M. C. Association 120.

The index includes some pages to be found in the completed volumn.

Calendar for the First 6,000 Years of the Christian Era.

We have seen that the centennial of our Independence is to be on Tuesday, 4 July, 1876. If Russia—which persists yet in Old Style, and had twenty-nine days in her February, 1800, and is now twelve days behind the age—should compliment us by making that day—4 July, 1876—the commencement of her New Style, what day of the month would her Monday next before be? Move the *Tu.* from opposite **||** to opposite 4, and Monday is seen to be June 21, 1876, O.S. May we then see the end of the confusion that can cease only with the abolition of the astronomical falsehood of Old Style.

Before attempting the solution of the Russian problem, the reader will please apply the rules and examples given on the accompanying page.

On what day of the week was George Washington born—it being 22 Feb., 1732, New Style? ☞ Economy is the right application of forces.

Last Two Figures of the Year.											Century. O.S. / N.S.	Days of the Month.						Day	Months
04	10	+	21	27	32	38	+	49	55	60	66	+	77	83	88	94	5 / 0	7	14	21	28		S.	Jan.? Oct.
																						29	M.	May.
+	09	15	20	26	+	37	43	48	54	+	65	71	76	82	+	93	99	6 /	1	8	15	22	29	Tu.	August.
																						30	W.	Feb.? Mar., Nov.
03	08	14	+	25	31	36	42	+	53	59	64	70	+	81	87	92	98	0 /	2	9	16	23	30	Th.	June.
																						31	F.	Sept., Dec.
02	+	13	19	24	30	+	41	47	52	58	+	69	75	80	86	+	97	1 /	3	10	17	24	31	Sa.	April, July.
+	07	12	18	+	29	35	40	46	+	57	63	68	74	+	85	91	96	2 / ‖	4	11	18	25		S.	Jan.? Oct.
01	06	+	17	23	28	34	+	45	51	56	62	+	73	79	84	90		3 /	5	12	19	26		M.	May.
00	+	11	16	22	+	33	39	44	50	+	61	67	72	78	+	89	95	III / 4	6	13	20	27		Tu.	August.

(SLIDE.)

W.	Feb.? Mar., Nov.
Th.	June.
F.	Sept., Dec.
Sa.	April, July.
S.	Jan.? Oct.
M.	May.
Tu.	August.
W.	Feb.? Mar., Nov.
Th.	June.
F.	Sept., Dec.
Sa.	April, July.
S.	Jan.? Oct.

Entered according to Act of Congress, in the year 1872, by D.-P.' HOLTON, M.D., in the Office of the Librarian of Congress, at Washington, D. C.

Deacon Benjamin Parsons was baptized 17th March, 1627–8, O. S., at Sandiford, near Great Milton, Oxford Co., England. On what day of the week? In English dates marked thus—1627–8, as in this Calendar the larger number.

DAVID-PARSONS' HOLTON, M.D.

CHRONOLOGY.

A few words on Chronology are unavoidable in a genealogical work prepared for general readers. They shall be as few as we can clearly make them.

By the ancient Romans, the year was reckoned as consisting of 365 days, but as the actual Solar year was deemed to be 365 days and 6 hours, Julius Cæsar ordered that every fourth year should have an intercalary day. A day was accordingly added to the month of February, or on the sixth of the calends of March, and thus making two *sixths*, or *bis sextus*, gave origin to the term Bissextile Year, corresponding to our present Leap-Year.

It was subsequently ascertained that the true solar year consisted of 365 days, 5 hours 48', 48'', and that the overplus of 11', 12'', had occasioned a grievous error in the calendar.

Up to 1582, every fourth year had contained 366 days in all civilized lands. It was then discovered that each four hundred years should have had, instead of 100 leap years, 97 only; and that the world was already ten days out of its proper reckoning in consequence. Without disturbing or correcting former dates, *ten* days were dropped by the command of Pope Gregory XIII., from October, 1582; so the next day after Thursday, 4th Oct., 1582, Old Style, was Friday, 15th Oct., 1582 New Style. Protestant countries did not receive this at once, and when England made the change—having perversely made a leap year of 1700—there were *eleven* days dropped from September, 1752, so the day after Wednesday, 2d Sept., 1752, O.S., was Thursday, 15th Sept., N.S. It was also enacted that the year 1752, and all after, should begin on the first day of January instead of the twenty-fifth of March, and that March should be called the *third* month instead of the *first*. For, up to this time, a child born on the last day of the year, was recorded as born on the 24th day of the first month (March). For some time there had been "a historical year," beginning with January: so that an event occurring, as the birth of Josias Wynslow did, in the legal year 1604, on 16 Feb., is recorded as 16 Feb., 1604-5, or 1604(5), or 1604-5.

Forgetting the beginning of the year, sometimes leads to the tampering with dates. Thus we read that Magdalen Wynslow was born "on 26 Dec., 1604," and Josias was born of the same mother "on 16 Feb., 1605," meaning 1605-6,—when Magdalen was 13 months and 20 days old.

LEAP-YEARS.—In Old Style, every year the number of which can be *divided* by 4, is a leap year or bissextile year. In New Style, all centurial years *divisible* by 400, and all other years *divisible* by 4, are leap years, and no others. Thus the centurial year 1800, though *divisible* by 4, was not a leap year, as it is not *divisible* by 400. The above, with the substitution *measured* for *divided* and *divisible*, is a brief and perfect rule.

TO FIND THE DAY OF THE WEEK.—To ascertain which style is used and which year, and to control the accuracy of statements, every date ought to be tested whenever the day of the week is known. The well-known *Perpetual Calendar*—by use of the Dominical Letters—is a slow and sure way of accomplishing this. On the opposite page we give a much more ready means of doing this, and less liable to blunders. Let there be an exact copy of the "SLIDE" made, of the same size. Place its left hand edge opposite to the right hand end of the other, with the days of the week opposite any line of figures, and the slide is set for *some* month. But the problems are three, according to whether you wish to set it for a New Style date in this century, a New Style date in another century, or an Old Style date.

NEW STYLE FOR THE CENTURY FROM 1800 TO 1899, INCLUSIVE.—Bring the name of the month opposite to the number of the year. But in January or February of a leap-year, bring the month opposite the cross (+) next (Chronologically) before the year.* The "SLIDE" is then set for that month. Thus, if W be placed next to 30, the slide is set for Feb., 1896, Feb., 1876, March, 1896, Feb., Mar. and Nov., of 1870, Sept. and Dec., 1896, or 1801.

NEW STYLE, OTHER CENTURIES.—If you divide XVIII. by IV., you have a remainder of II. XVII. divided by IV., gives a remainder of I. So if you set the slide for July, 1876, *Tuesday* stands opposite II: move Tuesday to opposite the I., and the slide is ready for July, 1776, N.S. You now readily see that Independence was declared on Thursday. Our rule for new style is, therefore: Divide the hundreds of the year-number by 4, and against the remainder, expressed by a Roman numeral in the second century column, set the day of the week that comes against II., when the slide is arranged for the same year and month of that century.

FOR OLD STYLE.—Divide the hundreds of the year-number by 7, and against the Arabic figure for the remainder, in the first century column, set the day of the week that comes opposite 2 and II.

Now let us try an example or two. The Pilgrims, on 11th Dec., 1620, O.S., took possession of the strand of Plymouth as a home, though the landing is generally counted the next day; add the *ten* days (for it was our making a leap year of 1700 that made us *eleven* days wrong), and you have 21 Dec., N.S. In each case, if our contrivance be infallible, the day must come the same. Prove, then, by the slide that 11 Dec., O.S., and 21 Dec., N.S., in 1620, were both Monday. Now 1620, O.S., and 1820, N.S., are both alike, because the remainder is *two* when you divide 18 by 4, or 16 by 7. But for New Style, the III which comes opposite the II. must be placed opposite the O. and then it is also opposite the 21. But it is never safe to record events previous to Sept., 1752, in New Style, without writing the *N.S.* against the date EVERY TIME.

On Monday, 21st Dec., 1620, N. S., the shallop's party of exploration first visited Plymouth Rock; but it was Wednesday, *nine days later*, when upon this Rock occurred the memorable LANDING FROM THE MAYFLOWER, and its proper anniversary is the penultimate day of the New Year, the THIRTIETH OF DECEMBER.

On what day of the week will occur the tri-centennial of the "LANDING OF THE PILGRIMS," 30th Dec., 1920? Observe the above rule under "*New Style for other Centuries.*"

This arrangement will not apply to years before the Christian era, nor to any year later than 5999.

If needed, additional explanations will be given on application to

DAVID-PARSONS' HOLTON, M.D.,

20 SUTTON PLACE, NEW YORK.

---

* In the "SLIDE" an interrogation point is placed after the months *Feb.* and *Jan.*, to give caution in their leap-year application,—opposite the cross +.

It is hoped the readers of the Winslow, Parsons, Farwell and Holton Memorials will derive profitable amusement in the use of *this* Calendar, in conformity with these simple rules.

D-P.' H.

P.S.—AMERICAN PHILOLOGICAL SOCIETY.—Since the marginal announcement of the celebration, 5th Aug., 1882, the Executive Committee of the Am. Phil Society have entertained the proposition to hold, 1883, in New York City, a "World's Convention" in the interest of philology and an improved alphabet; and at its conclusion in the city to hold a mountain session on Tahawis of the Adirondacks. Should that proposition prevail, the celebration, 1882, will be postponed till said World's Convention, 1883.

WHY MANKIND ARE GENERALLY RIGHT-HANDED.

In 1870, on occasion of the fifth semi-centennial anniversary of the Landing of the Pilgrims, many commenced their examination of Forefathers' relics in Pilgrim Hall at Plymouth an hour or so before the procession to the Church for the oration and other exercises of the day. During this ante-past different speakers standing upon a table centrally placed, extemporized brief addresses.

Among the crowd some one recognized Dr. D-P'. Holton of New York, and called him to speak from the table. He said: The Mayflower passengers had proposed to be landed at or near the Hudson River; and when on the 8th or 9th of November, O. S., 1620, making southward, buffeting the troubled waters around the spit of land which had then been named Cape Malabarre or Tucker's Terror, Providence led them to retrace their steps, thus terminating their transatlantic voyage not southward to the *left*, but northward to the *right* . . . Do we not in this change see the right hand of the Lord ? . . . . . . Before leaving this platform, venerable from its historic surroundings, let me on this fifth return of the semi-centennial [holding up his right hand and counting in order the fingers, 1670, 1720, 1770, 1820, 1870] say a few words as to why mankind are generally right handed:

Accepting as true the statement that the original seat of human abode was north of the equator, and that the common form of pagan worship was that of the sun seen to the southward, coursing from east to west from its morning rising, moving westward to their right; thus facing southward, their right hand, in following the apparent movement of the sun, would obtain preeminent use in their adorations. A substitution of the left hand would have contravened organic economy; while the right, in its devotional acts, moving and developing in symmetrical harmony, would demand and obtain enlarged facilities for supply of nutriment through any change in direction or size of arteries requisite thereto.

A subsequent generation would have this right-handedness produced from two sources:

1. A hereditary force giving preeminence to the right hand.

2. A repetition of the devotional influences, working right-handward.

In like manner of any subsequent generation. Even should the worship of the sun give place to the worship of the true God, the superiority of the right hand would remain and by heredity would be transmitted in perpetuity.

Farwell Memorial Volumes.

The records of HENRY[1] FARWELL, an early settler of Concord, Mass., have been collected with the same degree of care given to those of the WINSLOW MEMORIAL. It is proposed to print the work in separate booklets of some 100 or 125 pages, each adapted to a particular branch of his descendants. The branches will be printed as severally ordered by those embraced in the respective parts. To the FARWELL MEMORIAL, published 18 June, 1879, we here add reviews of the *Winslow Memorial*, printed 1877, the two being executed in similar style.

From Joseph-Jackson Howard, LL.D., F.S.A., Editor of the Miscellanea Genealogica et Heraldica, London, England.

DARTMOUTH ROW, Blackheath, Kent, England,
Nov. 17, 1877.

MY DEAR SIR: I received the parcel of books, and will see that those intended for Mr. Winslow and Colonel Chester are duly sent. I am truly obliged for your kind remembrance.

The WINSLOW MEMORIAL contains a vast mass of most important genealogical data. I shall have the greatest pleasure in placing you on the *free* list of *Miscellanea Genealogica et Heraldica* subscribers, and will date this back, so that if you do not already possess all the parts of the monthly series, I will, on hearing from you what parts you require, send them.

I like much the RADIAL CHARTS and consider that proposed book of Charts will be of great value to genealogists.

It occurs to me that an advertisement of the WINSLOW MEMORIAL, if inserted in the *Miscellanea Genealogica*, would be the means of increasing the sale. If you would draw out a short advertisement, mentioning specially the pedigrees, &c., I will have it put in type at once and inserted in the January part of the *Miscellanea*, of course *without* expense to you.

If you approve, one or two copies of the book might be sent to Messrs. Mitchell & Hughes (the publishers) 24 Wardour Street, London, and it can be stated that the book can be obtained from them. Please also state the price in English money in the advertisement.

Again thanking you for the valuable addition to my collection, and with good wishes,

Believe me, ever sincerely yours,
J.-J. HOWARD.

From Col. Joseph-Lemuel[8] Chester.

LINDEN VILLAS, 124 Blue Anchor Road, Bermondsey, S.E.
London, England, 24 Nov. 1877.

MY DEAR SIR: I beg to acknowledge the receipt, through my friend Dr. Howard, of the first volume of the "Winslow Memorial," and to return you my most hearty thanks for it. It was indeed very kind of you to thus remember me. Of the book itself I can only speak in terms of the highest praise. As you well know, no one can comprehend better than myself the vast amount of careful, patient, and persevering labor it represents. I have looked through it very carefully, and you appear to have done your work admirably, and produced a volume that must stand for all time. I trust that nothing will prevent the continuance of the work. An enterprise so well commenced ought not to stop for lack of means—lack of material I know there is not. I shall look for the second volume with the greatest interest. If I had come across any thing of importance during its progress I should have sent it to you, and I can only say now that if at any time there is any thing special you want from here, I will endeavor to obtain it for you.

I am very much interested also in the smaller papers you enclosed, and shall give them a permanent place among my collections. Since the completion of my labors on the "Westminster Abbey Registers," I have returned to my work on the "Washington Family," and hope sooner or later to bring that to a successful completion. Hoping that you will be spared many years, and amply encouraged in your most interesting labors,

Believe me, very truly yours,

Dr. D-P[7]. Holton, New York.
JOSEPH-L. CHESTER.

HOLIDAY AND ANNIVERSARY PRESENTS.

Miss JULIA-AMELIA[8] WINSLOW, West Brewster, Mass.

Dear Friend: Your valued letter, in appreciation of Volume I. of the Pilgrim Series, some weeks since bought by you; and your enclosure of $6, the 11th inst., for another copy of the same book, as a *Christmas Present* to your friend, counting your payment for the book as a *Salvage Gift* to Mrs. Holten and myself for our years of research and for our great financial outlays in collecting and gracefully transmitting the records of your ancestors, is gratefully acknowledged.

In the mail carrying this acknowledgment I place the volume directed as you order. I trust the gilded inscription of the recipient's name may be satisfactory.

You regard your acts as an equitable salvage paid for our long labors and attendant expenses. If now *one thousand persons*, following your example, would, with commendable promptness, thus add to our *Working Publication Fund* five thousand dollars, the manuscripts of succeeding volumes would in a few days thereafter be put into the hands of the printer......... Without such or some equivalent co-operation we *cannot* go forward with our genealogical works.

John[7] Winslow, Esq., of 59 Liberty Street, New York, who has done much to advance the work, and knows its expensiveness, hearing of your appreciative view of the situation, desires me to express to you his personal thanks.

If your example is not largely followed—if this call for aid be unheeded, we shall, in sadness, be compelled to abandon all. Very gratefully, yours truly,

DAVID-P[7]. HOLTON.

17 HARGRAVE PARK ROAD, near Highgate, N }
LONDON, 19 Feb., 1878.

Sir: Should you have a copy of your valuable Memorial of the Winslows to spare, I shall esteem it a great favor if you will kindly exchange works with me.

I have issued to subscribers three volumes *Cansick's Epitaphs of Middlesex,* J.-R. Smith, publisher, Soho Square.

I am, Sir, Your Humble Sv't,

DAVID-P. HOLTON, M.D.,   F-TEAGUE CANSICK.
Secretary of Pilgrim Record Society, New York.

F-TEAGUE CANSICK, Esq., London.

Dear Sir: For some twenty years Mrs. Holton and myself have been investigating the genealogy of descendants of the Pilgrims of the Mayflower of Plymouth, and now our longings go instinctively to the MOTHER COUNTRY for their more remote ancestry.

Your proposition is more than welcome. Your researches will doubtless facilitate our progress, which we deliberately resolve shall be lifelong.

It is highly gratifying to us to know that many English Genealogists appreciate our work and kindly propose exchange akin to yours.

The Pilgrim Record Society of the City of New York have secured a beautiful location, No. 20 Eastern Boulevard, S.W. corner of East 59th street, overlooking the East River for miles of its course, constantly the moving scene of voyaging, mercantile, and excursional transport, and offering an eastern view of Long Island residences on a circuit of many miles.

The view very naturally carries us to Plymouth Rock and the Mother Land. . . . .

We hope long here to quietly co-operate with you and other European and American Genealogists in constructing sure bases on which posterity may erect truthful and enduring structures.

Yours truly,

DAVID-P⁷. HOLTON,
20 Eastern Boulevard (Sutton Place), cor. E. 59th St.,   Secretary of the Pilgrim Record Society.
New York, 4 March, 1878.

1879. PILGRIM RECORD SOCIETY, 1879.

Removed to 20 Eastern Boulevard (Sutton Place), cor. East 59th Street.

Formal and informal meetings of the PILGRIM RECORD SOCIETY are held at its rooms, on the SECOND TUESDAY afternoon and evening of each month, as specified below. Descendants of New Englanders and others interested in the early Pilgrim times are invited to attend, and bring what family records they can severally furnish.

Regular sessions will be the second Tuesday of each month during the year 1879, viz.:

1879.
January 14	May 13	September 9
February 11	June 10	October 14
March 11		November 11
April 8		December 9

The Fourth Anniversary of the Pilgrim Record Society will be held Tuesday, Dec. 30, 1879, 8 p.m., at 20 Sutton Place, Eastern Boulevard, N. Y., corner of East 59th Street.

☞ The recipient is respectfully invited to attend with friends.

DAVID-P⁷. HOLTON, *Secretary.*

While Volume I is especially for the records of Kenelm[1] Winslow and his descendants, the "INTRODUCTION," consisting of seventy pages, is of great interest to the descendants of his brothers John[1], Josiah[1], and Governor Edward[1]—to those bearing the patronymic, and to those of other names through female lines.

Of letters in commendation, we present one from a gentleman of the seventh generation, in the line of John[1] who was an eminent merchant of Boston and died there 1674:

52 PINCKNEY STREET, BOSTON, 20 Dec. 1877.

DAVID-P⁷. HOLTON, M.D.

Dear Sir: Enclosed please find ten dollars, postal order, in payment for the two volumes of Winslow Memorial.

I think you and your wife are deserving of great credit. Have not had time to look it through; as far as I have gone, am much pleased. It is a beautiful volume.

Very truly yours,

SAMUEL-W⁷. WINSLOW.

The books of the Memorial Series, large octavo, bound in cloth, may be purchased at Dr. Holton's Genealogical Studio, 20 Eastern Boulevard, New York; price five dollars ($5) for five hundred pages. Volume I. contains 656 pages, price five dollars, thirty cents extra for postage prepaid on the book. Remittances by postal orders should be payable to the order of David-P⁷. Holton, M.D., at Station H, Branch P.O., N.Y. City. Copies of any of our radial charts, photo-lithographed or printed, may, as samples, be had at $1 each, while the sale price of most of them is $2 each.

The recipient is invited to consult those relatives who would probably unite in raising the $200 requisite for a family chart analogous to that of Carpenter[3] Winslow, or of Thomas[4] Parsons, and make early report to Dr. Holton, as above.

JAMES-EDWARD OLIVER, Professor of Mathematics in Cornell University, having examined some advance sheets of VOLUME II, on returning them writes:
LYNN, Mass., 28 July, 1878.
· · · · The beauty, compactness, and accuracy of these pages are admirable.
JAMES-EDWARD OLIVER.

PILGRIM RECORD SOCIETY.

At the Second Anniversary, 30 December, 1877, was read the ROBERT CUSHMAN SERMON, the first one in New England which was printed; and the Society now purpose to reprint it as soon as funds therefor are obtained.

From several letters written by Honorary Members invited to attend, we give that of Rev. Dr. Henry-Martyn Dexter:

1 SOMERSET STREET, BOSTON, MASS.
January 11, 1878.

MY DEAR SIR: An unusual press of work prevented me from immediately replying to yours requesting my presence in New York at the anniversary of the Pilgrim Record Society.

I shall be very glad to do what I can to aid you in every endeavor you may make to shed light upon Pilgrim History.

I have in my library one of the very few known copies of Cushman Sermon in its original edition.*

I am not at this moment able to refer accurately to your publications. But if you will send me a complete set of your "Bulletin" to date, and of the "Winslow Memorial," so far as published, I will send you the money on receipt of the bill, and will be glad to have you consider me a permanent subscriber for every publication of the sort which you may issue.

Faithfully yours,
HENRY-M. DEXTER,
Editor of the Congregationalist.

DAVID-P⁷. HOLTON, M.D., 20 Eastern Boulevard, cor. East 59th St., N.Y.

*The loan of this original print is obtained, that from it our edition may be set. We hope it may be publicly read in all the villages and towns of the Union. The Secretary of the Society will occasionally read it, if thereto invited.

D-P⁷. HOLTON, Secretary.

From Thomas Spooner, Esq., Author of the Spooner Genealogy.

130 DAYTON STREET, CINCINNATI, 25 Aug. 1877.

DAVID-P⁷. HOLTON, M.D.

My Dear Sir: The WINSLOW MEMORIAL, Vol. I., reached me last week. I treasure it highly. You have made a grand success. The second volume, now in course of printing, I must have. Be pleased to send it by express, C.O.D.; or, if you prefer, I will send you the value in advance.

I notice that you run pretty largely into the Spooner, Holland, Gale, Graves, and Averill of my family. . . . I congratulate you on the beginning of the completion of your long and great toil—and, too, on the eminent success you have made of the book in its matter, the arrangement, the excellence of typography, paper, etc., etc.

With thanks and best wishes, I am, very truly,
THOMAS SPOONER.

A Bequest, Currently, Prospectively and Increasingly Beneficial.

The first *five* American semi-zones have analagous showings in the chart facing the 100th page of Vol. I. of the Pilgrim Record series, (Winslow Memorial) of which a copy may be seen at the rooms of the New England Historic-Genealogical Society, 18 Somerset St., Boston, in the Library of Congress, and in many of the public libraries of the Union.

1. For the construction of our GRAND RADIAL CHARTS, giving the open spaced, perpendicular, ancestral chain to the fifth American generation, with the brothers and sisters of each representative link placed upon the right and left; and giving for the member placed in the central section of the fifth whorl a full development of ALL his or her known descendants to the present time, we refer to our circulars and to our published MEMORIAL VOLUMES and RADIALS.

2. It will be observed that our plan is to place some member of the fifth (5th) generation in the upward extension of the direct line of his ancestors, [See James⁴ in the Kingsboro Parsons Chart] and then give a full development of all his descendants, *only*, instead of immensely enlarging the chart to admit of the full records of the descendants of ALL the brothers and sisters of that generation.

3. In like manner any parent of the seventh generation thus centrally placed, bequeathing in trust for his posterity a goodly number of copies of his chart, may provide for the records of all his descendants for a century to come in the following manner:

4. Let the grand and great-grand children of the said party cut off all the chart paper beyond the semi-zone of his or her children in the eighth American belt; also, cut out the space now appropriated to said children, making a notch which may be re-occupied in accordance with the respective demands of their completed records.

5. The printed chart thus cut may be smoothly pasted on a vellum sheet of size sufficient for four or five additional whorls, that thereon may be skilfully placed by a master penman the records of successive generations, harmoniously arranged, from the said party of the seventh whorl to the BI-CENTENNIAL OF THE GREAT REPUBLIC, 1976—an elegantly framed typo-script Radial Chart, an esteemed ornament for the parlors of posterity.

6. While the types of the chart of any person of the fifth American generation are yet standing each of his grand-children having descendants may at comparatively little expense be properly set in the central section of the seventh whorl preparatory to the above-named arrangement for the future records of his or her posterity.

DAVID-PARSONS⁷ HOLTON, M.A.,
No. 20 Sutton Place, Eastern Boulevard,
Corner of East 59th St., New York, July 4, 1878.

FARWELL MEMORIAL.

THE numerous descendants of Henry[1] Farwell, an early settler of Concord, Mass., have for many years been aware that their memorial volume has been in a state of great forwardness for the press.

June 18th, 1879, we issue a part which will be of *common interest* to all the branches, containing records of their several Farwell ancestors of the first four generations in America, and generally of descendants born prior to 1760. This little book will bring the record down to include the birth of most of the descendants who participated in the struggle for the Independence of the United States—an ANCESTRAL BOOK OF AMERICAN FARWELLS. To these pages of COMMON INTEREST to all Farwells, have been added samples of branch development to the present date, 1879. This booklet when generously purchased at $3.00 per copy, will become a way of co-operation by which it is hoped the three thousand dollars requisite to bring out the full volume will soon be secured.

Special advances towards the $3000 may be forwarded to William-D[s]. Farwell, 115 Worth Street, New York, who has kindly consented to act as Trustee for the contributors. Postal orders, checks, and drafts designed for the FARWELL MEMORIAL PUBLICATION FUND, should be made payable to the order of William-D[s]. Farwell; but ordinary correspondence, genealogical and biographical items, may be addressed to DAVID-P[r]. HOLTON, M.D.
20 Sutton Place, Eastern Boulevard, Cor. East 59th St.

NEW YORK, May 12th, 1879.

AMERICAN PHILOLOGICAL SOCIETY.—Its sessions are in Room 36, Cooper Institute, N.E. Corner, on the floor of the Public Reading Room; entrance by the eastern passage through the series of *adjunct reading rooms*, the third Wednesday of each month, commencing at 8 P.M. Dr. John-A. Weisse, author of "Origin, Progress, and Destiny of the English Language and Literature," President.

Prof. Seyffarth delivered a lecture on Egyptian Archæology and Hieroglyphics, 19 March, 1879, which he continued on the 16th of April, and by request of the Society, will give a resume of the two lectures in Association Hall, corner of Fourth Avenue and 23d Street, or in some other suitable hall, of which due announcement will be made. The Professor, now 83 years of age, was a pioneer in this department of study, *The Interpretation of Egyptian Hieroglyphics.*

Few of our citizens know that the venerable Dr. Seyffarth has been for twenty-four years a resident of the United States, and for six or seven years, of this city, where he lives in a very retired manner, occupied with the prosecution of the Oriental studies to which he has given more than half a century of laborious research. Born at Ubigan, Saxony, July 13, 1796, Dr. Seyffarth was educated at Leipsic, and became Professor of Archæology in the famous university of that city in 1825. He was a pupil of the eminent Egyptologist Spohn, after whose death he edited his Egyptian manuscripts and has since published above fifty works upon the same branch of study. He is the oldest of living philologists of eminence, was a contemporary and associate of Champollion and Dr. Young, and divides with them the credit of the magnificent Oriental discoveries which gave such lustre to the earlier half of the century. Dr. Seyffarth has views of his own about all Oriental subjects, which, in some cases, are widely opposed to present accepted doctrines. A long biographical sketch of Dr. Seyffarth may be found in Vapereau's "Dictionnaire des Contemporains," Other accounts may be found in Appleton and Johnson's Cyclopedias, and in Allibone's "Dictionary of Authors," where a full list of his numerous works may be found. It is to the credit of the American Philological Society that it has drawn this interesting veteran from his retirement, elected him an honorary member and proposes to recall to a forgetful generation the fact that one of the founders of Comparative Philology still lives among us.

May 21, 1879, Prof. Edwin-H. Davis, M.D., delivered before the American Philological Society Room 36, Cooper Institute as above, a lecture on "American Antiquities, and the Mound Builders of the Mississippi Valley."

June 18th, 1879, Charles Sotheran, Esq., will deliver, as above, a lecture on "The Origin of our Popular Surnames."

Sessions of the American Philological Society, third Wednesdays, at Room 36 as above, will be during the remainder of the year 1879: June 18th; October 15th; November 19th; and December 17th. ☞ The recipient is invited to attend.

May, 1879. DAVID-P[r]. HOLTON, M.D., Cor. Secretary.

NEW YORK GENEALOGICAL AND BIOGRAPHICAL SOCIETY.—For ten years its sessions, twice each month, have been held with great regularity at the MOTT MEMORIAL HALL, 64 Madison Avenue. From this date, the second and fourth Friday evenings of each month, except July, August, and September, are the times of meeting. Sessions for the remainder of the year 1879, on Fridays: April 11th, 25th; May 9th, 23d; June 13th, 27th; October 10th, 24th; November 14th, 28th; and December 12th, 26th. These sessions are open to all interested in Genealogy.

Sessions of the PILGRIM RECORD SOCIETY, the second Tuesday of each month, are open to the public at 20 Sutton Place, Eastern Boulevard, corner of East 59th street.

89066138637

b89066138637a

CPSIA information can be obtained
at www.ICGtesting.com
Printed in the USA
LVHW021503240619
622190LV00006B/222/P